50% OFF Online Praxis 5901 Prep Course!

Dear Customer,

We consider it an honor and a privilege that you chose our Praxis 5901 Study Guide. **Included with your purchase is discounted access to the Mometrix Praxis 5901 Prep Course.** Many Praxis 5901 courses are needlessly expensive and don't deliver enough value. That is why Test Prep Books has partnered with Mometrix. With their course, you get access to the best Praxis 5901 prep material, and **you only pay half price**.

Mometrix has structured their online course to perfectly complement your printed study guide. The Praxis Elementary Education (5901) Prep Course contains **in-depth lessons** that cover all the most important topics, **230+ video reviews** that explain difficult concepts, over **1,150 practice questions** to ensure you feel prepared, and more than **500 digital flashcards**, so you can study while you're on the go.

Online Praxis 5901 Prep Course

Topics Included:
- Mathematics
    - Numbers and Operations
    - Algebraic Thinking
    - Geometry and Measurement
- Social Studies
    - United States History
    - United States Government and Citizenship
    - Geography, Anthropology, and Sociology
- Science
    - Earth Science
    - Physical Science
    - Scientific Inquiry and Impact

Course Features:
- Praxis 5901 Study Guide
    - Get content that complements our best-selling study guide.
- Full-Length Practice Tests
    - With over 1,150 practice questions, you can test yourself again and again.
- Mobile Friendly
    - If you need to study on the go, the course is easily accessible from your mobile device.
- Praxis 5901 Flashcards
    - Our course includes a flashcard mode with over 500 content cards to help you study.

To lock in this discounted access, visit mometrix.com/university/praxis5901/ or simply scan this QR code with your smartphone. At the checkout page, enter the discount code: **TPBPR5901**.

If you have any questions or concerns, please contact them at support@mometrix.com.

Sincerely,

 In Partnership with

Online Resources

Included with your purchase are multiple online resources. This includes the practice tests in an interactive format and a convenient study timer to help you manage your time.

Instructions for accessing these resources can be found on the last page of this book.

Praxis Elementary Education Multiple Subjects 5901 Study Guide

4 Practice Tests and Exam Prep for All Three Subjects (5903, 5904, 5905) [Includes Detailed Answer Explanations]

Lydia Morrison

Copyright © 2025 by TPB Publishing

All rights reserved. No part of this publication may be reproduced, distributed, or transmitted in any form or by any means, including photocopying, recording, or other electronic or mechanical methods, without the prior written permission of the publisher, except in the case of brief quotations embodied in critical reviews and certain other noncommercial uses permitted by copyright law.

Written and edited by TPB Publishing.

TPB Publishing is not associated with or endorsed by any official testing organization. TPB Publishing is a publisher of unofficial educational products. All test and organization names are trademarks of their respective owners. Content in this book is included for utilitarian purposes only and does not constitute an endorsement by TPB Publishing of any particular point of view.

ISBN 13: 9781637756041

Table of Contents

Welcome -- *1*

Quick Overview -- *2*

Test-Taking Strategies -- *3*

Introduction --- *7*

Study Prep Plan -- *9*

Math Reference Sheet --- *11*

Mathematics -- *13*

   Numbers and Operations --- 13

   Algebraic Thinking --- 29

   Geometry & Measurement, Data, Statistics, and Probability ------------ 40

   Practice Quiz --- 80

   Answer Explanations --- 81

Social Studies -- *82*

   United States History, Government, and Citizenship -------------------- 82

   Geography, Anthropology, and Sociology -------------------------------- 93

   World History and Economics -- 101

   Practice Quiz -- 109

   Answer Explanations -- 110

Science -- *111*

   Earth Science -- 111

   Life Science --- 129

   Physical Science --- 149

   Practice Quiz -- 164

Answer Explanations ———————————————————————— 165

Practice Test #1 ————————————————————————*166*
Mathematics ———————————————————————— 166
Social Studies ———————————————————————— 175
Science ———————————————————————— 184

Answer Explanations #1 ————————————————————*192*
Mathematics ———————————————————————— 192
Social Studies ———————————————————————— 199
Science ———————————————————————— 207

Practice Test #2 ————————————————————————*214*
Mathematics ———————————————————————— 214
Social Studies ———————————————————————— 223
Science ———————————————————————— 232

Answer Explanations #2 ————————————————————*240*
Mathematics ———————————————————————— 240
Social Studies ———————————————————————— 248
Science ———————————————————————— 257

Practice Test #3 & #4 ————————————————————*263*

Index ————————————————————————*264*

Online Resources ————————————————————*272*

Welcome

Dear Reader,

Welcome to your new Test Prep Books study guide! We are pleased that you chose us to help you prepare for your exam. There are many study options to choose from, and we appreciate you choosing us. Studying can be a daunting task, but we have designed a smart, effective study guide to help prepare you for what lies ahead.

Whether you're a parent helping your child learn and grow, a high school student working hard to get into your dream college, or a nursing student studying for a complex exam, we want to help give you the tools you need to succeed. We hope this study guide gives you the skills and the confidence to thrive, and we can't thank you enough for allowing us to be part of your journey.

In an effort to continue to improve our products, we welcome feedback from our customers. We look forward to hearing from you. Suggestions, success stories, and criticisms can all be communicated by emailing us at support@testprepbooks.com.

Sincerely,

Test Prep Books Team

Quick Overview

As you draw closer to taking your exam, effective preparation becomes more and more important. Thankfully, you have this study guide to help you get ready. Use this guide to help keep your studying on track and refer to it often.

This study guide contains several key sections that will help you be successful on your exam. The guide contains tips for what you should do the night before and the day of the test. Also included are test-taking tips. Knowing the right information is not always enough. Many well-prepared test takers struggle with exams. These tips will help equip you to accurately read, assess, and answer test questions.

A large part of the guide is devoted to showing you what content to expect on the exam and to helping you better understand that content. In this guide are practice test questions so that you can see how well you have grasped the content. Then, answer explanations are provided so that you can understand why you missed certain questions.

Don't try to cram the night before you take your exam. This is not a wise strategy for a few reasons. First, your retention of the information will be low. Your time would be better used by reviewing information you already know rather than trying to learn a lot of new information. Second, you will likely become stressed as you try to gain a large amount of knowledge in a short amount of time. Third, you will be depriving yourself of sleep. So be sure to go to bed at a reasonable time the night before. Being well-rested helps you focus and remain calm.

Be sure to eat a substantial breakfast the morning of the exam. If you are taking the exam in the afternoon, be sure to have a good lunch as well. Being hungry is distracting and can make it difficult to focus. You have hopefully spent lots of time preparing for the exam. Don't let an empty stomach get in the way of success!

When travelling to the testing center, leave earlier than needed. That way, you have a buffer in case you experience any delays. This will help you remain calm and will keep you from missing your appointment time at the testing center.

Be sure to pace yourself during the exam. Don't try to rush through the exam. There is no need to risk performing poorly on the exam just so you can leave the testing center early. Allow yourself to use all of the allotted time if needed.

Remain positive while taking the exam even if you feel like you are performing poorly. Thinking about the content you should have mastered will not help you perform better on the exam.

Once the exam is complete, take some time to relax. Even if you feel that you need to take the exam again, you will be well served by some down time before you begin studying again. It's often easier to convince yourself to study if you know that it will come with a reward!

Test-Taking Strategies

1. Predicting the Answer

When you feel confident in your preparation for a multiple-choice test, try predicting the answer before reading the answer choices. This is especially useful on questions that test objective factual knowledge. By predicting the answer before reading the available choices, you eliminate the possibility that you will be distracted or led astray by an incorrect answer choice. You will feel more confident in your selection if you read the question, predict the answer, and then find your prediction among the answer choices. After using this strategy, be sure to still read all of the answer choices carefully and completely. If you feel unprepared, you should not attempt to predict the answers. This would be a waste of time and an opportunity for your mind to wander in the wrong direction.

2. Reading the Whole Question

Too often, test takers scan a multiple-choice question, recognize a few familiar words, and immediately jump to the answer choices. Test authors are aware of this common impatience, and they will sometimes prey upon it. For instance, a test author might subtly turn the question into a negative, or he or she might redirect the focus of the question right at the end. The only way to avoid falling into these traps is to read the entirety of the question carefully before reading the answer choices.

3. Looking for Wrong Answers

Long and complicated multiple-choice questions can be intimidating. One way to simplify a difficult multiple-choice question is to eliminate all of the answer choices that are clearly wrong. In most sets of answers, there will be at least one selection that can be dismissed right away. If the test is administered on paper, the test taker could draw a line through it to indicate that it may be ignored; otherwise, the test taker will have to perform this operation mentally or on scratch paper. In either case, once the obviously incorrect answers have been eliminated, the remaining choices may be considered. Sometimes identifying the clearly wrong answers will give the test taker some information about the correct answer. For instance, if one of the remaining answer choices is a direct opposite of one of the eliminated answer choices, it may well be the correct answer. The opposite of obviously wrong is obviously right! Of course, this is not always the case. Some answers are obviously incorrect simply because they are irrelevant to the question being asked. Still, identifying and eliminating some incorrect answer choices is a good way to simplify a multiple-choice question.

4. Don't Overanalyze

Anxious test takers often overanalyze questions. When you are nervous, your brain will often run wild, causing you to make associations and discover clues that don't actually exist. If you feel that this may be a problem for you, do whatever you can to slow down during the test. Try taking a deep breath or counting to ten. As you read and consider the question, restrict yourself to the particular words used by the author. Avoid thought tangents about what the author *really* meant, or what he or she was *trying* to say. The only things that matter on a multiple-choice test are the words that are actually in the question. You must avoid reading too much into a multiple-choice question, or supposing that the writer meant

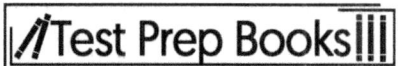

something other than what he or she wrote.

5. No Need for Panic

It is wise to learn as many strategies as possible before taking a multiple-choice test, but it is likely that you will come across a few questions for which you simply don't know the answer. In this situation, avoid panicking. Because most multiple-choice tests include dozens of questions, the relative value of a single wrong answer is small. As much as possible, you should compartmentalize each question on a multiple-choice test. In other words, you should not allow your feelings about one question to affect your success on the others. When you find a question that you either don't understand or don't know how to answer, just take a deep breath and do your best. Read the entire question slowly and carefully. Try rephrasing the question a couple of different ways. Then, read all of the answer choices carefully. After eliminating obviously wrong answers, make a selection and move on to the next question.

6. Confusing Answer Choices

When working on a difficult multiple-choice question, there may be a tendency to focus on the answer choices that are the easiest to understand. Many people, whether consciously or not, gravitate to the answer choices that require the least concentration, knowledge, and memory. This is a mistake. When you come across an answer choice that is confusing, you should give it extra attention. A question might be confusing because you do not know the subject matter to which it refers. If this is the case, don't

eliminate the answer before you have affirmatively settled on another. When you come across an answer choice of this type, set it aside as you look at the remaining choices. If you can confidently assert that one of the other choices is correct, you can leave the confusing answer aside. Otherwise, you will need to take a moment to try to better understand the confusing answer choice. Rephrasing is one way to tease out the sense of a confusing answer choice.

7. Your First Instinct

Many people struggle with multiple-choice tests because they overthink the questions. If you have studied sufficiently for the test, you should be prepared to trust your first instinct once you have carefully and completely read the question and all of the answer choices. There is a great deal of research suggesting that the mind can come to the correct conclusion very quickly once it has obtained all of the relevant information. At times, it may seem to you as if your intuition is working faster even than your reasoning mind. This may in fact be true. The knowledge you obtain while studying may be retrieved from your subconscious before you have a chance to work out the associations that support it. Verify your instinct by working out the reasons that it should be trusted.

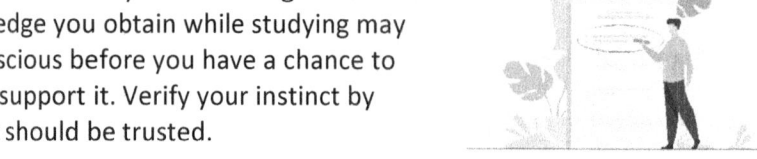

8. Key Words

Many test takers struggle with multiple-choice questions because they have poor reading comprehension skills. Quickly reading and understanding a multiple-choice question requires a mixture of skill and experience. To help with this, try jotting down a few key words and phrases on a piece of scrap paper. Doing this concentrates the process of reading and forces the mind to weigh the relative importance of the question's parts. In selecting words and phrases to write down, the test taker thinks about the question more deeply and carefully. This is especially true for multiple-choice questions that are preceded by a long prompt.

9. Subtle Negatives

One of the oldest tricks in the multiple-choice test writer's book is to subtly reverse the meaning of a question with a word like *not* or *except*. If you are not paying attention to each word in the question, you can easily be led astray by this trick. For instance, a common question format is, "Which of the following is...?" Obviously, if the question instead is, "Which of the following is not...?," then the answer will be quite different. Even worse, the test makers are aware of the potential for this mistake and will include one answer choice that would be correct if the question were not negated or reversed. A test taker who misses the reversal will find what he or she believes to be a correct answer and will be so confident that he or she will fail to reread the question and discover the original error. The only way to avoid this is to practice a wide variety of multiple-choice questions and to pay close attention to each and every word.

10. Reading Every Answer Choice

It may seem obvious, but you should always read every one of the answer choices! Too many test takers fall into the habit of scanning the question and assuming that they understand the question because they recognize a few key words. From there, they pick the first answer choice that answers the question they believe they have read. Test takers who read all of the answer choices might discover that one of the latter answer choices is actually *more* correct. Moreover, reading all of the answer choices can remind you of facts related to the question that can help you arrive at the correct answer. Sometimes, a misstatement or incorrect detail in one of the latter answer choices will trigger your memory of the subject and will enable you to find the right answer. Failing to read all of the answer choices is like not reading all of the items on a restaurant menu: you might miss out on the perfect choice.

11. Spot the Hedges

One of the keys to success on multiple-choice tests is paying close attention to every word. This is never truer than with words like *almost*, *most*, *some*, and *sometimes*. These words are called "hedges" because they indicate that a statement is not totally true or not true in every place and time. An absolute statement will contain no hedges, but in many subjects, the answers are not always straightforward or absolute. There are always exceptions to the rules in these subjects. For this reason,

you should favor those multiple-choice questions that contain hedging language. The presence of qualifying words indicates that the author is taking special care with his or her words, which is certainly important when composing the right answer. After all, there are many ways to be wrong, but there is only one way to be right! For this reason, it is wise to avoid answers that are absolute when taking a multiple-choice test. An absolute answer is one that says things are either all one way or all another. They often include words like *every*, *always*, *best*, and *never*. If you are taking a multiple-choice test in a subject that doesn't lend itself to absolute answers, be on your guard if you see any of these words.

12. Long Answers

In many subject areas, the answers are not simple. As already mentioned, the right answer often requires hedges. Another common feature of the answers to a complex or subjective question are qualifying clauses, which are groups of words that subtly modify the meaning of the sentence. If the question or answer choice describes a rule to which there are exceptions or the subject matter is complicated, ambiguous, or confusing, the correct answer will require many words in order to be expressed clearly and accurately. In essence, you should not be deterred by answer choices that seem excessively long. Oftentimes, the author of the text will not be able to write the correct answer without offering some qualifications and modifications. Your job is to read the answer choices thoroughly and completely and to select the one that most accurately and precisely answers the question.

13. Restating to Understand

Sometimes, a question on a multiple-choice test is difficult not because of what it asks but because of how it is written. If this is the case, restate the question or answer choice in different words. This process serves a couple of important purposes. First, it forces you to concentrate on the core of the question. In order to rephrase the question accurately, you have to understand it well. Rephrasing the question will concentrate your mind on the key words and ideas. Second, it will present the information to your mind in a fresh way. This process may trigger your memory and render some useful scrap of information picked up while studying.

14. True Statements

Sometimes an answer choice will be true in itself, but it does not answer the question. This is one of the main reasons why it is essential to read the question carefully and completely before proceeding to the answer choices. Too often, test takers skip ahead to the answer choices and look for true statements. Having found one of these, they are content to select it without reference to the question above. The savvy test taker will always read the entire question before turning to the answer choices. Then, having settled on a correct answer choice, he or she will refer to the original question and ensure that the selected answer is relevant. The mistake of choosing a correct-but-irrelevant answer choice is especially common on questions related to specific pieces of objective knowledge.

15. No Patterns

One of the more dangerous ideas that circulates about multiple-choice tests is that the correct answers tend to fall into patterns. These erroneous ideas range from a belief that B and C are the most common right answers, to the idea that an unprepared test-taker should answer "A-B-A-C-A-D-A-B-A." It cannot be emphasized enough that pattern-seeking of this type is exactly the WRONG way to approach a multiple-choice test. To begin with, it is highly unlikely that the test maker will plot the correct answers according to some predetermined pattern. The questions are scrambled and delivered in a random order. Furthermore, even if the test maker was following a pattern in the assignation of correct answers, there is no reason why the test taker would know which pattern he or she was using. Any attempt to discern a pattern in the answer choices is a waste of time and a distraction from the real work of taking the test. A test taker would be much better served by extra preparation before the test than by reliance on a pattern in the answers.

Introduction

Function of the Test

The Praxis Elementary Education 5901 exams are intended to measure knowledge of more than ninety specific subjects taught by educators in kindergarten through twelfth grade classrooms. These tests also aim to teach skills and knowledge in those subject areas. The tests are offered worldwide but are primarily used in the United States mostly as a required part of the certification and licensing procedure in certain individual states. They are also used as part of the licensing process by some professional associations and organizations.

The Elementary Education 5901 exams cover three individual subjects: Mathematics, Social Studies, and Science. States that require the test typically require that a test-taker reach a minimum passing score on each of the three sub-tests in order to pass and receive the license or certification sought. Individuals taking the test are usually beginning teachers, either freshly out of college, having recently decided to seek a particular license or certification, or having recently moved to a state where the test is required or preferred.

Test Administration

The test is administered by computer through an international system of testing centers, including Prometric centers, some colleges and universities, and a variety of other locations. Although it is primarily used in the United States, the test is available at locations throughout the world. However, the test is not available at all times. Instead, there is a window of approximately two weeks per month during which the test may be taken. The individual subtests can be taken separately, but the fee for taking them together offers a significant discount from the combined cost of the three individual tests.

Accommodations for test-takers meeting the requirements of the Americans with Disabilities Act include extended testing time, additional rest breaks, a separate testing room, a writer/recorder of answers, a test reader, and large print test materials. Alternate forms of the test are available in sign language, Braille, or audio format.

Test takers may opt to retake the test at any time after twenty-eight days have passed from the initial attempt. An individual wishing to retake one of the three tests that comprise the Multiple Subjects exam must also wait twenty-one days from the initial attempt of that exam.

Test Format

All questions are selected response (in which the test-taker chooses from multiple choice options or chooses a particular word, sentence or part of a graphic), and numeric entry (in which the test-taker gives a numeric answer). In all cases, the test-taker will receive a question from the computer and be prompted to select a response from the options on the screen or enter a number. Questions may be answered in any order, and test takers may mark questions to return to them later.

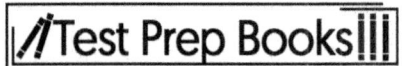

The four sub-tests of the exam break down as follows:

Subject	Minutes	Questions
Mathematics	65	50
Social Studies	50	55
Science	50	50
Total	165	155

Scoring

Raw scores are based on the number of correct responses with no penalty for incorrect answers or guesses. The raw scores are then converted to a scaled score from 100 to 200. The required passing scaled score varies from state to state and from sub-test to sub-test. On the Reading and Language Arts sub-test, the required score ranges from a low of 154 to a high of 165 with most states requiring at least a 157. The median score in 2015 was a 169. On the Mathematics sub-test, the required score ranges from a low of 143 to a high of 171 with most states requiring at least a 157. The median score in 2015 was a 170. On the Social Studies sub-test, the required score ranges from a low of 142 to 166 with most states requiring at least a 155. The median score in 2015 was a 163. Finally, on the Science sub-test, the required score ranges from a low of 144 to 170 with most states requiring at least a 159. The median score in 2015 was a 167.

ETS also offers a "Recognition of Excellence" to test takers who perform exceptionally well on the exam. The award is typically given to test takers whose scores fall in the top 15 percent of scores on the exam.

Study Prep Plan

1 **Schedule** - Use one of our study schedules below or come up with one of your own.

2 **Relax** - Test anxiety can hurt even the best students. There are many ways to reduce stress. Find the one that works best for you.

3 **Execute** - Once you have a good plan in place, be sure to stick to it.

One Week Study Schedule		
Day 1	Mathematics
Day 2	Geometry & Measurement, Data, Statistics...
Day 3	Social Studies
Day 4	Science
Day 5	Practice Test #1
Day 6	Practice Test #2
Day 7	Take Your Exam!

Two Week Study Schedule				
Day 1	Mathematics	Day 8	Science
Day 2	Algebraic Thinking	Day 9	Earth History
Day 3	Geometry & Measurement...	Day 10	Life Science
Day 4	Perimeter, Area, Surface Area, and Volume	Day 11	Physical Science
Day 5	Solving Problems Involving Measurement	Day 12	Practice Test #1
Day 6	Social Studies	Day 13	Practice Test #2
Day 7	Geography, Anthropolog...	Day 14	Take Your Exam!

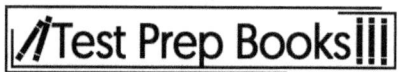

Study Prep Plan

One Month Study Schedule

Day 1	Mathematics	Day 11	Connections between Causes and Effects	Day 21	Interactions of Energy
Day 2	Understanding Proportional...	Day 12	Geography, Anthropology...	Day 22	Practice Test #1
Day 3	Algebraic Thinking	Day 13	World History and Economics	Day 23	Answer Explanations #1
Day 4	Solutions to Linear Equations...	Day 14	Science	Day 24	Practice Test #2
Day 5	Geometry & Measurement...	Day 15	Earth History	Day 25	Answer Explanations #2
Day 6	Perimeter, Area, Surface Area...	Day 16	Earth Patterns	Day 26	Practice Test #3
Day 7	Components of the Coordinate Plane	Day 17	Life Science	Day 27	Answer Explanations #3
Day 8	Solving Problems Involving...	Day 18	Reproduction and Heredity	Day 28	Practice Test #4
Day 9	Representing and Interpreting Data	Day 19	Interdependence of Organisms	Day 29	Answer Explanations #4
Day 10	Social Studies	Day 20	Physical Science	Day 30	Take Your Exam!

Build your own prep plan by visiting the Online Resources page.

Instructions and a QR code can be found on the last page of this guide.

Math Reference Sheet

Symbol	Phrase
+	added to, increased by, sum of, more than
-	decreased by, difference between, less than, take away
×	multiplied by, 3 (4, 5 . . .) times as large, product of
÷	divided by, quotient of, half (third, etc.) of
=	is, the same as, results in, as much as
x, t, n, etc.	a variable which is an unknown value or quantity
<	is under, is below, smaller than, beneath
>	is above, is over, bigger than, exceeds
≤	no more than, at most, maximum; less than or equal to
≥	no less than, at least, minimum; greater than or equal to
√	square root of, exponent divided by 2

Geometry	Description
$P = 2l + 2w$	for perimeter of a rectangle
$P = 4 \times s$	for perimeter of a square
$P = a + b + c$	for perimeter of a triangle
$A = \frac{1}{2} \times b \times h = \frac{bh}{2}$	for area of a triangle
$A = b \times h$	for area of a parallelogram
$A = \frac{1}{2} \times h(b_1 + b_2)$	for area of a trapezoid
$A = \frac{1}{2} \times a \times P$	for area of a regular polygon
$C = 2 \times \pi \times r$	for circumference (perimeter) of a circle
$A = \pi \times r^2$	for area of a circle
$c^2 = a^2 + b^2; c = \sqrt{a^2 + b^2}$	for finding the hypotenuse of a right triangle
$SA = 2xy + 2yz + 2xz$	for finding surface area
$V = \frac{1}{3}xyh$	for finding volume of a rectangular pyramid
$V = \frac{4}{3}\pi r^3; \frac{1}{3}\pi r^2 h; \pi r^2 h$	for volume of a sphere; a cone; and a cylinder

Radical Expressions	Description
$\sqrt[n]{a} = a^{\frac{1}{n}}; \sqrt[n]{a^m} = (\sqrt[n]{a})^m = a^{\frac{m}{n}}$	a is the radicand, n is the index, m is the exponent
$\sqrt{x^2} = (x^2)^{\frac{1}{2}} = x$	to convert square root to exponent
$a^m \times a^n = a^{m+n}$	multiplying radicands with exponents
$(a^m)^n = a^{m \times n}$	multiplying exponents
$(a \times b)^m = a^m \times b^m$	parentheses with exponents

Property	Addition	Multiplication
Commutative	$a + b = b + a$	$a \times b = b \times a$
Associative	$(a + b) + c = a + (b + c)$	$(a \times b) \times c = a \times (b \times c)$
Identity	$a + 0 = a; 0 + a = a$	$a \times 1 = a; 1 \times a = a$
Inverse	$a + (-a) = 0$	$a \times \frac{1}{a} = 1; a \neq 0$
Distributive		$a(b + c) = ab + ac$

Data	Description
Mean	equal to the total of the values of a data set, divided by the number of elements in the data set
Median	middle value in an odd number of ordered values of a data set, or the mean of the two middle values in an even number of ordered values in a data set
Mode	the value that appears most often
Range	the difference between the highest and the lowest values in the set

Graphing	Description
(x, y)	ordered pair, plot points in a graph
$y = mx + b$	slope-intercept form; m represents the slope of the line and b represents the y-intercept
$f(x)$	read as f of x, which means it is a function of x
(x_2, y_2) and (x_2, y_2)	two ordered pairs used to determine the slope of a line
$m = \frac{y_2 - y_1}{x_2 - x_1}$	to find the slope of the line, m, for ordered pairs
$Ax + By = C$	standard form of an equation, also for solving a system of equations through the elimination method
$M = (\frac{x_1 + x_2}{2}, \frac{y_1 + y_2}{2})$	for finding the midpoint of an ordered pair
$y = ax^2 + bx + c$	quadratic function for a parabola
$y = a(x - h)^2 + k$	quadratic function for a parabola with vertex
$y = ab^x; y = a \times b^x$	function for exponential curve
$y = ax^2 + bx + c$	standard form of a quadratic function
$x = \frac{-b}{2a}$	for finding axis of symmetry in a parabola; given quadratic formula in standard form
$f = \sqrt{\frac{\Sigma(x - \bar{x})^2}{n - 1}}$	function for standard deviation of the sample; where $\bar{x}$ = sample mean and n = sample size

Proportions and Percentage	Description
$\frac{gallons}{cost} = \frac{gallons}{cost}; \frac{7 \text{ gallons}}{\$14.70} = \frac{x}{\$20}$	written as equal ratios with a variable representing the missing quantity
$\frac{y_1}{x_1} = \frac{y_2}{x_2}$	for direct proportions
$(y_1)(x_1) = (y_2)(x_2)$	for indirect proportions
$\frac{change}{original\ value} \times 100 = percent\ change$	for finding percentage change in value
$\frac{new\ quantity - old\ quantity}{old\ quantity} \times 100$	for calculating the increase or decrease in percentage

Mathematics

Numbers and Operations

Place Value System

Base-10 Numerals, Number Names, and Expanded Form
Numbers used in everyday life are constituted in a base-10 system. Each digit in a number, depending on its location, represents some multiple of 10, or quotient of 10 when dealing with decimals. Each digit to the left of the decimal point represents a higher multiple of 10. Each digit to the right of the decimal point represents a quotient of a higher multiple of 10 for the divisor. For example, consider the number 7,631.42. The digit one represents simply the number one. The digit 3 represents 3×10. The digit 6 represents $6 \times 10 \times 10$ (or 6×100). The digit 7 represents $7 \times 10 \times 10 \times 10$ (or 7×1000). The digit 4 represents $4 \div 10$. The digit 2 represents $(2 \div 10) \div 10$, or $2 \div (10 \times 10)$ or $2 \div 100$.

A number is written in **expanded form** by expressing it as the sum of the value of each of its digits. The expanded form in the example above, which is written with the highest value first down to the lowest value, is expressed as:

$$7{,}000 + 600 + 30 + 1 + 0.4 + .02$$

When verbally expressing a number, the **integer** part of the number (the numbers to the left of the decimal point) resembles the expanded form without the addition between values. In the above example, the numbers read "seven thousand six hundred thirty-one." When verbally expressing the decimal portion of a number, the number is read as a whole number, followed by the place value of the furthest digit (non-zero) to the right. In the above example, 0.42 is read "forty-two hundredths." Reading the number 7,631.42 in its entirety is expressed as "seven thousand six hundred thirty-one and forty-two hundredths." The word *and* is used between the integer and decimal parts of the number.

Composing and Decomposing Multi-Digit Numbers
Composing and decomposing numbers aids in conceptualizing what each digit of a multi-digit number represents. The standard, or typical, form in which numbers are written consists of a series of digits representing a given value based on their place value. Consider the number 592.7. This number is composed of 5 hundreds, 9 tens, 2 ones, and 7 tenths.

Composing a number requires adding the given numbers for each place value and writing the numbers in standard form. For example, composing 4 thousands, 5 hundreds, 2 tens, and 8 ones consists of adding as follows: $4{,}000 + 500 + 20 + 8$, to produce 4,528 (standard form).

Decomposing a number requires taking a number written in standard form and breaking it apart into the sum of each place value. For example, the number 83.17 is decomposed by breaking it into the sum of 4 values (for each of the 4 digits): 8 tens, 3 ones, 1 tenth, and 7 hundredths. The decomposed or "expanded" form of 83.17 is:

$$80 + 3 + 0.1 + 0.07$$

Place Value of a Given Digit
The decimal system consists of only ten different digits, 0 to 9, and is used to represent an infinite number of values. The place value system makes this infinite number of values possible. The position in which a digit is

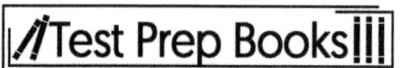

written corresponds to a given value. Starting from the decimal point (which is implied, if not physically present), each subsequent place value to the left represents a value greater than the one before it. Conversely, starting from the decimal point, each subsequent place value to the right represents a value less than the one before it.

The names for the place values to the left of the decimal point are as follows:

...	Billions	Hundred-Millions	Ten-Millions	Millions	Hundred-Thousands	Ten-Thousands	Thousands	Hundreds	Tens	Ones

Note that this table can be extended infinitely further to the left.

The names for the place values to the right of the decimal point are as follows:

Decimal Point (.)	Tenths	Hundredths	Thousandths	Ten-Thousandths	...

Note that this table can be extended infinitely further to the right.

When given a multi-digit number, the value of each digit depends on its place value. Consider the number 682,174.953. Referring to the chart above, it can be determined that the digit 8 is in the ten-thousands place. It is in the fifth place to the left of the decimal point. Its value is 8 ten-thousands or 80,000. The digit 5 is two places to the right of the decimal point. Therefore, the digit 5 is in the hundredths place. Its value is 5 hundredths or $\frac{5}{100}$ (equivalent to .05).

Value of Digits
In accordance with the base-10 system, the value of a digit increases by a factor of ten each place it moves to the left. For example, consider the number 7. Moving the digit one place to the left (70) increases its value by a factor of 10 ($7 \times 10 = 70$). Moving the digit two places to the left (700) increases its value by a factor of 10 twice ($7 \times 10 \times 10 = 700$). Moving the digit three places to the left (7,000) increases its value by a factor of 10 three times ($7 \times 10 \times 10 \times 10 = 7,000$), and so on.

Conversely, the value of a digit decreases by a factor of ten each place it moves to the right. (Note that multiplying by $\frac{1}{10}$ is equivalent to dividing by 10). For example, consider the number 40. Moving the digit one place to the right (4) decreases its value by a factor of 10 ($40 \div 10 = 4$). Moving the digit two places to the right (0.4), decreases its value by a factor of 10 twice ($40 \div 10 \div 10 = 0.4$) or ($40 \times \frac{1}{10} \times \frac{1}{10} = 0.4$). Moving the digit three places to the right (0.04) decreases its value by a factor of 10 three times ($40 \div 10 \div 10 \div 10 = 0.04$) or ($40 \times \frac{1}{10} \times \frac{1}{10} \times \frac{1}{10} = 0.04$), and so on.

Exponents to Denote Powers of 10
The value of a given digit of a number in the base-10 system can be expressed utilizing powers of 10. A **power of 10** refers to 10 raised to a given exponent such as 10^0, 10^1, 10^2, 10^3, etc. For the number 10^3, 10 is the base and 3 is the exponent. A base raised by an exponent represents how many times the base is multiplied by itself. Therefore, $10^1 = 10$, $10^2 = 10 \times 10 = 100$, $10^3 = 10 \times 10 \times 10 = 1,000$, $10^4 = 10 \times 10 \times 10 \times 10 = 10,000$, etc. Any base with a zero-exponent equals one.

Powers of 10 are utilized to decompose a multi-digit number without writing all the zeroes. Consider the number 872,349. This number is decomposed to $800,000 + 70,000 + 2,000 + 300 + 40 + 9$. When utilizing powers of 10, the number 872,349 is decomposed to:

$$(8 \times 10^5) + (7 \times 10^4) + (2 \times 10^3) + (3 \times 10^2) + (4 \times 10^1) + (9 \times 10^0)$$

Mathematics

The power of 10 by which the digit is multiplied corresponds to the number of zeroes following the digit when expressing its value in standard form. For example, 7×10^4 is equivalent to 70,000 or 7 followed by four zeros.

Rounding Multi-Digit Numbers

Rounding numbers changes the given number to a simpler and less accurate number than the exact given number. Rounding allows for easier calculations which estimate the results of using the exact given number. The accuracy of the estimate and ease of use depends on the place value to which the number is rounded. Rounding numbers consists of:

- Determining what place value the number is being rounded to
- Examining the digit to the right of the desired place value to decide whether to round up or keep the digit
- Replacing all digits to the right of the desired place value with zeros

To round 746,311 to the nearest ten thousands, the digit in the ten thousands place should be located first. In this case, this digit is 4 (7<u>4</u>6,311). Then, the digit to its right is examined. If this digit is 5 or greater, the number will be rounded up by increasing the digit in the desired place by one. If the digit to the right of the place value being rounded is 4 or less, the number will be kept the same. For the given example, the digit being examined is a 6, which means that the number will be rounded up by increasing the digit to the left by one. Therefore, the digit 4 is changed to a 5. Finally, to write the rounded number, any digits to the left of the place value being rounded remain the same and any to its right are replaced with zeros. For the given example, rounding 746,311 to the nearest ten thousand will produce 750,000.

To round 746,311 to the nearest hundred, the digit to the right of the three in the hundreds place is examined to determine whether to round up or keep the same number. In this case, that digit is a one, so the number will be kept the same and any digits to its right will be replaced with zeros. The resulting rounded number is 746,300.

Rounding place values to the right of the decimal follows the same procedure, but digits being replaced by zeros can simply be dropped. To round 3.752891 to the nearest thousandth, the desired place value is located (3.75<u>2</u>891) and the digit to the right is examined. In this case, the digit 8 indicates that the number will be rounded up, and the 2 in the thousandths place will increase to a 3. Rounding up and replacing the digits to the right of the thousandths place produces 3.753000 which is equivalent to 3.753. Therefore, the zeros are not necessary, and the rounded number should be written as 3.753.

When rounding up, if the digit to be increased is a 9, the digit to its left is increased by 1 and the digit in the desired place value is changed to a zero. For example, the number 1,598 rounded to the nearest ten is 1,600. Another example shows the number 43.72961 rounded to the nearest thousandth is 43.730 or 43.73.

Understanding Operations

Solving Multistep Mathematical and Real-World Problems
Problem Situations for Operations

Addition and subtraction are **inverse operations**. Adding a number and then subtracting the same number will cancel each other out, resulting in the original number, and vice versa. For example, $8 + 7 - 7 = 8$ and $137 - 100 + 100 = 137$. Similarly, multiplication and division are inverse operations. Therefore, multiplying by a number and then dividing by the same number results in the original number, and vice versa. For example, $8 \times 2 \div 2 = 8$ and $12 \div 4 \times 4 = 12$. Inverse operations are used to work backwards to solve problems. In the case that 7 and a number add to 18, the inverse operation of subtraction is used to find the

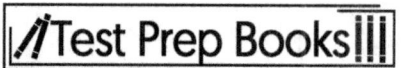

unknown value ($18 - 7 = 11$). If a school's entire 4th grade was divided evenly into 3 classes each with 22 students, the inverse operation of multiplication is used to determine the total students in the grade ($22 \times 3 = 66$). Additional scenarios involving inverse operations are included in the tables below.

There are a variety of real-world situations in which one or more of the operators is used to solve a problem. The tables below display the most common scenarios.

Addition & Subtraction

	Unknown Result	Unknown Change	Unknown Start
Adding to	5 students were in class. 4 more students arrived. How many students are in class? $5 + 4 = ?$	8 students were in class. More students arrived late. There are now 18 students in class. How many students arrived late? $8 + ? = 18$ Solved by inverse operations $18 - 8 = ?$	Some students were in class early. 11 more students arrived. There are now 17 students in class. How many students were in class early? $? + 11 = 17$ Solved by inverse operations $17 - 11 = ?$
Taking from	15 students were in class. 5 students left class. How many students are in class now? $15 - 5 = ?$	12 students were in class. Some students left class. There are now 8 students in class. How many students left class? $12 - ? = 8$ Solved by inverse operations $8 + ? = 12 \rightarrow 12 - 8 = ?$	Some students were in class. 3 students left class. Then there were 13 students in class. How many students were in class before? $? - 3 = 13$ Solved by inverse operations $13 + 3 = ?$

	Unknown Total	Unknown Addends (Both)	Unknown Addends (One)
Putting together/ taking apart	The homework assignment is 10 addition problems and 8 subtraction problems. How many problems are in the homework assignment? $10 + 8 = ?$	Bobby has $9. How much can Bobby spend on candy and how much can Bobby spend on toys? $9 = ? + ?$	Bobby has 12 pairs of pants. 5 pairs of pants are shorts, and the rest are long. How many pairs of long pants does he have? $12 = 5 + ?$ Solved by inverse operations $12 - 5 = ?$

Mathematics

	Unknown Difference	Unknown Larger Value	Unknown Smaller Value
Comparing	Bobby has 5 toys. Tommy has 8 toys. How many more toys does Tommy have than Bobby? $5+?=8$ Solved by inverse operations $8-5=?$ Bobby has \$6. Tommy has \$10. How many fewer dollars does Bobby have than Tommy? $10-6=?$	Tommy has 2 more toys than Bobby. Bobby has 4 toys. How many toys does Tommy have? $2+4=?$ Bobby has 3 fewer dollars than Tommy. Bobby has \$8. How many dollars does Tommy have? $?-3=8$ Solved by inverse operations $8+3=?$	Tommy has 6 more toys than Bobby. Tommy has 10 toys. How many toys does Bobby have? $?+6=10$ Solved by inverse operations $10-6=?$ Bobby has \$5 less than Tommy. Tommy has \$9. How many dollars does Bobby have? $9-5=?$

Multiplication and Division

	Unknown Product	Unknown Group Size	Unknown Number of Groups
Equal groups	There are 5 students, and each student has 4 pieces of candy. How many pieces of candy are there in all? $5\times 4=?$	14 pieces of candy are shared equally by 7 students. How many pieces of candy does each student have? $7\times?=14$ Solved by inverse operations $14\div 7=?$	If 18 pieces of candy are to be given out 3 to each student, how many students will get candy? $?\times 3=18$ Solved by inverse operations $18\div 3=?$

	Unknown Product	Unknown Factor	Unknown Factor
Arrays	There are 5 rows of students with 3 students in each row. How many students are there? $5\times 3=?$	If 16 students are arranged into 4 equal rows, how many students will be in each row? $4\times?=16$ Solved by inverse operations $16\div 4=?$	If 24 students are arranged into an array with 6 columns, how many rows are there? $?\times 6=24$ Solved by inverse operations $24\div 6=?$

	Larger Unknown	Smaller Unknown	Multiplier Unknown
Comparing	A small popcorn costs \$1.50. A large popcorn costs 3 times as much as a small popcorn. How much does a large popcorn cost? $1.50\times 3=?$	A large soda costs \$6 and that is 2 times as much as a small soda costs. How much does a small soda cost? $2\times?=6$ Solved by inverse operations $6\div 2=?$	A large pretzel costs \$3 and a small pretzel costs \$2. How many times as much does the large pretzel cost as the small pretzel? $?\times 2=3$ Solved by inverse operations $3\div 2=?$

Remainders in Division Problems

If a given total cannot be divided evenly into a given number of groups, the amount left over is the **remainder**. Consider the following scenario: 32 textbooks must be packed into boxes for storage. Each box holds 6 textbooks. How many boxes are needed? To determine the answer, 32 is divided by 6, resulting in 5 with a remainder of 2. A remainder may be interpreted three ways:

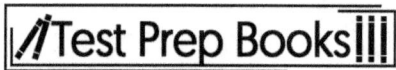

- Add 1 to the quotient
  How many boxes will be needed? Six boxes will be needed because five will not be enough.

- Use only the quotient
  How many boxes will be full? Five boxes will be full.

- Use only the remainder
  If you only have 5 boxes, how many books will not fit? Two books will not fit.

Strategies and Algorithms to Perform Operations on Rational Numbers

A rational number is any number that can be written in the form of a ratio or fraction. Integers can be written as fractions with a denominator of 1 ($5 = \frac{5}{1}$; $-342 = \frac{-342}{1}$; etc.). Decimals that terminate and/or repeat can also be written as fractions ($47 = \frac{47}{100}$; $.\overline{33} = \frac{1}{3}$). For more on converting decimals to fractions, see the section *Converting Between Fractions, Decimals,* and *Percent*.

When adding or subtracting fractions, the numbers must have the same denominators. In these cases, numerators are added or subtracted, and denominators are kept the same. For example, $\frac{2}{7} + \frac{3}{7} = \frac{5}{7}$ and $\frac{4}{5} - \frac{3}{5} = \frac{1}{5}$. If the fractions to be added or subtracted do not have the same denominator, a common denominator must be found. This is accomplished by changing one or both fractions to a different but equivalent fraction. Consider the example $\frac{1}{6} + \frac{4}{9}$. First, a common denominator must be found. One method is to find the least common multiple (LCM) of the denominators 6 and 9. This is the lowest number that both 6 and 9 will divide into evenly. In this case the LCM is 18. Both fractions should be changed to equivalent fractions with a denominator of 18.

To obtain the numerator of the new fraction, the old numerator is multiplied by the same number by which the old denominator is multiplied. For the fraction $\frac{1}{6}$, 6 multiplied by 3 will produce a denominator of 18. Therefore, the numerator is multiplied by 3 to produce the new numerator $\left(\frac{1 \times 3}{6 \times 3} = \frac{3}{18}\right)$. For the fraction $\frac{4}{9}$, multiplying both the numerator and denominator by 2 produces $\frac{8}{18}$. Since the two new fractions have common denominators, they can be added:

$$\frac{3}{18} + \frac{8}{18} = \frac{11}{18}$$

When multiplying or dividing rational numbers, these numbers may be converted to fractions and multiplied or divided accordingly. When multiplying fractions, all numerators are multiplied by each other and all denominators are multiplied by each other. For example,

$$\frac{1}{3} \times \frac{6}{5} = \frac{1 \times 6}{3 \times 5} = \frac{6}{15}$$

and

$$\frac{-1}{2} \times \frac{3}{1} \times \frac{11}{100} = \frac{-1 \times 3 \times 11}{2 \times 1 \times 100} = \frac{-33}{200}$$

When dividing fractions, the problem is converted by multiplying by the reciprocal of the divisor. This is done by changing division to multiplication and "flipping" the second fraction, or divisor. For example, $\frac{1}{2} \div \frac{3}{5} \to \frac{1}{2} \times \frac{5}{3}$ and $\frac{5}{1} \div \frac{1}{3} \to \frac{5}{1} \times \frac{3}{1}$. To complete the problem, the rules for multiplying fractions should be followed.

Mathematics

Note that when adding, subtracting, multiplying, and dividing mixed numbers (ex. $4\frac{1}{2}$), it is easiest to convert these to improper fractions (larger numerator than denominator). To do so, the denominator is kept the same. To obtain the numerator, the whole number is multiplied by the denominator and added to the numerator. For example, $4\frac{1}{2} = \frac{9}{2}$ and $7\frac{2}{3} = \frac{23}{3}$. Also, note that answers involving fractions should be converted to the simplest form.

Rational Numbers and Their Operations
Irregular Products and Quotients
The following shows examples where multiplication does not result in a product greater than both factors, and where division does not result in a quotient smaller than the dividend.

If multiplying numbers where one or more has a value less than one, the product will not be greater than both factors. For example, $6 \times \frac{1}{2} = 3$ and $0.75 \times 0.2 = .15$. When dividing by a number less than one, the resulting quotient will be greater than the dividend. For example, $8 \div \frac{1}{2} = 16$, because division turns into a multiplication problem:

$$8 \div \frac{1}{2} \rightarrow 8 \times \frac{2}{1}$$

Another example is $0.5 \div 0.2$, which results in 2.5. The problem can be stated by asking how many times 0.2 will go into 0.5. The number being divided is larger than the number that goes into it, so the result will be a number larger than both factors.

Composing and Decomposing Fractions

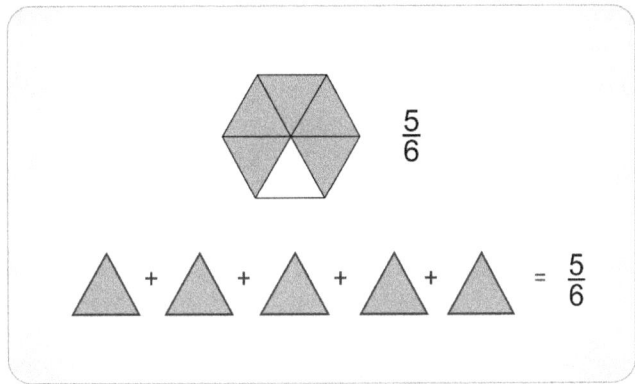

Fractions can be broken apart into sums of fractions with the same denominator. For example, the fraction $\frac{5}{6}$ can be decomposed into sums of fractions with all denominators equal to 6 and the numerators adding to 5. The fraction $\frac{5}{6}$ is decomposed as: $\frac{3}{6} + \frac{2}{6}$; or $\frac{2}{6} + \frac{2}{6} + \frac{1}{6}$; or $\frac{3}{6} + \frac{1}{6} + \frac{1}{6}$; or $\frac{1}{6} + \frac{1}{6} + \frac{1}{6} + \frac{2}{6}$; or:

$$\frac{1}{6} + \frac{1}{6} + \frac{1}{6} + \frac{1}{6} + \frac{1}{6}$$

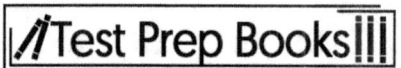

Mathematics

A **unit fraction** is a fraction in which the numerator is 1. If decomposing a fraction into unit fractions, the sum will consist of a unit fraction added the number of times equal to the numerator. For example, $\frac{3}{4} = \frac{1}{4} + \frac{1}{4} + \frac{1}{4}$ (unit fractions $\frac{1}{4}$ added 3 times). **Composing fractions** is simply the opposite of decomposing. It is the process of adding fractions with the same denominators to produce a single fraction. For example,

$$\frac{3}{7} + \frac{2}{7} = \frac{5}{7}$$

and

$$\frac{1}{5} + \frac{1}{5} + \frac{1}{5} = \frac{3}{5}$$

Decrease in Value of a Unit Fraction

A unit fraction is one in which the numerator is 1 ($\frac{1}{2}, \frac{1}{3}, \frac{1}{8}, \frac{1}{20}$, etc.). The **denominator** indicates the number of *equal pieces* that the whole is divided into. The greater the number of pieces, the smaller each piece will be. Therefore, the greater the denominator of a unit fraction, the smaller it is in value. Unit fractions can also be compared by converting them to decimals. For example, $\frac{1}{2}$ = 0.5, $\frac{1}{3}$ = 0.$\overline{3}$, $\frac{1}{8}$ = 0.125, $\frac{1}{20}$ = 0.05, etc.

Use of the Same Whole when Comparing Fractions

Fractions all represent parts of the same whole. Fractions may have different denominators, but they represent parts of the same one whole, like a pizza. For example, the fractions $\frac{5}{7}$ and $\frac{2}{3}$ can be difficult to compare because they have different denominators. The first fraction may represent a whole divided into seven parts, where five parts are used. The second fraction represents the same whole divided into three parts, where two are used. It may be helpful to convert one or more of the fractions so that they have common denominators for converting to equivalent fractions by finding the LCM of the denominator. Comparing is much easier if fractions are converted to the equivalent fractions of $\frac{15}{21}$ and $\frac{14}{21}$. These fractions show a whole divided into 21 parts, where the numerators can be compared because the denominators are the same.

Order of Operations

When reviewing calculations consisting of more than one operation, the order in which the operations are performed affects the resulting answer. Consider $5 \times 2 + 7$. Performing multiplication then addition results in an answer of 17 ($5 \times 2 = 10$; $10 + 7 = 17$). However, if the problem is written $5 \times (2 + 7)$, the order of operations dictates that the operation inside the parentheses must be performed first. The resulting answer is 45:

$$2 + 7 = 9, \text{ so } 5 \times 9 = 45$$

The order in which operations should be performed is remembered using the acronym **PEMDAS**. PEMDAS stands for parentheses, exponents, multiplication/division, and addition/subtraction. Multiplication and division are performed in the same step, working from left to right with whichever comes first. Addition and subtraction are performed in the same step, working from left to right with whichever comes first.

Consider the following example: $8 \div 4 + 8(7 - 7)$. Performing the operation inside the parentheses produces $8 \div 4 + 8(0)$ or $8 \div 4 + 8 \times 0$. There are no exponents, so multiplication and division are performed next from left to right resulting in: $2 + 8 \times 0$, then $2 + 0$. Finally, addition and subtraction are performed to obtain an answer of 2. Now consider the following example: $6x3 + 3^2 - 6$. Parentheses are not applicable. Exponents are evaluated first, $6 \times 3 + 9 - 6$. Then multiplication/division forms $18 + 9 - 6$. At last, addition/subtraction leads to the final answer of 21.

Properties of Operations

Properties of operations exist that make calculations easier and solve problems for missing values. The following table summarizes commonly used properties of real numbers.

Property	Addition	Multiplication
Commutative	$a + b = b + a$	$a \times b = b \times a$
Associative	$(a + b) + c = a + (b + c)$	$(a \times b) \times c = a \times (b \times c)$
Identity	$a + 0 = a; 0 + a = a$	$a \times 1 = a; 1 \times a = a$
Inverse	$a + (-a) = 0$	$a \times \frac{1}{a} = 1; a \neq 0$
Distributive		$a(b + c) = ab + ac$

The **commutative property of addition** states that the order in which numbers are added does not change the sum. Similarly, the commutative property of multiplication states that the order in which numbers are multiplied does not change the product. The **associative property of addition and multiplication** state that the grouping of numbers being added or multiplied does not change the sum or product, respectively. The commutative and associative properties are useful for performing calculations. For example, $(47 + 25) + 3$ is equivalent to $(47 + 3) + 25$, which is easier to calculate.

The **identity property of addition** states that adding zero to any number does not change its value. The **identity property of multiplication** states that multiplying a number by one does not change its value. The **inverse property of addition** states that the sum of a number and its opposite equals zero. **Opposites** are numbers that are the same with different signs (ex. 5 and -5; $-\frac{1}{2}$ and $\frac{1}{2}$). The **inverse property of multiplication** states that the product of a number (other than zero) and its reciprocal equals one. **Reciprocal numbers** have numerators and denominators that are inverted (ex. $\frac{2}{5}$ and $\frac{5}{2}$). Inverse properties are useful for canceling quantities to find missing values (see algebra content). For example, $a + 7 = 12$ is solved by adding the inverse of 7 (which is -7) to both sides in order to isolate a.

The **distributive property** states that multiplying a sum (or difference) by a number produces the same result as multiplying each value in the sum (or difference) by the number and adding (or subtracting) the products. Consider the following scenario: You are buying three tickets for a baseball game. Each ticket costs $18. You are also charged a fee of $2 per ticket for purchasing the tickets online. The cost is calculated: $3 \times 18 + 3 \times 2$. Using the distributive property, the cost can also be calculated $3(18 + 2)$.

Representing Rational Numbers and Their Operations

Concrete Models

Concrete objects are used to develop a tangible understanding of operations of rational numbers. Tools such as tiles, blocks, beads, and hundred charts are used to model problems. For example, a hundred chart (10×10) and beads can be used to model multiplication. If multiplying 5 by 4, beads are placed across 5 rows and down 4 columns producing a product of 20. Similarly, tiles can be used to model division by splitting the total into equal groups. If dividing 12 by 4, 12 tiles are placed one at a time into 4 groups. The result is 4 groups of 3. This is also an effective method for visualizing the concept of remainders.

Representations of objects can be used to expand on the concrete models of operations. Pictures, dots, and tallies can help model these concepts. Utilizing concrete models and representations creates a foundation upon which to build an abstract understanding of the operations.

Rational Numbers on a Number Line

A **number line** typically consists of integers (...3,2,1,0,-1,-2,-3...), and is used to visually represent the value of a rational number. Each rational number has a distinct position on the line determined by comparing its value with the displayed values on the line. For example, if plotting -1.5 on the number line below, it is necessary to recognize that the value of -1.5 is .5 less than -1 and .5 greater than -2. Therefore, -1.5 is plotted halfway between -1 and -2.

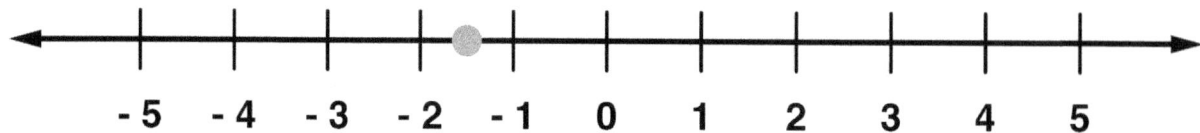

Number lines can also be useful for visualizing sums and differences of rational numbers. Adding a value indicates moving to the right (values increase to the right), and subtracting a value indicates moving to the left (numbers decrease to the left). For example, $5 - 7$ is displayed by starting at 5 and moving to the left 7 spaces, if the number line is in increments of 1. This will result in an answer of -2.

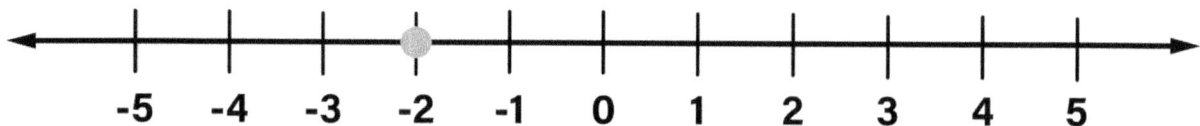

Multiplication and Division Problems

Multiplication and division are inverse operations that can be represented by using rectangular arrays, area models, and equations. Rectangular arrays include an arrangement of rows and columns that correspond to the factors and display product totals.

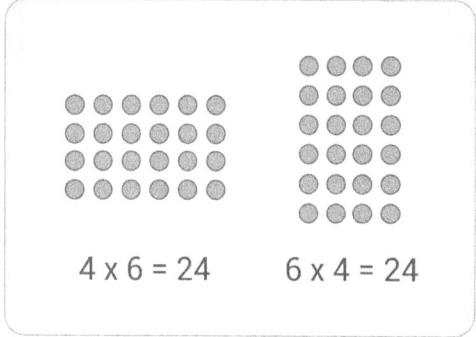

Another method of multiplication can be done with the use of an **area model**. An area model is a rectangle that is divided into rows and columns that match up to the number of place values within each number. Take the example 29×65. These two numbers can be split into simpler numbers: $29 = 25 + 4$ and $65 = 60 + 5$. The products of those 4 numbers are found within the rectangle and then summed up to get the answer. The entire process is:

$$(60 \times 25) + (5 \times 25) + (60 \times 4) + (5 \times 4) = 1,500 + 240 + 125 + 20 = 1,885$$

Mathematics

Here is the actual area model:

	25	4
60	60x25 1,500	60x4 240
5	5x25 125	5x4 20

```
  1,500
    240
    125
+    20
  -----
  1,885
```

Dividing a number by a single digit or two digits can be turned into repeated subtraction problems. An area model can be used throughout the problem that represents multiples of the divisor. For example, the answer to 8580 ÷ 55 can be found by subtracting 55 from 8580 one at a time and counting the total number of subtractions necessary.

However, a simpler process involves using larger multiples of 55. First, $100 \times 55 = 5,500$ is subtracted from 8,580, and 3,080 is leftover. Next, $50 \times 55 = 2,750$ is subtracted from 3,080 to obtain 380. $5 \times 55 = 275$ is subtracted from 330 to obtain 55, and finally, $1 \times 55 = 55$ is subtracted from 55 to obtain zero. Therefore, there is no remainder, and the answer is:

$$100 + 50 + 5 + 1 = 156$$

Here is a picture of the area model and the repeated subtraction process:

8580 ÷ 55

	55
100	5500
50	2750
5	275
1	55

```
55 | 8580
    -5500  (100 x 55)
     3080
    -2750  (50 x 55)
      330
     -275  (5 x 55)
       55
      -55  (1 x 55)
        0
```

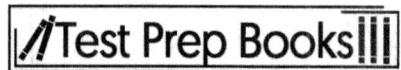

Comparing, Classifying, and Ordering Rational Numbers

A **rational number** is any number that can be written as a fraction or ratio. Within the set of rational numbers, several subsets exist that are referenced throughout the mathematics topics. Counting numbers are the first numbers learned as a child. Counting numbers consist of 1,2,3,4, and so on. **Whole numbers** include all counting numbers and zero (0,1,2,3,4,…). **Integers** include counting numbers, their opposites, and zero (…,-3,-2,-1,0,1,2,3,…). Rational numbers include integers, fractions, and decimals that terminate (1.7, 0.04213) or repeat (0.136).

When comparing or ordering numbers, the numbers should be written in the same format (decimal or fraction), if possible. For example, $\sqrt{49}$, 7.3, and $\frac{15}{2}$ are easier to order if each one is converted to a decimal: 7, 7.3, and 7.5 (converting fractions and decimals is covered in the following section). A number line is used to order and compare the numbers. Any number that is to the right of another number is greater than that number. Conversely, a number positioned to the left of a given number is less than that number.

Converting Between Fractions, Decimals, and Percent

To convert a fraction to a decimal, the numerator is divided by the denominator. For example, $\frac{3}{8}$ can be converted to a decimal by dividing 3 by 8 ($\frac{3}{8} = 0.375$). To convert a decimal to a fraction, the decimal point is dropped, and the value is written as the numerator. The denominator is the place value farthest to the right with a digit other than zero. For example, to convert .48 to a fraction, the numerator is 48, and the denominator is 100 (the digit 8 is in the hundredths place). Therefore,

$$0.48 = \frac{48}{100}$$

Fractions should be written in the simplest form, or reduced. To reduce a fraction, the numerator and denominator are divided by the largest common factor. In the previous example, 48 and 100 are both divisible by 4. Dividing the numerator and denominator by 4 results in a reduced fraction of $\frac{12}{25}$.

To convert a decimal to a percent, the number is multiplied by 100. To convert .13 to a percent, .13 is multiplied by 100 to get 13 percent. To convert a fraction to a percent, the fraction is converted to a decimal and then multiplied by 100. For example, $\frac{1}{5} = 0.20$ and 0.20 multiplied by 100 produces 20 percent.

To convert a percent to a decimal, the value is divided by 100. For example, 125 percent is equal to 1.25 ($\frac{125}{100}$). To convert a percent to a fraction, the percent sign is dropped, and the value is written as the numerator with a denominator of 100. For example, $80\% = \frac{80}{100}$. This fraction can be reduced ($\frac{80}{100} = \frac{4}{5}$).

Understanding Proportional Relationships and Percent

Applying Ratios and Unit Rates

A **ratio** is a comparison of two quantities that represent separate groups. For example, if a recipe calls for 2 eggs for every 3 cups of milk, this is expressed as a ratio. Ratios can be written three ways:

- With the word "to"
- Using a colon
- As a fraction

Mathematics

In the previous example, the ratio of eggs to cups of milk is written as 2 to 3, 2:3, or $\frac{2}{3}$. When writing ratios, the order is very important. The ratio of eggs to cups of milk is not the same as the ratio of cups of milk to eggs, 3:2.

In simplest form, both quantities of a ratio should be written as integers. These should also be reduced just as a fraction is reduced. For example, 5:10 is reduced to 1:2. Given a ratio where one or both quantities are expressed as a decimal or fraction, multiply both by the same number to produce integers. To write the ratio $\frac{1}{3}$ to 2 in simplest form, both quantities are multiplied by 3. The resulting ratio is 1 to 6.

A problem involving ratios may give a comparison between two groups. The problem may then provide a total and ask for a part, or provide a part and ask for a total. Consider the following: The ratio of boys to girls in the 11th grade class is 5:4. If there are a total of 270 11th grade students, how many are girls? The total number of **ratio pieces** should be determined first. The total number of 11th grade students is divided into 9 pieces. The ratio of boys to total students is 5:9, and the ratio of girls to total students is 4:9. Knowing the total number of students, the number of girls is determined by setting up a proportion:

$$\frac{4}{9} = \frac{x}{270}$$

A **rate** is a ratio comparing two quantities expressed in different units. A unit rate is a ratio in which the second quantity is one unit. Rates often include the word *per*. Examples include miles per hour, beats per minute, and price per pound. The word *per* is represented with a / symbol or abbreviated with the letter *p* and units abbreviated. For example, miles per hour is written as mi/h. When given a rate that is not in its simplest form (the second quantity is not one unit), both quantities are divided by the value of the second quantity. If 99 heartbeats were recorded in $1\frac{1}{2}$ minutes, both quantities are divided by $1\frac{1}{2}$ to determine the heart rate of 66 beats per minute.

Percent

The word **percent** means per hundred. Similar to a unit rate in which the second quantity is always one unit, a percent is a rate where the second quantity is always 100 units. If the results of a poll state that 47 percent of people support a given policy, this indicates that 47 out of every 100 individuals polled were in support. In other words, 47 per 100 support the policy. If an upgraded model of a car costs 110 percent of the cost of the base model, for every $100 that is spent for the base model, $110 must be spent to purchase the upgraded model. In other words, the upgraded model costs $110 per $100 for the cost of the base model.

When dealing with percentages, the numbers can be evaluated as a value in hundredths. For example, 15 percent is expressed as fifteen hundredths and is written as $\frac{15}{100}$ or 0.15.

Unit-Rate Problems

A rate is a ratio in which two terms are in different units. When rates are expressed as a quantity of one, they are considered **unit rates**. To determine a unit rate, the first quantity is divided by the second. Knowing a unit rate makes calculations easier than simply having a rate. For example, suppose a 3-pound bag of onions costs $1.77. To calculate the price of 5 pounds of onions, a proportion could show:

$$\frac{3}{1.77} = \frac{5}{x}$$

However, by knowing the unit rate, the value of pounds of onions is multiplied by the unit price. The unit price is calculated:

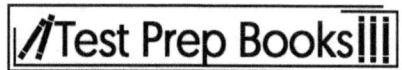

$$\frac{\$1.77}{3 \text{ lb}} = \$0.59/\text{lb}$$

Multiplying the weight of the onions by the unit price yields:

$$5 \text{ lb} \times \frac{\$0.59}{\text{lb}} = \$2.95$$

The *lb.* units cancel out.

Similar to unit-rate problems, unit conversions appear in real-world scenarios including cooking, measurement, construction, and currency. Given the conversion rate, unit conversions are written as a fraction (ratio) and multiplied by a quantity in one unit to convert it to the corresponding unit. To determine how many minutes are in $3\frac{1}{2}$ hours, the conversion rate of 60 minutes to 1 hour is written as $\frac{60 \text{ min}}{1 \text{ h}}$. Multiplying the quantity by the conversion rate results in:

$$3\frac{1}{2} \text{h} \times \frac{60 \text{ min}}{1 \text{h}} = 210 \text{ min}$$

(The *h* unit is canceled.)

To convert a quantity in minutes to hours, the fraction for the conversion rate is flipped to cancel the *min* unit. To convert 195 minutes to hours, $195 \text{ min} \times \frac{1 \text{ h}}{60 \text{ min}}$ is multiplied. The result is $\frac{195 \text{ h}}{60}$ which reduces to $3\frac{1}{4}$ h.

Converting units may require more than one multiplication. The key is to set up conversion rates so that units cancel each other out and the desired unit is left. To convert 3.25 yards to inches, given that 1 yd = 3 ft and 12 in = 1 ft, the calculation is performed by multiplying:

$$3.25 \text{ yd} \times \frac{3 \text{ft}}{1 \text{yd}} \times \frac{12 \text{in}}{1 \text{ft}}$$

The *yd* and *ft* units will cancel, resulting in 117 in.

Using Proportional Relationships

A **proportion** is a statement consisting of two equal ratios. Proportions will typically give three of four quantities and require solving for the missing value. The key to solving proportions is to set them up properly. Consider the following: 7 gallons of gas costs $14.70. How many gallons can you get for $20? The information is written as equal ratios with a variable representing the missing quantity:

$$\left(\frac{gallons}{cost} = \frac{gallons}{cost}\right) : \frac{7}{14.70} = \frac{x}{20}$$

To solve for x, the proportion is cross-multiplied. This means the numerator of the first ratio is multiplied by the denominator of the second, and vice versa. The resulting products are shown equal to each other. Cross-multiplying results in:

$$(7)(20) = (14.7)(x)$$

Mathematics

By solving the equation for x (see the algebra content), the answer is that 9.5 gallons of gas may be purchased for $20.

Percent problems can also be solved by setting up proportions. Examples of common percent problems are:

- a. What is 15% of 25?
- b. What percent of 45 is 3?
- c. 5 is $\frac{1}{2}$% of what number?

Setting up the proper proportion is made easier by following the format: $\frac{is}{of} = \frac{percent}{100}$. A variable is used to represent the missing value. The proportions for each of the three examples are set up as follows:

- a. $\frac{x}{25} = \frac{15}{100}$
- b. $\frac{3}{45} = \frac{x}{100}$
- c. $\frac{5}{x} = \frac{\frac{1}{2}}{100}$

By cross-multiplying and solving the resulting equation for the variable, the missing values are determined to be:

a. 3.75
b. $6.\overline{6}$%
c. 1,000

Basic Concepts of Number Theory

Prime and Composite Numbers

Whole numbers are classified as either prime or composite. A **prime number** can only be divided evenly by itself and one. For example, the number 11 can only be divided evenly by 11 and one; therefore, 11 is a prime number. A helpful way to visualize a prime number is to use concrete objects and try to divide them into equal piles. If dividing 11 coins, the only way to divide them into equal piles is to create 1 pile of 11 coins or to create 11 piles of 1 coin each. Other examples of prime numbers include 2, 3, 5, 7, 13, 17, and 19.

A **composite number** is any whole number that is not a prime number. A composite number is a number that can be divided evenly by one or more numbers other than itself and one. For example, the number 6 can be divided evenly by 2 and 3. Therefore, 6 is a composite number. If dividing 6 coins into equal piles, the possibilities are 1 pile of 6 coins, 2 piles of 3 coins, 3 piles of 2 coins, or 6 piles of 1 coin. Other examples of composite numbers include 4, 8, 9, 10, 12, 14, 15, 16, 18, and 20.

To determine if a number is a prime or composite number, the number is divided by every whole number greater than one and less than its own value. If it divides evenly by any of these numbers, then the number is composite. If it does not divide evenly by any of these numbers, then the number is prime. For example, when attempting to divide the number 5 by 2, 3, and 4, none of these numbers divide evenly. Therefore, 5 must be a prime number.

Factors and Multiples of Numbers

The **factors of a number** are all integers that can be multiplied by another integer to produce the given number. For example, 2 is multiplied by 3 to produce 6. Therefore, 2 and 3 are both factors of 6. Similarly, $1 \times 6 = 6$ and $2 \times 3 = 6$, so 1, 2, 3, and 6 are all factors of 6. Another way to explain a factor is to say that a given number divides evenly by each of its factors to produce an integer. For example, 6 does not divide evenly by 5. Therefore, 5 is not a factor of 6.

Multiples of a given number are found by taking that number and multiplying it by any other whole number. For example, 3 is a factor of 6, 9, and 12. Therefore, 6, 9, and 12 are multiples of 3. The multiples of any number are an infinite list. For example, the multiples of 5 are 5, 10, 15, 20, and so on. This list continues without end. A list of multiples is used in finding the least common multiple, or LCM, for fractions when a common denominator is needed. The denominators are written down and their multiples listed until a common number is found in both lists. This common number is the LCM.

Prime factorization breaks down each factor of a whole number until only prime numbers remain. All composite numbers can be factored into prime numbers. For example, the prime factors of 12 are 2, 2, and 3 ($2 \times 2 \times 3 = 12$). To produce the prime factors of a number, the number is factored, and any composite numbers are continuously factored until the result is the product of prime factors only. A factor tree, such as the one below, is helpful when exploring this concept.

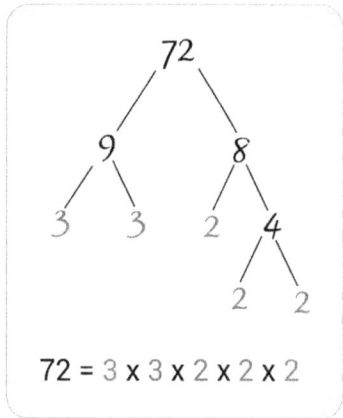

Determining the Reasonableness of Results

Reasonableness of Results within a Context

When solving math word problems, the solution obtained should make sense within the given scenario. The step of checking the solution will reduce the possibility of a calculation error or a solution that may be *mathematically* correct but not applicable in the real world. Consider the following scenarios:

A problem states that Lisa got 24 out of 32 questions correct on a test and asks to find the percentage of correct answers. To solve the problem, a student divided 32 by 24 to get 1.33, and then multiplied by 100 to get 133 percent. By examining the solution within the context of the problem, the student should recognize that getting all 32 questions correct will produce a perfect score of 100 percent. Therefore, a score of 133 percent with 8 incorrect answers does not make sense, and the calculations should be checked.

A problem states that the maximum weight on a bridge cannot exceed 22,000 pounds. The problem asks to find the maximum number of cars that can be on the bridge at one time if each car weighs 4,000 pounds. To solve this problem, a student divided 22,000 by 4,000 to get an answer of 5.5. By examining the solution within the context of the problem, the student should recognize that although the calculations are mathematically correct, the solution does not make sense. Half of a car on a bridge is not possible, so the student should determine that a maximum of 5 cars can be on the bridge at the same time.

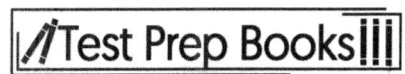

Mental Math Estimation
Once a result is determined to be logical within the context of a given problem, the result should be evaluated by its nearness to the expected answer. This is performed by approximating given values to perform mental math. Numbers should be rounded to the nearest value possible to check the initial results.

Consider the following example: A problem states that a customer is buying a new sound system for their home. The customer purchases a stereo for $435, 2 speakers for $67 each, and the necessary cables for $12. The customer chooses an option that allows him to spread the costs over equal payments for 4 months. How much will the monthly payments be?

After making calculations for the problem, a student determines that the monthly payment will be $145.25. To check the accuracy of the results, the student rounds each cost to the nearest ten $(440 + 70 + 70 + 10)$ and determines that the total is approximately $590. Dividing by 4 months gives an approximate monthly payment of $147.50. Therefore, the student can conclude that the solution of $145.25 is very close to what should be expected.

When rounding, the place-value that is used in rounding can make a difference. Suppose the student had rounded to the nearest hundred for the estimation. The result $(400 + 100 + 100 + 0 = 600; 600 \div 4 = 150)$ will show that the answer is reasonable but not as close to the actual value as rounding to the nearest ten.

Algebraic Thinking

Evaluating and Manipulating Algebraic Expressions and Equations

Differentiating between Algebraic Expressions and Equations
An **algebraic expression** is a statement about an unknown quantity expressed in mathematical symbols. A **variable** is used to represent the unknown quantity, usually denoted by a letter. An **equation** is a statement in which two expressions (at least one containing a variable) are equal to each other. An algebraic expression can be thought of as a mathematical phrase and an equation can be thought of as a mathematical sentence.

Algebraic expressions and equations both contain numbers, variables, and mathematical operations. The following are examples of algebraic expressions: $5x + 3$, $7xy - 8(x^2 + y)$, and $\sqrt{a^2 + b^2}$. An expression can be simplified or evaluated for given values of variables. The following are examples of equations: $2x + 3 = 7$, $a^2 + b^2 = c^2$, and $2x + 5 = 3x - 2$. An equation contains two sides separated by an equal sign. Equations can be solved to determine the value(s) of the variable for which the statement is true.

Adding and Subtracting Linear Algebraic Expressions
An algebraic expression is simplified by combining like terms. A **term** is a number, variable, or product of a number and variables separated by addition and subtraction. For the algebraic expression $3x^2 - 4x + 5 - 5x^2 + x - 3$, the terms are $3x^2$, $-4x$, 5, $-5x^2$, x, and -3. **Like terms** have the same variables raised to the same powers (exponents). The like terms for this example are $3x^2$ and $-5x^2$, $-4x$ and x, 5 and -3. To combine like terms, the coefficients (numerical factor of the term including sign) are added, and the variables and their powers are kept the same. Note that if a coefficient is not written, it is an implied coefficient of 1 $(x = 1x)$. The previous example will simplify to:

$$-2x^2 - 3x + 2$$

When adding or subtracting algebraic expressions, each expression is written in parentheses. The negative sign is distributed when necessary, and like terms are combined. Consider the following: add $2a + 5b - 2$ to $a - 2b + 8c - 4$. The sum is set as follows:

$$(a - 2b + 8c - 4) + (2a + 5b - 2)$$

In front of each set of parentheses is an implied positive one, which, when distributed, does not change any of the terms. Therefore, the parentheses are dropped and like terms are combined:

$$a - 2b + 8c - 4 + 2a + 5b - 2 = 3a + 3b + 8c - 6$$

Consider the following problem: Subtract $2a + 5b - 2$ from $a - 2b + 8c - 4$. The difference is set as follows:

$$(a - 2b + 8c - 4) - (2a + 5b - 2)$$

The implied one in front of the first set of parentheses will not change those four terms. However, distributing the implied -1 in front of the second set of parentheses will change the sign of each of those three terms:

$$a - 2b + 8c - 4 - 2a - 5b + 2$$

Combining like terms yields the simplified expression:

$$-a - 7b + 8c - 2$$

Distributive Property

The **distributive property** states that multiplying a sum (or difference) by a number produces the same result as multiplying each value in the sum (or difference) by the number and adding (or subtracting) the products. Using mathematical symbols, the distributive property states:

$$a(b + c) = ab + ac$$

The expression $4(3 + 2)$ is simplified using the order of operations. Simplifying inside the parentheses first produces 4×5, which equals 20. The expression $4(3 + 2)$ can also be simplified using the distributive property:

$$4(3 + 2) = 4 \times 3 + 4 \times 2 = 12 + 8 = 20$$

Consider the following example: $4(3x - 2)$. The expression cannot be simplified inside the parentheses because $3x$ and -2 are not like terms and therefore cannot be combined. However, the expression can be simplified by using the distributive property and multiplying each term inside of the parentheses by the term outside of the parentheses: $12x - 8$. The resulting equivalent expression contains no like terms, so it cannot be further simplified.

Mathematics

Consider the expression:

$$(3x + 2y + 1) - (5x - 3) + 2(3y + 4)$$

Again, there are no like terms, but the distributive property is used to simplify the expression. Note there is an implied one in front of the first set of parentheses and an implied -1 in front of the second set of parentheses. Distributing the 1, -1, and 2 produces:

$$1(3x) + 1(2y) + 1(1) - 1(5x) - 1(-3) + 2(3y) + 2(4)$$

$$3x + 2y + 1 - 5x + 3 + 6y + 8$$

This expression contains like terms that are combined to produce the simplified expression:

$$-2x + 8y + 12$$

Algebraic expressions are tested to be equivalent by choosing values for the variables and evaluating both expressions. For example, $4(3x - 2)$ and $12x - 8$ are tested by substituting 3 for the variable x and calculating to determine if equivalent values result.

Simple Expressions for Given Values

An **algebraic expression** is a statement written in mathematical symbols, typically including one or more unknown values represented by variables. For example, the expression $2x + 3$ states that an unknown number (x) is multiplied by 2 and added to 3. If given a value for the unknown number, or variable, the value of the expression is determined. For example, if the value of the variable x is 4, the value of the expression 4 is multiplied by 2, and 3 is added. This results in a value of 11 for the expression.

When given an algebraic expression and values for the variable(s), the expression is evaluated to determine its numerical value. To evaluate the expression, the given values for the variables are substituted (or replaced), and the expression is simplified using the order of operations. Parentheses should be used when substituting. Consider the following: Evaluate $a - 2b + ab$ for $a = 3$ and $b = -1$. To evaluate, any variable a is replaced with 3 and any variable b with -1, producing:

$$(3) - 2(-1) + (3)(-1)$$

Next, the order of operations is used to calculate the value of the expression, which is 2.

Parts of Expressions

Algebraic expressions consist of variables, numbers, and operations. A **term** of an expression is any combination of numbers and/or variables, and terms are separated by addition and subtraction. For example, the expression $5x^2 - 3xy + 4 - 2$ consists of 4 terms: $5x^2$, $-3xy$, $4y$, and -2. Note that each term includes its given sign (+ or −). The **variable** part of a term is a letter that represents an unknown quantity. The coefficient of a term is the number by which the variable is multiplied. For the term $4y$, the variable is y, and the coefficient is 4. Terms are identified by the power (or exponent) of its variable.

A number without a variable is referred to as a **constant**. If the variable is to the first power (x^1 or simply x), it is referred to as a **linear term**. A term with a variable to the second power (x^2) is quadratic, and a term to the third power (x^3) is cubic. Consider the expression $x^3 + 3x - 1$. The constant is -1. The linear term is $3x$. There is no quadratic term. The cubic term is x^3.

An algebraic expression can also be classified by how many terms exist in the expression. Any like terms should be combined before classifying. A **monomial** is an expression consisting of only one term. Examples of

31

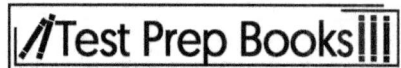

monomials are: 17, $2x$, and $-5ab^2$. A **binomial** is an expression consisting of two terms separated by addition or subtraction. Examples include $2x - 4$ and $-3y^2 + 2y$. A **trinomial** consists of 3 terms. For example, $5x^2 - 2x + 1$ is a trinomial.

Verbal Statements and Algebraic Expressions

An algebraic expression is a statement about unknown quantities expressed in mathematical symbols. The statement *five times a number added to forty* is expressed as $5x + 40$. An equation is a statement in which two expressions (with at least one containing a variable) are equal to one another. The statement *five times a number added to forty is equal to ten* is expressed as:

$$5x + 40 = 10$$

Real world scenarios can also be expressed mathematically. Suppose a job pays its employees $300 per week and $40 for each sale made. The weekly pay is represented by the expression $40x + 300$ where x is the number of sales made during the week.

Consider the following scenario: Bob had $20 and Tom had $4. After selling 4 ice cream cones to Bob, Tom has as much money as Bob. The cost of an ice cream cone is an unknown quantity and can be represented by a variable (x). The amount of money Bob has after his purchase is four times the cost of an ice cream cone subtracted from his original $20 → $20 - 4x$. The amount of money Tom has after his sale is four times the cost of an ice cream cone added to his original $4 → $4x + 4$. After the sale, the amount of money that Bob and Tom have is equal:

$$\rightarrow 20 - 4x = 4x + 4$$

When expressing a verbal or written statement mathematically, it is vital to understand words or phrases that can be represented with symbols. The following are examples:

Symbol	Phrase
+	Added to; increased by; sum of; more than
−	Decreased by; difference between; less than; take away
×	Multiplied by; 3(4, 5…) times as large; product of
÷	Divided by; quotient of; half (third, etc.) of
=	Is; the same as; results in; as much as; equal to
x, t, n, etc.	A number; unknown quantity; value of; variable

Use of Formulas

Formulas are mathematical expressions that define the value of one quantity, given the value of one or more different quantities. Formulas look like equations because they contain variables, numbers, operators, and an equal sign. All formulas are equations, but not all equations are formulas. A formula must have more than one variable. For example, $2x + 7 = y$ is an equation and a formula (it relates the unknown quantities x and y). However, $2x + 7 = 3$ is an equation but not a formula (it only expresses the value of the unknown quantity x).

Formulas are typically written with one variable alone (or isolated) on one side of the equal sign. This variable can be thought of as the *subject* in that the formula is stating the value of the *subject* in terms of the relationship between the other variables. Consider the distance formula: $distance = rate \times time$ or $d = rt$. The value of the subject variable d (distance) is the product of the variable r and t (rate and time). Given the rate and time, the distance traveled can easily be determined by substituting the values into the formula and evaluating.

Mathematics

The formula $P = 2l + 2w$ expresses how to calculate the perimeter of a rectangle (P) given its length (l) and width (w). To find the perimeter of a rectangle with a length of 3 ft and a width of 2 ft, these values are substituted into the formula for l and w:

$$P = 2(3 \text{ ft}) + 2(2 \text{ ft})$$

Following the order of operations, the perimeter is determined to be 10 ft. When working with formulas such as these, including units is an important step.

Given a formula expressed in terms of one variable, the formula can be manipulated to express the relationship in terms of any other variable. In other words, the formula can be rearranged to change which variable is the *subject*. To solve for a variable of interest by manipulating a formula, the equation may be solved as if all other variables were numbers. The same steps for solving are followed, leaving operations in terms of the variables instead of calculating numerical values. For the formula $P = 2l + 2w$, the perimeter is the subject expressed in terms of the length and width. To write a formula to calculate the width of a rectangle, given its length and perimeter, the previous formula relating the three variables is solved for the variable w. If P and l were numerical values, this is a two-step linear equation solved by subtraction and division. To solve the equation $P = 2l + 2w$ for w, $2l$ is first subtracted from both sides:

$$P - 2l = 2w$$

Then both sides are divided by 2:

$$\frac{P - 2l}{2} = w$$

Dependent and Independent Variables

A variable represents an unknown quantity and, in the case of a formula, a specific relationship exists between the variables. Within a given scenario, variables are the quantities that are changing. If two variables exist, one is dependent and one is independent. The value of one variable depends on the other variable. If a scenario describes distance traveled and time traveled at a given speed, distance is dependent and time is independent. The distance traveled depends on the time spent traveling. If a scenario describes the cost of a cab ride and the distance traveled, the cost is dependent and the distance is independent. The cost of a cab ride depends on the distance traveled. Formulas often contain more than two variables and are typically written with the dependent variable alone on one side of the equation. This lone variable is the *subject* of the statement. If a formula contains three or more variables, one variable is dependent and the rest are independent. The values of all independent variables are needed to determine the value of the dependent variable.

The formula $P = 2l + 2w$ expresses the dependent variable P in terms of the independent variables, l and w. The perimeter of a rectangle depends on its length and width. The formula $d = rt$ ($distance = rate \times time$) expresses the dependent variable d in terms of the independent variables, r and t. The distance traveled depends on the rate (or speed) and the time traveled.

Solutions to Linear Equations and Inequalities

Multistep One-Variable Linear Equations and Inequalities

Linear equations and linear inequalities are both comparisons of two algebraic expressions. However, unlike equations in which the expressions are equal, linear inequalities compare expressions that may be unequal. **Linear equations** typically have one value for the variable that makes the statement true. **Linear inequalities** generally have an infinite number of values that make the statement true.

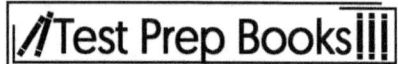

When solving a linear equation, the desired result requires determining a numerical value for the unknown variable. If given a linear equation involving addition, subtraction, multiplication, or division, working backwards isolates the variable. Addition and subtraction are inverse operations, as are multiplication and division. Therefore, they can be used to cancel each other out.

The first steps to solving linear equations are distributing, if necessary, and combining any like terms on the same side of the equation. Sides of an equation are separated by an *equal* sign. Next, the equation is manipulated to show the variable on one side. Whatever is done to one side of the equation must be done to the other side of the equation to remain equal. Inverse operations are then used to isolate the variable and undo the order of operations backwards. Addition and subtraction are undone, then multiplication and division are undone.

For example, solve $4(t-2) + 2t - 4 = 2(9 - 2t)$

Distributing: $4t - 8 + 2t - 4 = 18 - 4t$

Combining like terms: $6t - 12 = 18 - 4t$

Adding $4t$ to each side to move the variable: $10t - 12 = 18$

Adding 12 to each side to isolate the variable: $10t = 30$

Dividing each side by 10 to isolate the variable: $t = 3$

The answer can be checked by substituting the value for the variable into the original equation and ensuring that both sides calculate to be equal.

Linear inequalities express the relationship between unequal values. More specifically, they describe in what way the values are unequal. A value can be greater than ($>$), less than ($<$), greater than or equal to ($\geq$), or less than or equal to ($\leq$) another value. $5x + 40 > 65$ is read as *five times a number added to forty is greater than sixty-five.*

When solving a linear inequality, the solution is the set of all numbers that make the statement true. The inequality $x + 2 \geq 6$ has a solution set of 4 and every number greater than 4 (4.01; 5; 12; 107; etc.). Adding 2 to 4 or any number greater than 4 results in a value that is greater than or equal to 6. Therefore, $x \geq 4$ is the solution set.

To algebraically solve a linear inequality, follow the same steps as those for solving a linear equation. The inequality symbol stays the same for all operations *except* when multiplying or dividing by a negative number. If multiplying or dividing by a negative number while solving an inequality, the relationship reverses (the sign flips). In other words, $>$ switches to $<$ and vice versa. Multiplying or dividing by a positive number does not change the relationship, so the sign stays the same. An example is shown below.

Solve $-2x - 8 \leq 22$ for the value of x.

Add 8 to both sides to isolate the variable:

$$-2x \leq 30$$

Divide both sides by -2 to solve for x:

$$x \geq -15$$

Mathematics

Solutions of a linear equation or a linear inequality are the values of the variable that make a statement true. In the case of a linear equation, the solution set (list of all possible solutions) typically consists of a single numerical value. To find the solution, the equation is solved by isolating the variable. For example, solving the equation $3x - 7 = -13$ produces the solution $x = -2$. The only value for x which produces a true statement is -2. This can be checked by substituting -2 into the original equation to check that both sides are equal. In this case, $3(-2) - 7 = -13 \rightarrow -13 = -13$; therefore, -2 is a solution.

Although linear equations generally have one solution, this is not always the case. If there is no value for the variable that makes the statement true, there is no solution to the equation. Consider the equation:

$$x + 3 = x - 1$$

There is no value for x in which adding 3 to the value produces the same result as subtracting one from the value. Conversely, if substituting any value for the variable makes a true statement, the equation has an infinite number of solutions. Consider the equation:

$$3x + 6 = 3(x + 2)$$

Any number substituted for x will result in a true statement (both sides of the equation are equal).

By manipulating equations like the two above, the variable of the equation will cancel out completely. If the remaining constants express a true statement (ex. $6 = 6$), then all real numbers are solutions to the equation. If the constants left express a false statement (ex. $3 = -1$), then no solution exists for the equation.

Interpreting Solutions on a Number Line

Solving a linear inequality requires all values that make the statement true to be determined. For example, solving $3x - 7 \geq -13$ produces the solution $x \geq -2$. This means that -2 and any number greater than -2 produces a true statement. Solution sets for linear inequalities will often be displayed using a number line. If a value is included in the set ($\geq$ or $\leq$), a shaded dot is placed on that value and an arrow extending in the direction of the solutions. For a variable $>$ or $\geq$ a number, the arrow will point right on a number line, the direction where the numbers increase. If a variable is $<$ or $\leq$ a number, the arrow will point left on a number line, which is the direction where the numbers decrease. If the value is not included in the set ($>$ or $<$), an open (unshaded) circle on that value is used with an arrow in the appropriate direction.

Like this:

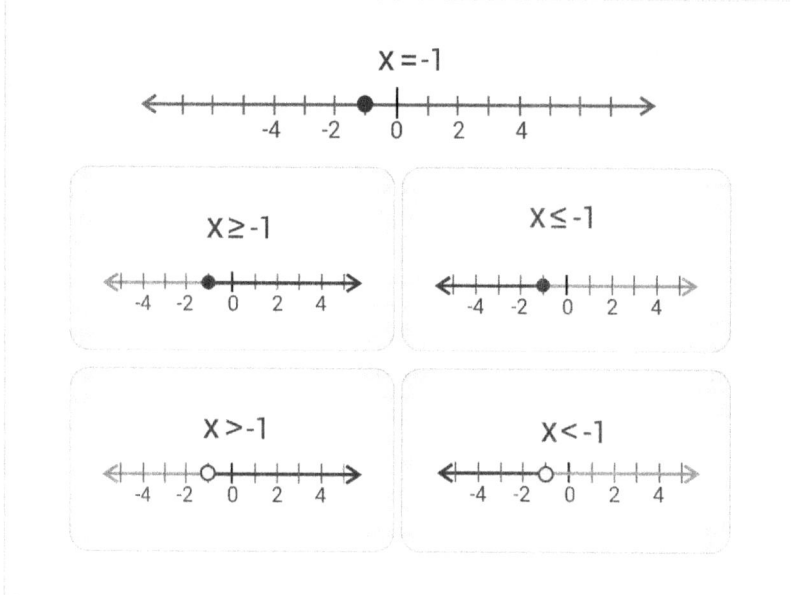

Similar to linear equations, a linear inequality may have a solution set consisting of all real numbers or contain no solution. When solved algebraically, a linear inequality in which the variable cancels out and results in a true statement (ex. $7 \geq 2$) has a solution set of all real numbers. A linear inequality in which the variable cancels out and results in a false statement (ex. $7 \leq 2$) has no solution.

Linear Relationships

Linear relationships describe the way two quantities change with respect to each other. The relationship is defined as linear because a line is produced if all the sets of corresponding values are graphed on a coordinate grid. When expressing the linear relationship as an equation, the equation is often written in the form $y = mx + b$ (slope-intercept form) where m and b are numerical values and x and y are variables (for example, $y = 5x + 10$). Given a linear equation and the value of either variable (x or y), the value of the other variable can be determined.

Suppose a teacher is grading a test containing 20 questions with 5 points given for each correct answer, adding a curve of 10 points to each test. This linear relationship can be expressed as the equation $y = 5x + 10$ where x represents the number of correct answers, and y represents the test score. To determine the score of a test with a given number of correct answers, the number of correct answers is substituted into the equation for x and evaluated. For example, for 10 correct answers, 10 is substituted for x:

$$y = 5(10) + 10 \rightarrow y = 60$$

Therefore, 10 correct answers will result in a score of 60. The number of correct answers needed to obtain a certain score can also be determined. To determine the number of correct answers needed to score a 90, 90 is substituted for y in the equation (y represents the test score) and solved:

$$90 = 5 + 10 \rightarrow 80 = 5x \rightarrow 16 = x$$

Therefore, 16 correct answers are needed to score a 90.

Mathematics

Linear relationships may be represented by a table of 2 corresponding values. Certain tables may determine the relationship between the values and predict other corresponding sets. Consider the table below, which displays the money in a checking account that charges a monthly fee:

Month	0	1	2	3	4
Balance	$210	$195	$180	$165	$150

An examination of the values reveals that the account loses $15 every month (the month increases by one and the balance decreases by 15). This information can be used to predict future values. To determine what the value will be in month 6, the pattern can be continued, and it can be concluded that the balance will be $120. To determine which month the balance will be $0, $210 is divided by $15 (since the balance decreases $15 every month), resulting in month 14.

Similar to a table, a graph can display corresponding values of a linear relationship.

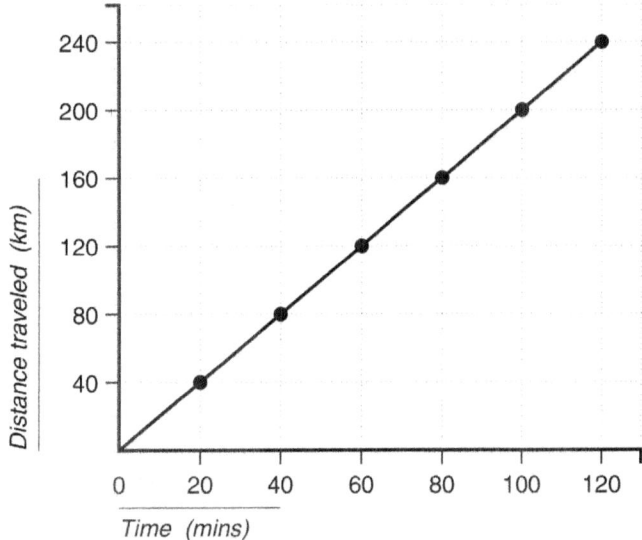

The graph above represents the relationship between distance traveled and time. To find the distance traveled in 80 minutes, the mark for 80 minutes is located at the bottom of the graph. By following this mark directly up on the graph, the corresponding point for 80 minutes is directly across from the 150 kilometer mark. This information indicates that the distance travelled in 80 minutes is 160 kilometers. To predict information not displayed on the graph, the way in which the variables change with respect to one another is determined. In this case, distance increases by 40 kilometers as time increases by 20 minutes. This information can be used to continue the data in the graph or convert the values to a table.

Recognizing and Representing Patterns

Number and Shape Patterns

Patterns within a sequence can come in two distinct forms: the items (shapes, numbers, etc.) either repeat in a constant order, or the items change from one step to another in some consistent way. The core is the smallest unit, or number of items, that repeats in a repeating pattern. For example, the pattern oo▲oo▲o... has a core that is oo▲. Knowing only the core, the pattern can be extended. Knowing the number of steps in the core allows the identification of an item in each step without drawing/writing the entire pattern out. For example, suppose the tenth item in the previous pattern must be determined. Because the core consists of three items (oo▲), the core repeats in multiples of 3. In other words, steps 3, 6, 9, 12, etc. will be ▲

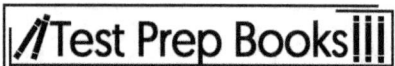

completing the core with the core starting over on the next step. For the above example, the 9th step will be ▲ and the 10th will be ○.

The most common patterns in which each item changes from one step to the next are arithmetic and geometric sequences. An **arithmetic sequence** is one in which the items increase or decrease by a constant difference. In other words, the same thing is added or subtracted to each item or step to produce the next. To determine if a sequence is arithmetic, determine what must be added or subtracted to step one to produce step two. Then, check if the same thing is added/subtracted to step two to produce step three. The same thing must be added/subtracted to step three to produce step four, and so on.

Consider the pattern 13, 10, 7, 4 . . . To get from step one (13) to step two (10) requires subtracting by 3. The next step is checking if subtracting 3 from step two (10) will produce step three (7), and subtracting 3 from step three (7) will produce step four (4). In this case, the pattern holds true. Therefore, this is an arithmetic sequence in which each step is produced by subtracting 3 from the previous step. To extend the sequence, 3 is subtracted from the last step to produce the next. The next three numbers in the sequence are 1, −2, −5.

A **geometric sequence** is one in which each step is produced by multiplying or dividing the previous step by the same number. To determine if a sequence is geometric, decide what step one must be multiplied or divided by to produce step two. Then check if multiplying or dividing step two by the same number produces step three, and so on. Consider the pattern 2, 8, 32, 128 . . . To get from step one (2) to step two (8) requires multiplication by 4. The next step determines if multiplying step two (8) by 4 produces step three (32), and multiplying step three (32) by 4 produces step four (128). In this case, the pattern holds true. Therefore, this is a geometric sequence in which each step is produced by multiplying the previous step by 4. To extend the sequence, the last step is multiplied by 4 and repeated. The next three numbers in the sequence are 512; 2,048; 8,192.

Although arithmetic and geometric sequences typically use numbers, these sequences can also be represented by shapes. For example, an arithmetic sequence could consist of shapes with three sides, four sides, and five sides (add one side to the previous step to produce the next). A geometric sequence could consist of eight blocks, four blocks, and two blocks (each step is produced by dividing the number of blocks in the previous step by 2).

Conjectures, Predictions, or Generalizations Based on Patterns

An arithmetic or geometric sequence can be written as a formula and used to determine unknown steps without writing out the entire sequence. (Note that a similar process for repeating patterns is covered in the previous section.) An arithmetic sequence progresses by a **common difference**. To determine the common difference, any step is subtracted by the step that precedes it. In the sequence 4, 9, 14, 19 . . . the common difference, or d, is 5. By expressing each step as a_1, a_2, a_3, etc., a formula can be written to represent the sequence. a_1 is the first step. To produce step two, step 1 (a_1) is added to the common difference (d):

$$a_2 = a_1 + d$$

Mathematics

To produce step three, the common difference (d) is added twice to a_1:

$$a_3 = a_1 + 2d$$

To produce step four, the common difference (d) is added three times to a_1:

$$a_4 = a_1 + 3d$$

Following this pattern allows a general rule for arithmetic sequences to be written. For any term of the sequence (a_n), the first step (a_1) is added to the product of the common difference (d) and one less than the step of the term ($n-1$):

$$a_n = a_1 + (n-1)d$$

Suppose the 8th term (a_8) is to be found in the previous sequence. By knowing the first step (a_1) is 4 and the common difference (d) is 5, the formula can be used:

$$a_n = a_1 + (n-1)d \to a_8 = 4 + (7)5 \to a_8 = 39$$

In a geometric sequence, each step is produced by multiplying or dividing the previous step by the same number. The **common ratio**, or (r), can be determined by dividing any step by the previous step. In the sequence 1, 3, 9, 27 ... the common ratio (r) is 3 ($\frac{3}{1} = 3$ or $\frac{9}{3} = 3$ or $\frac{27}{9} = 3$). Each successive step can be expressed as a product of the first step (a_1) and the common ratio (r) to some power. For example:

$$a_2 = a_1 \times r$$

$$a_3 = a_1 \times r \times r \text{ or } a_3 = a_1 \times r^2$$

$$a_4 = a_1 \times r \times r \times r \text{ or } a_4 = a_1 \times r^3$$

Following this pattern, a general rule for geometric sequences can be written. For any term of the sequence (a_n), the first step (a_1) is multiplied by the common ratio (r) raised to the power one less than the step of the term ($n-1$):

$$a_n = a_1 \times r^{(n-1)}$$

Suppose for the previous sequence, the 7th term (a_7) is to be found. Knowing the first step (a_1) is one, and the common ratio (r) is 3, the formula can be used:

$$a_n = a_1 \times r^{(n-1)} \to a_7 = (1) \times 3^6 \to a_7 = 729$$

Corresponding Terms of Two Numerical Patterns

When given two numerical patterns, the corresponding terms should be examined to determine if a relationship exists between them. **Corresponding terms** between patterns are the pairs of numbers that appear in the same step of the two sequences. Consider the following patterns 1, 2, 3, 4 ... and 3, 6, 9, 12 ... The corresponding terms are: 1 and 3; 2 and 6; 3 and 9; and 4 and 12. To identify the relationship, each pair of corresponding terms is examined and the possibilities of performing an operation ($+, -, \times, \div$) to the term from the first sequence to produce the corresponding term in the second sequence are determined.

In this case:

$$1 + 2 = 3 \quad \text{or} \quad 1 \times 3 = 3$$

$2 + 4 = 6$	or	$2 \times 3 = 6$	
$3 + 6 = 9$	or	$3 \times 3 = 9$	
$4 + 8 = 12$	or	$4 \times 3 = 12$	

The consistent pattern is that the number from the first sequence multiplied by 3 equals its corresponding term in the second sequence. By assigning each sequence a label (input and output) or variable (x and y), the relationship can be written as an equation. If the first sequence represents the inputs, or x, and the second sequence represents the outputs, or y, the relationship can be expressed as: $y = 3x$.

Consider the following sets of numbers:

a	2	4	6	8
b	6	8	10	12

To write a rule for the relationship between the values for a and the values for b, the corresponding terms (2 and 6; 4 and 8; 6 and 10; 8 and 12) are examined. The possibilities for producing b from a are:

$2 + 4 = 6$ or $2 \times 3 = 6$

$4 + 4 = 8$ or $4 \times 2 = 8$

$6 + 4 = 10$

$8 + 4 = 12$ or $8 \times 1.5 = 12$

The consistent pattern is that adding 4 to the value of a produces the value of b. The relationship can be written as the equation $a + 4 = b$.

Geometry & Measurement, Data, Statistics, and Probability

Classifying One-, Two-, and Three-Dimensional Figures

Lines, Rays, and Line Segments

The basic unit of geometry is a **point**. A point represents an exact location on a plane, or flat surface. The position of a point is indicated with a dot and usually named with a single uppercase letter, such as point A or point T. A point is a place, not a thing, and therefore has no dimensions or size. A set of points that lies on the same line is called **collinear**.

A set of points that lies on the same plane is called **coplanar**.

The image above displays point A, point B, and point C.

Mathematics

A **line** is as series of points that extends in both directions without ending. It consists of an infinite number of points and is drawn with arrows on both ends to indicate it extends infinitely. Lines can be named by two points on the line or with a single, cursive, lower case letter. The two lines below could be named line AB or line BA or $\overleftrightarrow{AB}$ or $\overleftrightarrow{BA}$; and line m.

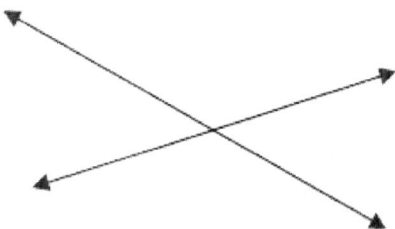

Two lines are considered parallel to each other if, while extending infinitely, they will never intersect (or meet). **Parallel lines** point in the same direction and are always the same distance apart. Two lines are considered perpendicular if they intersect to form right angles. Right angles are 90°. Typically, a small box is drawn at the intersection point to indicate the right angle.

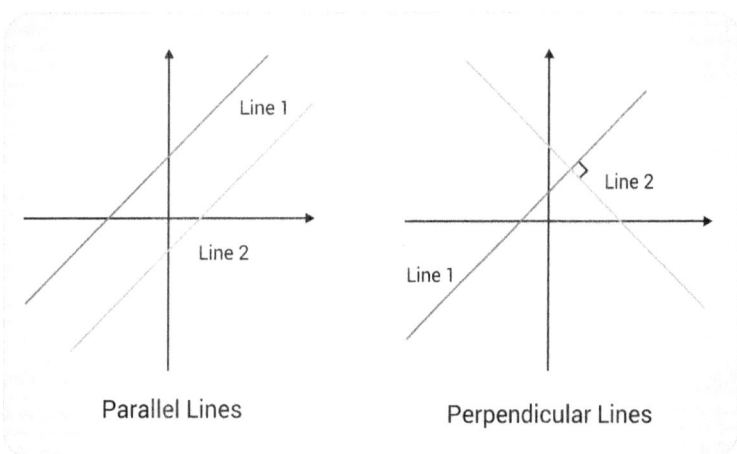

Line 1 is parallel to line 2 in the left image and is written as line 1 || line 2. Line 1 is perpendicular to line 2 in the right image and is written as line 1 ⊥ line 2.

A **ray** has a specific starting point and extends in one direction without ending. The endpoint of a ray is its starting point. Rays are named using the endpoint first, and any other point on the ray. The following ray can be named ray AB and written $\overrightarrow{AB}$.

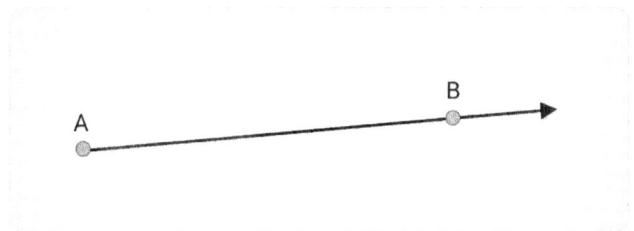

A **line segment** has specific starting and ending points. A line segment consists of two endpoints and all the points in between. Line segments are named by the two endpoints. The example below is named segment KL or segment LK, written $\overline{KL}$ or $\overline{LK}$.

Classification of Angles

An **angle** consists of two rays that have a common endpoint. This common endpoint is called the **vertex of the angle**. The two rays can be called **sides of the angle**. The angle below has a vertex at point B and the sides consist of ray BA and ray BC. An angle can be named in three ways:

- 1. Using the vertex and a point from each side, with the vertex letter in the middle.
- 2. Using only the vertex. This can only be used if it is the only angle with that vertex.
- 3. Using a number that is written inside the angle.

The angle below can be written $\angle ABC$ (read angle ABC), $\angle CBA$, $\angle B$, or $\angle 1$.

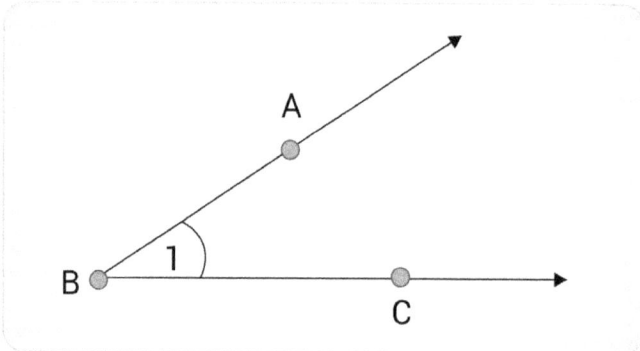

An angle divides a plane, or flat surface, into three parts: the angle itself, the interior (inside) of the angle, and the exterior (outside) of the angle. The figure below shows point M on the interior of the angle and point N on the exterior of the angle.

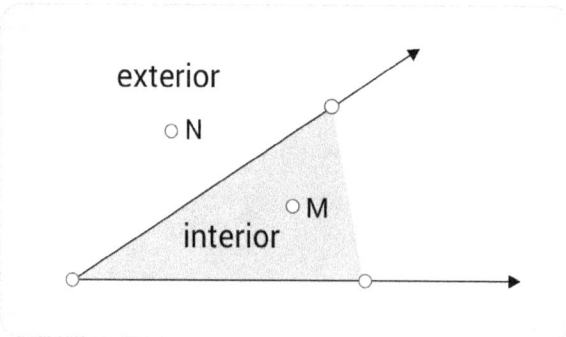

Angles can be measured in units called **degrees**, with the symbol °. The degree measure of an angle is between 0° and 180° and can be obtained by using a protractor.

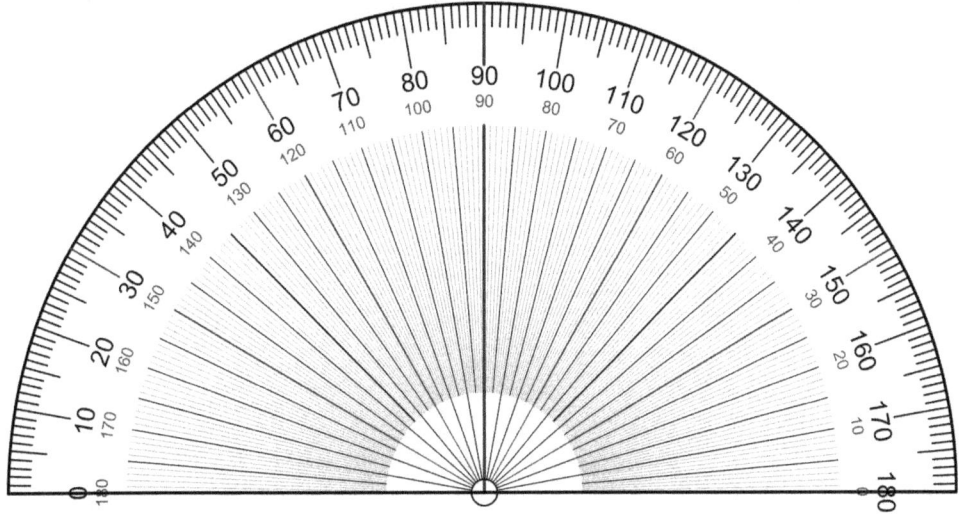

A **straight angle** (or simply a line) measures exactly 180°. A right angle's sides meet at the vertex to create a square corner. A **right angle** measures exactly 90° and is typically indicated by a box drawn in the interior of the angle. An **acute angle** has an interior that is narrower than a right angle. The measure of an acute angle is any value less than 90° and greater than 0°. For example, 89.9°, 47°, 12°, and 1°. An **obtuse angle** has an interior that is wider than a right angle. The measure of an obtuse angle is any value greater than 90° but less than 180°. For example, 90.1°, 110°, 150°, and 179.9°.

- Acute angles: Less than 90°
- Obtuse angles: Greater than 90°
- Right angles: 90°
- Straight angles: 180°

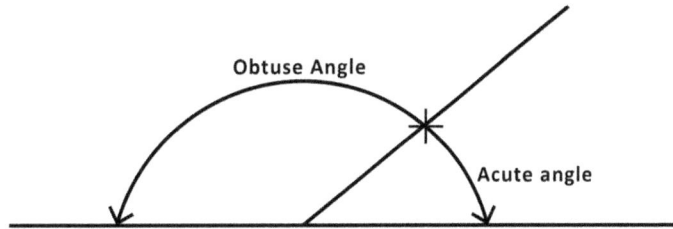

Two- and Three-Dimensional Shapes

A **polygon** is a closed geometric figure in a plane (flat surface) consisting of at least 3 sides formed by line segments. These are often defined as **two-dimensional shapes**. Common two-dimensional shapes include circles, triangles, squares, rectangles, pentagons, and hexagons. Note that a circle is a two-dimensional shape without sides.

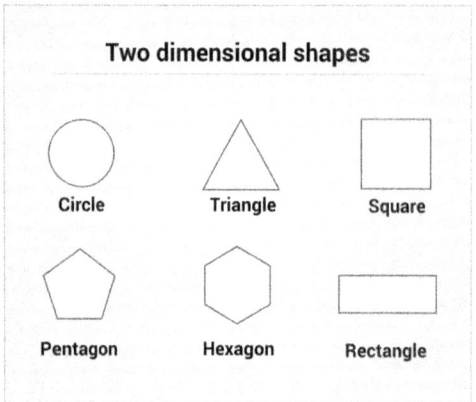

A solid figure, or simply solid, is a figure that encloses a part of space. Some solids consist of flat surfaces only while others include curved surfaces. Solid figures are often defined as **three-dimensional shapes**. Common three-dimensional shapes include spheres, prisms, cubes, pyramids, cylinders, and cones.

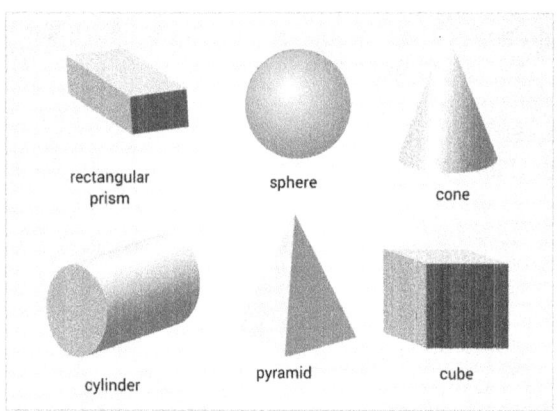

Mathematics

Composing two- or three-dimensional shapes involves putting together two or more shapes to create a new larger figure. For example, a semi-circle (half circle), rectangle, and two triangles can be used to compose the figure of the sailboat shown below.

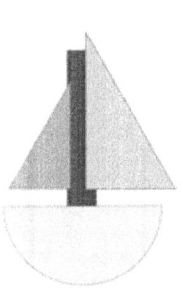

Similarly, solid figures can be placed together to compose an endless number of three-dimensional objects.

Decomposing two- and three-dimensional figures involves breaking the shapes apart into smaller, simpler shapes. Consider the following two-dimensional representations of a house:

This complex figure can be decomposed into the following basic two-dimensional shapes: large rectangle (body of house); large triangle (roof); small rectangle and small triangle (chimney). Decomposing figures is often done more than one way. To illustrate, the figure of the house could also be decomposed into: two large triangles (body); two medium triangles (roof); two smaller triangles of unequal size (chimney).

Polygons and Solids

A **polygon** is a closed two-dimensional figure consisting of three or more sides. Polygons can be either convex or concave. A polygon that has interior angles all measuring less than 180° is **convex**. A **concave** polygon has one or more interior angles measuring greater than 180°. Examples are shown below.

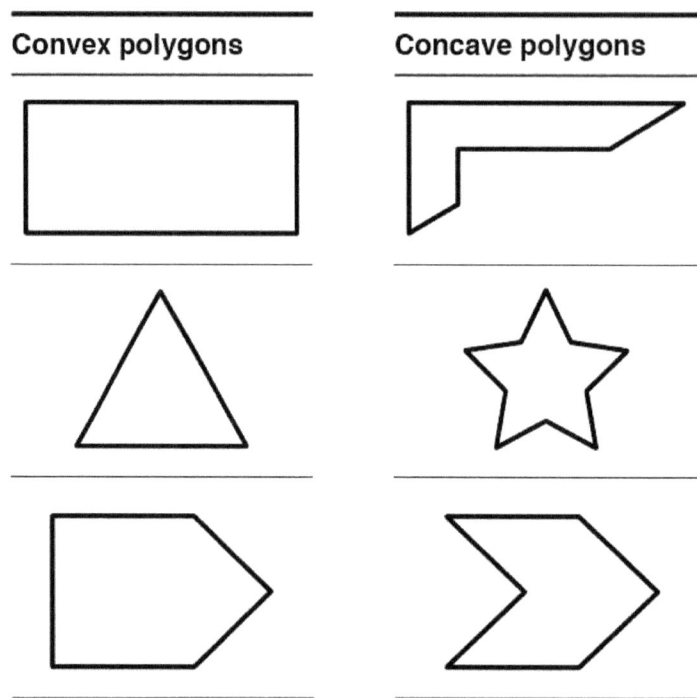

Polygons can be classified by the number of sides (also equal to the number of angles) they have. The following are the names of polygons with a given number of sides or angles:

# of sides	3	4	5	6	7	8	9	10
Name of polygon	Triangle	Quadrilateral	Pentagon	Hexagon	Septagon (or heptagon)	Octagon	Nonagon	Decagon

Equiangular polygons are polygons in which the measure of every interior angle is the same. The sides of **equilateral polygons** are always the same length. If a polygon is both equiangular and equilateral, the polygon is defined as a **regular polygon**. Examples are shown below.

Mathematics

Triangles can be further classified by their sides and angles. A triangle with its largest angle measuring 90° is a **right triangle**. A triangle with the largest angle less than 90° is an **acute triangle**. A triangle with the largest angle greater than 90° is an **obtuse triangle**. Below is an example of a right triangle.

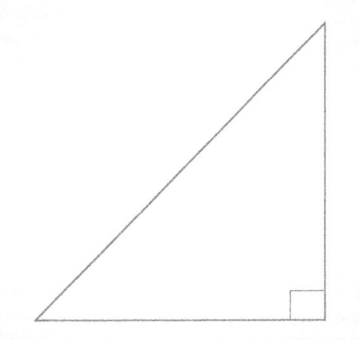

A triangle consisting of two equal sides and two equal angles is an **isosceles triangle**. A triangle with three equal sides and three equal angles is an **equilateral triangle**. A triangle with no equal sides or angles is a **scalene triangle**.

Isosceles triangle:

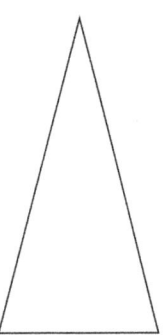

Equilateral triangle:

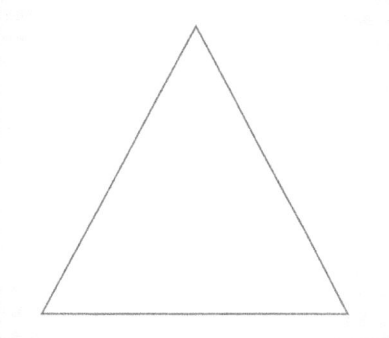

Scalene triangle:

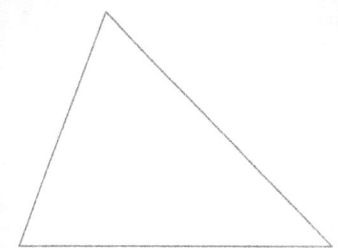

Quadrilaterals can be further classified according to their sides and angles. A quadrilateral with exactly one pair of parallel sides is called a **trapezoid**. A quadrilateral that shows both pairs of opposite sides parallel is a **parallelogram**. Parallelograms include rhombuses, rectangles, and squares. A **rhombus** has four equal sides. A **rectangle** has four equal angles (90° each). A **square** has four 90° angles and four equal sides. Therefore, a square is both a rhombus and a rectangle.

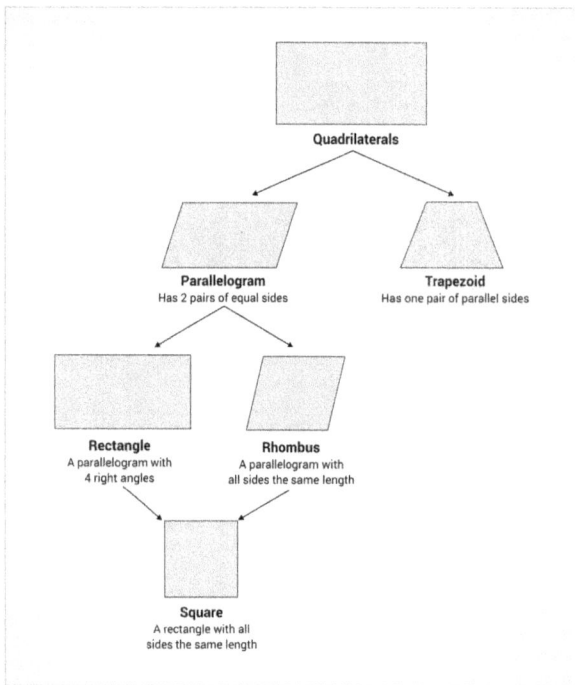

A **solid** is a three-dimensional figure that encloses a part of space. Solids consisting of all flat surfaces that are polygons are called **polyhedrons**. The two-dimensional surfaces that make up a polyhedron are called **faces**. Types of polyhedrons include prisms and pyramids. A **prism** consists of two parallel faces that are congruent (or the same shape and same size) and lateral faces going around (which are parallelograms).

A **prism** is further classified by the shape of its base, as shown below:

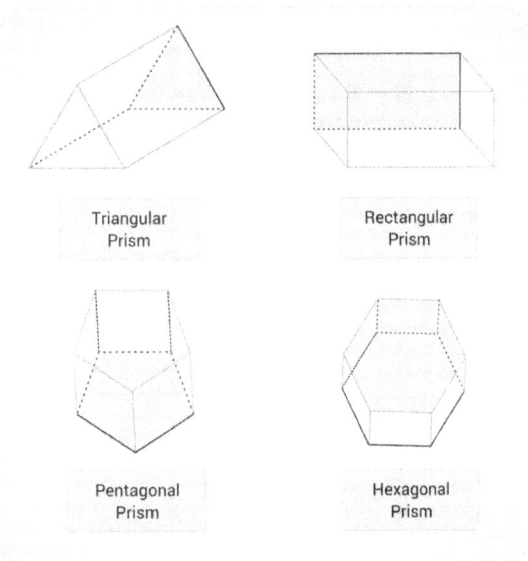

A **pyramid** consists of lateral faces (triangles) that meet at a common point called the **vertex** and one other face that is a polygon, called the **base**. A pyramid can be further classified by the shape of its base, as shown below.

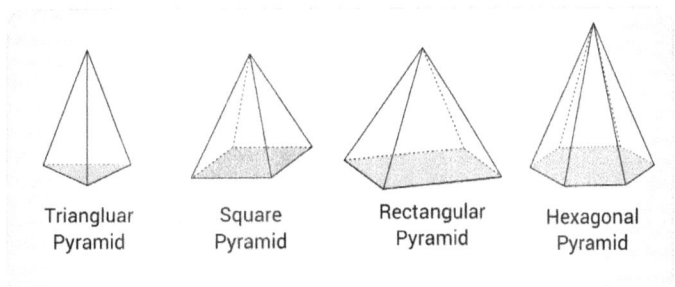

A **tetrahedron** is another name for a triangular pyramid. All the faces of a tetrahedron are triangles.

Solids that are not polyhedrons include spheres, cylinders, and cones. A **sphere** is the set of all points a given distance from a given center point. A sphere is commonly thought of as a three-dimensional circle. A **cylinder** consists of two parallel, **congruent** (same size) circles and a lateral curved surface. A **cone** consists of a circle as its base and a lateral curved surface that narrows to a point called the vertex.

Similar polygons are the same shape but different sizes. More specifically, their corresponding angle measures are congruent (or equal) and the length of their sides is proportional. For example, all sides of one polygon may be double the length of the sides of another. Likewise, similar solids are the same shape but different sizes. Any corresponding faces or bases of similar solids are the same polygons that are proportional by a consistent value.

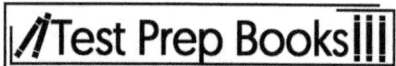

Mathematics

Perimeter, Area, Surface Area, and Volume

Three-Dimensional Figures with Nets

A **net** is a construction of two-dimensional figures that can be folded to form a given three-dimensional figure. More than one net may exist to fold and produce the same solid, or three-dimensional figure. The bases and faces of the solid figure are analyzed to determine the polygons (two-dimensional figures) needed to form the net.

Consider the following triangular prism:

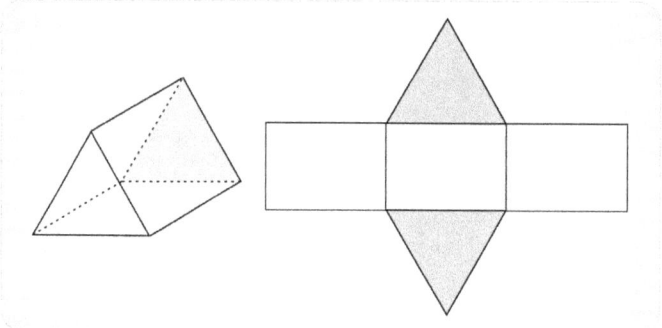

The surface of the prism consists of two triangular bases and three rectangular faces. The net beside it can be used to construct the triangular prism by first folding the triangles up to be parallel to each other, and then folding the two outside rectangles up and to the center with the outer edges touching.

Consider the following cylinder:

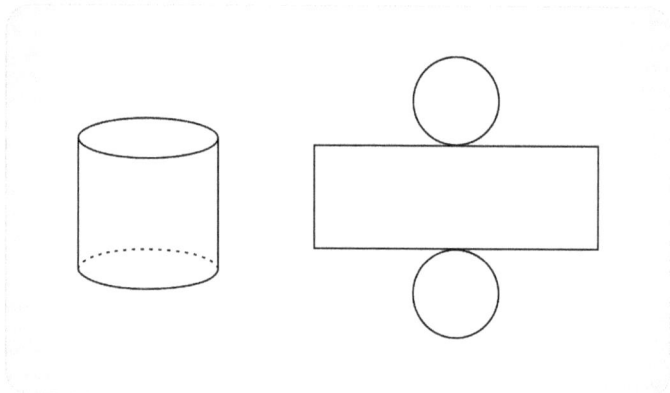

The surface consists of two circular bases and a curved lateral surface that can be opened and flattened into a rectangle. The net beside the cylinder can be used to construct the cylinder by first folding the circles up to be parallel to each other, and then curving the sides of the rectangle up to touch each other. The top and bottom of the folded rectangle should be touching the outside of both circles.

Mathematics

Consider the following square pyramid below on the left. The surface consists of one square base and four triangular faces. The net below on the right can be used to construct the square pyramid by folding each triangle towards the center of the square. The top points of the triangle meet at the vertex.

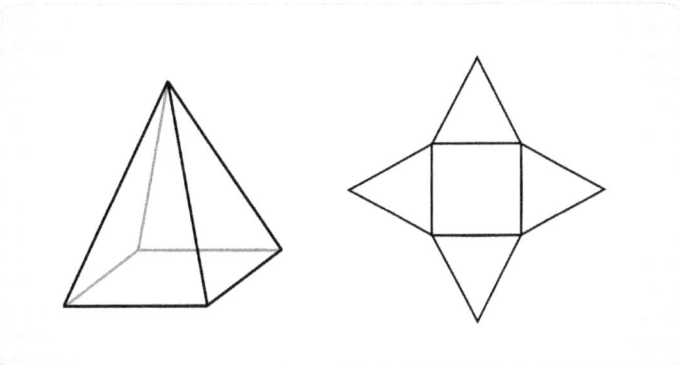

Surface Area of Three-Dimensional Figures

The **area of a two-dimensional figure** refers to the number of square units needed to cover the interior region of the figure. This concept is similar to wallpaper covering the flat surface of a wall. For example, if a rectangle has an area of 10 square centimeters (written 10 cm^2), it will take 10 squares, each with sides one centimeter in length, to cover the interior region of the rectangle. Note that area is measured in square units such as: square centimeters or cm^2; square feet or ft^2; square yards or yd^2; square miles or mi^2.

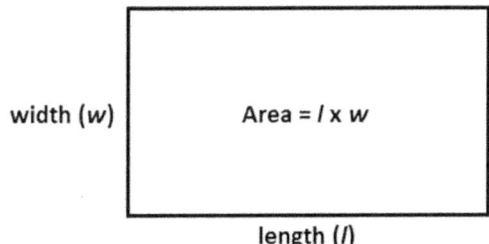

The **surface area of a three-dimensional figure** refers to the number of square units needed to cover the entire surface of the figure. This concept is similar to using wrapping paper to completely cover the outside of a box. For example, if a triangular pyramid has a surface area of 17 square inches (written 17 in^2), it will take 17 squares, each with sides one inch in length, to cover the entire surface of the pyramid. Surface area is also measured in square units.

Many three-dimensional figures (solid figures) can be represented by nets consisting of rectangles and triangles. The surface area of such solids can be determined by adding the areas of each of its faces and bases. Finding the surface area using this method requires calculating the areas of rectangles and triangles. To find the area (A) of a rectangle, the length (l) is multiplied by the width:

$$(w) \rightarrow A = l \times w$$

The area of a rectangle with a length of 8 cm and a width of 4 cm is calculated:

$$A = (8 \text{ cm}) \times (4 \text{ cm}) \rightarrow A = 32 \text{ cm}^2$$

To calculate the area (A) of a triangle, the product of $\frac{1}{2}$, the base (b), and the height (h) is found:

$$A = \frac{1}{2} \times b \times h$$

Note that the height of a triangle is measured from the base to the vertex opposite of it forming a right angle with the base. The area of a triangle with a base of 11 cm and a height of 6 cm is calculated:

$$A = \frac{1}{2} \times (11 \text{ cm}) \times (6 \text{ cm}) \rightarrow A = 33 \text{ cm}^2$$

Consider the following triangular prism, which is represented by a net consisting of two triangles and three rectangles.

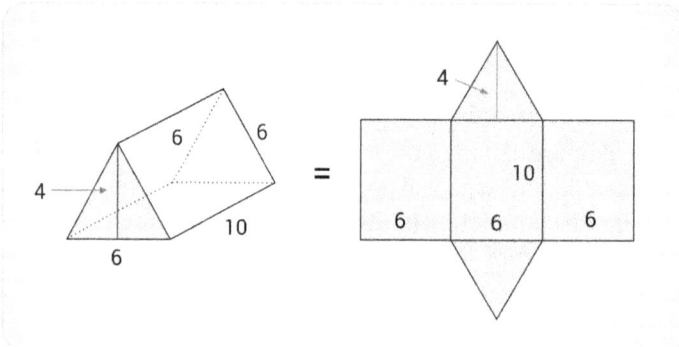

The **surface area of the prism** can be determined by adding the areas of each of its faces and bases. The surface area:

$$SA = area\ of\ triangle + area\ of\ triangle + area\ of\ rectangle$$
$$+ area\ of\ rectangle + area\ of\ rectangle$$

$$SA = \left(\frac{1}{2} \times b \times h\right) + \left(\frac{1}{2} \times b \times h\right) + (l \times w) + (l \times w) + (l \times w)$$

$$SA = \left(\frac{1}{2} \times 6 \times 4\right) + \left(\frac{1}{2} \times 6 \times 4\right) + (6 \times 10) + (6 \times 10) + (6 \times 10)$$

$$SA = (12) + (12) + (60) + (60) + (60)$$

$$SA = 204 \text{ square units}$$

Area and Perimeter of Polygons

Perimeter is the measurement of a distance around something or the sum of all sides of a polygon. Think of perimeter as the length of the boundary, like a fence. In contrast, **area** is the space occupied by a defined enclosure, like a field enclosed by a fence.

When thinking about perimeter, think about walking around the outside of something. When thinking about area, think about the amount of space or **surface area** something takes up.

Mathematics

Squares

The **perimeter of a square** is measured by adding together all of the sides. Since a square has four equal sides, its perimeter can be calculated by multiplying the length of one side by 4. Thus, the formula is $P = 4 \times s$, where s equals one side. For example, the following square has side lengths of 5 meters:

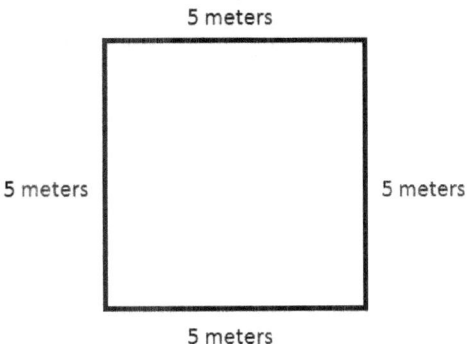

The perimeter is 20 meters because 4 times 5 is 20.

The **area of a square** is the length of a side squared. For example, if a side of a square is 7 centimeters, then the area is 49 square centimeters. The formula for this example is $A = s^2 = 7^2 = 49$ square centimeters. An example is if the rectangle has a length of 6 inches and a width of 7 inches, then the area is 42 square inches:

$$A = lw = 6(7) = 42 \text{ square inches}$$

Rectangles

Like a square, a **rectangle's perimeter** is measured by adding together all of the sides. But as the sides are unequal, the formula is different. A rectangle has equal values for its lengths (long sides) and equal values for its widths (short sides), so the perimeter formula for a rectangle is:

$$P = l + l + w + w = 2l + 2w$$

l equals length
w equals width

The area is found by multiplying the length by the width, so the formula is $A = l \times w$.

For example, if the length of a rectangle is 10 inches and the width 8 inches, then the perimeter is 36 inches because:

$$P = 2l + 2w = 2(10) + 2(8) = 20 + 16 = 36 \text{ inches}$$

Triangles

A **triangle's perimeter** is measured by adding together the three sides, so the formula is $P = a + b + c$, where a, b, and c are the values of the three sides. The area is the product of one-half the base and height so the formula is:

$$A = \frac{1}{2} \times b \times h$$

It can be simplified to:

$$A = \frac{bh}{2}$$

The base is the bottom of the triangle, and the height is the distance from the base to the peak. If a problem asks to calculate the area of a triangle, it will provide the base and height.

For example, if the base of the triangle is 2 feet and the height 4 feet, then the area is 4 square feet. The following equation shows the formula used to calculate the area of the triangle:

$A = \frac{1}{2} bh = \frac{1}{2}(2)(4) = 4$ square feet

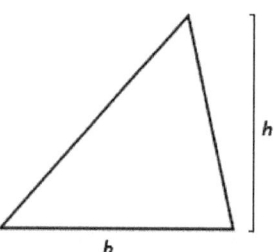

Circles

A circle's perimeter—also known as its **circumference**—is measured by multiplying the diameter by π.

Diameter is the straight line measured from a point on one side of the circle to a point directly across on the opposite side of the circle.

π is referred to as **pi** and is equal to 3.14 (with rounding).

So, the formula is $\pi \times d$.

This is sometimes expressed by the formula $C = 2 \times \pi \times r$, where r is the radius of the circle. These formulas are equivalent, as the radius equals half of the diameter.

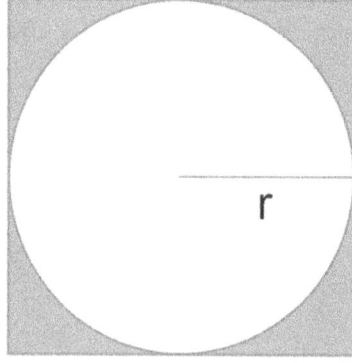

Mathematics

The area of a circle is calculated through the formula:

$$A = \pi \times r^2$$

The test will indicate either to leave the answer with π attached or to calculate to the nearest decimal place, which means multiplying by 3.14 for π.

Arc

The **arc of a circle** is the distance between two points on the circle. The length of the arc of a circle in terms of **degrees** is easily determined if the value of the central angle is known. The length of the arc is simply the value of the central angle. In this example, the length of the arc of the circle in degrees is 75°.

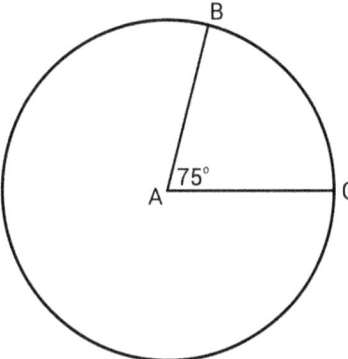

To determine the length of the arc of a circle in distance, the values for both the central angle and the radius must be known. This formula is:

$$\frac{central\ angle}{360°} = \frac{arc\ length}{2\pi r}$$

The equation is simplified by cross-multiplying to solve for the arc length. In the following example, to solve for arc length, substitute the values of the central angle (75°) and the radius (10 inches) into the equation above.

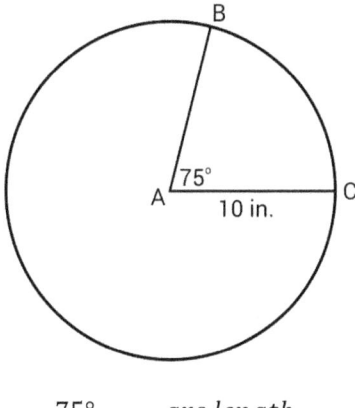

$$\frac{75°}{360°} = \frac{arc\ length}{2(3.14)(10\ in)}$$

To solve the equation, first cross-multiply: $4,710 = 360(arc\ length)$. Next, divide each side of the equation by 360. The result of the formula is that the arc length is 13.1 (rounded).

Parallelograms

Similar to triangles, the height of the parallelogram is measured from one base to the other at a 90° angle (or perpendicular).

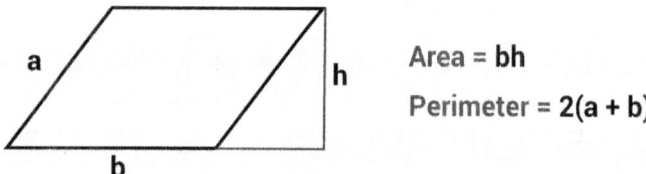

Trapezoid

The **area of a trapezoid** can be calculated using the formula: $A = \frac{1}{2} \times h(b_1 + b_2)$, where h is the height and b_1 and b_2 are the parallel bases of the trapezoid:

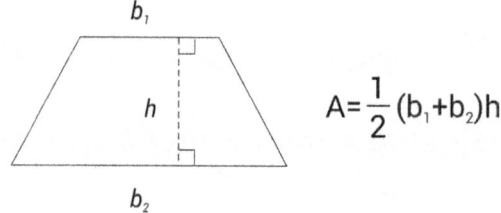

Regular Polygon

The area of a regular polygon can be determined by using its perimeter and the length of the apothem. The **apothem** is a line from the center of the regular polygon to any of its sides at a right angle. (Note that the perimeter of a regular polygon can be determined given the length of only one side.) The formula for the area (A) of a regular polygon is $A = \frac{1}{2} \times a \times P$, where a is the length of the apothem, and P is the perimeter of the figure. Consider the following regular pentagon:

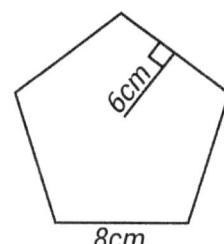

Mathematics

To find the area, the perimeter (P) is calculated first: $8 \text{ cm} \times 5 \to P = 40 \text{ cm}$. Then the perimeter and the apothem are used to find the area (A):

$$A = \frac{1}{2} \times a \times P \to A = \frac{1}{2} \times (6 \text{ cm}) \times (40 \text{ cm}) \to A = 120 \text{ cm}^2$$

Note that the unit is:

$$\text{cm}^2 \to \text{cm} \times \text{cm} = \text{cm}^2$$

Irregular Shapes

The perimeter of an irregular polygon is found by adding the lengths of all of the sides. In cases where all of the sides are given, this will be very straightforward, as it will simply involve finding the sum of the provided lengths. Other times, a side length may be missing and must be determined before the perimeter can be calculated.

Consider the example below:

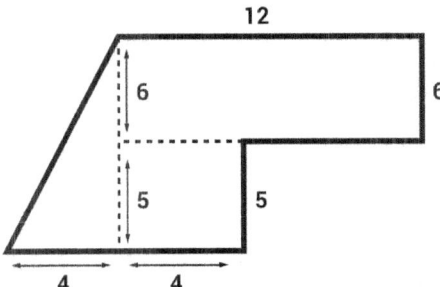

All of the side lengths are provided except for two: the horizontal line on the right between the vertical sides that measure 5 and 6, and the angled side on the left.

The horizontal side is easiest to solve, as test takers can identify that the length of the missing side, s, plus the length of the bottom horizontal side (4) are equal to the length of the top side (12). This could also be written as the formula $4 + s = 12$, and solved with an answer of 8.

Next, it's time to solve for the angled side on the left. Test takers should notice that this is the hypotenuse of a right triangle. The other two sides of the triangle are provided (the base is 4 and the height is $6 + 5 = 11$). The Pythagorean Theorem can be used to find the length of the hypotenuse of a right triangle, using the equation $a^2 + b^2 = c^2$, where c represents the hypotenuse.

Substituting the side values provided yields:

$$(4)^2 + (11)^2 = c^2$$

Therefore,

$$c = \sqrt{16 + 121} = 11.7$$

Finally, the perimeter can be found by adding this new side length with the other provided lengths to get the total length around the figure:

$$4 + 4 + 5 + 8 + 6 + 12 + 11.7 = 50.7$$

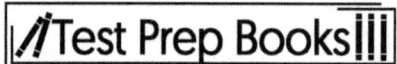

Mathematics

Although units are not provided in this figure, remember that reporting units with a measurement is important.

The area of irregular polygons is found by decomposing, or breaking apart, the figure into smaller shapes. When the area of the smaller shapes is determined, the area of the smaller shapes will produce the area of the original figure when added together. Consider the earlier example:

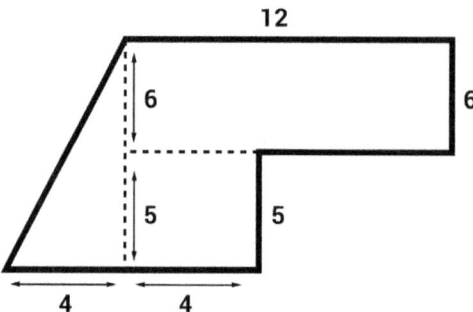

The irregular polygon is decomposed into two rectangles and a triangle. The area of the large rectangle ($A = l \times w \rightarrow A = 12 \times 6$) is 72 square units. The area of the small rectangle is 20 square units ($A = 4 \times 5$). The area of the triangle ($A = \frac{1}{2} \times b \times h \rightarrow A = \frac{1}{2} \times 4 \times 11$) is 22 square units. The sum of the areas of these figures produces the total area of the original polygon:

$A = 72 + 20 + 22 \rightarrow A = 114$ square units

Here's another example:

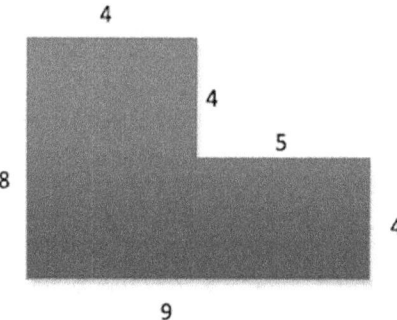

This irregular polygon is decomposed into two rectangles. The area of the large rectangle ($A = l \times w \rightarrow A = 8 \times 4$) is 32 square units. The area of the small rectangle is 20 square units ($A = 4 \times 5$). The sum of the areas of these figures produces the total area of the original polygon:

$A = 32 + 20 \rightarrow A = 52$ square units

Right Rectangular Prisms
A **right rectangular prism** consists of:

- Two congruent (same size and shape) rectangles as the parallel *bases* (top and bottom).
- Two congruent rectangles as the *side* faces.
- Two congruent rectangles as the *front and back* faces.

Mathematics

It is called a right prism because the base and sides meet at right angles.

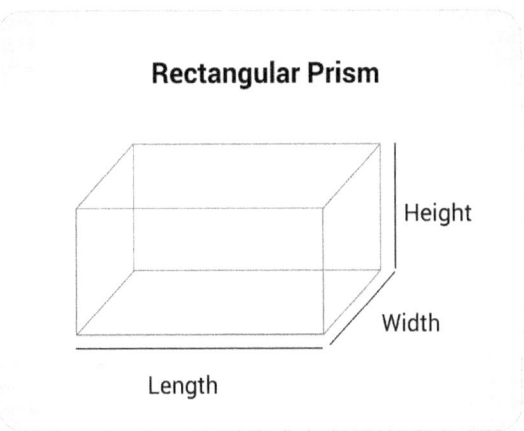

Rectangular Prism

The length and width of the prism is the length and width of the rectangular base. The height of the prism is the measure from one base to the other.

The surface area of three-dimensional figures can be found by adding the areas of each of its bases and faces. The areas of a right rectangular prism are found as follows: two bases → $A = l \times w$; front and back faces → $A = l \times h$; two side faces → $A = w \times h$. The sum of these six areas will equal the surface area of the prism.

$$Surface\ area = area\ of\ 2\ bases + area\ of\ front\ and\ back + area\ of\ 2\ sides$$

This is true for all right rectangular prisms leading to the formula for surface area:

$$SA = 2 \times l \times w + 2 \times l \times h + 2 \times w \times h$$

$$SA = 2(l \times w + l \times h + w \times h)$$

Given the right rectangular prism below, the surface area is calculated as follows:

$$SA = 2\left(3\frac{1}{2}\text{ft}\right)\left(2\frac{1}{2}\text{ft}\right) + 2\left(3\frac{1}{2}\text{ft}\right)\left(1\frac{1}{2}\text{ft}\right) + 2\left(2\frac{1}{2}\text{ft}\right)\left(1\frac{1}{2}\text{ft}\right) \rightarrow SA = 35.5\text{ ft}^2$$

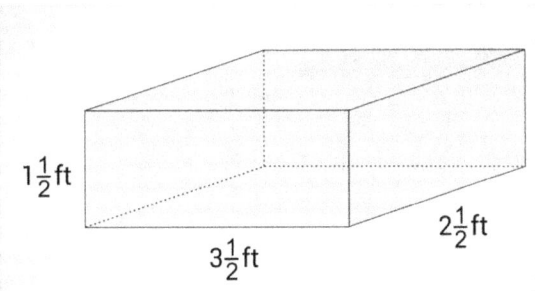

The **volume of a solid** (three-dimensional figure) is the number of cubic units needed to fill the space that the figure occupies. This concept is similar to filling a box with blocks. Volume is a three-dimensional measurement. Therefore, volume is expressed in cubic units such as cubic centimeters (cm^3), cubic feet (ft^3), and cubic yards (yd^3). If a rectangular prism has a volume of 30 cubic meters ($30\ m^3$), it will take 30 cubes, each with sides one meter in length, to fill the space occupied by the prism. A simple formula can be used to determine the volume of a right rectangular prism. The area of the base of the prism ($l \times w$) will indicate how many "blocks" are needed to cover the base. The height (h) of the prism will indicate how many "levels" of blocks are needed to construct the prism.

Therefore, to find the volume (V) of a right rectangular prism, the area of the base ($l \times w$) is multiplied by the height (h):

$$V = l \times w \times h$$

The volume of the prism shown above is calculated:

$$V = \left(3\frac{1}{2}\text{ft}\right) \times \left(2\frac{1}{2}\text{ft}\right) \times \left(1\frac{1}{2}\text{ft}\right) \rightarrow V = 13.125 \text{ ft}^3$$

Effects of Changes to Dimensions on Area and Volume

Similar polygons are figures that are the same shape but different sizes. Likewise, similar solids are different sizes but are the same shape. In both cases, corresponding angles in the same positions for both figures are congruent (equal), and corresponding sides are proportional in length. For example, the triangles below are similar. The following pairs of corresponding angles are congruent: $\angle A$ and $\angle D$; $\angle B$ and $\angle E$; $\angle C$ and $\angle F$. The corresponding sides are proportional:

$$\frac{AB}{DE} = \frac{6}{3} = 2$$

$$\frac{BC}{EF} = \frac{9}{4.5} = 2$$

$$\frac{CA}{FD} = \frac{10}{5} = 2$$

In other words, triangle ABC is the same shape but twice as large as triangle DEF.

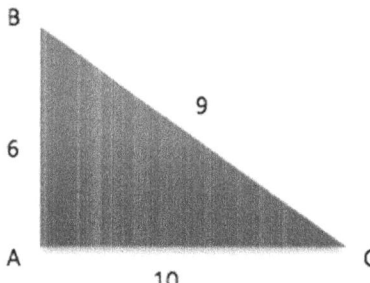
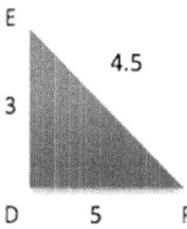

Mathematics

An example of similar triangular pyramids is shown below.

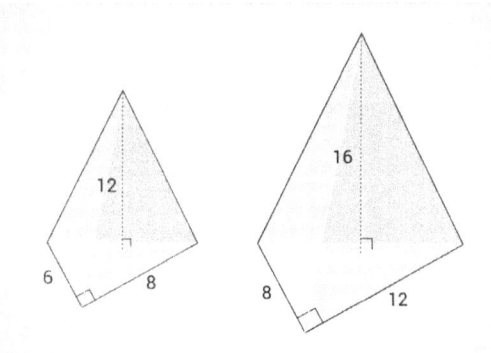

Given the nature of two- and three-dimensional measurements, changing dimensions by a given scale (multiplier) does not change the area of volume by the same scale. Consider a rectangle with a length of 5 centimeters and a width of 4 centimeters. The area of the rectangle is 20 cm². Doubling the dimensions of the rectangle (multiplying by a scale factor of 2) to 10 centimeters and 8 centimeters *does not* double the area to 40 cm². Area is a two-dimensional measurement (measured in square units). Therefore, the dimensions are multiplied by a scale that is squared (raised to the second power) to determine the scale of the corresponding areas. For the previous example, the length and width are multiplied by 2. Therefore, the area is multiplied by 2^2, or 4. The area of a 5 cm × 4 cm rectangle is 20 cm². The area of a 10 cm × 8 cm rectangle is 80 cm².

Volume is a three-dimensional measurement, which is measured in cubic units. Therefore, the scale between dimensions of similar solids is cubed (raised to the third power) to determine the scale between their volumes. Consider similar right rectangular prisms: one with a length of 8 inches, a width of 24 inches, and a height of 16 inches; the second with a length of 4 inches, a width of 12 inches, and a height of 8 inches. The first prism, multiplied by a scalar of $\frac{1}{2}$, produces the measurement of the second prism. The volume of the first prism, multiplied by $(\frac{1}{2})^3$, which equals $\frac{1}{8}$, produces the volume of the second prism. The volume of the first prism is 8 in × 24 in × 16 in which equals 3,072 in³. The volume of the second prism is 4 in × 12 in × 8 in which equals 384 in³:

$$3{,}072 \text{ in}^3 \times \frac{1}{8} = 384 \text{ in}^3$$

The rules for squaring the scalar for area and cubing the scalar for volume only hold true for similar figures. In other words, if only one dimension is changed (changing the width of a rectangle but not the length) or dimensions are changed at different rates (the length of a prism is doubled and its height is tripled) the figures are not similar (same shape). Therefore, the rules above do not apply.

Components of the Coordinate Plane

X-Axis, Y-Axis, Origin, and Four Quadrants

The **coordinate plane**, sometimes referred to as the **Cartesian plane**, is a two-dimensional surface consisting of a horizontal and a vertical number line. The horizontal number line is referred to as the *x*-**axis**, and the vertical number line is referred to as the *y*-**axis**. The *x*-axis and *y*-axis intersect (or cross) at a point called the **origin**. At the origin, the value of the *x*-axis is zero, and the value of the *y*-axis is zero. The coordinate plane identifies the exact location of a point that is plotted on the two-dimensional surface. Like a map, the location of all points on the plane are in relation to the origin. Along the *x*-axis (horizontal line), numbers to the right of the origin are positive and increasing in value (1, 2, 3,...) and to the left of the origin numbers are negative and decreasing in value (−1, −2, −3,...). Along the y-axis (vertical line), numbers above the origin are positive and increasing in value and numbers below the origin are negative and decreasing in value.

The x- and y-axis divide the coordinate plane into four sections. These sections are referred to as quadrant one, quadrant two, quadrant three, and quadrant four, and are often written with Roman numerals I, II, III, and IV.

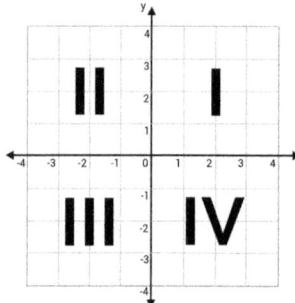

The upper right section is **Quadrant I** and consists of points with positive x-values and positive y-values. The upper left section is **Quadrant II** and consists of points with negative x-values and positive y-values. The bottom left section is **Quadrant III** and consists of points with negative x-values and negative y-values. The bottom right section is **Quadrant IV** and consists of points with positive x-values and negative y-values.

Solving Problems in the Coordinate Plane

The location of a point on a coordinate grid is identified by writing it as an ordered pair. An **ordered pair** is a set of numbers indicating the x-and y-coordinates of the point. Ordered pairs are written in the form (x, y) where x and y are values which indicate their respective coordinates. For example, the point $(3, -2)$ has an x-coordinate of 3 and a y-coordinate of -2.

Mathematics

Plotting a point on the coordinate plane with a given coordinate means starting from the origin $(0, 0)$. To determine the value of the x-coordinate, move right (positive number) or left (negative number) along the x-axis. Next, move up (positive number) or down (negative number) to the value of the y-coordinate. Finally, plot and label the point. For example, plotting the point $(1, -2)$ requires starting from the origin and moving right along the x-axis to positive one, then moving down until straight across from negative 2 on the y-axis. The point is plotted and labeled. This point, along with three other points, are plotted and labeled on the graph below.

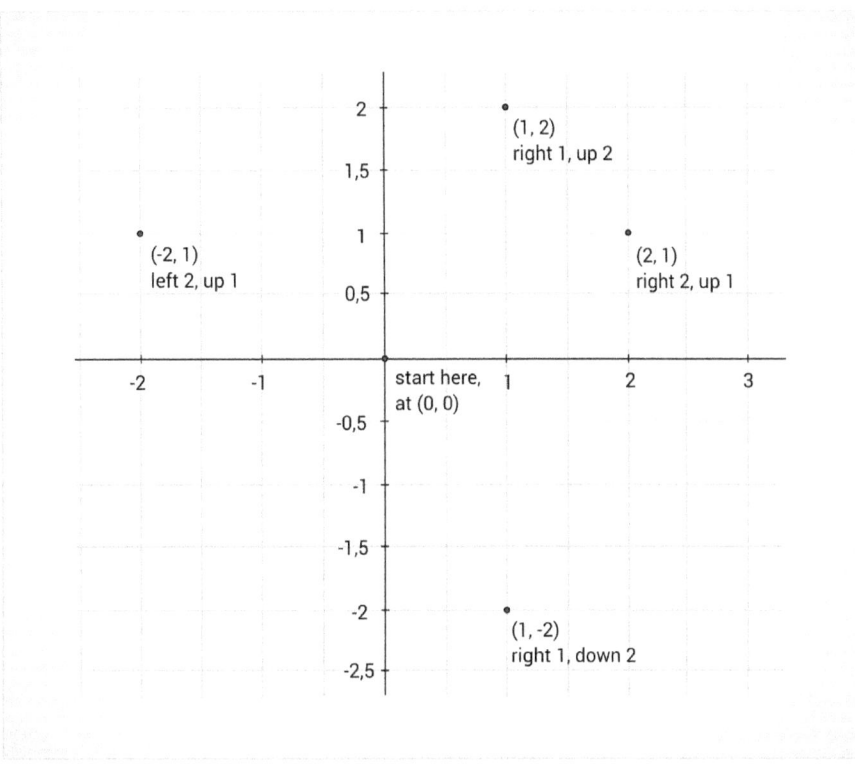

To write the coordinates of a point on the coordinate grid, a line should be traced directly above or below the point until reaching the x-axis (noting the value on the x-axis). Then, returning to the point, a line should be traced directly to the right or left of the point until reaching the y-axis (noting the value on the y-axis). The ordered pair (x, y) should be written with the values determined for the x- and y-coordinates.

Polygons can be drawn in the coordinate plane given the coordinates of their vertices. These coordinates can be used to determine the perimeter and area of the figure. Suppose triangle RQP has vertices located at the points: $R(-4, 2)$, $Q(1, 6)$, and $P(1, 2)$. By plotting the points for the three vertices, the triangle can be constructed as follows:

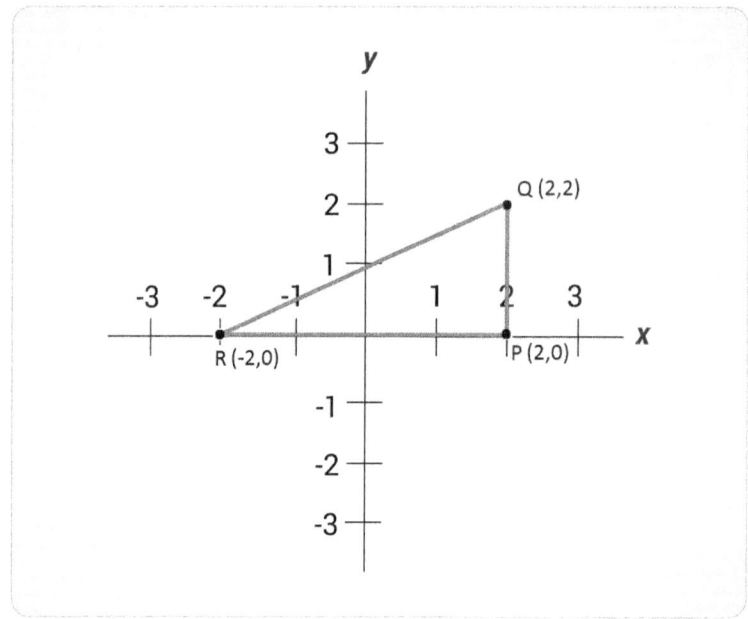

Because points R and P have the same y-coordinates (they are directly across from each other), the distance between them is determined by subtracting their x-coordinates (or simply counting units from one point to the other): $2 - (-2) = 4$. Therefore, the length of side RP is 4 units. Because points Q and P have the same x-coordinate (they are directly above and below each other), the distance between them is determined by subtracting their y-coordinates (or counting units between them): $2 - 0 = 2$. Therefore, the length of side PQ is 2 units. Knowing the length of side RP, which is the base of the triangle, and the length of side PQ, which is the height of the triangle, the area of the figure can be determined by using the formula $A = \frac{1}{2}bh$.

To determine the perimeter of the triangle, the lengths of all three sides are needed. Points R and Q are neither directly across nor directly above and below each other. Therefore, the distance formula must be used to find the length of side RQ.

The distance formula is as follows:

$$d = \sqrt{(x_2 - x_1)^2 + (y_2 - y_1)^2}$$

$$d = \sqrt{(2 - (-2))^2 + (2 - 0)^2}$$

$$d = \sqrt{(4)^2 + (2)^2}$$

$$d = \sqrt{16 + 4}$$

$$= \sqrt{20}$$

The perimeter is determined by adding the lengths of the three sides of the triangle.

Mathematics

Solving Problems Involving Measurement

Elapsed Time, Money, Length, Volume, and Mass

Word problems involving elapsed time, money, length, volume, and mass require determining which operations (addition, subtraction, multiplication, and division) should be performed, and using and/or converting the proper unit for the scenario.

The following table lists key words that can be used to indicate the proper operation:

Addition	Sum, total, in all, combined, increase of, more than, added to
Subtraction	Difference, change, remaining, less than, decreased by
Multiplication	Product, times, twice, triple, each
Division	Quotient, goes into, per, evenly, divided by half, divided by third, split

Identifying and utilizing the proper units for the scenario requires knowing how to apply the conversion rates for money, length, volume, and mass. For example, given a scenario that requires subtracting 8 inches from $2\frac{1}{2}$ feet, both values should first be expressed in the same unit (they could be expressed $\frac{2}{3}$ ft & $2\frac{1}{2}$ ft, or 8 in and 30 in). The desired unit for the answer may also require converting back to another unit.

Consider the following scenario: A parking area along the river is only wide enough to fit one row of cars and is $\frac{1}{2}$ kilometers long. The average space needed per car is 5 meters. How many cars can be parked along the river? First, all measurements should be converted to similar units: $\frac{1}{2}$ km = 500 m. The operation(s) needed should be identified. Because the problem asks for the number of cars, the total space should be divided by the space per car. 500 meters divided by 5 meters per car yields a total of 100 cars. Written as an expression, the meters unit cancels and the cars unit is left: $\frac{500 \text{ m}}{5 \text{ m/car}}$ the same as $500 \text{ m} \times \frac{1 \text{ car}}{5 \text{ m}}$ yields 100 cars.

When dealing with problems involving elapsed time, breaking the problem down into workable parts is helpful. For example, suppose the length of time between 1:15pm and 3:45pm must be determined. From 1:15pm to 2:00pm is 45 minutes (knowing there are 60 minutes in an hour). From 2:00pm to 3:00pm is 1 hour. From 3:00pm to 3:45pm is 45 minutes. The total elapsed time is 45 minutes plus 1 hour plus 45 minutes. This sum produces 1 hour and 90 minutes. 90 minutes is over an hour, so this is converted to 1 hour (60 minutes) and 30 minutes. The total elapsed time can now be expressed as 2 hours and 30 minutes.

Measuring Lengths of Objects

The length of an object can be measured using standard tools such as rulers, yard sticks, meter sticks, and measuring tapes. The following image depicts a yardstick:

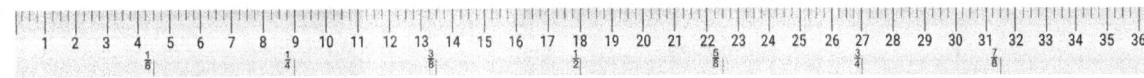

Choosing the right tool to perform the measurement requires determining whether United States customary units or metric units are desired, and having a grasp of the approximate length of each unit and the approximate length of each tool. The measurement can still be performed by trial and error without the knowledge of the approximate size of the tool.

For example, to determine the length of a room in feet, a United States customary unit, various tools can be used. These include a ruler (typically 12 inches/1 foot long), a yardstick (3 feet/1 yard long), or a tape measure displaying feet (typically either 25 feet or 50 feet). Because the length of a room is much larger than the length of a ruler or a yardstick, a tape measure should be used to perform the measurement.

When the correct measuring tool is selected, the measurement is performed by first placing the tool directly above or below the object (if making a horizontal measurement) or directly next to the object (if making a vertical measurement). The next step is aligning the tool so that one end of the object is at the mark for zero units, then recording the unit of the mark at the other end of the object. To give the length of a paperclip in metric units, a ruler displaying centimeters is aligned with one end of the paper clip to the mark for zero centimeters.

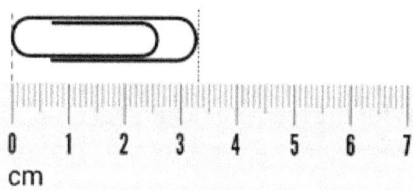

Directly down from the other end of the paperclip is the mark that measures its length. In this case, that mark is two small dashes past the 3 centimeter mark. Each small dash is 1 millimeter (or .1 centimeters). Therefore, the length of the paper clip is 3.2 centimeters.

To compare the lengths of objects, each length must be expressed in the same unit. If possible, the objects should be measured with the same tool or with tools utilizing the same units. For example, a ruler and a yardstick can both measure length in inches. If the lengths of the objects are expressed in different units, these different units must be converted to the same unit before comparing them. If two lengths are expressed in the same unit, the lengths may be compared by subtracting the smaller value from the larger value. For example, suppose the lengths of two gardens are to be compared. Garden A has a length of 4 feet, and garden B has a length of 2 yards. 2 yards is converted to 6 feet so that the measurements have similar units. Then, the smaller length (4 feet) is subtracted from the larger length (6 ft): 6 ft − 4 ft = 2 ft. Therefore, garden B is 2 feet larger than garden A.

Relative Sizes of United States Customary Units and Metric Units

The United States customary system and the metric system each consist of distinct units to measure lengths and volume of liquids. The U.S. customary units for length, from smallest to largest, are: inch (in), foot (ft), yard (yd), and mile (mi). The metric units for length, from smallest to largest, are: millimeter (mm), centimeter (cm), decimeter (dm), meter (m), and kilometer (km). The relative size of each unit of length is shown below.

U.S. Customary	Metric	Conversion
12 in = 1 ft	10 mm = 1 cm	1 in = 2.54 cm
36 in = 3 ft = 1 yd	10 cm = 1 dm (decimeter)	1 m ≈ 3.28 ft ≈ 1.09 yd
5,280 ft = 1,760 yd = 1 mi	100 cm = 10 dm = 1 m	1 mi ≈ 1.6 km
	1,000 m = 1 km	

The U.S. customary units for volume of liquids, from smallest to largest, are: fluid ounces (fl oz), cup (c), pint (pt), quart (qt), and gallon (gal). The metric units for volume of liquids, from smallest to largest, are: milliliter

Mathematics

(mL), centiliter (cL), deciliter (dL), liter (L), and kiloliter (kL). The relative size of each unit of liquid volume is shown below.

U.S. Customary	Metric	Conversion
8 fl oz = 1 c	10 mL = 1 cL	1 pt ≈ 0.473 L
2 c = 1 pt	10 cL = 1 dL	1 L ≈ 1.057 qt
4 c = 2 pt = 1 qt	1,000 mL = 100 cL = 10 dL = 1 L	1 gal ≈ 3.785 L
4 qt = 1 gal	1,000 L = 1 kL	

The U.S. customary system measures weight (how strongly Earth is pulling on an object) in the following units, from least to greatest: ounce (oz), pound (lb), and ton. The metric system measures mass (the quantity of matter within an object) in the following units, from least to greatest: milligram (mg), centigram (cg), gram (g), kilogram (kg), and metric ton (MT). The relative sizes of each unit of weight and mass are shown below.

U.S. Measures of Weight	Metric Measures of Mass
16 oz = 1 lb	10 mg = 1 cg
2,000 lbs = 1 ton	100 cg = 1 g
	1,000 g = 1 kg
	1,000 kg = 1 MT

Note that weight and mass DO NOT measure the same thing.

Time is measured in the following units, from shortest to longest: second (sec), minute (min), hour (h), day (d), week (wk), month (mo), year (yr), decade, century, millennium. The relative sizes of each unit of time is shown below.

- 60 sec = 1 min
- 60 min = 1 h
- 24 hr = 1 d
- 7 d = 1 wk
- 52 wk = 1 yr
- 12 mo = 1 yr
- 10 yr = 1 decade
- 100 yrs = 1 century
- 1,000 yrs = 1 millennium

Conversion of Units

When working with different systems of measurement, conversion from one unit to another may be necessary. The conversion rate must be known to convert units. One method for converting units is to write and solve a proportion. The arrangement of values in a proportion is extremely important. Suppose that a problem requires converting 20 fluid ounces to cups. To do so, a proportion can be written using the conversion rate of 8 fl oz = 1 c with x representing the missing value. The proportion can be written in any of the following ways:

$$\frac{1}{8} = \frac{x}{20} \left(\frac{c \text{ for conversion}}{fl \text{ oz for conversion}} = \frac{\text{unknown } c}{fl \text{ oz given}} \right)$$

$$\frac{8}{1} = \frac{20}{x} \left(\frac{fl \text{ oz for conversion}}{c \text{ for conversion}} = \frac{fl \text{ oz given}}{\text{unknown } c} \right)$$

$$\frac{1}{x} = \frac{8}{20} \left(\frac{c \text{ for conversion}}{\text{unknown } c} = \frac{fl \text{ oz for conversion}}{fl \text{ oz given}} \right)$$

$$\frac{x}{1} = \frac{20}{8} \left(\frac{\text{unknown } c}{c \text{ for conversion}} = \frac{fl \text{ oz given}}{fl \text{ oz for conversion}} \right)$$

To solve a proportion, the ratios are cross-multiplied and the resulting equation is solved. When cross-multiplying, all four proportions above will produce the same equation:

$$(8)(x) = (20)(1) \rightarrow 8x = 20$$

Divide by 8 to isolate the variable x, the result is $x = 2.5$. The variable x represented the unknown number of cups. Therefore, the conclusion is that 20 fluid ounces converts (is equal) to 2.5 cups.

Sometimes converting units requires writing and solving more than one proportion. Suppose an exam question asks to determine how many hours are in 2 weeks. Without knowing the conversion rate between hours and weeks, this can be determined knowing the conversion rates between weeks and days, and between days and hours. First, weeks are converted to days, then days are converted to hours. To convert from weeks to days, the following proportion can be written:

$$\frac{7}{1} = \frac{x}{2} \left(\frac{\text{days conversion}}{\text{weeks conversion}} = \frac{\text{days unknown}}{\text{weeks given}} \right)$$

Cross-multiplying produces: $(7)(2) = (x)(1) \rightarrow 14 = x$. Therefore, 2 weeks is equal to 14 days. Next, a proportion is written to convert 14 days to hours:

$$\frac{24}{1} = \frac{x}{14} \left(\frac{\text{conversion hours}}{\text{conversion days}} = \frac{\text{unknown hours}}{\text{given days}} \right)$$

Cross-multiplying produces:

$$(24)(14) = (x)(1) \rightarrow 336 = x$$

Therefore, the answer is that there are 336 hours in 2 weeks.

Statistical Concepts

Identifying Statistical Questions

The field of **statistics** describes relationships between quantities that are related, but not necessarily in a deterministic manner. For example, a graduating student's salary will often be higher when the student graduates with a higher GPA, but this is not always the case. Likewise, people who smoke tobacco are more likely to develop lung cancer, but, in fact, it is possible for non-smokers to develop the disease as well. Statistics describes these kinds of situations, where the likelihood of some outcome depends on the starting data.

Descriptive statistics involves analyzing a collection of data to describe its broad properties such average (or mean), what percent of the data falls within a given range, and other such properties. An example of this would be taking all of the test scores from a given class and calculating the average test score. Inferential statistics attempts to use data about a subset of some population to make inferences about the rest of the population. An example of this would be taking a collection of students who received tutoring and comparing their results to a collection of students who did not receive tutoring, then using that comparison to try to predict whether the tutoring program in question is beneficial.

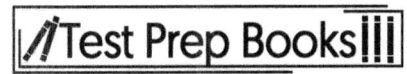

Mathematics

Measures of Center and Range

The center of a set of data (statistical values) can be represented by its mean, median, or mode. These are sometimes referred to as **measures of central tendency**.

Mean

The first property that can be defined for this set of data is the **mean**. This is the same as the average. To find the mean, add up all the data points, then divide by the total number of data points. For example, suppose that in a class of 10 students, the scores on a test were 50, 60, 65, 65, 75, 80, 85, 85, 90, 100. Therefore, the average test score will be:

$$\frac{50 + 60 + 65 + 65 + 75 + 80 + 85 + 85 + 90 + 100}{10} = 75.5$$

The mean is a useful number if the distribution of data is normal (more on this later), which means that the frequency of different outcomes has a single peak and is roughly equally distributed on both sides of that peak. However, it is less useful in some cases where the data might be split or where there are some outliers. **Outliers** are data points that are far from the rest of the data. For example, suppose there are 10 executives and 90 employees at a company. The executives make $1000 per hour, and the employees make $10 per hour.

Therefore, the average pay rate will be:

$$\frac{\$1000 \times 10 + \$10 \times 90}{100} = \$109 \text{ per hour}$$

In this case, this average is not very descriptive since it's not close to the actual pay of the executives or the employees.

Median

Another useful measurement is the **median**. In a data set, the median is the point in the middle. The **middle** refers to the point where half the data comes before it and half comes after, when the data is recorded in numerical order. For instance, these are the speeds of the fastball of a pitcher during the last inning that he pitched (in order from least to greatest):

$$90, 92, 93, 93, 95, 96, 97, 97, 97$$

There are nine total numbers, so the middle or *median* number is the 5th one, which is 95.

In cases where the number of data points is an even number, then the average of the two middle points is taken. In the previous example of test scores, the two middle points are 75 and 80. Since there is no single point, the average of these two scores needs to be found.

The average is:

$$\frac{75 + 80}{2} = 77.5$$

The median is generally a good value to use if there are a few outliers in the data. It prevents those outliers from affecting the "middle" value as much as when using the mean.

Since an outlier is a data point that is far from most of the other data points in a data set, this means an outlier also is any point that is far from the median of the data set. The outliers can have a substantial effect

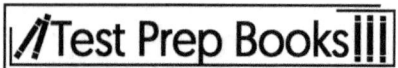

on the mean of a data set, but they usually do not change the median or mode, or do not change them by a large quantity. For example, consider the data set (3, 5, 6, 6, 6, 8). This has a median of 6 and a mode of 6, with a mean of $\frac{34}{6} \approx 5.67$. Now, suppose a new data point of 1000 is added so that the data set is now (3, 5, 6, 6, 6, 8, 1000). The median and mode, which are both still 6, remain unchanged. However, the average is now $\frac{1034}{7}$, which is approximately 147.7. In this case, the median and mode will be better descriptions for most of the data points.

Outliers in a given data set are sometimes the result of an error by the experimenter, but oftentimes, they are perfectly valid data points that must be taken into consideration.

Mode
One additional measure to describe a set of data is the **mode**. This is the data point that appears most frequently. If two or more data points all tie for the most frequent appearance, then each of them is considered a mode. In the case of the test scores, where the numbers were 50, 60, 65, 65, 75, 80, 85, 85, 90, 100, there are two modes: 65 and 85.

The **range of a data set** is the difference between the highest and the lowest values in the set. The range can be considered the span of the data set. To determine the range, the smallest value in the set is subtracted from the largest value. The ranges for the data sets A, B, and C above are calculated as follows: A: $14 - 7 = 7$; B: $51 - 33 = 18$; C: $173 - 151 = 22$.

Best Description of a Set of Data
Measures of central tendency, namely mean, median, and mode, describe characteristics of a set of data. Specifically, they are intended to represent a *typical* value in the set by identifying a central position of the set. Depending on the characteristics of a specific set of data, different measures of central tendency are more indicative of a typical value in the set.

When a data set is grouped closely together with a relatively small range and the data is spread out somewhat evenly, the mean is an effective indicator of a typical value in the set. Consider the following data set representing the height of sixth grade boys in inches: 61 inches, 54 inches, 58 inches, 63 inches, 58 inches. The mean of the set is 58.8 inches. The data set is grouped closely (the range is only 9 inches) and the values are spread relatively evenly (three values below the mean and two values above the mean). Therefore, the mean value of 58.8 inches is an effective measure of central tendency in this case.

When a data set contains a small number of values either extremely large or extremely small when compared to the other values, the mean is not an effective measure of central tendency. Consider the following data set representing annual incomes of homeowners on a given street: $71,000; $74,000; $75,000; $77,000; $340,000. The mean of this set is $127,400. This figure does not indicate a typical value in the set, which contains four out of five values between $71,000 and $77,000. The median is a much more effective measure of central tendency for data sets such as these. Finding the middle value diminishes the influence of outliers, or numbers that may appear out of place, like the $340,000 annual income. The median for this set is $75,000 which is much more typical of a value in the set.

Mathematics

The **mode of a data set** is a useful measure of central tendency for categorical data when each piece of data is an option from a category. Consider a survey of 31 commuters asking how they get to work with results summarized below.

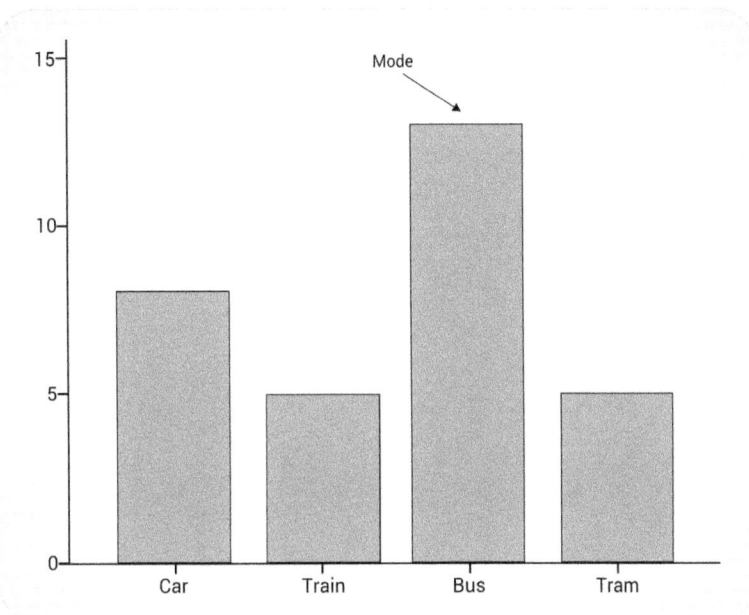

The mode for this set represents the value, or option, of the data that repeats most often. This indicates that the bus is the most popular method of transportation for the commuters.

Effects of Changes in Data

Changing all values of a data set in a consistent way produces predictable changes in the measures of the center and range of the set. A linear transformation changes the original value into the new value by either adding a given number to each value, multiplying each value by a given number, or both. Adding (or subtracting) a given value to each data point will increase (or decrease) the mean, median, and any modes by the same value. However, the range will remain the same due to the way that range is calculated. Multiplying (or dividing) a given value by each data point will increase (or decrease) the mean, median, and any modes, and the range by the same factor.

Consider the following data set, call it set P, representing the price of different cases of soda at a grocery store: $4.25, $4.40, $4.75, $4.95, $4.95, $5.15. The mean of set P is $4.74. The median is $4.85. The mode of the set is $4.95. The range is $0.90. Suppose the state passes a new tax of $0.25 on every case of soda sold. The new data set, set T, is calculated by adding $0.25 to each data point from set P. Therefore, set T consists of the following values: $4.50, $4.65, $5.00, $5.20, $5.20, $5.40. The mean of set T is $4.99. The median is $5.10. The mode of the set is $5.20. The range is $.90. The mean, median and mode of set T is equal to $0.25 added to the mean, median, and mode of set P. The range stays the same.

Now suppose, due to inflation, the store raises the cost of every item by 10 percent. Raising costs by 10 percent is calculated by multiplying each value by 1.1. The new data set, set I, is calculated by multiplying each data point from set T by 1.1. Therefore, set I consists of the following values: $4.95, $5.12, $5.50, $5.72, $5.72, $5.94. The mean of set I is $5.49. The median is $5.61. The mode of the set is $5.72. The range is $0.99. The mean, median, mode, and range of set I is equal to 1.1 multiplied by the mean, median, mode, and range of set T because each increased by a factor of 10 percent.

Describing a Set of Data

A set of data can be described in terms of its center, spread, shape and any unusual features. The **center of a data** set can be measured by its mean, median, or mode. Measures of central tendency are covered in the *Measures of Center and Range* section. The **spread of a data set** refers to how far the data points are from the center (mean or median). The spread can be measured by the range or by the quartiles and interquartile range. A data set with all its data points clustered around the center will have a small spread. A data set covering a wide range of values will have a large spread.

When a data set is displayed as a histogram or frequency distribution plot, the shape indicates if a sample is normally distributed, symmetrical, or has measures of skewness or kurtosis. When graphed, a data set with a normal distribution will resemble a bell curve.

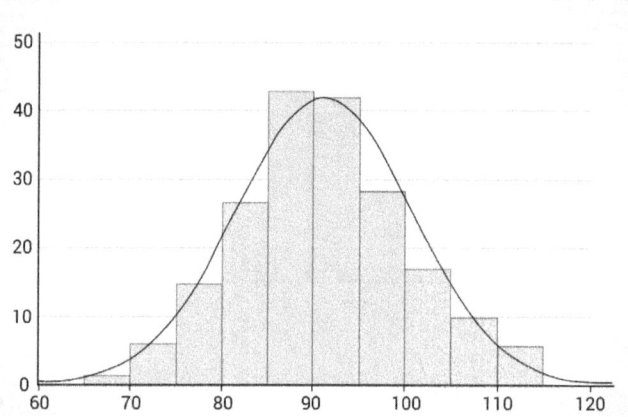

If the data set is symmetrical, each half of the graph when divided at the center is a mirror image of the other. If the graph has fewer data points to the right, the data is skewed right. If it has fewer data points to the left, the data is skewed left.

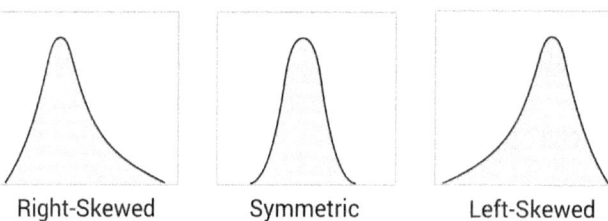

Right-Skewed   Symmetric   Left-Skewed

Kurtosis is a measure of whether the data is heavy-tailed with a high number of outliers, or light-tailed with a low number of outliers.

A description of a data set should include any unusual features such as gaps or outliers. A **gap** is a span within the range of the data set containing no data points. An outlier is a data point with a value either extremely large or extremely small when compared to the other values in the set.

Representing and Interpreting Data

Interpreting Displays of Data

A set of data can be visually displayed in various forms allowing for quick identification of characteristics of the set. **Histograms**, such as the one shown below, display the number of data points (vertical axis) that fall into given intervals (horizontal axis) across the range of the set. The histogram below displays the heights of black cherry trees in a certain city park. Each rectangle represents the number of trees with heights between a given five-point span. For example, the furthest bar to the right indicates that two trees are between 85 and 90 feet. Histograms can describe the center, spread, shape, and any unusual characteristics of a data set.

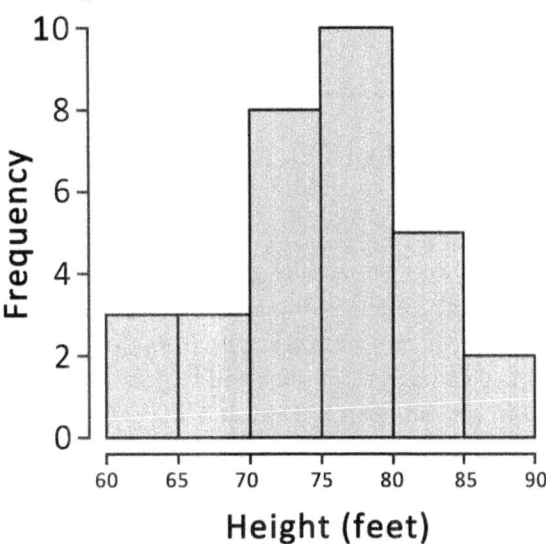

A **box plot**, also called a **box-and-whisker plot**, divides the data points into four groups and displays the five-number summary for the set as well as any outliers. The five-number summary consists of:

- The lower extreme: the lowest value that is not an outlier
- The higher extreme: the highest value that is not an outlier
- The median of the set: also referred to as the second quartile or Q_2
- The first quartile or Q_1: the median of values below Q_2
- The third quartile or Q_3: the median of values above Q_2

Calculating each of these values is covered in the next section, *Graphical Representation of Data*.

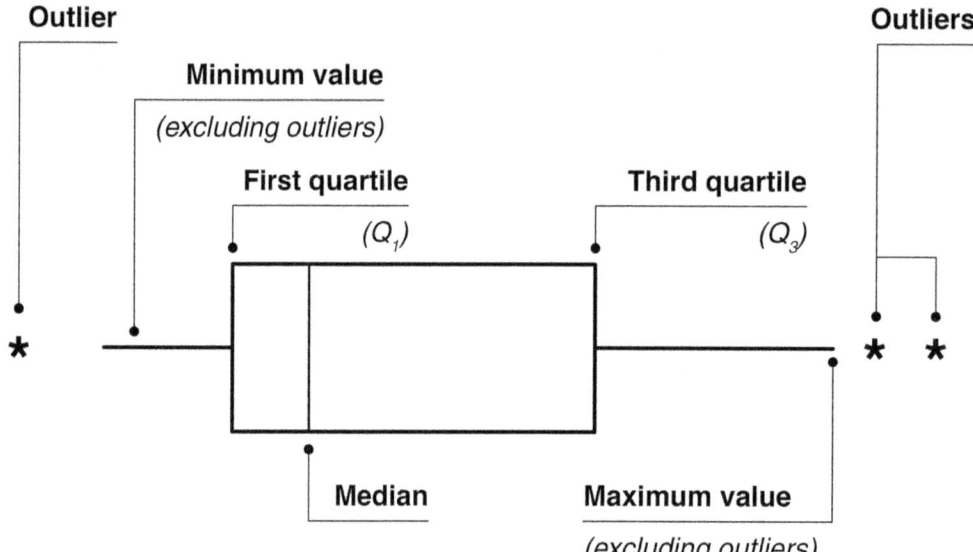

Suppose the box plot displays IQ scores for 12th grade students at a given school. The five number summary of the data consists of: lower extreme (67); upper extreme (127); Q_2 or median (100); Q_1 (91); Q_3 (108); and outliers (135 and 140). Although all data points are not known from the plot, the points are divided into four quartiles each, including 25% of the data points. Therefore, 25% of students scored between 67 and 91, 25% scored between 91 and 100, 25% scored between 100 and 108, and 25% scored between 108 and 127. These percentages include the normal values for the set and exclude the outliers. This information is useful when comparing a given score with the rest of the scores in the set.

Mathematics

A **scatter plot** is a mathematical diagram that visually displays the relationship or connection between two variables. The independent variable is placed on the x-axis, or horizontal axis, and the dependent variable is placed on the y-axis, or vertical axis. When visually examining the points on the graph, if the points model a linear relationship, or if a line of best-fit can be drawn through the points with the points relatively close on either side, then a correlation exists. If the line of best-fit has a positive slope (rises from left to right), then the variables have a positive correlation. If the line of best-fit has a negative slope (falls from left to right), then the variables have a negative correlation. If a line of best-fit cannot be drawn, then no correlation exists. A positive or negative correlation can be categorized as strong or weak, depending on how closely the points are graphed around the line of best-fit.

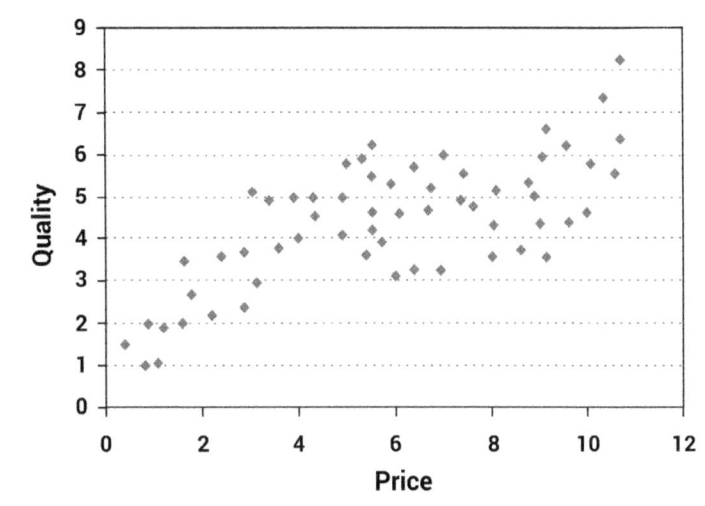

Graphical Representation of Data

Various graphs can be used to visually represent a given set of data. Each type of graph requires a different method of arranging data points and different calculations of the data. Examples of histograms, box plots, and scatter plots are discussed in the previous section *Interpreting Displays of Data*. To construct a histogram, the range of the data points is divided into equal intervals. The frequency for each interval is then determined, which reveals how many points fall into each interval. A graph is constructed with the vertical axis representing the frequency and the horizontal axis representing the intervals. The lower value of each interval should be labeled along the horizontal axis. Finally, for each interval, a bar is drawn from the lower value of each interval to the lower value of the next interval with a height equal to the frequency of the interval. Because of the intervals, histograms do not have any gaps between bars along the horizontal axis.

A scatter plot displays the relationship between two variables. Values for the independent variable, typically denoted by x, are paired with values for the dependent variable, typically denoted by y. Each set of corresponding values are written as an ordered pair (x, y). To construct the graph, a coordinate grid is labeled with the x-axis representing the independent variable and the y-axis representing the dependent variable.

Each ordered pair is graphed.

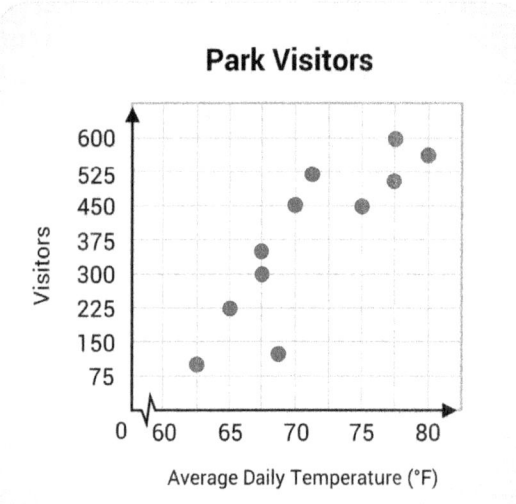

Like a scatter plot, a **line graph** compares variables that change continuously, typically over time. Paired data values (ordered pairs) are plotted on a coordinate grid with the x- and y-axis representing the variables. A line is drawn from each point to the next, going from left to right. The line graph below displays cell phone use for given years (two variables) for men, women, and both sexes (three data sets).

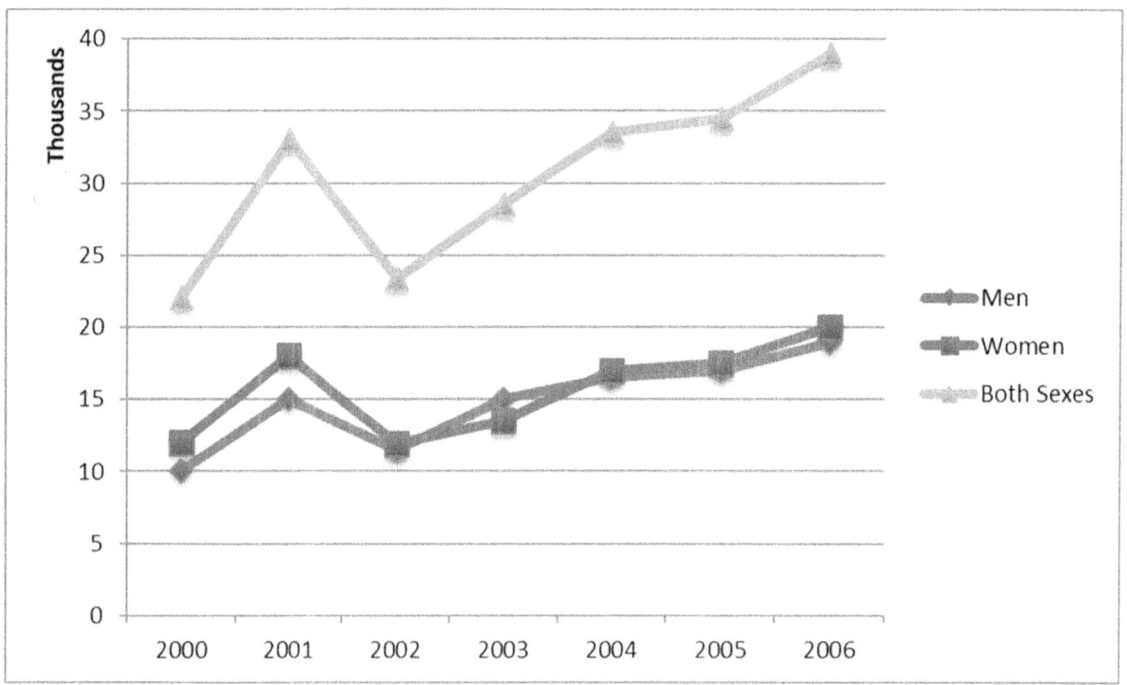

Mathematics

A **line plot**, also called **dot plot**, displays the frequency of data (numerical values) on a number line. To construct a line plot, a number line is used that includes all unique data values. It is marked with x's or dots above the value the number of times that the value occurs in the data set.

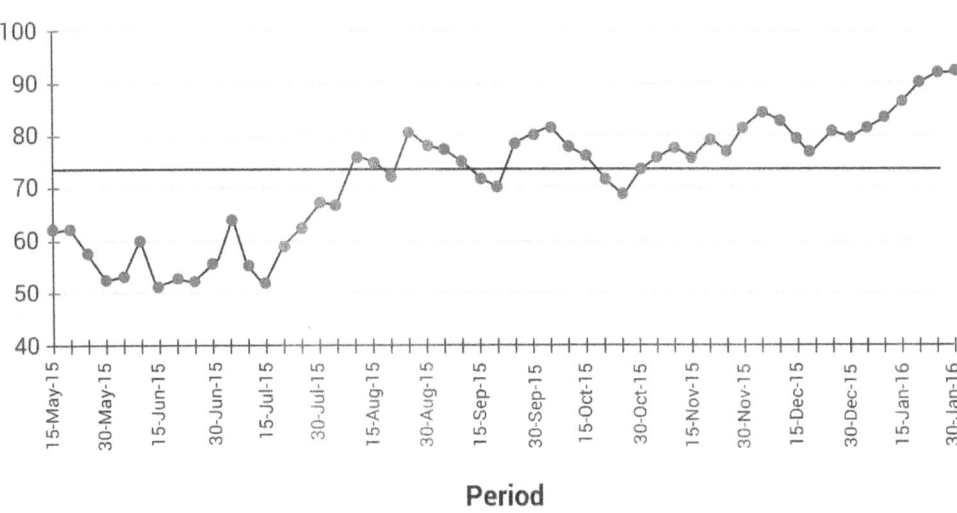

A **bar graph** looks similar to a histogram but displays categorical data. The horizontal axis represents each category and the vertical axis represents the frequency for the category. A bar is drawn for each category (often different colors) with a height extending to the frequency for that category within the data set. A **double bar graph** displays two sets of data that contain data points consisting of the same categories. The double bar graph below indicates that two girls and four boys like Pad Thai the most out of all the foods, two boys and five girls like pizza, and so on.

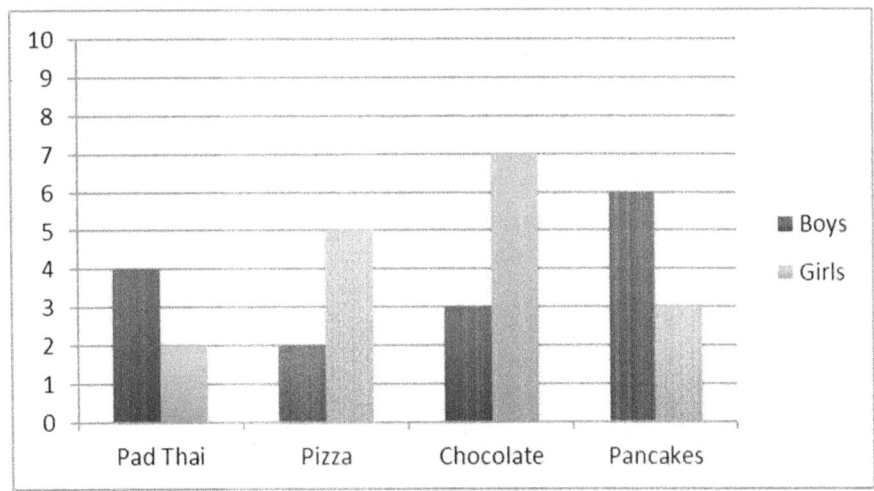

A circle graph, also called a **pie chart**, displays categorical data with each category representing a percentage of the whole data set. To construct a circle graph, the percent of the data set for each category must be determined. To do so, the frequency of the category is divided by the total number of data points and converted to a percent. For example, if 80 people were asked their favorite pizza topping and 20 responded cheese, then cheese constitutes 25% of the data ($\frac{20}{80} = 0.25 = 25\%$). Each category in a data set is represented by a *slice* of the circle proportionate to its percentage of the whole.

Choice of Graphs to Display Data

Choosing the appropriate graph to display a data set depends on what type of data is included in the set and what information must be displayed. Histograms and box plots can be used for data sets consisting of individual values across a wide range. Examples include test scores and incomes. Histograms and box plots will indicate the center, spread, range, and outliers of a data set. A histogram will show the shape of the data set, while a box plot will divide the set into quartiles (25% increments), allowing for comparison between a given value and the entire set.

Scatter plots and line graphs can be used to display data consisting of two variables. Examples include height and weight, or distance and time. A correlation between the variables is determined by examining the points on the graph. Line graphs are used if each value for one variable pairs with a distinct value for the other variable. Line graphs show relationships between variables.

Line plots, bar graphs, and circle graphs are all used to display categorical data, such as surveys. Line plots and bar graphs both indicate the frequency of each category within the data set. A line plot is used when the categories consist of numerical values. For example, the number of hours of TV watched by individuals is displayed on a line plot. A bar graph is used when the categories consist of words. For example, the favorite ice cream of individuals is displayed with a bar graph. A circle graph can be used to display either type of categorical data. However, unlike line plots and bar graphs, a circle graph does not indicate the frequency of each category. Instead, the circle graph represents each category as its percentage of the whole data set.

Interpreting the Probability of Events

Probabilities Relative to Likelihood of Occurrence

Probability is a measure of how likely an event is to occur. Probability is written as a fraction between zero and one. If an event has a probability of zero, the event will never occur. If an event has a probability of one, the event will definitely occur. If the probability of an event is closer to zero, the event is unlikely to occur. If the probability of an event is closer to one, the event is more likely to occur. For example, a probability of $\frac{1}{2}$ means that the event is equally as likely to occur as it is not to occur. An example of this is tossing a coin. To calculate the probability of an event, the number of favorable outcomes is divided by the number of total

Mathematics

outcomes. For example, suppose you have 2 raffle tickets out of 20 total tickets sold. The probability that you win the raffle is calculated:

$$\frac{number\ of\ favorable\ outcomes}{total\ number\ of\ outcomes} = \frac{2}{20} = \frac{1}{10}$$

Therefore, the probability of winning the raffle is $\frac{1}{10}$ or 0.1.

Chance is the measure of how likely an event is to occur, written as a percent. If an event will never occur, the event has a 0% chance. If an event will certainly occur, the event has a 100% chance. If an event will sometimes occur, the event has a chance somewhere between 0% and 100%. To calculate chance, probability is calculated, and the fraction is converted to a percent.

The probability of multiple events occurring can be determined by multiplying the probability of each event. For example, suppose you flip a coin with heads and tails, and roll a six-sided die numbered one through six. To find the probability that you will flip heads AND roll a two, the probability of each event is determined, and those fractions are multiplied. The probability of flipping heads is $\frac{1}{2} \left(\frac{1\ side\ with\ heads}{2\ sides\ total} \right)$, and the probability of rolling a two is $\frac{1}{6} \left(\frac{1\ side\ with\ a\ 2}{6\ total\ sides} \right)$. The probability of flipping heads AND rolling a 2 is:

$$\frac{1}{2} \times \frac{1}{6} = \frac{1}{12}$$

The above scenario with flipping a coin and rolling a die is an example of independent events. Independent events are circumstances in which the outcome of one event does not affect the outcome of the other event. Conversely, dependent events are ones in which the outcome of one event affects the outcome of the second event. Consider the following scenario: a bag contains 5 black marbles and 5 white marbles. What is the probability of picking 2 black marbles without replacing the marble after the first pick?

The probability of picking a black marble on the first pick is $\frac{5}{10} \left(\frac{5\ black\ marbles}{10\ total\ marbles} \right)$. Assuming that a black marble was picked, there are now 4 black marbles and 5 white marbles for the second pick. Therefore, the probability of picking a black marble on the second pick is $\frac{4}{9} \left(\frac{4\ black\ marbles}{9\ total\ marbles} \right)$. To find the probability of picking two black marbles, the probability of each is multiplied:

$$\frac{5}{10} \times \frac{4}{9} = \frac{20}{90} = \frac{2}{9}$$

Practice Quiz

1. If $-3(x + 4) \geq x + 8$, what is the value of x?
   a. $x = 4$
   b. $x \geq 2$
   c. $x \geq -5$
   d. $x \leq -5$

2. Which inequality represents the values displayed on the number line?

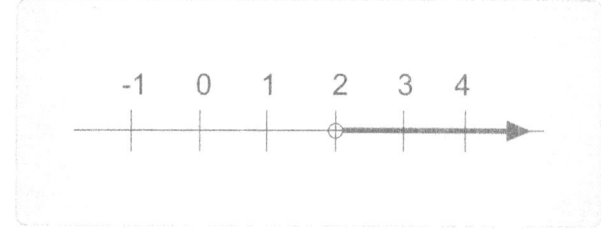

   a. $x < 2$
   b. $x \leq 2$
   c. $x > 2$
   d. $x \geq 2$

3. What is the 42nd item in the pattern: ▲○○□▲○○□▲...?
   a. ○
   b. ▲
   c. □
   d. None of the above

4. If a car can travel 300 miles in four hours, how far can it go in an hour and a half?
   a. 100 miles
   b. 112.5 miles
   c. 135.5 miles
   d. 150 miles

5. Greg buys a $10 lunch with 5% sales tax. He leaves a $2 tip after paying his bill. How much money does he spend?
   a. $12.50
   b. $12.00
   c. $13.00
   d. $13.25

See answers on next page.

Answer Explanations

1. D: Solve a linear inequality in a similar way to solving a linear equation. First, start by distributing the −3 on the left side of the inequality.

$$-3x - 12 \geq x + 8$$

Then, add 12 to both sides.

$$-3x \geq x + 20$$

Next, subtract x from both sides.

$$-4x \geq 20$$

Finally, divide both sides of the inequality by −4. Don't forget to flip the inequality sign because you are dividing by a negative number.

$$x \leq -5$$

2. C: $x > 2$. The open dot on one indicates that the value is not included in the set. The arrow pointing right indicates that numbers greater than two (numbers get larger to the right) are included in the set. Therefore, the set includes numbers greater than two, which can be written as $x > 2$.

3. A: The core of the pattern consists of 4 items: ▲○○□. Therefore, the core repeats in multiples of 4, with the pattern starting over on the next step. The highest multiple of 4 below 42 is 40. Step 40 is the end of the core (□), so step 41 will start the core over (▲) and step 42 is ○.

4. B: 300 miles in four hours is $\frac{300}{4} = 75$ miles per hour. In 1.5 hours, the car will go 1.5×75 miles, or 112.5 miles.

5. A: The tip is not taxed, so he pays 5% tax only on the $10. To find 5% of $10, calculate $0.05 \times \$10 = \$0.50$. Add up $\$10 + \$0.50 + \$2$ to get $\$12.50$.

Social Studies

United States History, Government, and Citizenship

Colonization and Expansion in U.S. History

When examining how Europeans explored what would become the United States of America, one must first examine why Europeans came to explore the New World as a whole. In the fifteenth century, tensions increased between the Eastern and Mediterranean nations of Europe and the expanding Ottoman Empire to the east. As war and piracy spread across the Mediterranean, the once-prosperous trade routes across Asia's Silk Road began to decline, and nations across Europe began to explore alternative routes for trade.

Italian explorer **Christopher Columbus** proposed a westward route. Contrary to popular lore, the main challenge that Columbus faced in finding backers was not proving that the world was round. In fact, much of Europe's educated elite knew that the world was round; the real issue was that they rightly believed that a westward route to Asia, even assuming a lack of obstacles, would be too long to be practical. Nevertheless, Columbus set sail in 1492 after obtaining support from Spain and arrived in the West Indies three months later.

Spain launched further expeditions to the new continents and established **New Spain**. The colony consisted not only of Central America and Mexico, but also the American Southwest and Florida. France claimed much of what would become Canada, along with the Mississippi River region and the Midwest. In addition, the Dutch established colonies that covered New Jersey, New York, and Connecticut. Each nation managed its colonies differently, and thus influenced how they would assimilate into the United States. For instance, Spain strove to establish a system of Christian missions throughout its territory, while France focused on trading networks and had limited infrastructure in regions such as the Midwest.

Even in cases of limited colonial growth, the land of America was hardly vacant, because a diverse array of Native American nations and groups were already present. Throughout much of colonial history, European settlers commonly misperceived native peoples as a singular, static entity. In reality, Native Americans had a variety of traditions depending on their history and environment. Additionally, their culture continued to change through the course of interactions with European settlers; for instance, tribes such as the Cheyenne and Comanche used horses, which were introduced by white settlers, to become powerful warrior nations. However, a few generalizations can be made: many, but not all, tribes were matrilineal, which gave women a fair degree of power, and land was commonly seen as belonging to everyone. These differences, particularly European settlers' continual focus on land ownership, contributed to increasing prejudice and violence.

Situated on the Atlantic Coast, the Thirteen Colonies that would become the United States of America constituted only a small portion of North America. Even those colonies had significant differences that stemmed from their different origins. For instance, the Virginia colony under John Smith in 1607 started with male bachelors seeking gold, whereas families of Puritans settled Massachusetts. As a result, the Thirteen Colonies—Virginia, Massachusetts, Connecticut, Maryland, New York, New Jersey, Pennsylvania, Delaware, Rhode Island, New Hampshire, Georgia, North Carolina, and South Carolina—had different structures and customs that would each influence the United States.

Competition among several imperial powers in eastern areas of North America led to conflicts that would later bring about the independence of the United States. The French and Indian War from 1754 to 1763, which was a subsidiary war of the Seven Years' War, ended with Great Britain claiming France's Canadian territories as well as the Ohio Valley. The war was costly for all the powers involved, which led to increased taxes on the Thirteen Colonies. In addition, the new lands to the west of the colonies attracted new settlers, and they came into conflict with Native Americans and British troops that were trying to maintain the boundaries laid out by treaties between Great Britain and the Native American tribes. These growing tensions with Great Britain, as well as other issues, eventually led to the American Revolution, which ended with Britain relinquishing its control of the colonies.

Britain continued to hold onto its other colonies, such as Canada and the West Indies, which reflects the continued power of multiple nations across North America, even as the United States began to expand across the continent. Many Americans advocated expansion regardless of the land's current inhabitants, but the results were often mixed. Still, events both abroad and within North America contributed to the growth of the United States. For instance, the French Revolution and rise of Napoleon led to the Louisiana Purchase in 1803, when France sold a large chunk of land consisting of Louisiana and much of the Midwest to the United States. Meanwhile, as Spanish power declined, Mexico claimed independence in 1821, but the new nation became increasingly vulnerable to foreign pressure. In the Mexican-American War (1846-1848), Mexico surrendered territory to the United States that eventually became California, Nevada, Utah, and New Mexico, as well as parts of Arizona, Colorado, and Wyoming.

Even as the United States sought new inland territory, American interests were also expanding overseas via trade. As early as 1784, the ship **Empress of China** traveled to China to establish trading connections. American interests had international dimensions throughout the nation's history. For instance, during the presidency of Andrew Jackson, the **Potomac** was dispatched to Sumatra in 1832 to avenge the deaths of American sailors. This incident exemplifies how U.S. foreign trade connected with imperial expansion.

This combination of continental and seaward growth adds a deeper layer to American development, because it was not purely focused on western expansion. For example, take the 1849 Gold Rush; a large number of Americans and other immigrants traveled to California by ship and settled western territories before more eastern areas, such as Nevada and Idaho. Therefore, the United States' early history of colonization and expansion is a complex network of diverse cultures.

American Revolution and the Founding of the Nation

The **American Revolution** largely occurred as a result of changing values in the Thirteen Colonies that broke from their traditional relationship with England. Early on in the colonization of North America, the colonial social structure tried to mirror the stratified order of Great Britain. In England, the landed elites were seen as intellectually and morally superior to the common man, which led to a paternalistic relationship. This style of governance was similarly applied to the colonial system; government was left to the property-owning upper class, and the colonies as a whole could be seen as a child dutifully serving "Mother England."

However, the colonies' distance from England meant that actual, hereditary aristocrats from Britain only formed a small percentage of the overall population and did not even fill all the positions of power. By the mid-eighteenth century, much of the American upper class consisted of local families who acquired status through business rather than lineage. Despite this, representatives from Britain were appointed to govern the colonies. As a result, a rift began to form between the colonists and British officials.

Tensions began to rise in the aftermath of the French and Indian War of 1754 to 1763. To recover the financial costs of the long conflict, Great Britain drew upon its colonies to provide the desired resources. Since the American colonists did not fully subscribe to the paternal connection, taxation to increase British revenue, such as the **Stamp Act of 1765**, was met with increasing resistance. Britain sent soldiers to the colonies and enacted the **1765 Quartering Act** to require colonists to house the troops. In 1773, the **Tea Act**, which legitimized Britain's taxing of the colonies, led disgruntled colonists to raid ships importing tea and destroy their contents in an act known as the **Boston Tea Party**.

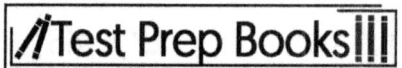

Uncertain about whether they should remain loyal to Britain, representatives from twelve colonies formed the First Continental Congress in 1774 to discuss what they should do next. When Patriot militiamen at Lexington and Concord fought British soldiers in April 1775, the **Revolutionary War** began. While the rebel forces worked to present the struggle as a united, patriotic effort, the colonies remained divided throughout the war. Thousands of colonists, known as **Loyalists** or **Tories**, supported Britain. Even the revolutionaries proved to be significantly fragmented, and many militias only served in their home states. The Continental Congress was also divided over whether to reconcile with Britain or push for full separation. These issues hindered the ability of the revolutionary armies to resist the British, who had superior training and resources at their disposal.

Even so, the **Continental Army**, under **General George Washington**, gradually built up a force that utilized Prussian military training and backwoods guerrilla tactics to make up for their limited resources. Although the British forces continued to win significant battles, the Continental Army gradually reduced Britain's will to fight as the years passed. Furthermore, Americans appealed to the rivalry that other European nations had with the British Empire. The support was initially limited to indirect assistance, but aid gradually increased. After the American victory at the Battle of Saratoga in 1777, France and other nations began to actively support the American cause by providing much-needed troops and equipment.

In 1781, the primary British army under **General Cornwallis** was defeated by an American and French coalition at Yorktown, Virginia, which paved the way for peace negotiations. The **Treaty of Paris in 1783** ended the war, recognized the former colonies' independence from Great Britain, and gave America control over territory between the Appalachian Mountains and Mississippi River. However, the state of the new nation was still uncertain. The new nation's government initially stemmed from the state-based structure of the Continental Congress and was incorporated into the Articles of Confederation in 1777.

The **Articles of Confederation** emphasized the ideals of the American Revolution, particularly the concept of freedom from unjust government. Unfortunately, the resulting limitations on the national government left most policies—even ones with national ramifications—up to individual states. For instance, states sometimes simply decided to not pay taxes. Many representatives did not see much value in the National Congress and simply did not attend the meetings. Some progress was still made during the period, such as the **Northwest Ordinance of 1787**, which organized the western territories into new states; nevertheless, the disjointed links in the state-oriented government inhibited significant progress.

Although many citizens felt satisfied with this decentralized system of government, key intellectuals and leaders in America became increasingly disturbed by the lack of unity. An especially potent fear among them was the potential that, despite achieving official independence, other powers could threaten America's autonomy. In 1786, poor farmers in Massachusetts launched an insurrection, known as **Shays' Rebellion**, which sparked fears of additional uprisings and led to the creation of the **Constitutional Convention in 1787**.

While the convention initially intended to correct issues within the Articles of Confederation, speakers, such as **James Madison**, compellingly argued for the delegates to devise a new system of government that was more centralized than its predecessor. The Constitution was not fully supported by all citizens, and there was much debate about whether or not to support the new government. Even so, in 1788, the Constitution was ratified. Later additions, such as the **Bill of Rights**, would help protect individual liberty by giving specific rights to citizens. In 1789, **George Washington** became the first president of the newly created executive branch of the government, and America entered a new stage of history.

U.S. History from Founding to Present

One early development was the growth of political parties—something that Washington tried and failed to stop from forming. Federalists, such as **Alexander Hamilton**, wanted to expand the national government's power, while Democratic-Republicans, such as **Thomas Jefferson**, favored states' rights. The United States suffered multiple defeats by Britain in the War of 1812, but individual American victories, such as the **Battle of New Orleans**, still strengthened nationalistic pride.

In the aftermath of the war, the Federalists were absorbed into the Democratic-Republicans, which began the **Era of Good Feelings**. However, two new parties eventually emerged. The Democrats, whose leader **Andrew Jackson** became president in 1828, favored "Jacksonian" democracy, which emphasized mass participation in elections. However, Jackson's policies largely favored white male landowners and suppressed opposing views. The Whigs supported Federalist policies but also drew on democratic principles, particularly with marginalized groups such as African Americans and women.

At the same time, settlers continued to expand west in search of new land and fortune. The Louisiana Purchase of 1803 opened up large amounts of land west of the Mississippi River, and adventurers pushed past even those boundaries toward the western coast. The vision of westward growth into the frontier is a key part of American popular culture, but the expansion was often erratic and depended on a combination of incentives and assurances of relative security. Hence, some areas, such as California and Oregon, were settled more quickly than other areas to the east. Some historians have pointed to the growth of the frontier as a means through which American democracy expanded.

However, the matter of western lands became an increasingly volatile issue as the controversy over slavery heightened. Not all northerners supported abolition, but many saw the practice as outdated and did not want it to expand. Abolitionists formed the Republican Party, and their candidate, **Abraham Lincoln**, was elected as president in 1860. In response, southern states seceded and formed the **Confederate States of America**. The ensuing **Civil War** lasted from 1861 to 1865 and had significant consequences. Slavery was abolished in the United States, and the power of individual states was drastically curtailed. After being reunified, southern states worked to retain control over freed slaves, and the Reconstruction period was followed by **Jim Crow** segregation. As a result, blacks were barred from public education, unable to vote, and forced to accept their status as second-class citizens.

After the Civil War, the United States increasingly industrialized and became part of the larger Industrial Revolution, which took place throughout the western world. Steps toward industrialization had already begun as early as Jackson's presidency, but the full development of American industry took place in the second half of the nineteenth century. Railroads helped link cities like Chicago to locations across the West, which allowed for rapid transfer of materials. New technologies, such as electricity, allowed leisure time for those with enough wealth. Even so, the **Gilded Age** was also a period of disparities, and wealthy entrepreneurs rose while impoverished workers struggled to make their voices heard.

The late nineteenth and early twentieth century not only marked U.S. expansion within North America but also internationally. For instance, after the **Spanish-American War in 1898**, the United States claimed control over Guam, Puerto Rico, and the Philippines. Rivalries in Europe culminated in World War I, in which great powers ranging from France to Russia vied for control in a bloody struggle. Americans did not enter the war until 1917, but we had a critical role in the final phase of the war. During the peace treaty process, **President Woodrow Wilson** sought to establish a **League of Nations** in order to promote global harmony, but his efforts only achieved limited success.

After World War I, the United States largely stayed out of international politics for the next two decades. Still, American businesses continued overseas ventures and strengthened the economy in the 1920s. However, massive speculation in the stock market in 1929 triggered the **Great Depression**—a financial crisis that spread worldwide as nations withdrew from the global economy. The crisis shepherded in the presidency of **Franklin D. Roosevelt**, who reformed the Democratic Party and implemented new federal programs known as the **New Deal**.

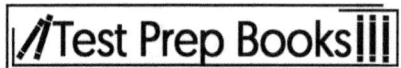

The Great Depression had ramifications worldwide and encouraged the rise of fascist governments in Italy and Germany. Highly dictatorial, fascism emphasized nationalism and militarism. World War II began when the Axis powers of Germany, Italy, and Japan built up their military forces and launched invasions against neighboring nations in 1939. As part of the Allies, which also included Britain, France, and the Soviet Union, America defeated the Axis powers in 1945 and asserted itself as a global force.

The **Union of Soviet Socialist Republics** had emerged through the **Bolshevik Revolution in 1917** in Russia and militantly supported **Communism**—a socialist system of government that called for the overthrow of capitalism. Although the Soviet Union formed an alliance with the United States during World War II, relations chilled, and the Cold War began in 1947. Although no true war was declared between the two nations, both the Union of Soviet Socialist Republics and the United States engaged in indirect conflict by supporting and overthrowing foreign governments.

Meanwhile, the **Civil Rights Movement** began to grow as marginalized groups objected to racial segregation and abuse by whites across the nation. Civil rights leaders, such as **Martin Luther King Jr.**, argued for nonviolent resistance, but others, such as **Malcolm X**, advocated more radical approaches. Civil rights groups became increasingly discontented during the Vietnam War because they felt they were being drafted for a foreign war that ignored domestic problems. Even so, significant reforms, such as the **Voting Rights Act of 1965**, opened up new opportunities for freedom and equality in America.

In 1991, the Soviet Union collapsed, leaving the United States as the dominant global power. However, as the United States struggled to fill the void left by the Soviet Union, questions arose about America's role in the world. Terrorist acts, such as the 9/11 attack on the World Trade Center in 2001, have shed doubt on the United States' ability to enforce its authority on an international scale.

Twentieth-Century Developments in the United States

Although the United States began industrializing in the second half of the nineteenth century, American technology continued to develop in new directions throughout the course of the twentieth century. A key example was the invention of the modern assembly line. Assembly lines and conveyor belts had already become a prominent part of industrial work, but **Henry Ford** combined conveyor belts with the system of assembly workers in 1913 in order to produce Model T automobiles. This streamlined production system, in which multiple parts were assembled by different teams along the conveyors, allowed industries in the United States to grow ever larger.

Ford's assembly lines also promoted the growth of the automobile as a means of transportation. Early cars were an expensive and impractical novelty and were primarily the toys of the rich. The Model T, on the other hand, was relatively affordable, which made the car available to a wider array of consumers. Many of the automobiles' early issues, such as radiator leaks and fragile tires, were gradually corrected, and this made the car more appealing than horses. With the support of **President Eisenhower**, the **Federal Aid Highway Act of 1956** paved the way for a network of interstates and highways across the nation.

At the same time, a revolutionary approach to transportation was emerging: flight. Blimps and balloons were already gaining popularity by the turn of the twentieth century, but aviators struggled to create an airplane. The first critical success was by the **Wright Brothers** in 1903, and they demonstrated that aircrafts did not need to be lighter than air. In time, airplanes surpassed the popularity of balloons and blimps, which tended to be more volatile. Aircraft also added a new dimension to warfare, and aircraft carriers became an integral piece of the American navy during World War II.

Furthermore, by demonstrating that heavier-than-air vehicles could actually carry passengers upward, the stage was set for the space race in the second half of the twentieth century. In 1958, the U.S. government created the **National Aeronautics and Space Administration (NASA)** to head the budding initiative to extend American power into space. After the Soviet Union successfully launched the **Sputnik satellite** into Earth's orbit in 1957 and sent the first human in space in 1961, the United States intensified its own space program through the **Apollo missions. Apollo 11** successfully landed on the moon in 1969 with **Buzz Aldrin** and **Neil Armstrong**. Later ventures into space would focus on space shuttles and satellites, and the latter significantly enhanced communications worldwide.

Indeed, the twentieth century also made considerable advancements in communications and media. Inventions such as the radio greatly boosted communication across the nation and world, such that news could be reported immediately rather than take days. Furthermore, motion pictures evolved from black-and-white movies at theaters to full-color television sets in households. From animation to live films, television matured into a compelling art form in popular culture. Live-action footage gave a new layer to news broadcasts and proved instrumental in the public's reaction to events, such as the Civil Rights Movement and the Vietnam War. With the success of the space program, satellites became a fundamental piece of Earth's communications network by transmitting signals across the planet instantaneously.

Further communications advancements resulted from the development of computer technology. The early computers in the twentieth century were enormous behemoths that were too bulky and expensive for anything but government institutions. However, computers gradually became smaller while still storing large amounts of data. A turning point came with the 1976 release of the Apple computer by entrepreneurs **Steve Wozniak** and **Steve Jobs**. The computer had a simplistic design that made it marketable for a mass consumer audience, and computers eventually became household items. Similarly, the networks that would become the Internet originated as government systems, but in time they were extended to commercial avenues that became a vibrant element of modern communications.

However, other advancements in American science during the twentieth century were aimed toward more lethal purposes. In response to the multiple wars throughout the century, the United States built up a powerful military force, and new technologies were devised for that purpose. One of the deadliest creations was the **atomic bomb**, which split molecular atoms to produce powerful explosions; in addition to the sheer force of the bombs, the aftereffects included toxic radiation and electronic shutdowns. Developed and used in the last days of World War II, the nuclear bomb was the United States' most powerful weapon during the Cold War.

On the other hand, the twentieth century also marked new approaches to the natural environments in America. In reaction to the depletion of natural habitats by industrialization and overhunting, **President Theodore Roosevelt** helped preserve areas for what would become the National Parks in 1916. Laws, such as the **Clean Water Act of 1972**, helped improve the health of ecosystems, which benefitted not only wildlife but people across the nation. This also led to the development of alternative energy sources such as wind and solar power.

America continues to change and grow into the twenty-first century by building on preexisting ideas but also pioneering new concepts. As globalization becomes an increasingly prominent phenomenon, American businesses strive to adapt their products to consumers worldwide while also funneling in new ideas from other nations. Yet many of the current developments in American enterprises stem in part from earlier events in American history. For instance, the environmental movement has expanded to address new issues such as global warming. NASA continues its space exploration endeavors, but entrepreneurs hope one day to travel to Mars. Therefore, the history of technology within the United States remains an engaging and relevant subject in the present.

Connections between Causes and Effects

When examining the historical narratives of events, it is important to understand the relationship between causes and effects. A **cause** can be defined as something, whether an event, social change, or other factor, that contributes to the occurrence of certain events; the results of causes are called **effects**. Those terms may seem simple enough, but they have drastic implications on how one explores history. Events such as the American Revolution or the Civil Rights Movement may appear to occur spontaneously, but a closer examination will reveal that these events depended on earlier phenomena and patterns that influenced the course of history.

For example, although the battles at Concord and Lexington may seem to be instantaneous eruptions of violence during the American Revolution, they stemmed from a variety of factors. The most obvious influences behind those two battles were the assortment of taxes and policies imposed on the Thirteen Colonies following the French and Indian War from 1754 to 1763. Taxation without direct representation, combined with the deployment of British soldiers to enforce these policies, greatly increased American resistance. Earlier events, such as the Boston Massacre and the Boston Tea Party, similarly stemmed from conflicts between British soldiers and local colonists over perceived tyranny and rebelliousness. Therefore, the start of the American Revolution progressed from preceding developments.

Furthermore, there can be multiple causes and effects for any situation. The existence of multiple causes can be seen through the settling of the American West. Many historians have emphasized the role of Manifest Destiny—the national vision of expanding across the continent—as a driving force behind the growth of the United States. Yet there were many different influences behind the expansion westward. Northern abolitionists and southern planters saw the frontier as a way to either extend or limit slavery. Economic opportunities in the West also encouraged travel westward, as did the gradual pacification of Native American tribes.

Even an individual cause can be subdivided into smaller factors or stretched out in a gradual process. Although there were numerous issues that led to the Civil War, slavery was the primary cause. However, that topic stretched back to the very founding of the nation, and the existence of slavery was a controversial topic during the creation of the Declaration of Independence and the Constitution. The abolition movement as a whole did not start until the 1830s, but nevertheless, slavery is a cause that gradually grew more important over the following decades. In addition, opponents of slavery were divided by different motivations—some believed that it stifled the economy, while others focused on moral issues.

On the other end of the spectrum, a single event can have numerous results. The rise of the telegraph, for example, had several effects on American history. The telegraph allowed news to travel much quicker and turned events into immediate national news, such as the sinking of the USS Maine, which sparked the Spanish-American War. In addition, the telegraph helped make railroads run more efficiently by improving the links between stations. The faster speed of both travel and communications led to a shift in time itself, and localized times were replaced by standardized time zones across the nation.

The importance of grasping cause-and-effect relationships is critical in interpreting the growth and development of the Civil Rights Movement. Historical narratives of the movement often focus on charismatic individuals, such as Martin Luther King Jr., and they certainly played a key leadership role. Even so, elements of the movement had already emerged in previous decades through the growth of the **National Association for the Advancement of Colored People (NAACP)** and other organizations. Several factors proved critical to the formation of civil rights organizations during the 1950s. African American veterans returning from World War II, as well as those continuing to serve in the military, called for equal rights. Furthermore, the United States' role as a key member of the United Nations, which included African countries, required the federal government to take racial discrimination seriously.

A specific example in the Civil Rights Movement is the sit-ins during 1960, in which black and white students defied segregation policies in restaurants and other establishments. The wave is often thought to originate from spontaneous activism by students in Greensboro, North Carolina. However, there had already been other sit-ins, such as at **Royal Ice Cream Parlor** in Durham, North Carolina, in 1957. In fact, the sit-ins would not have spread as quickly without a preexisting network of activists across the nation, which in part stemmed from the growth of organizations through various local and national movements. By looking at such cases closely, it becomes clear that no event occurs without one—if not multiple—causes behind it, and that each historical event can have a variety of direct and indirect consequences.

One of the most critical elements of cause-and-effect relationships is how they are relevant not only in studying history but also in contemporary events. Much of the current political debate about social security and healthcare stems from FDR's New Deal in the 1930s, and at the time some people criticized the programs for being too extensive, while others argued that he did not go far enough with his vision. Current environmental concerns have their origins in long-term issues that reach back centuries. The United States' mixed history of global isolation and foreign intervention continues to influence foreign policy approaches today. Most of all, people must realize that events and developments today will likely have a number of consequences later on. Therefore, the study of cause and effect remains vital in understanding the past, the present, and the future.

Nature, Purpose, and Forms of Government

The United States of America's government, as outlined by the **Constitution**, is designed to serve as a compromise between democracy and preceding monarchical systems. The American Revolution brought independence from Britain and freedom from its aristocratic system of governance. On the other hand, the short-lived Articles of Confederation revealed the significant weaknesses of state-based governance with limited national control. By dividing power between local, state, and federal governments, the United States can uphold its value of individual liberties while, nevertheless, giving a sense of order to the country.

The **federal government**, which is in charge of laws that affect the entire nation, is split into three main branches: executive, judicial, and legislative. It is important to realize that the three segments of the federal government are intended to stand as equal counterparts to the others, and that none of them are "in charge." The **executive branch** centers on the president, the vice president, and the cabinet. The president and vice president are elected every four years. Also known as the **commander-in-chief**, the **president** is the official head of state and serves as the nation's head diplomat and military leader. The **vice president** acts as the president of the Senate in the legislative branch, while the president appoints members of the cabinet to lead agencies, including the Treasury and Department of Defense. However, the president can only sign and veto laws and cannot initiate them himself.

Instead, the **legislative branch**, specifically Congress, proposes and debates laws. **Congress** is bicameral because it is divided into two separate legislative houses. Each state's representation in the **House of Representatives** is determined proportionally by population, with the total number of voting seats limited to 435. The **Senate**, in contrast, has only two members per state and a total of one hundred senators. Members of both houses are intended to represent the interests of the constituents in their home states and to bring their concerns to a national level while also being consistent with the interests of the nation as a whole. Drafts of laws, called **bills**, are proposed in one chamber and then are voted upon according to that chamber's rules; should the bill pass the vote in the first house of Congress, the other legislative chamber must approve it before it can be sent to the president. Congress also has a variety of other powers, such as the rights to declare war, collect taxes, and impeach the president.

The **judicial branch**, though it cannot pass laws itself, serves to interpret the laws. At the federal level, this is done through several tiers of judicial bodies. At the top, the **Supreme Court** consists of judges appointed by

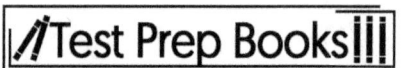

the president; these judges serve for life, unless they resign from their position or are removed by Congress for improper behavior. The Supreme Court's decisions in trials and other judgments rest on the justices' interpretations of the Constitution and enacted laws. As the Constitution remains fundamental to the American legal system, the Supreme Court's rulings on how laws follow or fail to uphold the Constitution have powerful implications on future rulings. Beneath the Supreme Court, there are a number of other federal judicial bodies—courts of appeals, district courts, and courts of special jurisdiction.

While the federal government manages the nation as a whole, state governments address issues pertaining to their specific territory. In the past, states claimed the right, known as **nullification**, to refuse to enforce federal laws that they considered unconstitutional. However, conflicts between state and federal authority, particularly in the South in regard to first, slavery, and later, discrimination, have led to increased federal power, and states cannot defy federal laws. Even so, the **Tenth Amendment** limits federal power to those specifically granted in the Constitution, and the rest of the powers are retained by the states and citizens. Therefore, individual state governments are left in charge of decisions with immediate effects on their citizens, such as state laws and taxes. Like the federal government, state governments consist of executive, judicial, and legislative branches, but the exact configuration of those branches varies between states. For instance, while most states follow the bicameral structure of Congress, Nebraska has only a single legislative chamber. **State governments** have considerable authority within their states, but they cannot impose their power on other states, nor can they secede from the United States.

Local governments, which include town governments, county boards, library districts, and other agencies, are especially variable in their composition. They often reflect the overall views of their state governments but also have their own values, rules, and structures. Generally, local governments function in a democratic fashion, although the exact form of government depends on its role. Depending on the location within the state, local government may have considerable or minimal authority based on the population and prosperity of the area; some counties may have strong influence in the state, while others may have a limited impact.

Native American tribes are treated as dependent nations that answer to the federal government but may be immune to state jurisdiction. As with local governments, the exact form of governance is left up to the tribes, which ranges from small councils to complex systems of government. Other U.S. territories, including the District of Columbia (site of Washington, D.C.) and acquired islands, such as Guam and Puerto Rico, have representation within Congress, but their legislators cannot vote on bills.

As members of a democracy, U.S. citizens are empowered to elect most government leaders, but the process varies between branch and level of government. Presidential elections at the national scale use the **Electoral College system**. Rather than electing the president directly, citizens cast their ballots to select electors, who generally vote for a specific candidate, that represent each state in the college. Legislative branches at the federal and state level are also determined by elections, albeit without an Electoral College. In some areas, judges are elected, but in other states judges are appointed by elected officials. It should also be noted that the two-party system was not built into the Constitution but gradually emerged over time.

Key Documents and Speeches in U.S. History

With more than two hundred years of history, American leaders have produced a number of important documents and speeches. One of the most essential is the **Declaration of Independence**, which the **Second Continental Congress** ratified on **July 4, 1776**. Although many historians and politicians have drawn upon the words of the Declaration to demonstrate the American ideal of freedom, most of them focus on the **preamble**, which focuses on the necessity of fair government and the right to overthrow tyrants. The main body of the document consists of a set of grievances against **King George III**. Still, this document was instrumental in American history because it asserted American independence from Great Britain. Even so, it is important to note that the Declaration did not immediately lead to the United States; the document does

Social Studies

not outline the government of the soon-to-be independent colonies, and independence would not become reality until Britain agreed.

The colonies' first blueprint for government was the **Articles of Confederation**, which was ratified in 1777. The document declared that the confederacy would be called the United States of America and that the individual states would have "a firm league of friendship" with each other. The emphasis on friendship and cooperation highlights how the confederation was a voluntary effort that states could follow or ignore as they saw fit. Still, the document also revealed the importance of obeying decisions made by Congress as a whole; while this was not very effective during the confederation period, the framework would live on to a degree in the following Constitution.

Much like the Declaration of Independence, the **1787 Constitution of the United States** is most remembered for the preamble, which takes a more philosophical approach. However, the body of the Constitution is highly complex, and it covers the framework and responsibilities of the different branches of the federal government and the limits to state power. These details are very important and help to define the key institutions within the government. To resolve later issues not addressed in the Constitution, the fifth article in the document establishes a process to modify the government, and the first ten amendments are known as the **Bill of Rights**. Under the Tenth Amendment, powers not specifically allotted to Congress by the Constitution are reserved for the people and to individual states.

George Washington was the first president of the United States, and his administration set many precedents for the nation, particularly with his **Farewell Address**. In it, he noted the rise of regional feelings, and he urged citizens to uphold their duty to the nation above sectionalism because he felt that America was strongest when united. The issue of regional conflicts and national identity would become increasingly important in years to come, especially during the Civil War. Washington also argued against intervention in European affairs, and this warning would become the cornerstone for advocates of American isolation. On the other hand, his advice that political parties are detrimental to democracy failed to halt the development of the party system.

Washington's fears about sectional conflict were confirmed at the start of the Civil War, when the southern states violently seceded from the Union. As the president during that tumultuous time, Abraham Lincoln was seen by many to embody the Union as a whole. This can be demonstrated through his **Gettysburg Address** in November of 1863. After the difficult and bloody **Battle of Gettysburg** ended in a Union victory, crowds gathered for the dedication of the Soldiers' National Cemetery. Although he was not the main speaker of the event, Lincoln's short yet eloquent speech proved to be the most significant. Drawing upon the Declaration of Independence's assertion that "all men are created equal," he argued that the current war was a test of that ideal. More than that, he emphasized the importance of the United States as a whole and argued that it must endure as a Union for the sake of the world.

Earlier that year in January, Lincoln had already indicated his opposition to slavery through the **Emancipation Proclamation**. Although it was an executive order instead of a law passed by Congress, this document was not challenged by the courts and helped determine the objectives of the Civil War. The proclamation asserted that all slaves in Confederate territories were free. One must note that some southern states remained in the Union, and therefore, were not affected by this proclamation. Even so, the order helped establish a basis for later laws and amendments that would end slavery in the United States.

Another presidential attempt to set a new precedent for American policy was **Woodrow Wilson's Fourteen Points**, which were outlined in a speech he gave to Congress in 1918 after the United States had entered World War I. Wilson saw the United States as a protector of democracy in the world and said that we could reform world policy by fighting in the war. For instance, Wilson called for an end to private negotiations, which had contributed to the secret alliances behind the war. Most of all, he argued for nations to come

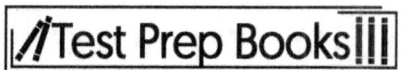

together in an international body to determine world policies. The negotiations after the war only partially fulfilled Wilson's ambitions by creating a weak League of Nations, but his vision of U.S. involvement in global affairs would become a key aspect of American foreign policy.

Even as the United States began playing a more active role on the international stage of politics, internal issues such as civil rights remained important, as shown in **Martin Luther King Jr.**'s "I Have a Dream" speech. A leader in the Civil Rights Movement, King gave his speech as part of the 1963 March on Washington. Drawing on Lincoln's past speech at Gettysburg, King argued that America's journey to true equality was not over. His references to biblical passages gave the speech a spiritual tone, but he also mentioned specific locations across the nation to emphasize that local struggles were tied with national consequences. Through its optimistic tone, Dr. King's speech reflects not only civil rights activism but also the American dream of freedom and progress.

Rights and Responsibilities of Citizenship in a Democracy

Citizens living in a democracy have several rights and responsibilities to uphold. The first duty is that they uphold the established laws of the government. In a democracy, a system of nationwide laws is necessary to ensure that there is some degree of order. Therefore, citizens must try to obey the laws and also help enforce them because a law that is inadequately enforced, such as early civil rights laws in the South, is almost useless. Optimally, a democratic society's laws will be accepted and followed by the community as a whole.

However, conflict can occur when an unjust law is passed. For instance, much of the civil rights movement centered around **Jim Crow laws** in the South that supported segregation between black and whites. Yet these practices were encoded in state laws, which created a dilemma for African Americans who wanted equality but also wanted to respect the law. Fortunately, a democracy offers a degree of protection from such laws by creating a system in which government leaders and policies are constantly open to change in accordance with the will of citizens. Citizens can influence the laws that are passed by voting for and electing members of the legislative and executive branches to represent them at the local, state, and national levels.

This, however, requires citizens to be especially vigilant in protecting their liberties because they cannot depend solely on the existing government to meet their needs. To assert their role in a democracy, citizens should be active voters and speak out on issues that concern them. Even with these safeguards, it is possible for systems to be implemented that inhibit active participation. For instance, many southern states had laws that prevented blacks from voting. Under such circumstances, civil rights leaders felt that they had no choice but to resist the laws in order to defend their personal rights. Once voting became possible, civil rights groups strove to ensure that their votes counted by changing state and national policy.

An extension of citizens' voting rights is their ability to run as elected officials. By becoming leaders in the government, citizens can demonstrate their engagement and help determine government policy. The involvement of citizens as a whole in the selection of leaders is vital in a democracy because it helps to prevent the formation of an elite cadre that does not answer to the public. Without the engagement of citizens who run for office, voters are limited in their ability to select candidates that appeal to them. In this case, voting options would become stagnant, which inhibits the ability of the nation to grow and change over time. As long as citizens are willing to take a stand for their vision of America, America's government will remain dynamic and diverse.

These features of a democracy give it the potential to reshape itself continually in response to new developments in society. In order for a democracy to function, it is of the utmost importance that citizens care about the course of politics and be aware of current issues. Apathy among citizens is a constant problem that threatens the endurance of democracies. Citizens should have a desire to take part in the political process, or else they simply accept the status quo and fail to fulfill their role as citizens.

Moreover, they must have acute knowledge of the political processes and the issues that they can address as citizens. A fear among the Founding Fathers was the prevalence of mob rule, in which the common people did not take interest in politics except to vote for their patrons; this was the usual course of politics in the colonial era, as the common people left the decisions to the established elites. Without understanding the world around them, citizens may not fully grasp the significance of political actions and thereby fail to make wise decisions in that regard. Therefore, citizens must stay informed about current affairs, ranging from local to national or global matters, so that they can properly address them as voters or elected leaders.

Furthermore, knowledge of the nation's history is essential for healthy citizenship. History continues to have an influence on present political decisions. For instance, Supreme Court rulings often take into account previous legal precedents and verdicts, so it is important to know about those past events and how they affect the current processes. It is especially critical that citizens are aware of the context in which laws were established because it helps clarify the purpose of those laws. For instance, an understanding of the problems with the Articles of Confederation allows people to comprehend some of the reasons behind the framework of the Constitution. In addition, history as a whole shapes the course of societies and the world; therefore, citizens should draw on this knowledge of the past to realize the full consequences of current actions. Issues such as climate change, conflict in the Middle East, and civil rights struggles are rooted in events and cultural developments that reach back centuries and should be addressed.

Therefore, education is a high priority in democracies because it has the potential to instill generations of citizens with the right mindset and knowledge required to do their part in shaping the nation. Optimally, education should cover a variety of different subjects, ranging from mathematics to biology, so that individuals can explore whatever paths they wish to take in life. Even so, social studies are especially important because students should understand how democracies function and understand the history of the nation and world. Historical studies should cover national and local events as well because they help provide the basis for the understanding of contemporary politics. Social studies courses should also address the histories of foreign nations because contemporary politics increasingly has global consequences. In addition, history lessons should remain open to multiple perspectives, even those that might criticize a nation's past actions, because citizens should be exposed to diverse perspectives that they can apply as voters and leaders.

Geography, Anthropology, and Sociology

World and Regional Geography

Geography is essential in understanding the world as a whole. This requires a study of spatial distribution, which examines how various locations and physical features are arranged in the world. The most common element in geography is the **region**, which refers to a specific area that is separate from surrounding ones. Regions can be defined based on a variety of factors, including environmental, economic, or political features, and these different kinds of regions can overlap with each other.

It is also important to know the difference between location and place. A **location**, defined either through its physical position or through its relation to other locations, determines where something is, and this characteristic is static. A **place**, on the other hand, describes a combination of physical and human elements in relation to each other; the determination of place is therefore changeable depending on the movement of individuals and groups.

Geography is visually conveyed using maps, and a collection of maps is called an **atlas**. To illustrate some key points about geography, please refer to the map below.

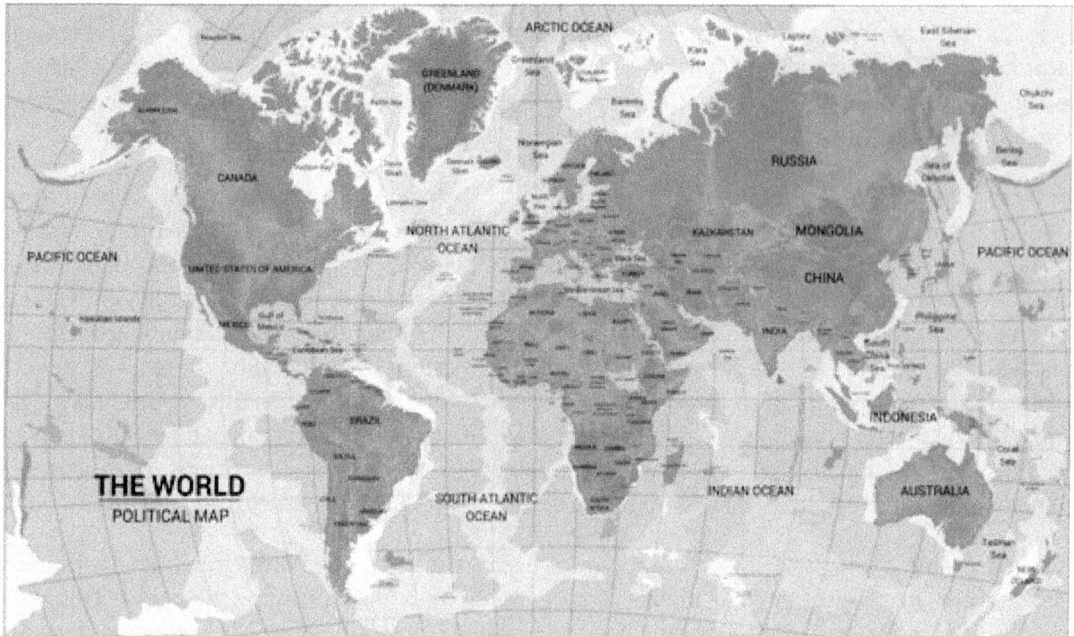

This is a traditional map of the world that displays all of the countries and six of the seven continents. **Countries**, the most common approach to political regions, can be identified by their labels. The **continents** are not identified on this map, with the exception of Australia, but they are larger landmasses that encompass most of the countries in their respective areas; the other five visible continents are North America, South America, Europe, Africa, and Asia. The seventh continent, Antarctica, is found at the South Pole and has been omitted from the map.

The absence of Antarctica leads into the issues of distortion, in which geographical features are altered on a map. Some degree of distortion is to be expected with a two-dimensional flat map of the world because the earth is a sphere. A map projection transforms a spherical map of the world into a flattened perspective, but the process generally alters the spatial appearance of landmasses. For instance, Greenland often appears, such as in the map above, larger than it really is.

Furthermore, Antarctica's exclusion from the map is, in fact, a different sort of distortion—that of the mapmakers' biases. Mapmakers determine which features are included on the map and which ones are not. Antarctica, for example, is often missing from maps because, unlike the other continents, it has a limited human population. Moreover, a study of the world reveals that many of the distinctions on maps are human constructions.

Even so, maps can still reveal key features about the world. For instance, the map above has areas that seem almost three-dimensional and jut out. They represent mountains and are an example of **topography**, which is a method used to display the differing elevations of the terrain. A more detailed topographical map can be viewed below.

On some colored maps, the oceans, represented in blue between the continents, vary in coloration depending on depth. The differences demonstrate **bathymetry**, which is the study of the ocean floor's depth. Paler areas represent less depth, while darker spots reflect greater depth.

Please also note the many lines running horizontally and vertically along the map. The horizontal lines, known as **parallels**, mark the calculated latitude of those locations and reveal how far north or south these areas are from the equator, which bisects the map horizontally. Generally, with exceptions depending on specific environments, climates closer to the equator are warmer because this region receives the most direct sunlight. The **equator** also serves to split the globe between the Northern and Southern hemispheres.

Longitude, as signified by the vertical lines, determines how far east or west different regions are from each other. The lines of longitude, known as **meridians**, are also the basis for time zones, which allocate different times to regions depending on their position eastward and westward of the prime meridian. As one travels west between time zones, the given time moves backward accordingly. Conversely, if one travels east, the time moves forward.

There are two particularly significant longitude-associated dividers in this regard. The **prime [Greenwich] meridian**, as displayed below, is defined as zero degrees in longitude, and thus determines the other lines. The line, in fact, circles the globe north and south, and it therefore divides the world into the Eastern and Western hemispheres. It is important to not confuse the Greenwich meridian with the **International Date Line**, which is an invisible line in the Pacific Ocean that was created to represent the change between calendar days. By traveling westward across the International Date Line, a traveler would essentially leap forward a day. For example, a person departing from the United States on Sunday would arrive in Japan on

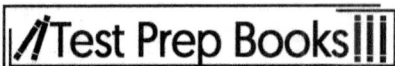

Monday. By traveling eastward across the line, a traveler would go backward a day. For example, a person departing from China on Monday would arrive in Canada on Sunday.

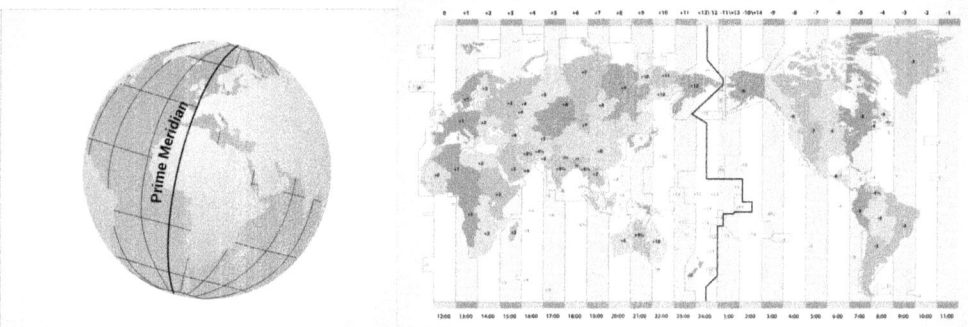

Although world maps are useful in showing the overall arrangement of continents and nations, it is also important at times to look more closely at individual countries because they have unique features that are only visible on more detailed maps.

For example, take the following map of the United States of America. It should be noted that the country is split into multiple states that have their own culture and localized governments. Other countries are often split into various divisions, such as provinces, and while these features are ignored for the sake of clarity on larger maps, they are important when studying specific nations. Individual states can be further subdivided into counties and townships, and they may have their own maps that can be examined for closer analysis.

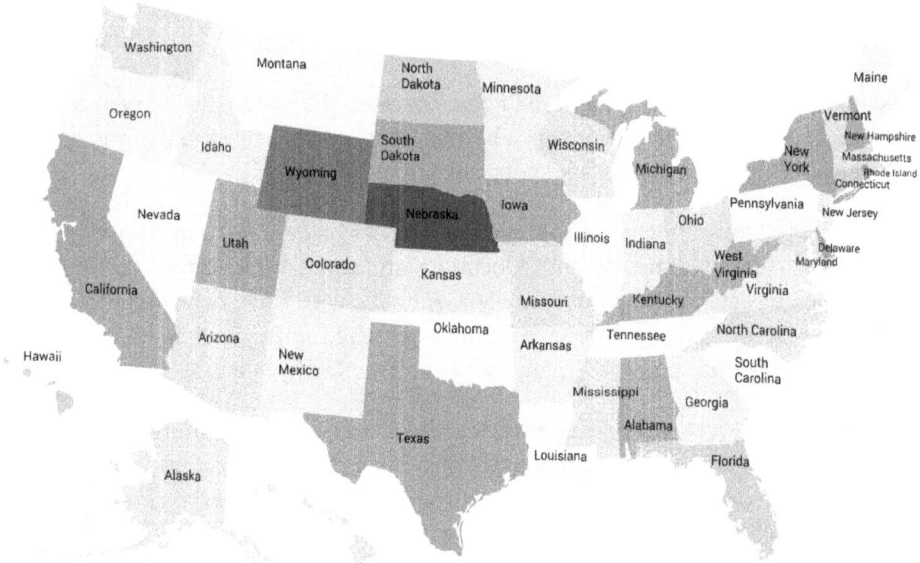

Finally, one of the first steps in examining any map should be to locate the map's key or legend, which will explain what features different symbols represent on the map. As these symbols can be arbitrary depending on the maker, a key will help to clarify the different meanings.

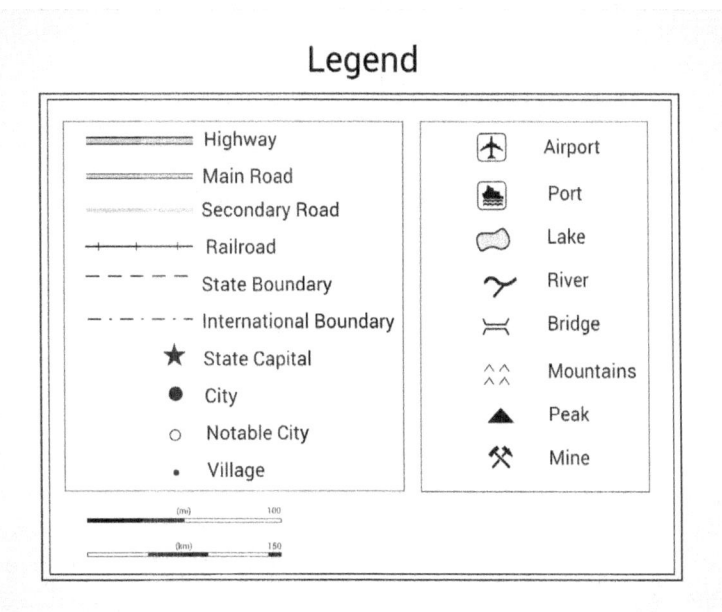

Interaction of Physical and Human Systems

Humans have always interacted with nature, and humanity has been shaped by, and, in turn, reshaped environments. Using tools to accomplish things they cannot do on their own, humans have proven highly adaptable to different environments. However, the specific ecosystems have helped to shape human development as individuals and as groups. The earth is highly diverse and has many different ecosystems, each with its own flora and fauna. The specific resources available in different places have, therefore, influenced how humans develop.

Water, in particular, has proved vital in determining the course of human civilizations. As humans require water daily to survive, even more than they do food, proximity to water has always been of utmost necessity. Many human settlements originated adjacent to sources, and only in time expanded to other areas. Water is also essential for the growth of plants, which form a considerable portion of the human diet. In the wild, edible plants grow in places where they can thrive but may not be conveniently located for harvesting by humans. Therefore, humans gradually learned to grow plants themselves in places of their own choice. Humans also diverted water sources to new areas for themselves and to irrigate crops, thus transforming ecosystems.

Another important factor in the relationships between humans and nature has been the role of other animals. From small pests, such as weevils and rodents, to predators, including crocodiles and bears, many species of animals have often posed threats to humans, and conflict increased as humans expanded into environments inhabited by other creatures. On the other hand, animals are invaluable to humans because they can provide sustenance and clothing. This led to hunting and domestication of animal species. Domestication of both plants and animals involves humans breeding species to fit their own needs, which leads to new qualities that would normally not appear in the wild.

However, despite the considerable role that humans can play in altering environments, these changes have remained limited to local levels for much of human history. This does not mean that humans did not affect

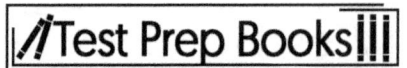

their ecosystems; some Native American tribes, for instance, used regular fires or hunting methods to maintain environments suitable for their needs. Even so, for much of human existence, nature was seen not simply as an obstacle but rather a power of its own right that was above human interference. **Natural phenomena** such as severe weather, diseases, and famine all kept human populations in check. Many pantheons of deities center on the gods' roles as arbitrary powers in the natural world, which reflects the lack of influence that humans had in the larger course of environmental changes.

Therefore, **natural resources** such as water and food were often seen as forces to be respected. Natural environments were recognized as vital regions, and alterations to fully exploit the resources were limited so that the resources could remain adequately sustainable. **Riparian customs** meant that water was the right of those with immediate access to it, and ownership changed accordingly with who lived nearby. However, increasing **industrialization** meant that natural resources such as water and lumber became resources that could be commoditized. In addition, appropriation gave water rights to those individuals or businesses that had first used the resource instead of being based on physical proximity.

Another instrumental change in the relationship between humans and nature is the increasing global connections worldwide. In many cases, earlier changes to environments occurred at local levels, with travel between different regions requiring considerable time and effort. The ability to travel around the world quickly has sharply altered that dynamic. Many local ecosystems, and the human cultures that developed accordingly, originated in separate circumstances that created unique plants and animals. Now products from one part of the world can be transported to entirely different environments and create new exchanges of goods. In some cases, the transferred species escape into the wild, and they often have traits for which the local environments are not prepared. This can result in invasive species that quickly grow and overpower native species.

A key symbol of artificial environments created by humans since early civilization has been the city, which is a human center of habitation that exists separate from the countryside around it. The creation of cities usually requires significant changes to the environment in which it is located, and the city must provide for the needs of residents without being compromised by nature. Yet the city has always remained connected to the rest of the world and to nature. Because a city generally lacks the capacity for agriculture and few natural resources are located within its confines, urban populations rely on resources from outlying areas for nourishment. The city, in turn, acts as a processing center for nearby settlements and offers rural workers and farmers the opportunity to sell their goods to a larger market.

Furthermore, the city, while an artificial construct, is still an environment in its own right. Although many species of animals have perished with the creation of cities, others, such as coyotes and pigeons, have adapted to urban life, thereby creating new ecosystems within cities. Natural connections within cities used to be stronger and more common because people would raise livestock within the city and regularly reuse garbage for livestock feed. While less hygienic, this helped stimulate natural cycles within the city. Recent efforts in many cities to create natural pockets, such as parks and community gardens, have also strengthened the ties between cities and the natural world. In a sense, the city reflects humanity's mixed relationship with nature as a whole: while humans continue to reshape the environment, they also remain linked to nature.

Uses of Geography

Geography helps people better understand the role that location plays in the past, present, and future. Historians make frequent use of maps in their studies to get a clearer picture of how history unfolded. Since the beginning of history, many different groups have fought conflicts that originated from struggles for land or other resources; therefore, knowing the location and borders of different empires and kingdoms helps reveal how they interacted with each other. In addition, environmental factors, such as access to water and

Social Studies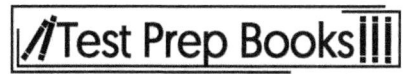

the proximity of mountains, often help to shape the course of civilizations. Even single events and battles make more sense with maps that show how the warring sides met and maneuvered.

Furthermore, determining the geography of historical events, in particular geographical change over time, is essential due to the role that physical settings play in the present. Many important geographic landmarks continue to exist in the world, and they are often commemorated for their roles in history. Yet the physical geography has sometimes changed significantly. For instance, the **Aswan Dam** significantly reshaped the flow of the **Nile River**, which was the heart of ancient Egyptian society; without knowledge of the past geography, it is difficult to fully understand the civilization's context and how it differs from the present reality.

History also depends on archaeology, the study of human artifacts, for the evidence necessary to make conclusions about cultures. These items are generally buried, which helps preserve the artifacts yet makes it difficult to locate them. Historical geography helps in that regard by ascertaining key sites of human activity that could potentially retain artifacts. These insights help archaeologists discover new aspects of ancient cultures, which in turn strengthen historical arguments. Maps themselves sometimes serve as artifacts in their own right because they help reveal how humans of earlier periods viewed the world.

Along with the historical implications, knowledge of the world's geography remains important for people in the present day. The most immediate use of geography is in navigation. Tools such as Global Positioning Systems have helped improve navigation, but they too represent an approach to geography that demonstrates how it continues to have a fundamental role in human society. Humans have even begun mapping the trajectories of planets and even their individual terrains.

However, beyond the direct uses for navigation, geography is invaluable in comprehending modern cultures and events. Whether through their proximity to other nations or their relation to environmental features, such as forests and deserts, societies remain deeply connected to their geographical settings. Therefore, to fully understand current affairs, such as wars and poverty, people must have a firm grasp on geographic settings. For instance, a study of nations in Africa, many of which continue to suffer from poverty, would require a close examination of geographic factors. The borders of many African countries were arbitrarily determined during the colonial period, and the conflicts of ethnic groups divided by these borders have influenced current struggles. On the environmental end, some nations have been significantly affected by desertification and deforestation, which makes studies of their ecological geography important as well.

Two recent key developments have made geography more important than ever before. The first change is the globalization of culture, economics, and politics. For much of human history, geography was most important at localized scales. Many people spent their entire lives in isolated communities, with intermittent trade between different centers. Geography was still important, but many people did not need to be familiar with anything other than their immediate locations. Today, on the other hand, places around the world are intricately connected to each other. Travel is relatively easy and quick and enables people to venture between different regions like never before. Areas that used to be geographically isolated from each other can now exchange ideas and products on an unprecedented scale.

In addition, due to the multinational relationship of politics, conflicts that would have been geographically isolated in the past can have international ramifications. Latin American revolutions, such as in Nicaragua during the Cold War, were seen as having larger implications in the struggle between American democracy and Soviet communism, which led to foreign interventions and wars that affected multiple countries. Therefore, geography is critical to not only addressing the current effects of globalization but also understanding how global interactions may influence international politics and economics in the future.

The second major factor in geography's role in modern events is the rising importance of environmental policies and climate change. Scientific developments have increasingly revealed how the planet as a whole

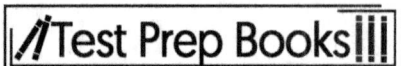

can be considered a large ecosystem in its own right, with its own strengths and frailties. A change in one part of the environment, such as industrialization in India and China, can have larger consequences for neighboring regions and for the world as a whole. Geographical insights help to show how the world functions and how humans can work to improve their relationship with the natural world.

Moreover, as climate changes become more evident in the world, geography helps illustrate the effects of new environmental phenomena. For instance, scientists have studied the topography of nations to determine how rising sea levels will alter the land via flooding, and local and national governments are using these findings to prepare for the coming changes. Furthermore, the continued scrutiny of the state of the earth's geography reveals how climate change is transforming the planet at this very moment, as regional climates shift and islands vanish under the sea. As a result, geography will continue to have a role in future developments.

Different Cultural Backgrounds

When studying different cultures, it is important to realize that cultures are always changing in response to individuals and groups within it. Therefore, one must avoid stereotyping members of a certain culture or overgeneralizing. For example, American culture is highly diverse with multiple ethnic groups. Many ethnic communities have resided in the United States for generations, so it is incorrect to label them as a foreign culture, yet each group must be closely examined to understand American culture as a whole.

This diversity within larger classifications of cultures can be seen with Native Americans. There are many different tribes of Native Americans, and each has its own unique history and characteristics. Nevertheless, a few general qualities describe most Native American groups. First of all, Native Americans continue to struggle to escape the poverty that they were historically forced into during white settlement of the United States. Many, but not all, tribes have been traditionally matrilineal—with ancestry defined through female lineage—and emphasized communal sharing and a sustainable relationship with nature, but the American government often suppressed these customs. This has led many Native Americans to begin protecting their surviving heritage, including their rights to traditional religious practices and access to historical artifacts.

South of the United States, Mexico has a vibrant yet troubled culture. Mexico was one of the principal colonies of Spain, and the culture is therefore a diverse blend of Spanish and native customs. One enduring legacy of Spain's rule is the prominence of Roman Catholicism, albeit mixed with pre-Spanish concepts; for instance, the traditional Day of the Dead embodies both pre-Columbian and Christian ideals. On the other hand, the Spanish system of large estates created significant class disparities. Furthermore, Mexico's war for independence and conflicts with other nations drastically destabilized its government, and the nation continues to struggle with corruption and violence. Still, Mexico retains a rich culture that celebrates its complex history. Mexican families are generally large and cooperate to help each other.

French national identity is relatively new because regional ties were prevalent until the French Revolution in the 1790s. A rising sense of nationalism unites French culture today, but various regions maintain their own local traditions. Much of France has been traditionally agricultural, but the globalization of the food trade has disrupted local markets and led to mass migration to cities. Reflecting Catholic values, most of France's families follow a nuclear model of a two-parent household with children.

South Africa is culturally and ethnically diverse, but historically white settlers used apartheid to oppress and isolate other groups. However, previously marginalized ethnic groups are now actively working to assert their own identity within South Africa. Rural communities tend to be more traditional, while people within cities have adopted new values. South Africa is largely patriarchal with defined gender roles that give men dominance over women. Efforts to strengthen South Africa's industries have depleted many of its natural resources and created a growing environmental crisis that is particularly devastating to rural populations.

Social Studies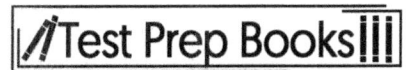

Laying claim to the legacies of ancient Persia, Iran's culture was at the crossroads of trade routes between multiple continents for centuries, which gave it a long and diverse background. Iran is primarily Islamic, with the majority of Muslims belonging to the Shi'a faith. They believe that their religious leaders, imams, are divinely appointed as the religious successors, known as **caliphs**, to the prophet Muhammad; even so, other religions such as Judaism and Zoroastrianism are also practiced in the country. Iran's patriarchal culture generally restricts the role of women, but women have nevertheless become more involved in the civil service, sciences, and other fields.

Russia's culture is built on a rich history but has been especially influenced by the dominance of communism until the Soviet Union's dissolution in 1991. The use of state police and other agents to enforce government policies led to a sense of paranoia and distrust of anyone outside the family. On the other hand, this situation created strong support networks within families that led to strong relationships with relatives. The Soviet Union's drive to industrialize also led to numerous current environmental issues across Russia.

As with Russia, the People's Republic of China's modern culture is deeply influenced by decades of Communist rule. Under the leadership of Mao, China enacted massive efforts to strengthen Chinese industry and agriculture at the cost of environmental damage; China continues to undergo intense industrial operations in the present, which has caused pollution in the cities. On the other hand, China takes great pride in its long traditions and history that date back thousands of years. China has been traditionally patriarchal, and children have been expected to respect and care for their elders. Chinese culture is not monolithic, and there are many different ethnic groups within the country, including the Han, Manchu, and Uyghur. However, the one-child policy from 1978 to 2015 has destabilized long-term family dynamics by putting considerable pressure on single children to look after their parents.

Japan's family structure has also been disrupted in the modern era. Japanese culture is built on a sense of interdependence within families and the community as a whole, but a low birthrate has led to a rising number of elderly relatives and few children, which has unsettled the traditional foundation. Even so, Japan embraces a blend of modern advancements and traditional customs. Japanese culture is built on multiple layers of social status, and people use different forms of language depending on their relationship with others. As a result, traditional Japanese society is highly formal, but recent generations have become more open to new ideas. As Japan's islands have limited space and resources, it has been at the forefront of many natural conservation efforts, although some controversial traditions, such as whaling, still persist.

World History and Economics

Major Contributions of Classical Civilizations

There were a number of powerful civilizations during the classical period. **Mesopotamia** was home to one of the earliest civilizations between the Euphrates and the Tigris rivers in the Near East. The rivers provided water and vegetation for early humans, but they were surrounded by desert. This led to the beginning of irrigation efforts to expand water and agriculture across the region, which resulted in the area being known as the **Fertile Crescent**.

The organization necessary to initiate canals and other projects led to the formation of cities and hierarchies, which would have considerable influence on the structure of later civilizations. For instance, the new hierarchies established different classes within the societies, such as kings, priests, artisans, and workers. Over time, these city-states expanded to encompass outside territories, and the city of Akkad became the world's first empire in 2350 B.C. In addition, Mesopotamian scribes developed systemized drawings called **pictograms**, which were the first system of writing in the world; furthermore, the creation of wedge-shaped **cuneiform tablets** preserved written records for multiple generations.

Later, Mesopotamian kingdoms made further advancements. For instance, **Babylon** established a sophisticated mathematical system based on numbers from one to sixty; this not only influenced modern concepts, such as the number of minutes in each hour, but also created the framework for math equations and theories. In addition, the Babylonian king Hammurabi established a complex set of laws, known as the **Code of Hammurabi**, which would set a precedent for future legal systems.

Meanwhile, another major civilization began to form around the Nile River in Africa. The Nile's relatively predictable nature allowed farmers to use the river's water and the silt from floods to grow many crops along its banks, which led to further advancements in irrigation. Egyptian rulers mobilized the kingdom's population for incredible construction projects, including the famous pyramids. Egyptians also improved pictographic writing with their more complex system of **hieroglyphs**, which allowed for more diverse styles of writing. The advancements in writing can be seen through the Egyptians' complex system of religion, with documents such as the **Book of the Dead** outlining not only systems of worship and pantheons of deities but also a deeper, more philosophical concept of the afterlife.

While civilizations in Egypt and Mesopotamia helped to establish class systems and empires, other forms of government emerged in Greece. Despite common ties between different cities, such as the Olympic Games, each settlement, known as a **polis**, had its own unique culture. Many of the cities were oligarchies, in which a council of distinguished leaders monopolized the government; others were dictatorships ruled by tyrants. Athens was a notable exception by practicing an early form of democracy in which free, landholding men could participate, but it offered more freedom of thought than other systems.

Taking advantage of their proximity to the Mediterranean Sea, Greek cities sent expeditions to establish colonies abroad that developed their own local traditions. In the process, Greek merchants interacted with Phoenician traders, who had developed an alphabetic writing system built on sounds instead of pictures. This diverse network of exchanges made Greece a vibrant center of art, science, and philosophy. For example, the Greek doctor Hippocrates established a system of ethics for doctors called the **Hippocratic Oath**, which continues to guide the modern medical profession. Complex forms of literature were created, including the epic poem "The Iliad," and theatrical productions were also developed. Athens in particular sought to spread its vision of democratic freedom throughout the world, which led to the devastating Peloponnesian War between allies of Athens and those of oligarchic Sparta from 431 to 404 B.C.

Alexander the Great helped disseminate Greek culture to new regions. Alexander was in fact an heir to the throne of Macedon, which was a warrior kingdom to the north of Greece. After finishing his father's work of unifying Greece under Macedonian control, Alexander successfully conquered Mesopotamia, which had been part of the Persian Empire. The spread of Greek institutions throughout the Mediterranean and Near East led to a period of Hellenization, during which various civilizations assimilated Greek culture; this allowed Greek traditions, such as architecture and philosophy, to endure into the present day.

Greek ideas were later assimilated, along with many other concepts, into the **Roman Empire**. Located west of Greece on the Italian peninsula, Rome greatly expanded its territories and grew to be a powerful empire through the conquering of its neighboring civilizations; by 44 B.C., Rome had conquered much of Western Europe, northern Africa, and the Near East. Romans were very creative, and they adapted new ideas and innovated new technologies to strengthen their power. For instance, Romans built on the engineering knowledge of Greeks to create arched pathways, known as **aqueducts**, to transport water for long distances and devise advanced plumbing systems.

One of Rome's greatest legacies was its system of government. Early Rome was a republic, a democratic system in which leaders are elected by the people. Although the process still heavily favored wealthy elites, the republican system was a key inspiration for later institutions such as the United States. Octavian "Augustus" Caesar later made Rome into an empire, and the senate had only a symbolic role in the government. The new imperial system built on the examples of earlier empires to establish a vibrant dynasty that used a sophisticated legal code and a well-trained military to enforce order across vast regions. Even after Rome itself fell to barbarian invaders in fifth century A.D., the eastern half of the empire survived as the Byzantine Empire until 1453 A.D. Furthermore, the Roman Empire's institutions continued to influence and inspire later medieval kingdoms, including the Holy Roman Empire; even rulers in the twentieth century called themselves Kaiser and Tsar, titles which stem from the word "Caesar."

In addition, the Roman Empire was host to the spread of new religious ideas. In the region of Israel, the religion of **Judaism** presented a new approach to worship via **monotheism**, which is the belief in the existence of a single deity. An offshoot of Judaism called **Christianity** spread across the Roman Empire and gained popularity. While Rome initially suppressed the religion, it later backed Christianity and allowed the religious system to endure as a powerful force in medieval times.

Twentieth-Century Development in World History

At the turn of the twentieth century, imperialism had led to powers, such as France, the United States, and Japan, to establish spheres of influence throughout the world. The combination of imperial competition and military rivalries led to the outbreak of World War I when **Archduke Ferdinand of Austria** was assassinated in 1914. The war pitted **the Allies**, including England, France, and Russia, against the Central Powers of Austria-Hungary, Germany, and the **Ottoman Empire**—a large Islamic realm that encompassed Turkey, Palestine, Saudi Arabia, and Iraq. The rapid advances in military technology turned the war into a prolonged bloodbath that took its toll on all sides. By the end of the war in 1918, the Ottoman Empire had collapsed, the Austrian-Hungarian Empire was split into multiple countries, and Russia had descended into a civil war that would lead to the rise of the Soviet Union and Communism.

The **Treaty of Versailles** ended the war, but the triumphant Allies also levied heavy fines on Germany, which led to resentment that would be accentuated by the Great Depression of the 1930s. The **Great Depression** destabilized the global economy and led to the rise of fascism, a militarized and dictatorial system of government, in nations such as Germany and Italy. The rapid expansion of the Axis Powers of Germany, Italy, and Japan led to the outbreak of World War II. The war was even more global than the previous conflicts, with battles occurring in Europe, Africa, and Asia. World War II encouraged the development of new technologies, such as advanced radar and nuclear weapons, that would continue to influence the course of future wars.

In the aftermath of World War II, the **United Nations** was formed as a step toward promoting international cooperation. Based on the preceding League of Nations, the United Nations included countries from around the world and gave them a voice in world policies. The formation of the United Nations coincided with the independence of formerly colonized states in Africa and Asia, and those countries joined the world body. A primary goal of the United Nations was to limit the extent of future wars and prevent a third world war; while the United Nations could not prevent the outbreak of wars, it nevertheless tried to peacefully resolve them. In addition to promoting world peace, the United Nations also helped protect human rights.

Even so, the primary leadership in the early United Nations was held by the United States and its allies, which contributed to tensions with the Soviet Union. The United States and the Soviet Union, while never declaring war on each other, fueled a number of proxy wars and coups across the world in what would be known as the **Cold War**. Cold War divisions were especially noticeable in Europe, where communist regimes ruled the eastern region and democratic governments controlled the western portion. These indirect struggles often involved interference with foreign politics, and sometimes local people began to resent Soviet or American attempts to influence their countries. For instance, American and Soviet interventions in Iran and Afghanistan contributed to fundamentalist Islamic movements. The Cold War ended when the Soviet Union collapsed in 1991, but the conflict affected nations across the globe and continues to influence current issues.

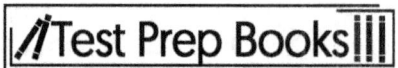

Another key development during the twentieth century, as noted earlier with the United Nations, was that most colonized nations broke free from imperial control and asserted their independence. Although these nations achieved autonomy and recognition in the United Nations, they still suffered from the legacies of imperialism. The borders of many countries in Africa and Asia were arbitrarily determined by colonists with little regard to the arrangement of native populations. Therefore, many former colonies have suffered conflicts between different ethnic groups; this was also the case with the British colony in India, which became independent in 1947. Violence occurred when it split into India and Pakistan because the borders were largely based on religious differences. In addition, former colonial powers continue to assert economic control that inhibits the growth of native economies. On the other hand, the end of direct imperialism has helped a number of nations, such as India and Iran, rise as world powers that have significant influence on the world as a whole.

Additionally, there were considerable environmental reforms worldwide during the twentieth century. In reaction to the growing effects of industrialization, organizations around the world protested policies that damaged the environment. Many of these movements were locally based, but others expanded to address various environmental threats across the globe. The United Nations helped carry these environmental reforms forward by making them part of international policies. For instance, in 1997, many members of the United Nations signed a treaty, known as the **Kyoto Protocol**, that tried to reduce global carbon dioxide emissions.

Most significantly, the twentieth century marked increasing globalization. The process had already been under way in the nineteenth century as technological improvements and imperial expansions connected different parts of the world, but the late twentieth century brought globalization to a new level. Trade became international, and local customs from different lands also gained prominence worldwide. Cultural exchanges occur on a frequent basis, and many people have begun to ponder the consequences of such rapid exchanges. One example of globalization was the 1993 establishment of the European Union—an economic and political alliance between several European nations.

Cross-Cultural Comparisons in World History Instruction

Cross-cultural interactions are the very heart of world history and must be closely examined to understand the world's historical patterns. One of the main reasons why cross-cultural studies are so important is because cultures are not necessarily synonymous with political entities, such as states. Many countries, ranging from China to Greece, historically have many subcultures that should be considered individually. For example, a study of culture in the United States would need to consider multiple ethnic and regional groups. Even individual states and cities have their own traditions. On the other hand, these multiple cultures often coalesce into a larger, national culture that defines the overall society and politics of the nation. Therefore, cross-cultural studies of different subgroups in a larger body allow people to understand how the different parts of a culture interact and connect with each other.

Furthermore, cultures are not always restricted by the borders of nations, and cultural phenomena may extend through multiple countries. This can be seen in the spread of the Spanish language across Central and South America as well as other regions. The Spanish language and other various traditions tie the different countries together with a common culture. Even so, each nation changes the culture and gives it a unique style. A study of the culture in a single nation may be very insightful, but it would be incomplete if it failed to account for aspects of the culture beyond that country. In addition, this means that different cultures can overlap with each other and that the cultures of different countries may intersect in ways that their borders do not. By examining multiple cultures and how they are linked with each other, larger cultural patterns become apparent, which makes these studies critical in world history.

Throughout history, cultures have not existed in isolation but rather have been affected by other traditions. A key influence in how different cultures develop is not only their setting and history but how they interact with neighboring cultures. For instance, the conflict from 499 to 449 B.C. between the Persian Empire and the Greek city-states helped to influence the course of Greek culture as a whole by creating a national sense of dichotomy between the Greek ideal of freedom and Persian autocracy. Aside from direct impacts such as wars, cultures can influence each other through interactions that spread some concepts while also adopting new ideas from their neighbors. Pasta became a phenomenon in Italy in part because the Silk Road linked Italy with China, which already had similar foods.

The pervasiveness of globalization in the present day has increased the importance of cross-cultural comparison and made it a topic of immediate relevance. The world now has a truly global market in which travel, communications, and trade function on an international scale. This means that people of different cultures can now interact with each other much more easily than in earlier centuries, which allows for a rapid exchange of ideas and goods between cultures. Furthermore, despite the international scope of modern trade, many globalized markets strive to build on the appeal of local cultures. Doing so gives the products a genuine and unique quality that resonates with consumers. Yet it is critical to realize how local cultures are transformed and combined with concepts from other cultures in the global market. For example, sushi is a traditional food in Japan, but its export to other nations has led chefs to create new culinary fusions, such as sushi tacos.

Cross-cultural comparisons also help to reveal common patterns in human society. Sometimes different cultures develop similar concepts without directly interacting with each other. For instance, both the Mayan culture in Central America and the ancient Egyptians independently developed pyramid structures. Although the similarities have sparked rumors that these civilizations were connected, it is most likely that each version originated independently. Close examination of the two types of pyramids and their respective cultures reveals significant differences amidst the similarities. These comparisons are important because they show how human cultures converge and diverge in their patterns of growth. A key function of historical study is to gain a better understanding and appreciation of how humanity develops. By examining the commonalities and differences between cultures, people can begin to theorize what factors influence the course of civilizations. However, such studies must account for the complex manners through which cultures interact with each other.

Terms and Concepts of Economics

Economics form a key component of human society. Studies of economies can be divided between **macroeconomics**, which considers the larger economy as a whole, and **microeconomics**, which focuses on the actions of smaller groups, households, and individuals. However, the most basic principle of economics comes down to resources. A **resource** can be defined as an object or material that can be used for some purpose. **Natural resources** come directly from the environment, whereas items altered through human activity are considered manufactured goods. Resources can be further divided into **renewable resources**, which are gradually replenished given enough time and proper circumstances, and **nonrenewable resources**, which regenerate slowly or not at all. In addition, there are four main types of economic resources: **land**, which includes most natural resources; **labor**, the services provided by individuals to create products; **capital**, which encompasses human-manufactured resources; and **entrepreneurship**, the process in which individuals utilize available resources for business ventures that generate new products.

Early on, human civilizations functioned using a **barter system**, where people would trade certain goods for other items. It remains common in some parts of the world today. However, the difficulty of storing and transporting products, such as livestock and minerals, for exchange, led to the development of monetary systems. **Money** is an object, such as a coin or a paper bill, which can be exchanged for any commercial

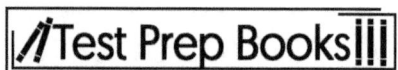

product. It is important to note that money on its own often has no worth; **paper money**, for example, is a rather flimsy material with little actual use outside of its monetary worth. It only has value when members of a society agree that it can be used to make purchases.

Due to the artificial nature of money within societies, prices fluctuate depending on the supply and demand of products. **Supply** refers to the available quantity of a specific good or resource. In contrast, demand accounts for the quantity that buyers wish to obtain. These two factors influence several economic patterns. The **law of supply** states that the quantity available for purchase is directly related to the price, while the **law of demand** states that the price of an item is inversely related to the demand for the item. Thus, raising prices increases supply and reduces demand.

Furthermore, the value of money in part depends on the amount that is circulated in the market. A surplus of money has the potential to devalue the currency, which lowers the worth of each unit of money. This process, called **inflation**, has a detrimental effect on the economy as prices generally increase. However, the opposite trend, **deflation**, can also be detrimental; thus, political leaders usually strive to find a stable balance between the two ends of the spectrum. By finding equilibrium between supply and demand, an economy's prices remain relatively stable.

Economies, by nature, have limited access to certain resources, which creates a conflict between supply and demand. **Scarcity** occurs when the demand for a product exceeds its availability. Scarcity in part depends on the choices of individuals as they determine which products they want more than others. **Choices**, in turn, are influenced by the perceived costs of pursuing certain options over others. The costs and benefits of specific choices often differ depending on the individuals' perceptions of the options. When people believe that a certain service's or product's benefits outweigh its necessary costs, they may choose to pay more for the desired benefits. It is important to realize that the laws of supply and demand are not absolute, and they may fluctuate depending on the situation.

Supply and demand can be further affected by **monopolies**, in which an individual or group holds sole or primary access to a given product or service. The individuals controlling a monopoly can limit the supply in a manner that best suits themselves but not necessarily the consumers. Monopolies are often asserted through the creation of barriers that limit access to the resources or services. For instance, patents give exclusive rights for inventions and discoveries to their respective creators or the firms that sponsored them. Without restraints, a monopoly can significantly limit economic development and prosperity of a society.

Effects of Economics on Population, Resources, and Technology

Economics are closely linked with the flow of resources, technology, and population in societies. The use of natural resources, such as water and fossil fuels, has always depended in part on the pressures of the economy. A supply of a specific good may be limited in the market, but with sufficient demand the sellers are incentivized to increase the available quantity. Unfortunately, the demand for certain objects can often be unlimited, and a high price or limited supply may prevent consumers from obtaining the product or service. If the sellers succumb to the consumers' demand and continue to exploit a scarce resource, supply could potentially be exhausted.

The resources for most products, both renewable and nonrenewable, are finite. This is a particularly difficult issue with nonrenewable resources, but even renewable resources often have limits: **organic products** such as trees and animals require stable populations and sufficient habitats to support those populations. Furthermore, the costs of certain decisions can have detrimental effects on other resources. For example, industrialization provides economic benefits in many countries but also has had the negative effect of polluting surrounding environments; the pollution, in turn, often eliminates or harms fish, plants, and other potential resources.

The control of resources within an economy is particularly important in determining how resources are used. While the demand may change with the choices of consumers, the range of supply depends on the objectives of the people producing the goods. They determine how much of their supply they allot for sale, and in the case of monopolies, they might have sole access to the resource. They might choose to limit their use of the resources or instead gather more to meet the demand. As they pay for the products, consumers can choose which sellers they rely on for the supply. In the case of a monopoly, though, consumers have little influence over the company's decision because there is no alternative supplier. Therefore, the function of supply within an economy can drastically influence how the resources are exploited.

The availability of resources, in turn, affects the human population. Humans require basic resources such as food and water for survival, as well as additional resources for healthy lifestyles. Therefore, access to these resources helps determine the survival rate of humans. For much of human existence, economies have had limited ability to extract resources from the natural world, which restricted the growth rate of populations. However, the development of new technologies, combined with increasing demand for certain products, has pushed resource use to a new level. On the one hand, this led to higher living standards that ensured that fewer people would die. However, this has also brought mass population growth. Admittedly, countries with higher standards of living often have lower birthrates. Even so, the increasing exploitation of resources has sharply increased the world's population as a whole to unsustainable levels. The rising population leads, in turn, to more demand for resources that cannot be met. This creates poverty, reduced living conditions, and higher death rates. As a result, economics can significantly influence local and world population levels.

Technology is also intricately related to population, resources, and economics. The role of demand within economies has incentivized people to innovate new technologies that enable societies to have a higher quality of life and greater access to resources. Entrepreneurs expand technologies by finding ways to create new products for the market. The **Industrial Revolution**, in particular, illustrates the relationship between economics and technology because the ambitions of businessmen led to new infrastructure that enabled more efficient and sophisticated use of resources. Many of these inventions reduced the amount of work necessary for individuals and allowed the development of leisure activities, which in turn created new economic markets. However, economic systems can also limit the growth of technology. In the case of monopolies, the lack of alternative suppliers reduces the incentive to meet and exceed consumer expectations. Moreover, as demonstrated by the effects of economics on resources, technology's increasing ability to extract resources can lead to their depletion and create significant issues that need to be addressed.

Government's Role in Economics and the Impact of Economics on Government

Governments have considerable influence over the flow of economies, which makes it important to understand the relationships between them. When a government has full control over the economic decisions of a nation, it is called a **command system**. This was the case in many absolute monarchies such as eighteenth-century France; **King Louis XIV** built his economy on the concept of **mercantilism**, which believed that the state should manage all resources, particularly by accumulating gold and silver. This system of economics discouraged exports and thereby limited trade.

In contrast, the **market system** is guided by the concept of capitalism, in which individuals and businesses have the freedom to manage their economic decisions. This allows for private property and increases the opportunities for entrepreneurship and trade. Early proponents of capitalism emphasized **laissez-faire** policies, which means "let it be," and argued that the government should not be involved with the economy at all. They believe the market is guided by the concept of self-interest and that individuals will optimally work for their personal success. However, individuals' interests do not necessarily correlate with the needs of the overall economy. For instance, during a financial recession, consumers may decide to save up their money rather than make purchases; doing so helps them in the short run but further reduces demand in a slumping economy. Therefore, most capitalist governments still assert a degree of control over their economies while still allowing for private business.

Likewise, many command system economies, such as monarchical France, still relied heavily on private businesses maintained by wealthy businessmen. With the end of most absolute monarchies, communism has been the primary form of command system economies in the modern era. **Communism** is a form of socialism that emphasizes communal ownership of property and government control over production. The high degree of government control gives more stability to the economy, but it also creates considerable flaws. The monopolization of the economy by the government limits its ability to respond to local economic conditions because certain regions often have unique resources and needs. With the collapse of the Soviet Union and other communist states, command systems have been largely replaced with market systems.

The U.S. government helps to manage the nation's economy through a market system in several ways. First and foremost, the federal government is responsible for the production of money for use within the economy; depending on how the government manages the monetary flow, it may lead to a stable economy, deflation, or inflation. Second, state and federal governments impose taxes on individuals, corporations, and goods. For instance, a tariff might be imposed on imports in order to stimulate demand for local goods in the economy. Third, the government can pass laws that require additional regulation or inspections. In addition, the government has passed antitrust laws to inhibit the growth of private monopolies, which could limit free growth in the market system. Debates continue over whether the government should take further action to manage private industries or reduce its control over the private sector.

Just as governments can affect the direction of the economy, the state of the economy can have significant implications on government policies. Financial stability is critical in maintaining a prosperous state. A healthy economy will allow for new developments that contribute to the nation's growth and create jobs. On the other hand, an economic crisis, such as a recession or depression, can gravely damage a government's stability. Without a stable economy, business opportunities plummet, and people begin to lose income and employment. This, in turn, leads to frustration and discontent in the population, which can lead to criticism of the government. This could very well lead to demands for new leadership to resolve the economic crisis.

The dangers of a destabilized economy can be seen with the downfall of the French monarchy. The mercantilist approach to economics stifled French trade. Furthermore, regional aristocracies remained exempt from government taxes, which limited the government's revenues. This was compounded by expensive wars and poor harvests that led to criticism of King Louis XIV's government. The problems persisted for decades, and Louis XIV was forced to convene the **Estates-General**, a legislative body of representatives from across France, to address the crisis. The economic crises at the end of the eighteenth century were critical in the beginning of the French Revolution. Those financial issues, in turn, at least partially stemmed from both the government's control of the economy through mercantilism and its inability to impose economic authority over local regions.

Practice Quiz

1. Which of the following civilizations developed the first democratic form of government?
    a. Roman Empire
    b. Ancient Greece
    c. Achaemenid Empire
    d. Zhou Dynasty

2. What is the difference between a primary source and a secondary source?
    a. Secondary sources are usually fictional, while primary sources are always true.
    b. Primary sources are context-specific, first-hand accounts, and secondary sources usually synthesize primary sources with some historical distance.
    c. Secondary sources are almost always first-hand accounts, while primary sources are second-hand fictional testimonies.
    d. There are no major differences between primary sources and secondary sources.

3. Which of the following was NOT a movement that was going on in the 1960s?
    a. Civil Rights Movement
    b. End the War Movement
    c. Women's Rights Movement
    d. LGBTQ Rights Movement

4. Which of the following is NOT one of the checks that individual branches have over another branch of government?
    a. The president may veto a bill passed by Congress
    b. The Supreme Court can try and remove the president for high crimes and misdemeanors committed in office
    c. Congress must approve all of the president's appointments to the Supreme Court
    d. Congress can pass a budget that limits what the president has to spend on defense

5. What was the Triple Entente?
    a. The Triple Entente was a free trade agreement between the United States, Britain, and France.
    b. The Triple Entente was a free trade agreement between Britain, France, and Germany.
    c. The Triple Entente was a military alliance between Austria-Hungary, Germany, and the Ottoman Empire.
    d. The Triple Entente was a military alliance between Britain, France, and Russia.

See answers on next page.

Answer Explanations

1. B: Ancient Greeks created many of the cultural and political institutions that form the basis of modern western civilization. Athens was an important Greek democracy, and all adult men could participate in politics after they had completed their military service. The Roman Empire, Choice A, evolved from the Roman Republic, but it was not democratic. The Achaemenid Empire and Zhou Dynasty, Choices C and D, were imperial monarchies that did not allow citizens to have much, if any, political voice.

2. B: Primary sources are context-specific, first-hand accounts, and secondary sources usually synthesize primary sources with some historical distance. Choice A is incorrect because both primary and secondary sources can be fictional or realistic. Choice C is wrong for two reasons. First, it confuses the fact that primary sources are first-hand accounts and secondary sources can be second-hand testimonies. Second, secondary sources aren't always fictional. Choice D is incorrect because primary sources and secondary sources are drastically different in scope and context.

3. B: End the War Movement. The 1960s were a time of growth for the United States. Everyone was pushing for rights and for changes to the system, and people were beginning to challenge the government. End the War was still a decade off, however, with Vietnam still around the corner. Choice A is incorrect because the Civil Rights Movement, led by leaders like Martin Luther King Jr., dominated the 1960s leading up to the Civil Rights Act. Choices C and D are incorrect because women's rights were also key throughout the decade, as well as the movement for LGBTQ rights.

4. B: By design, there are many checks and balances among the branches of government. The president does have the power to veto any law passed Congress, which Congress can override. Congress also has the power to consider and approve all of the president's picks for the Supreme Court and federal courts. Congress also controls the budget, which can limit what the president has to spend on the military. However, the Supreme Court does not get to try the president for high crimes and misdemeanors; that job belongs to Congress. The Chief Justice of the Supreme Court, however, does preside over the hearings.

5. D: During the early twentieth century, Britain sought military alliances with France and Russia after Germany militarized and expanded its colonies. The military alliance between Britain, France, and Russia was known as the **Triple Entente**, and it was one of the complex alliance systems that contributed to the start of World War I. Thus, Choice D is the correct answer. The Triple Entente was not a free trade agreement, so Choices A and B are both incorrect. The military alliance between Austria-Hungary, Germany, and the Ottoman Empire fought the Triple Entente as Central Powers during World War I. So, Choice C is incorrect.

Science

Earth Science

Structure of Earth System

Earth is a complex system of the **atmosphere** (air), **hydrosphere** (water), as well as continental land (land). All work together to support the **biosphere** (life).

The atmosphere is divided into several layers: the troposphere, stratosphere, mesosphere, and thermosphere. The **troposphere** is at the bottom and is about seven and a half miles thick. Above the troposphere is the 30-mile-thick **stratosphere**. Above the stratosphere is the **mesosphere**, a 20-mile layer, followed by the **thermosphere**, which is more than 300 miles thick.

The troposphere is closest to Earth and has the greatest pressure due to the pull of gravity on its gas particles as well as pressure from the layers above. 78 percent of the atmosphere is made of nitrogen. Surprisingly, the oxygen that we breathe only makes up 21 percent of the gases, and the carbon dioxide critical to insulating Earth makes up less than 1 percent of the atmosphere. There are other trace gases present in the atmosphere, including water vapor.

Although the stratosphere has minimal wind activity, it is critical for supporting the biosphere because it contains the ozone layer, which absorbs the sun's damaging ultra-violet rays and protects living organisms. Due to its low level of air movement, airplanes travel in the stratosphere. The mesosphere contains few gas particles, and the gas levels are so insignificant in the thermosphere that it is considered space.

Visible light is colors reflecting off particles. If all colors reflect, we see white; if no colors reflect, we see black. This means a colored object is reflecting only that color—a red ball reflects red light and absorbs other colors.

Because the thermosphere has so few particles to reflect light rays (photons), it appears black. The troposphere appears blue in the day, and various shades of yellow and orange at sunset due to the angle of the sun hitting particles that refract, or bend, the light. In certain instances, the entire visible spectrum can be seen in the form of rainbows. Rainbows occur when sunlight passes through water droplets and is refracted in many different directions by the water particles.

The **hydrosphere**, or water-containing portion of the Earth's surface, plays a major role in supporting the biosphere. In the picture below, a single water molecule (molecular formula H_2O) looks like a mouse head. The small ears of the mouse are the two hydrogen atoms connected to the larger oxygen atom in the middle.

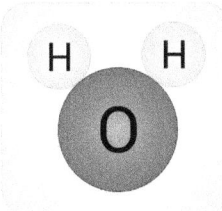

Each hydrogen atom has one **proton** (positively charged, like the plus end of a magnet) in its **nucleus** (center), while oxygen has eight protons in its center. Hydrogen also has only one electron (negatively charged, like the minus end of a magnet) orbiting around the nucleus. Because hydrogen has only one proton, its electron is pulled more toward the oxygen nucleus (more powerful magnet). This makes hydrogen exist without an electron most of the time, so it is positively charged. On the other hand, oxygen often has two extra electrons (one from each hydrogen), so it is negatively charged. These bonds between the oxygen and hydrogen are called **covalent bonds**.

This charged situation is what makes water such a versatile substance; it also causes different molecules of water to interact with each other.

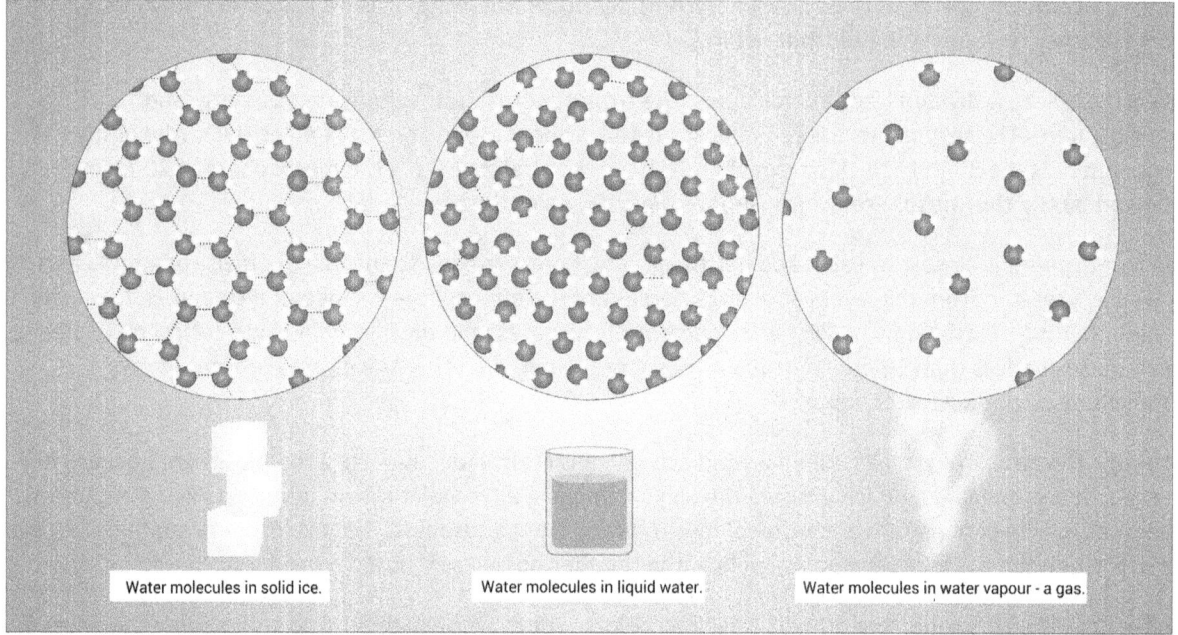

| Water molecules in solid ice. | Water molecules in liquid water. | Water molecules in water vapour - a gas. |

In a solid form (ice), water lines up in a crystal structure because the positive hydrogen atoms prefer to be next to the negative oxygen atoms that belong to other water molecules. These attractions are represented by the blue lines in the molecular picture of ice above. As heat is added and the ice melts, the water molecules have more kinetic energy and move faster; therefore, they are unable to perfectly arrange in the lattice structure of ice and turn into liquid. If enough heat is added, the water molecules will have so much kinetic energy they vaporize into gas. At this point, there are no bonds holding the water together because the molecules aren't close enough.

Notice how ice in its intricate arrangement has more space between the particles than liquid water, which shows that the ice is less dense than water. This contradicts the scientific fact that solids are denser than liquids. In water's case only, the solid will float due to a lower density! This is significant for the hydrosphere, because if temperatures drop to lower than freezing, frozen water will float to the surface of lakes or oceans and insulate the water underneath so that life can continue in liquid water. If ice was not less dense than liquid water, bodies of water would freeze from the bottom up and aquatic ecosystems would be trapped in a block of ice.

The hydrosphere has two components: **seawater** and **freshwater** (less than 5 percent of the hydrosphere). Water covers more than 70 percent of the Earth's surface.

The final piece of the biosphere is the **lithosphere**, the rocky portion of earth. **Geology** is the study of solid earth. Earth's surface is composed of elemental chunks called **minerals**, which are simply crystallized groups of bonded atoms. Minerals that have the same composition but different arrangements are called **polymorphs**, like graphite and diamonds. All minerals contain physical properties such as **luster** (shine), color, hardness, density, and boiling point. Their **chemical properties**, or how they react with other compounds, are also different. Minerals combine to form the rocks that make up Earth.

Earth has distinct layers—a thin, solid outer surface, a dense, solid core, and the majority of its matter between them. It is kind of like an egg: the thin crust is the shell, the inner core is the yolk, and the mantle and outer core that compose the space in between are like the egg white.

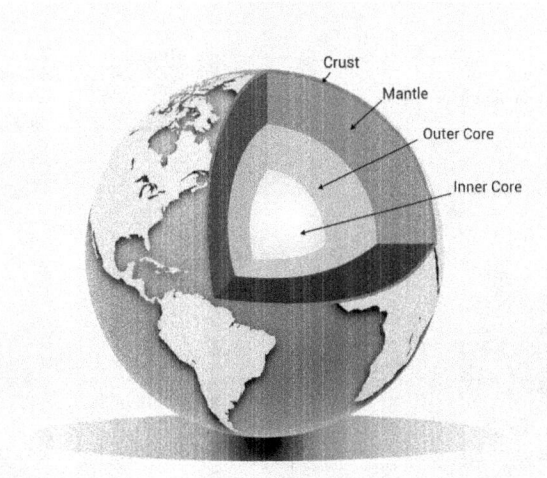

The outer crust of Earth consists of igneous or sedimentary rocks over metamorphic rocks (dense compacted rock underneath). The crust, combined with the upper portion of the mantle, forms the lithosphere, which is broken into several different plates, like puzzle pieces.

Major plates of the lithosphere

Major Plates of the Lithosphere

The **mantle** is divided in three zones. The thin zone adjacent to the crust is solid rock (the lower part of the lithosphere). Below that is the **asthenosphere**, which contains liquid magma (molten rock). The lower mantle is completely solid rock. Underneath the mantle is the outer core, a molten layer rich with iron and nickel, followed by the compact, solid, inner core.

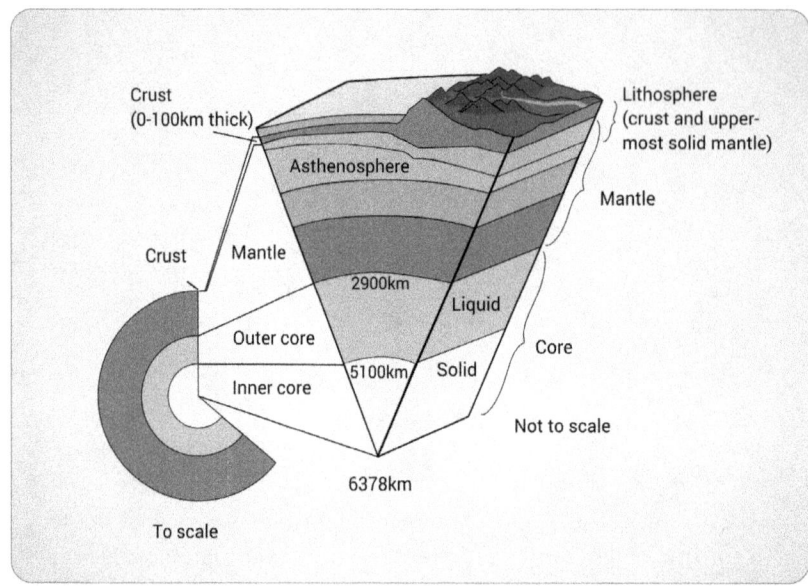

The inner and outer cores contain the densest elements (mostly iron with some nickel), which explains why they are at the center of earth: dense elements sink. Moving from outside in, Earth gets hotter and hotter, with inner core temperatures as hot as the surface of the sun. One source of this immense heat is **nuclear fission**, which occurs when a heavy element's nucleus breaks into smaller and smaller pieces and in the process produces huge amounts of energy. Some power plants that run on fission energy are used to produce electricity. The problem with fission is that it releases huge amounts of radiation. In Chernobyl, Ukraine in 1986, a power plant explosion killed thirty-one people and exposed hundreds to radiation, a known source of mutation and cancer.

Nuclear fusion is the opposite reaction, combining small elements into a larger atom. This process produces three to four times as much energy as fission. Nuclear fusion releases energy hotter than the sun, so some believe that finding a way to use it as an energy source may be a meaningful endeavor. Scientists haven't been able to construct a facility that can harness such high temperatures, but research is currently underway.

Even though the inner and outer cores contain the same elements, the inner core is solid while the outer core is liquid, indicating that they have different melting points. How can this be? This is because tremendous pressure (the weight of the world, literally) on the inner core is so forceful that the particles remain close together and stay in their solid form, making it harder to melt.

Processes of Earth

The **water cycle** is the cycling of water between its three physical states: solid, liquid, and gas. The Sun is a critical component of the water cycle because its thermal energy heats up surface liquid water so much that parts of it evaporate. **Transpiration** is a similar process that occurs when the sun evaporates water from plant pores called **stomata**. As water vapor rises into the atmosphere through **evaporation** and transpiration, it eventually condenses and forms clouds heavy with liquid water droplets. The liquid (or solid ice or snow) will precipitate back to Earth, collect on land, and either be absorbed by soil or run-off to the oceans and lakes where it will accumulate, circulate, and evaporate once again.

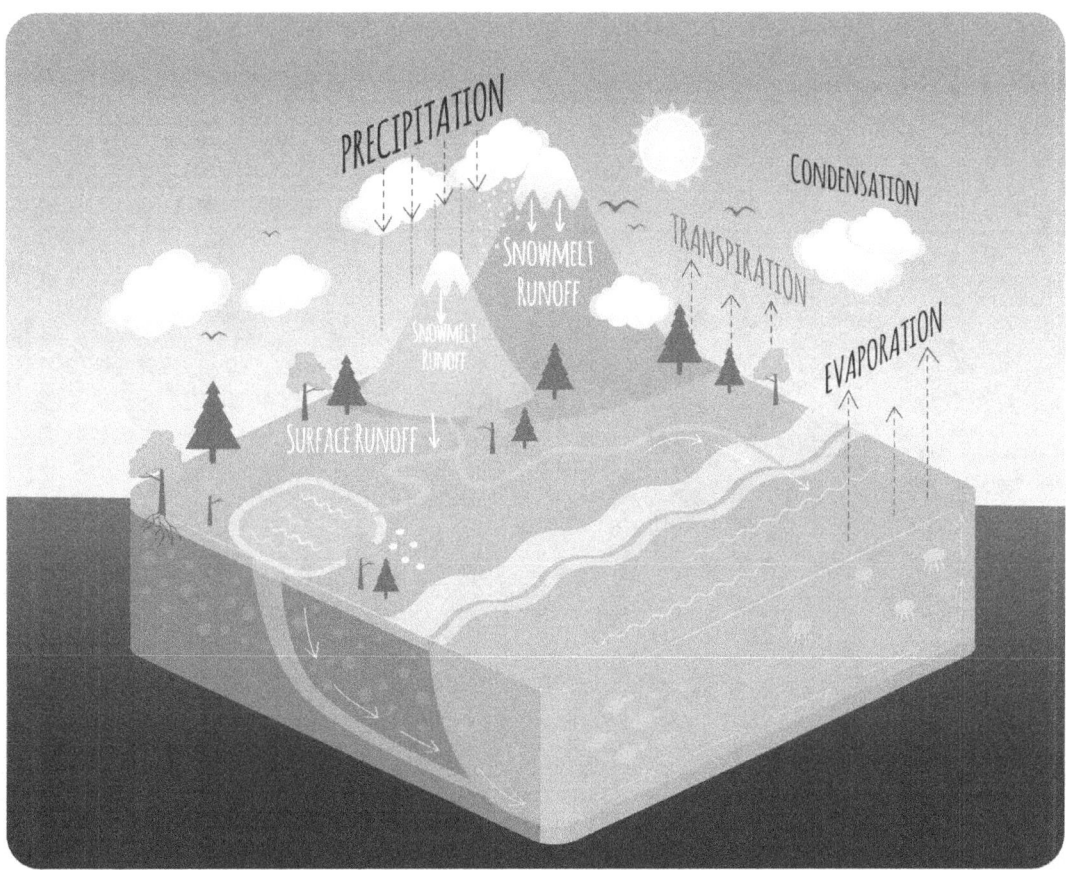

Clouds are condensed water vapor, which is water that has cooled from a gas to liquid, like the droplets on the outside of a glass of lemonade on a hot summer day. That water on the glass is water vapor that cooled enough to slow down the moving particles so that they become denser, forming a liquid. In the sky, water vapor combines in different ways so clouds appear in different forms. Cloud height, shape, and behavior results in a variety of different types:

- High-Clouds
    - Cirrus: wispy and thread-like
    - Cirrostratus: like cirrus clouds, but wider and thicker sheets. They have a halo effect where sunlight and moonlight refract through.
    - Cirrocumulus: a cross between cirrus and cirrostratus clouds. These have rows of round puffs like a cotton-ball stretched out.
    - Contrails: clouds made by jets
- Mid-Clouds
    - Altostratus: thick, stretched clouds that block sunlight and are blue-grayish in color
    - Nimbostratus: a thick altostratus cloud accompanied by rain
    - Altocumulus: layered rolls of clouds

- Low-Clouds
  - Cumulus: white, round, puffy clouds
  - Stratus: wide, thick, stretched-out, gray clouds that may cause drizzle
  - Fog: lazy stratus clouds that have drooped so low that they reach Earth's surface
  - Cumulonimbus: the angry cloud that brings thunderstorms, hail, and tornadoes. It looks like a thick mountain.
  - Stratocumulus: stretched-out, grayish, puffy, cumulus clouds

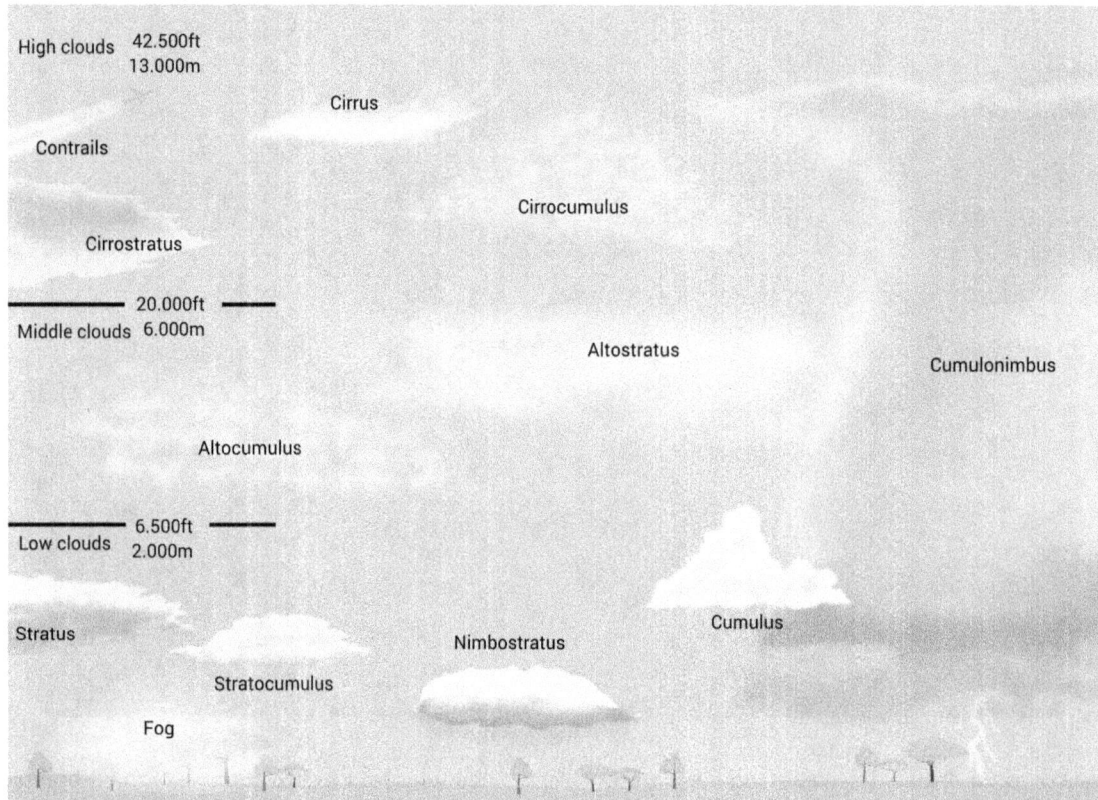

Precipitation comes in many different forms:

- **Rain** occurs due to water vapor condensing on dust particles in the troposphere. As more and more water condenses, the drops will eventually enlarge and accumulate mass, becoming so heavy that they fall to Earth.

- If the temperature is above the freezing point, the water falls as rain. Rain can freeze on the ground if the temperature on Earth's surface is colder than that of the troposphere. Freezing rain causes extremely dangerous driving conditions due to the slickness of the ice.

- **Sleet** freezes on its way down as opposed to freezing upon impact. Sleet starts as ice that melts as it falls through the atmosphere due to hitting spots of warmer temperature, and then it freezes again before hitting the ground.

- **Hail** is precipitation of balls of ice. Hail begins as ice at very cold temperatures in the atmosphere. Instead of precipitating sheets of ice like sleet storms, hailstorms precipitate ice that looks like rocks because hail is formed during thunderstorms. The massive winds throw hail up and down so more and more water vapor condenses and freezes on the original ice. Layer upon layer of ice combine, creating hail sometimes as large as golf balls.

- **Snow** forms as loosely packed ice crystals. Snow is less dangerous than the other frozen forms of precipitation and can produce beautiful snowflakes.

Even though seasons have predictable temperatures, there can be significant differences day to day. In the troposphere, the Sun's heat is trapped by the blanket of greenhouse gases and creates warm, low-pressure air. Because warm gas particles move faster and have less space between them, they are less dense than colder air, and they rise. Cool air moves below the warm air. This atmospheric movement is called **general circulation** and is the source of wind. Earth's spinning motion also causes wind.

Weather depends in a large part on temperature. Earth's equator is closest to the sun and receives more heat, so this area of earth is significantly warmer than the poles (Arctic and Antarctic). This warm air can form huge bubbles, as can the colder air at the poles. When warm air and cold air meet, the boundary is called a **front**. Fronts can be the site of extreme weather like thunderstorms, which are caused by water particles in clouds quickly rubbing against each other and transferring electrons, creating positive and negative regions. Lightning occurs when there is a massive electric spark due to the electrical current within a cloud, between two clouds, and even between a cloud and the ground.

While seasons are predictable trends in temperatures over a few months, **climate** describes the average weather and temperature patterns for a particular area over a long period of time, upwards of thirty years. While **fall** describes a season and **rain** describes weather, **rainforest** describes a climate. The climate of a rainforest, due to its proximity to the equator and oceans, consists of warm temperatures with humid air.

Even more extreme weather includes tornadoes and hurricanes. **Tornadoes** are spinning winds that can exceed 300 miles per hour and are caused by changing air pressure and quick winds. Hurricanes, typhoons, and tropical cyclones (the same phenomenon with different regional names) are storms with spinning winds that form over the ocean. **Hurricanes** are caused by warm ocean water quickly evaporating and rising to a colder, lower-pressure portion of the atmosphere. The fast movement of the warm air starts a cyclone around a central origination point (the eye of the storm). **Blizzards** are also caused by the clash of warm air and cold air. They occur when the cold Arctic air moves toward warmer air and involve massive amounts of snow.

Precipitation and run-off are constantly affecting the surface of Earth, as the run-off weathers rocks or breaks them down from the original bedrock into pieces called regolith. Regolith sizes range from microscopic to large and quickly form either soil or sediment. **Weathering** is the process of breaking rock while **erosion** is the process of moving rock. Weathering can be caused by both physical and chemical changes. Mechanical forces such as roots growing, animal contact, wind, and extreme weather cause weathering. Another cause is the water cycle, which includes flowing water, moving glaciers, and liquid ice seeping into rocks and cracking them as water freezes and expands. Chemical weathering actually transforms the regolith into clay and soft minerals. One consequence of chemical weathering is corrosive acid rain.

Rocks cover the surface of Earth. Igneous rock comes from the molten, hot, liquid magma circulating beneath Earth's surface in the upper mantle. Through vents called **volcanoes**, magma explodes or seeps onto the Earth's surface. Magma is not uniform; it varies in its elemental composition, gas composition, and thickness or viscosity. There are three main types of volcanoes: shield, cinder, and composite.

Shield volcanoes are the widest because their thin magma flows out of a central crater calmly and quietly, like a gentle fountain. This flowing magma results in layers of solid lava. The slow flow results in a convex hill that spans a wide area.

Like shield volcanoes, **cinder volcanoes** typically have a central crater and thin lava. In contrast to shield volcanoes, they are small, cone-shaped hills with steep sides. They are made of volcanic debris, or cinders. They are often found as secondary volcanoes near shield and composite volcanoes. In cinder volcanoes, the central vent spews lava that shatters into rock and debris and settles around it, resulting in its characteristic cone shape. Cinder volcanoes are surrounded by ashy, loose, magma dust.

Composite volcanoes (also called stratovolcanoes) are the most common and the tallest type of volcano. Their thick magma gets stuck at the vent, and as more and more builds up, the volcano eventually explodes and removes the clog. These eruptions generate loose debris, and once the plug has been violently expelled, the thick lava oozes out like a fountain. These volcanoes are the most dangerous with their extremely violent behavior and huge height. Most volcanoes are located around cracks in Earth's lithosphere.

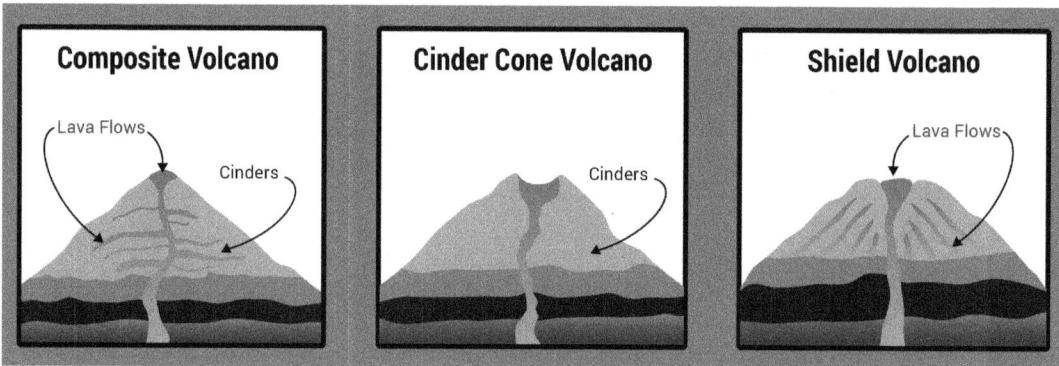

Once magma makes it to the surface, it is called **lava**. Once it cools, it solidifies into igneous rock. Common examples of igneous rock are obsidian, pumice, and granite. Weathering and erosion result in these rocks becoming soil or sediment and accumulating in layers mostly found in the ocean. These loose sediments settle over time and compress to become a uniform rock in a process called **lithification**. Examples of sedimentary rock include shale, limestone, and sandstone. As layers are piled atop each other, the bottom rock experiences an intense amount of pressure and transforms into metamorphic rock. Examples of metamorphic rocks are marble and slate. After long periods of time, the metamorphic rock moves closer to the asthenosphere and becomes liquid hot magma.

Magma's eventual fate is lava and igneous rock, and the cycle starts anew:

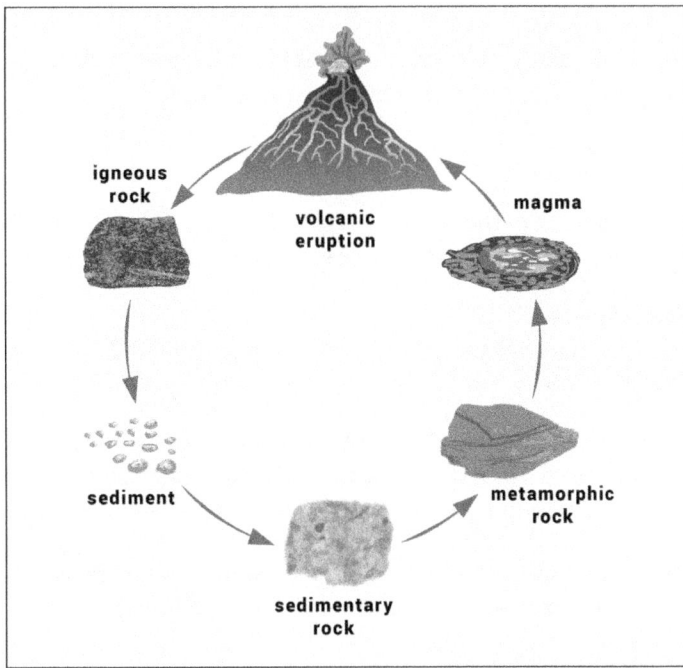

How does magma return to the surface if the lithosphere presses it down? Intense heat from the Earth's core travels to the upper mantle via **convection**. Convection involves thermal energy (heat) that converts into kinetic energy (movement), resulting in rapidly circulating molecules. Convection moves heat energy through fluids. In a pot of boiling water, the water closest to the burner becomes hot, causing its particles to move faster. Faster-moving molecules have more space between them and become less dense, so they rise. Some will vaporize, and some hit the cool air and slow down, becoming dense and sinking. Likewise, Earth's interior particles undergo convection (the heat source being the nuclear fission from the core), and the rock in the upper mantle will acquire so much kinetic energy that magma will be expelled from underneath Earth to the surface.

There are seven or eight major plates in the lithosphere and several minor plates. These tectonic plates explain the changing topography, or shape, of earth.

There are three types of boundaries between plates: divergent, convergent, and transform. All boundaries can be sites of volcanic activity. A **divergent boundary** occurs when plates separate. Lava fills in the space the plates create and hardens into rock, which creates oceanic crust. In a **convergent boundary**, if one of the plates is in the ocean, that plate is denser due to the weight of water. The dense ocean plate will slip under the land plate, causing a subduction zone where the plate moves underneath. Where plates converge on land, the continental crusts are both lighter with a similar density, and as a result they will buckle together and create mountains.

In **transform boundaries**, adjacent plates sliding past each other create friction and pressure that destroy the edges of the boundary and cause earthquakes. Transform boundaries don't produce magma, as they involve lateral movement.

Just as plates pushing together cause mountains, **canyons** are deep trenches caused by plates moving apart. Weather and erosion from rivers and precipitation run-off also create canyons. **Deltas** form when rivers dump their sediments and water into oceans. They are triangular flat stretches of land that are kind of like a triangular spatula; the handle represents the river and the triangle represents the mouth of a delta.

Sand dunes are another landform caused by wind or waves in combination with the absence of plants to hold sand in place. These are found in sandy areas like the desert or the ocean.

Earth History

A popular theory about the beginning of the universe is called the **Big Bang Theory**. It proposes that about fourteen billion years ago, a dense ball of matter exploded, releasing particles and energy.

From there, many scientists propose:

- Earth formed 4.6 billion years ago, and life didn't appear until approximately 3.5 billion years ago.

- At Earth's birth, it was an inhospitable place of active volcanoes, intense heat, lightning, and constant bombardment with space debris (rocks and dust). Heat vaporized all liquid water, and the anaerobic atmosphere (without oxygen) was composed of poisonous gases.

- Over time, the landscape changed, and once organic molecules (proteins, fats, carbohydrates, and DNA) and organisms came on the scene, water and oxygen became available, and the biosphere began.

- The last 542 million years have been divided into three eras: Paleozoic, Mesozoic, and Cenozoic. The **Paleozoic era** started with the **Cambrian Explosion**, when the animal kingdom expanded and diversified from invertebrates (simple animals without backbones) in the Pre-Cambrian Era. The era ended with the Permian mass extinction, where most animal species disappeared, probably due to volcanic eruptions.

- After the Permian extinction, the **Mesozoic era** began the reign of the dinosaurs. **Angiosperm** (flowering plants) life also exploded in the Mesozoic Era. The Cretaceous mass extinction ended the era, when nearly half of marine life and large portions of terrestrial species were decimated.

- Our most recent era is the **Cenozoic era**, and life continues to proliferate.

Our insight into the development of Earth has been fueled by fossil evidence. **Paleontology** is the study of fossils, which requires the study of rock layers. Sedimentary rocks exist as layers called **strata** and contain remains of once-living organisms. The depth at which a fossil is found within a layer of rock indicates the fossil's age. The lower the layer, the older the fossil.

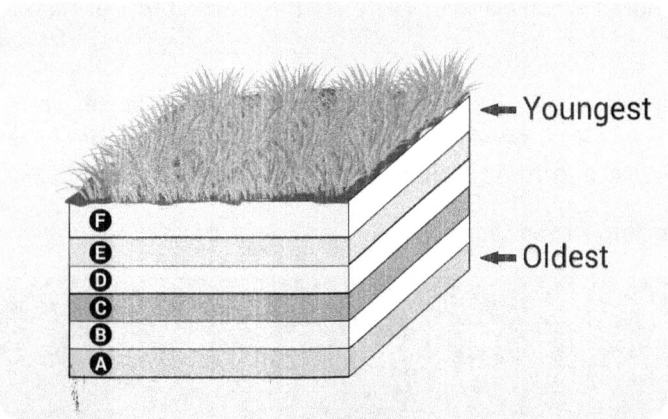

Fossils are remnants of organisms, such as teeth and bones. These structures, like petrified wood, have been preserved so well due to minerals seeping into the bone and acting as preservatives. Fossils can also be completely intact organisms found in glaciers or sap. Trace fossils are not actual parts of an organism but evidence that the organism was there, like a footprint or an imprint of a leaf.

Calculating the age of organisms in rock layers is based on the amounts of two different forms of radioactive elements like carbon. **Carbon-12** is the non-radioactive form, and **Carbon-14** is the radioactive form. In fossils, Carbon-12 won't decrease over time, but Carbon-14 will. Scientists can compare the amounts of Carbon-12 and Carbon-14 to estimate the age of fossils. The smaller the amount of Carbon-14, the older the fossil.

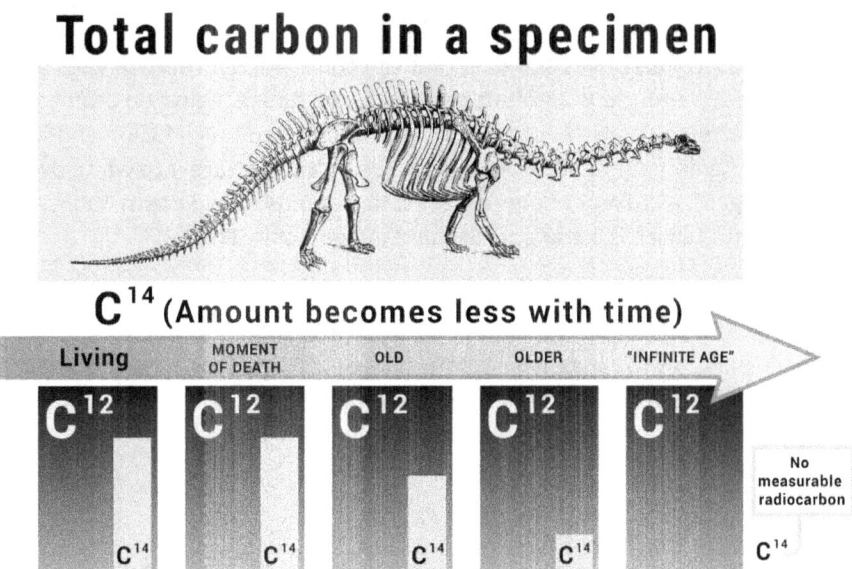

Earth and the Universe

Earth is part of a solar system that rotates around a star. Our solar system is a miniscule portion of the universe, with our Sun being just one of trillions upon trillions of stars. Almost every existing star belongs to a galaxy, clusters of stars, rocks, ice, and space dust. Between galaxies there is nothing, just darkness. There could be as many as a hundred billion galaxies. There are three main types of galaxies: spiral, elliptical, and irregular.

The majority of galaxies are spiral galaxies, with a large, central galactic bulge, which is a cluster of older stars. They look like a disk with arms circulating stars and gas. Elliptical galaxies have no particular rotation pattern. They can be spherical or extremely elongated and do not have circulating arms.

Irregular galaxies have no pattern and can vary significantly in size and shape:

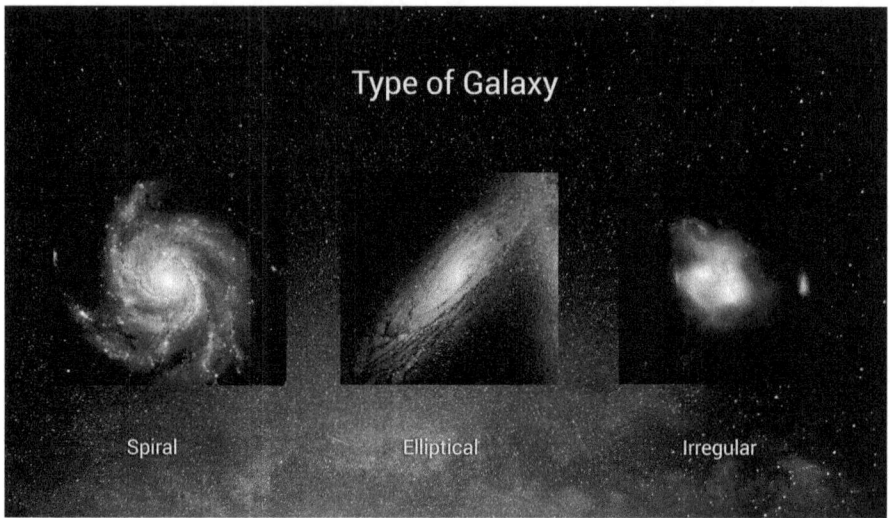

Earth's galaxy, the **Milky Way**, is a spiral galaxy and contains hundreds of billions of stars.

Pre-stars form from nebulas, clouds of gas and dust that can combine to form two types of small stars: brown and red dwarfs. **Stars** produce enormous amounts energy by combining hydrogen atoms to form helium via nuclear fusion. **Brown dwarfs** don't have enough hydrogen to undergo much fusion and fizzle out. **Red dwarfs** have plenty of gas (hydrogen) to undergo nuclear fusion and mature into white dwarfs. When they use all of their fuel (hydrogen), a burst of energy expands the star into a **red giant**. Red giants eventually condense into a **white dwarf**, which is a star approaching the end of its life.

Stars that undergo nuclear fusion will run out of gas quickly and burst in violent explosions called **supernovas**. This burst releases as much energy in a few seconds as the Sun will release in its entire lifetime. The particles from the explosion will condense into the smallest type of star, a **neutron star**; this will eventually condense into a **black hole**, which has such a high amount of gravity that not even light energy can escape.

Earth's sun is currently a red dwarf; it is early in its life cycle. As the center of Earth's solar system, the Sun has planets and space debris (rocks and ice) orbiting around it. The various forms of space debris include:

- **Comet**: made of rock and ice with a tail due to the melting ice

- **Asteroid**: a large rock orbiting a star. The asteroid belt lies between Mars and Jupiter and separates the smaller rocky planets (Mercury, Venus, Earth, and Mars) from the larger, gassy planets (Jupiter, Saturn, Uranus, and Neptune). Pluto is not considered a planet anymore due to its small size and distance from the Sun.

- **Meteoroid**: a mini-asteroid with no specific orbiting pattern

- **Meteor**: a meteoroid that has entered Earth's atmosphere and starts melting due to the warmth provided by our insulating greenhouse gases. These are commonly known as "falling stars."

- **Meteorite**: a meteor that hasn't completely burned away and lands on Earth. One is believed to have caused the Cretaceous mass extinction.

Each planet travels around the Sun in an **elliptic orbit**. The time it takes for one complete orbit is considered a year. The gravity of the massive Sun keeps the planets rotating, and the farther the planets are from the Sun, the slower they move and the longer their orbits. Earth's journey is little bit over 365 days a year. Because Mercury is so close to the Sun, one year for Mercury is actually only 88 Earth days. The farthest planet, Neptune, has a year that is about 60,255 Earth days long. Planets not only rotate around the Sun, but they also spin like a top. The time it takes for a planet to complete one spin is considered one day. On Earth, one day is about 24 hours. On Jupiter, one day is about nine Earth hours, while a day on Venus is 241 Earth days.

Planets may have natural satellites that rotate around them called **moons**. Some planets have no moons and some have dozens. In 1969, astronaut Neil Armstrong became the first man to set foot on Earth's only moon.

Earth Patterns

The temperature on the sun varies from its core to its atmosphere. Its atmospheric temperature is predicted at over one million degrees Fahrenheit. The sun accounts for two types of energy reaching earth: light energy and thermal (heat) energy.

Plants absorb the light energy and they use it to perform photosynthesis.

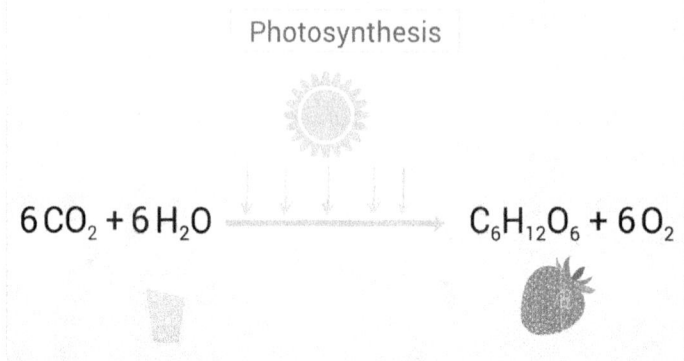

The thermal energy is transferred to earth's atmosphere through radiation. Unlike the transfer of heat through convection, radiation is a direct transfer—there are no particles in space to transfer the sun's heat. Once thermal energy reaches earth, the carbon dioxide in the atmosphere acts as a blanket to trap the heat.

The heat from the Sun as well as the orbit and position of Earth cause seasons. As discussed, Earth rotates around the sun and spins on an axis. Earth is slightly tilted on its side. An imaginary line around the middle called the **equator** splits the earth into the northern and southern hemispheres.

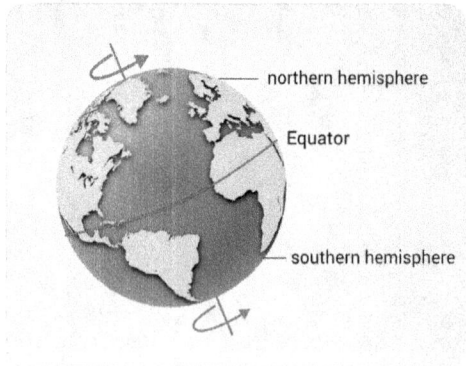

Science

To understand seasons and the heating of the planet, refer to this picture:

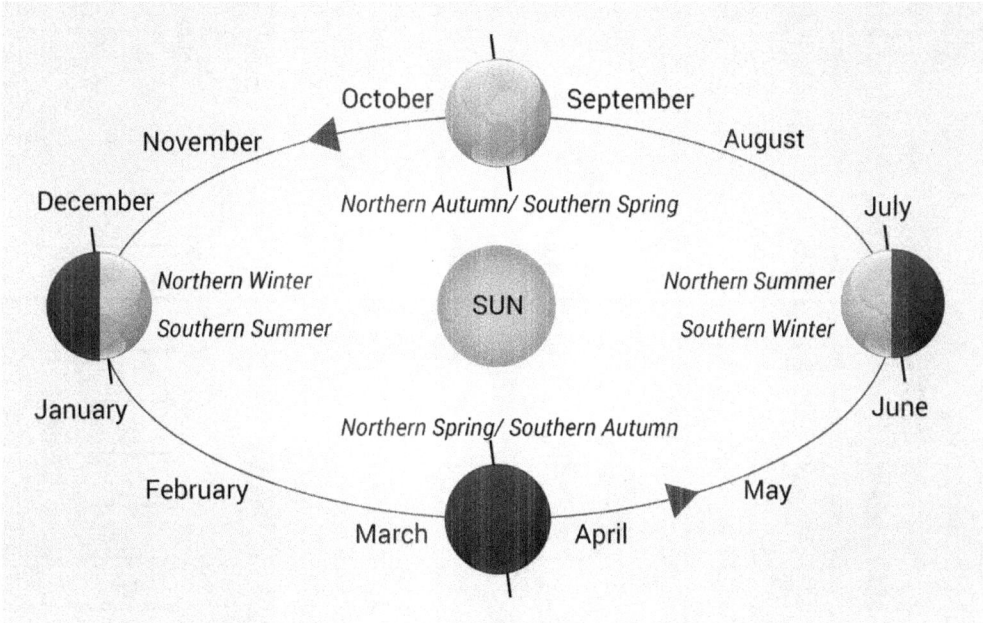

Observing July, these facts are apparent:

- Earth is tilted so that the northern hemisphere is pointing towards the sun. The southern hemisphere is pointed away.

- Because the north is tilted toward the sun, it gets more daylight in July than the southern hemisphere.

These observations explain why in July, the northern hemisphere experiences summer while the southern hemisphere experiences winter.

Notice in December that the opposite is true: the southern hemisphere gets more daylight compared to the northern hemisphere.

In spring and fall, both the north and the south get around the same sun exposure; therefore, those seasons have milder temperatures.

As the earth rotates, the distribution of light slowly changes, which explains why seasons gradually change. In June, the northern hemisphere experiences the summer solstice, the day with the most daylight. As the earth continues to orbit, its days will get shorter and shorter until the winter solstice, the shortest day of the year. Equinoxes occur in the fall and the spring and represent the days when the amount of daylight and darkness are relatively equal.

Just as the earth orbits the sun, the moon orbits the earth. The moon is much closer to earth than the sun. And even though the moon is so close to the earth, the moon contains no life because it lacks water and an atmosphere. Without greenhouse gases to blanket the sun's heat, temperatures on the moon are very low at night.

The moon is visible from the earth because it reflects sunlight at certain points in its orbit. The Moon's orbit has a predictable pattern. It has two main phases, waxing and waning. When the moon is waxing, it goes from a new moon to a full moon. Notice that only the left side of the moon is dark during the waxing phase. The waning phase goes from full moon to new moon. Only the right side of the moon is dark when it is waning.

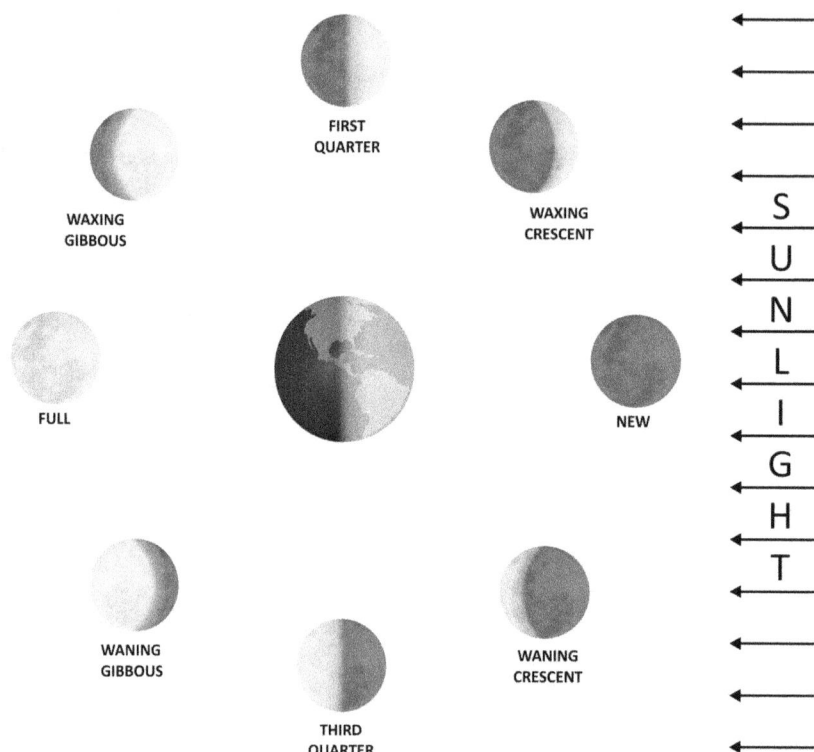

This picture shows that when the moon is behind the earth, then the moon's entire surface is reflected and we see a full moon. When the moon is between the earth and the sun, it is invisible at night, which is called a **new moon**.

Half-moons are visible when the moon and the earth are in a line that is perpendicular to the direction of sunlight. Only half of the moon reflects light to the earth at night, as seen in the figure above.

A moon that looks larger than a half-moon is called a **gibbous moon**, and a moon that looks smaller is called a **crescent moon**.

Eclipses occur when the earth, the sun, and the moon are all aligned—the earth blocks the others from seeing each other. If they are perfectly lined up, a total eclipse happens, and if they are only a little lined up, there is a partial eclipse.

There are two types of eclipses: lunar and solar. A **lunar eclipse** occurs when the earth interrupts the sun's light reflecting off of the full moon. Earth will then cast a shadow on the moon, and particles in earth's atmosphere refract the light so some reaches the surface of the moon, causing the moon to look yellow, brown, or red.

During a new moon, when the moon is between the earth and the sun, the moon will interrupt the sunlight, casting a shadow on earth. This is called a **solar eclipse**.

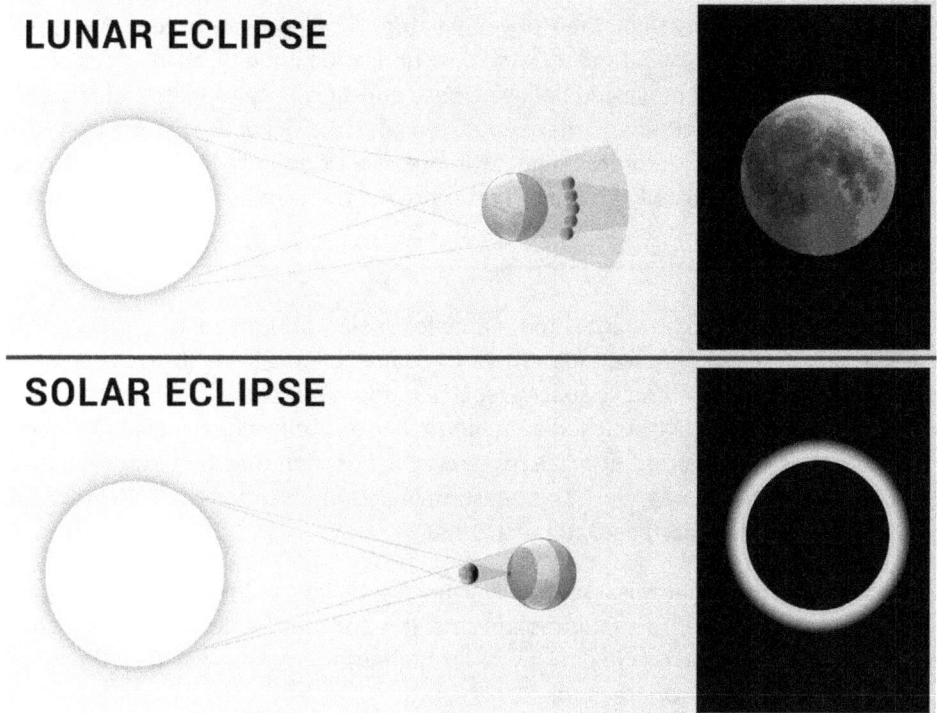

The moon also affects ocean tide due to gravity. Earth is much larger than the moon and has a very significant gravitational force that keeps us on the ground even though it is spinning very quickly. The moon is much smaller than earth, but because it is so close, it has a pulling effect on earth's oceans. When it is closest to earth, it pulls the water more, resulting in high tide. When the moon is farthest from earth, it pulls the ocean less and is called **low tide**.

Science as a Human Endeavor

Two of the worst earthquakes in history occurred in 1556 and 1976, causing 830,000 and 255,000 deaths, respectively. Earthquakes near the ocean cause massive tidal waves called tsunamis. In Indonesia in 2004, a tsunami resulted in 230,000 deaths. **Seismology** is the study of earthquakes. Understanding earthquakes can help predict them and possibly even prevent them.

Earthquakes have an initial source of plate movement called the **focus**. At the focus, there is a significant amount of tension, like the force of resistance generated by bending a wooden stick. Eventually, with enough pressure, there is so much tension that the stick breaks. The separate pieces that were once in a curved formation due to the strain will slip back into their original shape. This is called **elastic rebound** when it occurs at plate boundaries. After elastic rebound, the movement spreads outwards from the focus and causes waves of kinetic energy. These rolling vibrations are called **seismic waves**. Slipping back into place takes several adjustments called **aftershocks**, which are less severe than the initial movement but can still cause a significant amount of destruction. A logarithmic scale called the **Richter scale** measures the amplitude of seismic waves. An earthquake magnitude of 10 has the largest amplitude, and a magnitude of 1 has the smallest.

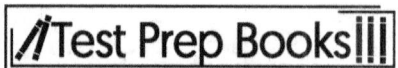

Science as an Inquiry

Science begins with questions—it is difficult to have an answer when there are no questions. A great source of inquiry for scientists has been weather. The study of weather is called **meteorology. Meteorologists** measure temperature, air pressure, wind speed, wind direction, and humidity, all in hopes of predicting how and where air and water vapor will move and behave. These questions inspire meteorologists to use weather balloons and satellites to study weather and make educated guesses. As knowledge grows, technologies also improve and facilitate better weather forecasting. The impressive **Doppler radar** has provided scientists with meaningful data since the 1980s, allowing them to better predict the weather with more certainty.

Research

Another aspect of science is **research**, which is the search for answers for a scientific inquiry. One of the largest areas of scientific research is space exploration. Of course, people have always wondered about the universe, but the United States didn't make space research a priority until the 1940s and 1950s "space race" with the Soviet Union. In 1957, Russia launched a satellite called **Sputnik**, which fueled the intense competition between the two countries. In space research, the question that accelerated space exploration was "How can man travel into space safely?" This question fueled the creation of NASA (the National Aeronautics and Space Administration) on October 1, 1958.

NASA research continues today. They observe the sky, launch satellites and telescopes into space, and study the data collected. Currently, there are a multitude of satellites and land vehicles or "rovers" on Mars collecting data with the hope of one day finding a way for humans to live there. In fact, the target date for human occupation on Mars is somewhere in the 2030s.

Process of Science

Theories are well-supported ideas that evolve from hypotheses and experimentation. A **hypothesis** is an educated guess about a scientific process or object. Once every angle of investigation has been examined and all evidence supports a hypothesis, only then can it be called a **theory**. It is important to know that theory development is a process. As technology advances and more aspects of science can be explored, evidence might no longer support a theory. With non-supportive data, either the theory can be modified or completely thrown out while new investigations are developed to examine other explanations.

For example, plate tectonic theory didn't appear until the early 20th century. People thought the earth was static and immobile. Only after many years of investigation and evidence did skeptics finally concede that the earth's surface was broken into plates. This theory wasn't universally accepted until the late 1960s and was considered revolutionary.

Early evidence that supported plate tectonics was publicized in the 1910s by Alfred Wegener, who observed that the South American and African borders to the Atlantic Ocean seemed like they could fit together like puzzle pieces. He proposed the idea of Pangaea, a massive supercontinent that existed long ago and must have broken into pieces due to a process called **continental drift**. Other evidence supporting plate tectonics were similar fossils found in Africa and South America, suggesting that they were once connected. But skeptics continued to scoff at the theory. Then, in the 1960s it was discovered, with the help of early computers, that a continental shelf (an underwater boundary between plates) between the two continents had a remarkable fit that was very unlikely to be due to chance.

Life Science

Structure and Function of Living Systems

Prokaryotes, Viruses, and Eukaryotes

Every living organism is made up of **cells**, and these cells come in various shapes and sizes, depending on the organism. There are two types of cells: **prokaryotes** and **eukaryotes**. The big difference between them is that eukaryotes have a nucleus and prokaryotes do not. The structures that will be covered in this section will be bacteria, protist, fungus, plant, and animal cells:

Bacteria	Protist, Fungus, Plant, Animal
DNA Ribosomes Cytoplasm Cell Membrane Cell Wall	DNA Ribosomes Cytoplasm Cell Membrane Cell Wall (except animal cells) Unique structures Nucleus Mitochondria Chloroplasts (only autotrophs, or organisms that can produce their own food. Only protists and plants are producers).

Below is an example of a plant cell:

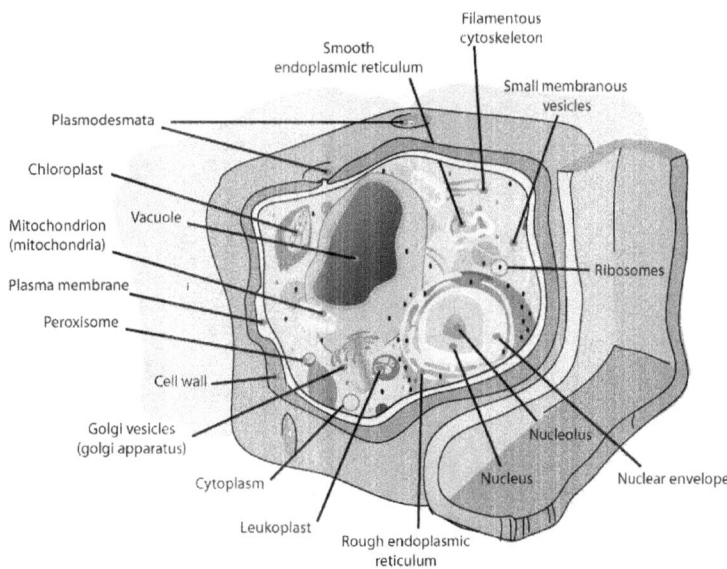

Animal cell

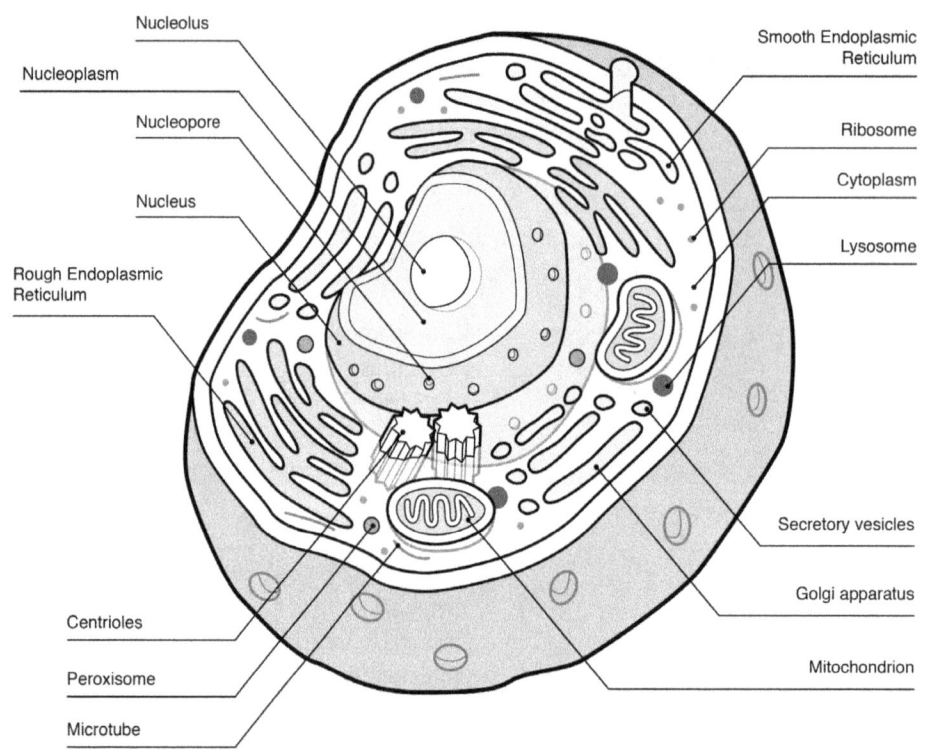

Below is an example of a bacteria cell:

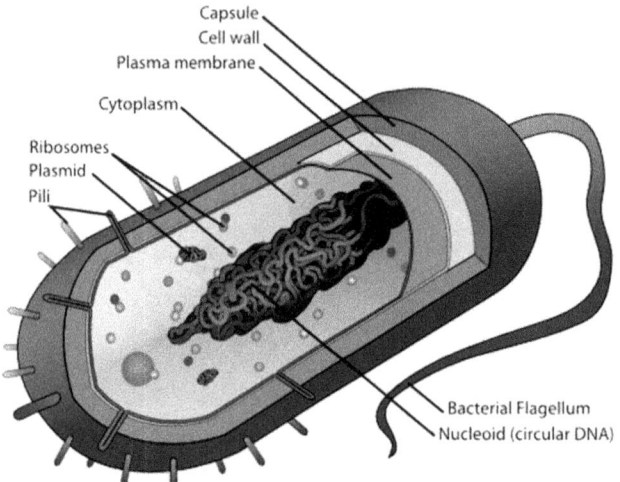

Like all cells, bacterial cells contain **DNA**, the genetic material that gives instructions for every single structure and process that the cell undergoes. DNA is a code made up of four letters: A (adenine), T (thymine), G (guanine), and C (cytosine). There are billions of these letters in DNA, and the order of these letters tells a cell exactly what to do and how to do it (just like reading a book of instructions).

Science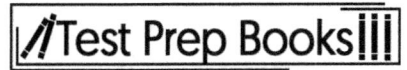

Because DNA doesn't do anything on its own, all cells must have a means of decoding DNA and turning it into the structure, which is the function of **ribosomes**—they are protein-makers. If DNA is like a recipe, then the ribosomes are like the chef.

DNA and ribosomes sit in a fluid called **cytoplasm**, which contains a **cytoskeleton** (a network of proteins) that holds them in place. All cells need a covering to contain everything inside—these are called **cell membranes** in animals or cell walls for plant cells.

Bacteria can also have a capsule and a **flagellum**, which are all external structures. A **capsule** is sticky and causes bacteria to cluster with other cells or on food. Only about 50 percent of bacteria can move, and those that do often have a **flagellum**, which is a whip-like structure like a tadpole's tail.

Viruses are commonly thought of as living organisms, but many scientists argue they aren't for two reasons: (1) they are not cells, and (2) they cannot reproduce by themselves. Both qualities are required for an organism to be considered alive. Viruses are unique in that they require a host in order to make proteins and reproduce, because viruses don't have all of the complex tools of a living cell. When a virus has infected a host, it acts like a living organism—it moves and reproduces—but outside of a host, it does nothing. A virus can survive outside of a host, but it cannot reproduce. Scientists are still trying to properly define a virus, so we can currently say that viruses are not like bacteria or any other living thing.

Eukaryotic cells are more complex than prokaryotic cells. They make up all the organisms in the kingdoms protist, fungus, plant, and animal. Eukaryotic cells are also larger than prokaryotes and contain a nucleus and other organelles.

Eukaryotic cells hold their DNA inside a nucleus in pieces called chromosomes. **Chromosomes** are a cell's way of organizing long strands of DNA in twisted-up bundles. Imagine a room filled with rolls of toilet paper compared to a room that has all of those rolls unraveled and thrown everywhere; it would be a mess!

Other important organelles include chloroplasts and mitochondria. **Chloroplasts** can be found in cells called autotrophs, which can convert sunlight into energy. Plants are autotrophs. **Mitochondria** are little energy factories found in almost every type of cell. They use chemical reactions to make little packets of energy that can be used by other parts of the cell.

Energy

Energy is everywhere and is one of the few things in the universe believed to be constant. That means that in the whole universe, if all the energy could be measured (energy in all the stars, atoms, etc.), the amount of energy that was present at the beginning of time is exactly the same as it is now. The only difference is that energy has been converted into different forms. For example, a plant gets its energy from the Sun, using it to grow bigger and stronger; therefore, the Sun's energy is converted and stored inside the plant. Then a person eats the plant, using its stored energy. In this example, energy exists in the form of light, growth, and movement (picking the plant and chewing it).

Only with the energy food provides an organism exist. Think of a construction team and a pile of bricks and mortar. The bricks are not going to just arrange themselves into a building. However, if a construction team uses their muscles and energy, the complex building can be built. If the construction team runs out of food, though, they will become exhausted and will be unable to construct the building.

The human body is the same way. Organs (heart, brain, stomach, etc.) are like the bricks. The chemical reactions in the body are like the workers. Energy is the food that the workers need to build the organism. The food of life is sugar, specifically glucose. A candy bar, soda, or a slice of birthday cake can provide a boost of energy because of all the sugar they contain. There are many bonds between the molecules of sugar,

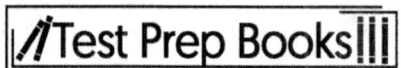

holding them in place (like the mortar holding the bricks in a building). When the bonds are broken in digestion, all that energy is released so that living things can invest that energy into chemical reactions.

Two chemical reactions are critical for living things: **photosynthesis** and **respiration**.

Any producer must have a chloroplast in order to convert light energy into food, usually in the form of a carbohydrate. **Chloroplasts** are organelles that look like little green beans because they contain the pigment **chlorophyll**, which is able to absorb the sunlight's energy in the form of photons, or light rays. Some prokaryotes are also photosynthetic, and although they don't have a chloroplast because they're too simple and don't contain organelles, they have a pigment in order to make their own food.

Plants need water and sunlight to live. Plants suck up water from their roots. The sunlight they need is absorbed by the chlorophyll in chloroplasts, which are clustered and concentrated in their leaves. Interestingly, the chlorophyll actually is able to absorb every color of light except for green, which is why leaves look green: they reflect green light. If the roots take in water and the leaves take in carbon dioxide and sunlight energy, why are stems important? The stems in plants are an example of how structure helps function. The stem is like a skeleton for plants; it holds the leaves high so they can be closer to the sun.

Plants are critical for life on earth because they absorb the energy from the sun and invest it in the bonds that make sugar. Sugar passes through the food chain to provide energy for all living organisms. Plants and other **autotrophs** can make their own energy, while **heterotrophs** (which cannot make their own energy) consume the sugar, break it down, and convert it into usable energy with their mitochondria.

Cellular Respiration in the Mitochondria

The **glucose** that provides energy does nothing by itself; it is the bonds between atoms holding these complex glucose molecules together that hold the energy. When the molecule is intact, the bonds between them hold energy in the form of potential energy. When the bonds are broken, that potential energy is released and becomes available to the workers in the cell to perform chemical reactions.

The process of cellular respiration breaks the bonds in an organelle called the **mitochondria** in eukaryotes (protists, fungi, plants, animals).

Note that the equation for cellular respiration is the almost exact opposite of photosynthesis:

$$C_6H_{12}O_6 + 6O_2 \rightarrow 6CO_2 + 6H_2O + 36ATP$$

The only difference between the above equation and photosynthesis is the new product: ATP. **ATP** is a conversion of light energy into usable pockets of energy that provide energy to all the workers in cells that do the chemical reactions. While glucose is like a $100 bill with lots of energy in its bonds, ATP is like one hundred $1 bills that can be invested here and there as needed.

Bacteria do not have mitochondria, so they perform different reactions in their cytoplasm that produce much less energy (2ATP).

Organisms Need Food for More than Just Energy

When we eat a hamburger, we're eating more than carbohydrates; we're also eating proteins and fats. Plants provide more than just carbohydrates when we eat them; they also are able to use the light energy to make proteins, fats, and, of course, their DNA, because if they didn't have DNA, they'd have no instructions to grow.

The following organic compounds and their atoms don't magically appear in organisms—life has to either grab the nutrients from soil or seeds or eat them.

- Carbohydrates, proteins, fats, and DNA/RNA have carbon, hydrogen, and oxygen
- DNA, proteins, and fats also have phosphorus
- DNA and proteins also have nitrogen
- Proteins also can have sulfur

Plants need all of these elements to make food. Where do they get them? Remember that Earth's atmosphere is a conglomerate of different gases, including nitrogen. Bacteria in the soil are able to convert that nitrogen into a usable form, and the roots of plants absorb the critical nitrogen. Carbon and oxygen get into the plant via photosynthesis (carbon dioxide), as does the element hydrogen, because plants take in water, which contains hydrogen. Phosphorus and sulfur are absorbed in plants through soil. Since heterotrophs cannot make their own food, they have to eat an autotroph (or eat something that ate an autotroph) in order to obtain these critical elements.

Cycles are a recurring pattern in science, and making food is no exception. When living things die, fungi and bacteria act as decomposers and break down the material. That's actually why dead things and rotten meat smell bad; the decomposers have broken them down so much that gases containing carbon, oxygen, phosphorus, nitrogen, and even smelly sulfur are released. Remember that sulfur is heavy in protein, and eggs are protein-rich. It makes sense that rotten eggs have an unpleasant smell as they release sulfur because they're mostly protein. Once living things decompose, all the elements eventually recycle back to the atmosphere or to the soil, and the atoms are available to construct molecules once again.

Cellular Organization

Prokaryotes contain ribosomes, DNA, cytoplasm, a cell membrane, a cytoskeleton, and a cell wall. Eukaryotes vary between kingdoms but contain all of these structures except a cell wall because animal cells require so much mobility. Large, land-dwelling animals typically compensate with an exoskeleton (like insects) or an endoskeleton (like humans and other mammals, reptiles, and birds) for structure.

All bacterial cells are **unicellular** (existing as just one cell). Almost all types of protist and some species in fungi kingdom are unicellular, but they still have the complicated organelles of eukaryotes. A few protists, almost all fungi, and all plants and animals are multicellular. Multicellularity leads to development of structures that are perfectly designed for their function.

Cells combine to form **tissue**. Tissue combines to form **organs**. Organs combine to form **organ systems**, and organ systems combine to form one **organism**. The structures of all of these combinations allow for the maximum functionality of an organism, as demonstrated by the nervous system.

A **neuron** is a cell in the nervous system designed to send and receive electrical impulses. Neurons have dendrites, which are sensors waiting to receive a message. Neurons also have an **axon**, a long arm that sends the message to the neighboring neuron. The axon also has insulation known as **myelin** that speeds the message along. Many neurons combine to form a **nerve**, the tissue of the nervous system, which is like a long wire. The structure of this nerve is perfect—it is a long cable whose function is to send signals to the brain so the brain can process the information and respond. Nerve tissue combines with other tissue to form the **brain**, a complex structure of many parts.

The brain also has glands (epithelial tissue) that release hormones to control processes in our body. The brain and spinal cord together form the central nervous system that controls the stimulus/response signaling in our body. The nervous system coordinates with the circulatory system to make our heart beat, the digestive system to control food digestion, the muscular system to move an arm, the respiratory system to facilitate breathing, and all other body systems to make the entire organism functional. Cells are the basic building block in our bodies, and their structure is critical for their function and the function of the tissues, organs, and systems that they comprise.

In the graphic below, the left depicts a neuron, and the right depicts the nervous system. A neuron is a nerve cell, and it is the basic building block of the nervous system. Cell, tissue, organ, and organ system structure are critical for function.

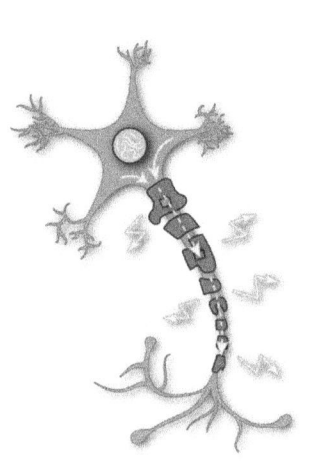
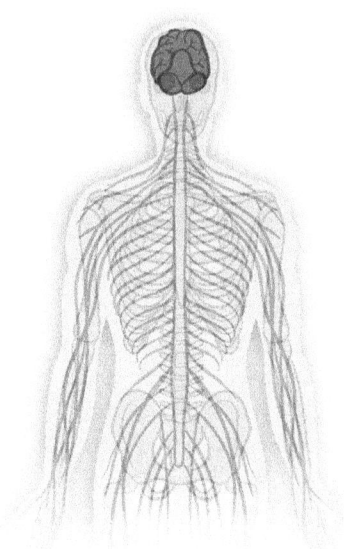

Science

The following table lists organ systems in the human body:

Name	Function	Main organs
Nervous	Detect stimuli and direct response	Brain and spinal cord
Circulatory	Pump blood to deliver oxygen to cells so they can perform cellular respiration	Heart
Respiratory	Breathe in oxygen (reactant for cellular respiration) and release carbon dioxide waste	Lungs
Muscular	Movement	Heart and muscles
Digestive	Break down food so that glucose can be delivered to cells for energy	Stomach, small intestine, lots of others
Skeletal	Support and organ protection	All sorts of joints, skull, ribcage

Reproduction and Heredity

Cellular Reproduction

Unlike viruses, all living organisms can independently reproduce, but reproduction occurs differently between bacteria and the more complex kingdoms. Bacteria reproduce via **binary fission**, which is a simpler process than eukaryotic division because it doesn't involve splitting a nucleus and doesn't have a web of proteins to pull chromosomes apart. Prokaryotes have simpler DNA compared to cells that have a much larger number of individual chromosomes (humans have two sets of 23 chromosomes—one set from mom and one set from dad, for a total of 46 chromosomes). Think of going from class to class with two identical binders (like bacteria) versus going from class to class with 23 identical pairs of binders (humans); it would be much more difficult to organize the large set of binders than the smaller one.

Binary fission in bacteria is therefore relatively easy. Bacteria copy their DNA in a process called **DNA replication**, grow, and then the replicated DNA moves to either side, and two new cells are made.

Eukaryotic cell division is part of a well-defined cycle with the following phases:

- **G1 phase**: The cell is growing and working.

- **S phase**: The cell is getting too large, so it copies its DNA because it wants to make sure the two new cells have the full instruction manual that is DNA.

- **G2 phase**: The cell uses its workers to get ready for cell division.

- **M phase**: Chromosomes condense and line up in the middle of the cell. The copies are sent to either side.

- **Cytokinesis**: The moment when the cytoplasm is officially split in two, and then two identical daughter cells are produced and enter G1 phase.

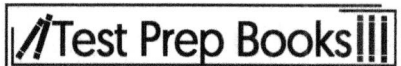

The M phase has subdivisions because it quickly goes through a series of events. Each sub-phase of events is described and illustrated below.

PHASE	PHASE EVENTS	ANIMAL CELL DIAGRAM	PLANT CELL DIAGRAM
Interphase (G1, S, and G2)	DNA is loose and spread out and contained in nucleus. This is important because it is actively growing and needs access to its instructions to do chemical reactions correctly. Chromosomes are replicated (copied) in S phase so that they look like an X. Each side of the X has identical DNA.		
Prophase	Nucleus disappears and DNA condenses into chromosomes		
Metaphase	Chromosomes line up in center and proteins from either side of cell attach to them		
Anaphase	Proteins shorten and pull chromosomes apart so that one half (either left side of X or right side of X) of DNA goes to each new cell		
Telophase and Cytokinesis	Nuclei reform and chromosomes start to spread out **Animal cells**: cytoplasm to split in half **Plant cells**: cell plate (new cell wall) forms between daughter cells and extends (animal cells don't have a cell wall)		

Organism Reproduction

For bacteria, cell reproduction is the same as organism reproduction; **binary fission** is an asexual process that produces two new cells that are clones of each other because they have identical DNA.

Eukaryotes are more complex than prokaryotes and can go through **sexual reproduction**. They produce **gametes** (sex cells). Females make eggs and males make sperm. The process of making gametes is called **meiosis**, which is similar to mitosis except for the following differences:

- There are two cellular divisions instead of one.

- Four genetically different haploid daughter cells (one set of chromosomes instead of two) are produced instead of two genetically identical diploid daughter cells.

- A process called crossing over (**recombination**) occurs, which makes the daughter cells genetically different. If chromosomes didn't cross over and rearrange genes, siblings could be identical clones. There would be no genetic variation, which is a critical factor in the theory of evolution of organisms.

In sexual reproduction, a sperm fertilizes an egg and creates the first cell of a new organism, called the **zygote**. The zygote will go through countless mitotic divisions over time to create the adult organism.

Heredity: Passing Genes Across Generations

All living things are a product of their DNA, specifically portions of their DNA called genes that code for different characteristics.

Learned behavior is not affected by DNA and is not hereditable. Changes in appearance like a woman painting her toenails, a bird whose feathers accidentally fall out due to a tornado, or a person getting a scar are also not heritable. Heritable characteristics are those coded by DNA like eye color, hair color, and height.

A man named **Gregor Mendel** is considered the father of genetics. He was a monk and a botanist, and through extensive experiments with pea plants, he figured out a great deal about heredity.

Our genetic code comes in pairs. Each chromosome contains many genes, and since we have one chromosome from our mom and one chromosome from our dad, we have two copies of each gene. Genes come in different forms called **alleles**, which determine the organism's traits, the way an organism looks or behaves. For some traits, there are only two alleles: a **dominant allele** and a **recessive allele**. Even though eye color is a bit more complicated, pretend that brown eyes are dominant over blue eyes, and there are the only two alleles:

- B = Brown eyes
- b = blue eyes

A child inherits these alleles from his parents. There are three possible combinations a child can inherit, dependent on his parents' alleles:

- BB (homozygous dominant)
- Bb (heterozygous)
- bb (homozygous recessive)

The combination of genes above will determine the trait in the offspring. If the child gets any combination with a B, the more powerful allele, his eyes will be brown. Only the bb combination will give the child blue eyes. In this example, the combination of alleles is called a **genotype**, and the actual eye color the child has is called a **phenotype**.

Change Over Time

The **theory of natural selection** is one of the fundamental tenets of evolution. It affects the **phenotype**, or visible characteristics, of individuals in a species, which ultimately affects the genotype, or genetic makeup, of those same individuals. **Charles Darwin** was the first to explain the theory of natural selection, and it is described by **Herbert Spencer** as favoring survival of the fittest.

Natural selection encompasses three assumptions:

- A species has heritable traits: All traits have some likelihood of being propagated to offspring.

- The traits of a species vary: Some traits are more advantageous than others.

- Individuals of a species are subject to differing rates of reproduction: Some individuals of a species may not get the opportunity to reproduce while others reproduce frequently.

Over time, certain variations in traits may increase both the survival and reproduction of certain individuals within a species. The desirable heritable traits are passed on from generation to generation. Eventually, the desirable traits will become more common and permeate the entire species.

Adaptation

The **theory of adaptation** is defined as an alteration in a species that causes it to become more well-suited to its environment. It increases the probability of survival, thus increasing the rate of successful reproduction. As a result, an adaptation becomes more common within the population of that species.

For examples, bats use reflected sound waves (echolocation) to prey on insects, and chameleons change colors to blend in with their surroundings to evade detection by its prey and predators. These adaptations are believed to be brought about by natural selection.

Adaptive radiation refers to the idea of rapid diversification within a species into an array of unique forms. It's thought to happen as a result of changes in a habitat creating new challenges, ecological niches, or natural resources.

Darwin's finches are often thought of as an example of the theory of adaptive radiation. Charles Darwin documented 13 varieties of finches on the Galapagos Islands. Each island in the chain presented a unique and changing environment, which was believed to cause rapid adaptive radiation among the finches. There was also diversity among finches inhabiting the same island. Darwin believed that as a result of natural selection, each variety of finch developed adaptations to fit into its native environment.

A major difference in Darwin's finches had to do with the size and shapes of beaks. The variation in beaks allowed the finches to access different foods and natural resources, which decreased competition and preserved resources. As a result, various finches of the same species were allowed to coexist, thrive, and diversify. Finches had:

- Short beaks, which were suited for foraging for seeds
- Thin, sharp beaks, which were suited for preying on insects
- Long beaks, which were suited for probing for food inside plants

Darwin believed that the finches on the Galapagos Islands resulted from chance mutations in genes transmitted from generation to generation.

Science

Life Cycle

Here's a look at the life cycles of many animals.

Chicken	Hens are female chickens, and they lay about one egg per day. If there is no rooster (male chicken) around to fertilize the egg, the egg never turns into a chick and instead becomes an egg that we can eat. If a rooster is around, he mates with the female chicken and fertilizes the egg. Once the egg is fertilized, the tiny little embryo (future chicken) will start as a white dot adjacent to the yolk and albumen (egg white) and will develop for 21 days. The mother hen sits on her clutch of eggs (several fertilized eggs) to incubate them and keep them warm. She will turn the eggs to make sure the embryo doesn't stick to one side of the shell. The embryo continues to develop, using the egg white and yolk nutrients, and eventually develops an "egg tooth" on its beak that it uses to crack open the egg and hatch. Before it hatches, it even chirps to let the mom know of its imminent arrival!
Frog	Frogs mate similar to the way chickens do, and then lay eggs in a very wet area. Sometimes, the parents abandon the eggs and let them develop on their own. The eggs, like chickens', will hatch around 21 days later. Just like chickens, a frog develops from a yolk, but when it hatches, it continues to use the yolk for nutrients. A chicken hatches and looks like a cute little chick, but a baby frog is actually a tadpole that is barely developed. It can't even swim around right away, although eventually it will develop gills, a mouth, and a tail. After more time, it will develop teeth and tiny legs and continue to change into a fully grown frog! This type of development is called **metamorphosis**.
Fish	Most fish also lay eggs in the water, but unlike frogs, their swimming sperm externally fertilize the eggs. Like frogs, when fish hatch, they feed on a yolk sac and are called **larvae**. Once the larvae no longer feed on their yolk and can find their own nutrients, they are called fry, which are basically baby fish that grow into adulthood.
Butterfly	Like frogs, butterflies go through a process called **metamorphosis**, where they completely change into a different looking organism. After the process of mating and internal fertilization, the female finds the perfect spot to lay her eggs, usually a spot with lots of leaves. When the babies hatch from the eggs, they are in the larva form, which for butterflies is called a **caterpillar**. The larvae eat and eat and then go through a process like hibernation and form into a **chrysalis**, or a **chrysalis**. When they hatch from the cocoon, the butterflies are in their adult form.
Bugs	After fertilization, other bugs go through incomplete metamorphosis, which involves three states: eggs that hatch, nymphs that look like little adults without wings and molt their exoskeleton over time, and adults.

All of these organisms depend on a proper environment for development, and that environment depends on their form. Frogs need water, caterpillars need leaves, and baby chicks need warmth in order to be born.

Regulation and Behavior

DNA is the instruction manual for every organism, including humans. It is identical in our cells (except for minor mutations); so why are neurons and heart muscles so different in function and appearance? The key is that in different cells, different parts of the DNA are read. Our DNA is an encyclopedia set with 46 volumes (chromosomes). The instructions for heart cells are different from instructions for neurons. And these instructions are scattered throughout the 46 volumes. It is still not completely understood how a cell chooses what parts of the encyclopedia to read, but it is known that different cells read different portions of our DNA.

Protein enzymes facilitate chemical reactions; they are the workers in the cell. Some unwind the DNA so that RNA can copy the genes in a process called **transcription**. **RNA** is similar to DNA except that it is single-stranded and has the base U, which stands for **uracil**, instead of the T in DNA. Another similarity between DNA and RNA is that they are both made of a base, a phosphate, and a sugar, though DNA is made of deoxyribose sugar and RNA is made of ribose sugar.

The final protein can have many destinations; it can become part of the cytoskeleton that holds the organelles in place, act as an enzyme, go to the cell membrane and act as a marker protein (a tag to identify the cell), act as a **transport protein** (allows materials to pass in and out of the cell), or as a **receptor protein** (can receive chemical messages like hormones and initiate reactions in the cell to respond), or leave the cell and become something else, like a person's hair and fingernails!

In the cell, processes are regulated at the DNA level because transcription and translation are tightly regulated. At the organism level, the entire nervous system controls activity. In humans, a stimulus is received by the sensory neuron, travels up the nerve to the brain, and a response travels down to whatever motor neuron is necessary for movement.

Sensory neurons detect environmental stimulus involving sight, sound, touch, taste, and smell.

Diversity of Life

Due to the speciation that has occurred over the last 3.5 billion years since life first appeared, the variety of organisms is astronomical. Scientists have identified about 2 million species, and they suspect that there are at least 8 million others out there.

A man named **Carolus Linnaeus** developed a naming system to try to create some order in classifying all species. For example, the classification of humans through the seven levels, from all-inclusive to the most specific, looks like this:

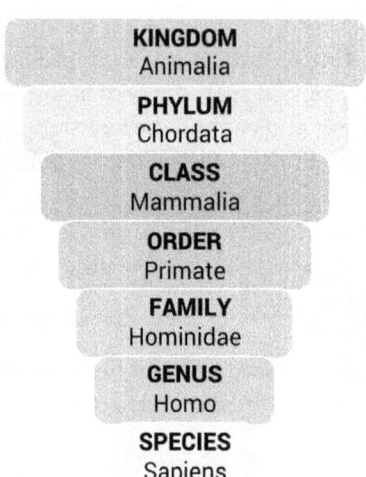

One benefit of this universal naming system is that because some organisms have different common names, like the roly-poly and doodlebug, or the cougar and panther, it allows scientists to have a common language. Due to the sheer magnitude of species, scientists need the seven levels, but when referring to organisms, their official names are just the last two: **genus** and **species**. Humans are simply referred to as **Homo sapiens**. This two-name system is called **binomial nomenclature**.

There are currently six kingdoms, although the prokaryotes (simpler cells) used to be lumped together into one kingdom called **Monera**. Currently, there are two prokaryotic kingdoms, **Archaebacteria** and **Eubacteria**.

Archaebacteria

Prokaryotes that have a cell membrane made of fats. They live in harsh places including extremely hot areas (volcanic vents or hot springs) and extremely salty locations (Utah's Salt Lake). These are the rarest prokaryotes.

Eubacteria

Common bacteria that have a cell membrane made of a protein-carbohydrate blend. They make up the vast majority of existing prokaryotes. An example is staphylococcus.

Protista

This kingdom consists of eukaryotes. Most are unicellular. This kingdom is the most diverse and can be divided into three types: fungus-like (including slime-molds), plant-like (including algae), and animal-like (including amoeba). Some scientists believe that there is so much diversity within the kingdom that they should be split into separate kingdoms, but so far they remain in one group.

Animal-like protists are **heterotrophs** (they do not make their own food), and plant-like protists are **autotrophs** (they make their own food). Fungus-like protists are heterotrophs. Like actual fungi, these organisms externally digest their food by acting as parasites and decomposers. Animal-like protists ingest their food via phagocytosis (cell eating) or by absorbing it.

Depending on the particular protists, some produce asexually via mitosis and others reproduce sexually.

Fungi

Fungi are eukaryotic heterotrophs that digest their food externally. Many of them, including common mushrooms and toadstools, act as decomposers by breaking down dead organisms then absorbing the broken down nutrients. Other fungi accomplish ingestion as parasites feeding off of living organisms, as in the case of a yeast infection. All fungi are multicellular with one exception—**yeast**. Fungi have cell walls made of a complex carbohydrate called **chitin**. Most fungi reproduce sexually and asexually.

Plantae

Plants are multicellular autotrophs like daisies, roses, and pine trees. They are closely related to the aquatic producer, algae, but different in that algae don't contain true roots, stems, or leaves. Plants are **photosynthesizers**, and their cells have surrounding cell walls made of the starch cellulose.

Animalia

Animals are multicellular heterotrophs, like fungi, except that animals move and internally ingest their food by consuming it. Animals are the only kingdom to not have cells with cell walls due to their flexibility and ability to move. The animal kingdom is very diverse and includes humans, jellyfish, and spiders, as well as all sorts of other organisms.

Interdependence of Organisms

The biosphere has layers and layers of complexity:

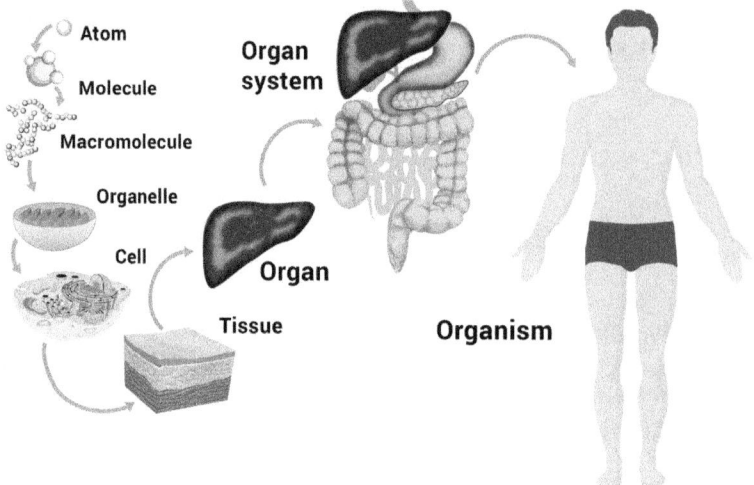

All organisms work together so that life can exist. An organism represents one of a species, like the fish below, and all organisms serve a particular function. The fish's niche is to eat aquatic producers and excrete waste that acts as fertilizer.

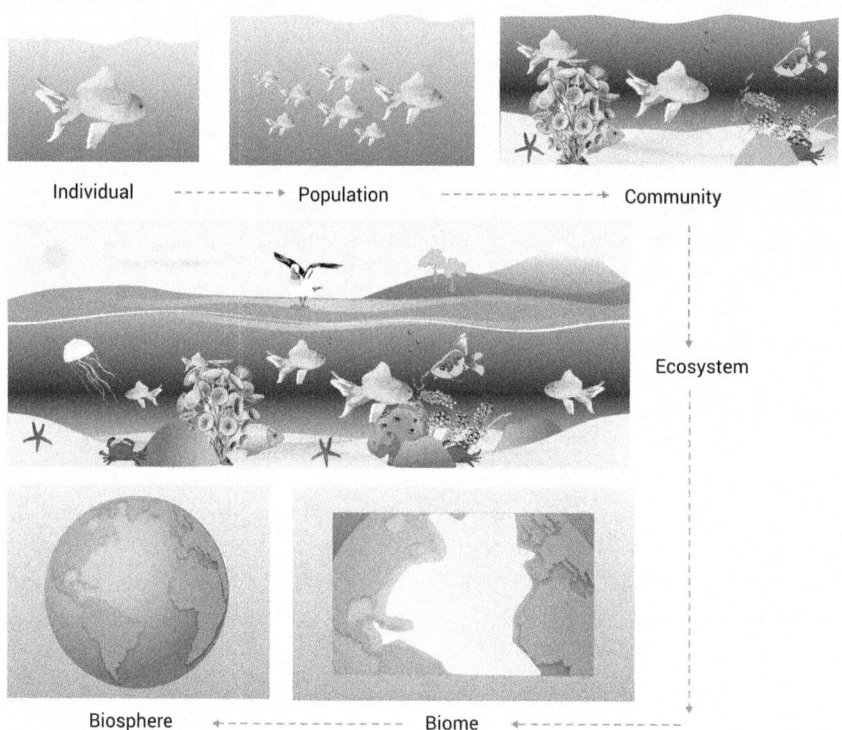

This fish is just one organism within a population. A **population** represents multiple individuals living in the same habitat. The community includes every biotic factor (living organism) within an ecosystem, in this case, the fish, jellyfish, algae, crab, bacteria, etc. An ecosystem includes all the biotic factors as well as the **abiotic**, which includes anything non-living—for the fish, that's a rock, a shipwreck, and a nearby glacier. For biomes, add weather and climate into the mix. The biosphere is all of Earth, which is the combination of all biomes.

We already discussed that producers (plants, protists, and even some bacteria) photosynthesize and make the food that provides energy required for all chemical reactions to occur and therefore all life to exist. A non-photosynthesizer must find and eat food, and this feeding relationship can be visualized in food chains. Consider this food chain:

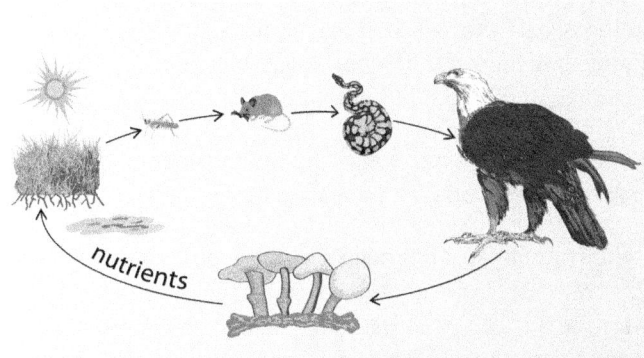

The true source of the energy for every living organism is the sun. Plants absorb the sun's energy to make glucose and are on the **first trophic level** (feeding level). The grasshopper on the **second trophic level** is an example of an herbivore and is a primary consumer, as he is the first eater in the food chain. Unfortunately, he receives only 10 percent of the energy that the plant absorbed (this is known as the 10 percent rule) because the other 90 percent of energy was either used by the plant to grow or will be lost as heat.

The mouse on the **third trophic level** is the secondary consumer, or second eater. Food chains are not as inclusive as **food webs**, which show all feeding relationships in an ecosystem. Looking at this food chain suggests that mice are carnivores (eaters of animals), but mice also eat berries and plants, so they are actually considered omnivores (eaters of both plants and animals). The mouse only gets 10 percent of the energy from the grasshopper, which is actually only 1 percent of the original energy provided by the Sun. The snake on the fourth trophic level is a carnivore, as is the hawk on the highest trophic level.

The arrows in the food chain show the transfer of energy, and fungi as well as bacteria act as decomposers, which break down organic material. Decomposers act at every trophic level because they feed on all organisms; they are non-discriminating omnivores. Decomposers are critical for life, as they recycle the atoms and building blocks of organisms.

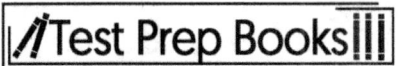

Feeding relationships and **predator-prey relationships** (hunter-hunted, like the hawk and the rabbit in the food web above) are not the only relationships in an ecosystem. There also can be competition within and between species. For example, in the food chain above, the rabbit and snail both eat grass, showing a relationship called **competition**, when two organisms want the same thing. Other relationships include symbiotic relationships, which represent two species living together. Symbiosis comes in three varieties:

- **Mutualism**: an arrangement where both organisms help each other. An example is the relationship between birds and flowers. When birds consume the nectar that the flower produces, pollen rubs on the bird's body so that when it travels to a neighboring plant, it helps with fertilization. The plant helps the bird by providing food, and the bird helps the plant by helping it reproduce. This is a win-win.

- **Parasitism**: when one organism is hurt while the other is helped. Fleas and dogs are a prime example. Fleas suck the dog's blood, and dogs are itchy and lose blood. This is a win-lose.

- **Commensalism**: when one organism is helped and the other is neither harmed nor helped. For example, barnacles are crusty little creatures that attach themselves to whales. They don't feed on the whale like a parasite. Instead, they use the whale to give them a free ride so they have access to food. The whales don't care about the barnacles. This is a win-do not care.

Personal Health

Humans appear to be the kings of nature, but unfortunately, disease can strike. Some protists (like the malaria-causing paramecium), fungi (yeast), and bacteria (strep) can make humans sick and can even be deadly.

The human body has an arsenal to help fight illness. Skin and the acid in our stomach are inhospitable to all sorts of disease-causing agents (pathogens) and fight them off without even trying. Eyebrows, eyelashes, nose hair, and cilia (tiny hairs) in the respiratory system trap any germs and prevent them from getting inside. Mucus is a defense to trap germs, which is why the human body overproduces it when sick—it acts like a spider web that catches germs, and when a person coughs or sneezes, the germs are expelled and unable to cause harm. If, however, the pathogen gets past these barriers, then the body has to start fighting them off. Inflammation and swelling, though annoying, actually help by increasing blood flow to an injured or infected area. And blood carries white blood cells that eat and destroy germs. Fevers are actually a body's natural response to killing pathogens.

If the germ is still not killed off, then the body makes massive amounts of white blood cells. One type of blood cell, the **plasma B-cell**, is particularly helpful because it makes structures called **antibodies**, little proteins that tag pathogens so that the other white blood cells can easily find and destroy them. Other types of white blood cells include **T-cells**, which destroy the pathogen as well as infected cells.

This picture shows how antibodies work:

The **antigen** on the germ is the part that attaches to cells in our body and destroys them. Think of the antigen like the key that attaches to a protein on the outside of our cell, tricking the cell to let it in. The antibody perfectly binds to the antigen (the key), making it so that the germ cannot open and enter our cells. And the immune system produces killer T-cells that eat these tagged pathogens.

An amazing thing about antibodies is that they are completely fashioned to match each germ they come across. And antibodies stay circulating in blood so that if they ever encounter the disease again, they can tag it for destruction and block its harmful effects, making a person immune to the pathogen.

For this reason, scientists have developed vaccines, which can save lives. For example, **polio** is a disease that attacks the brain and spinal cord, causing paralysis and death. The vaccine for polio is given to children. It is given in the inactive form of the virus (dead virus) but it still carries the same antigen. A person vaccinated will develop antibodies that are exactly matched to the polio antigens, so if they ever encounter polio in real life, the immune system will eradicate it before it can do any damage.

When a person gets infected and their body starts making massive amounts of antibodies and killer cells, they can feel sick due to the energy expended to create such an army. Usually, after a few days, the body effectively fights off the germ, and life goes back to normal. In the case of bacterial infections that don't resolve themselves, antibiotics (bacteria killers) can be taken to help the body fight the germs. Antibiotics, unfortunately, don't help with viruses.

Interestingly enough, antibiotics were discovered by accident in 1928 by **Alexander Fleming**. He was performing research of an entirely different nature when he noticed mold had killed the cells he was trying to study. Upon further investigation, he realized that the effect of the mold was reproducible and effectively killed a variety of bacteria. His discovery laid groundwork for a new field of medicine, which targeted the destruction of bacteria. Since then, a variety of antibiotics have been developed, and some of them are uniquely designed for different diseases. Biological research is critical for disease prevention because bacteria are always changing, and there is a need to continually improve the antibiotics already available.

Science as a Human Endeavor

In addition to learning about bacteria and viruses to save lives, an example of how increased scientific knowledge has helped society can be seen in the field of botany. **Flowers** are the reproductive structure of plants and are very complex structures that allow plants to create genetic diversity.

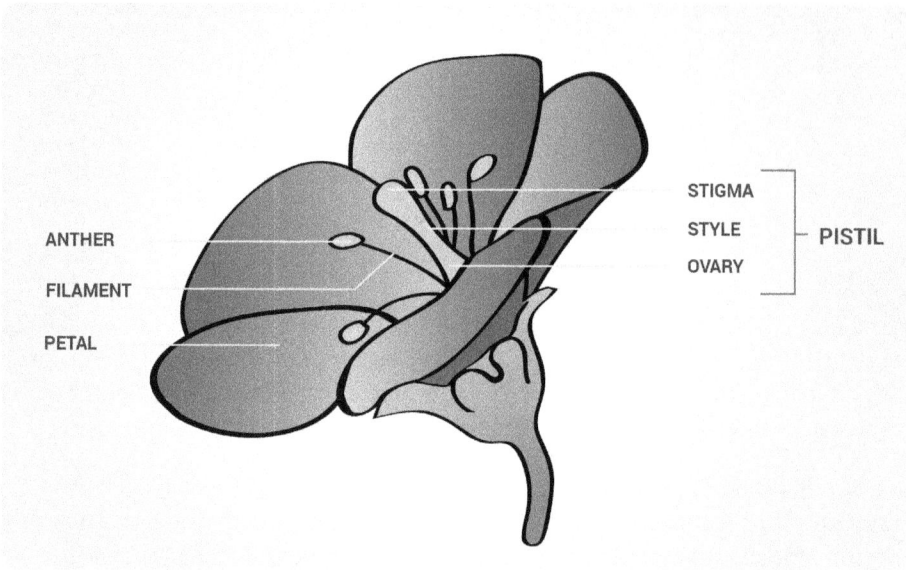

Scientists have determined the purpose for all of a flower's many parts:

- The **stamen** contains the pollen-holding **anther** (pollen is plant sperm) and the **filament** that holds it high.

- The **pistil** contains the sticky **stigma** at the top to which pollen sticks; the **style**, which holds up the stigma; and the **ovary**, or egg that will eventually be fertilized.

- The petals are colored and even have infrared patterns we cannot see to attract pollinators like birds and bees.

Note how structure aids function in the flower: the pollen is lightweight and easily attaches to pollinators. The stigma is sticky and easily catches the pollen. The petals are beautiful landing pads designed to attract different animals.

Scientists are using their knowledge of flowers and genetics to genetically engineer flowers. They are working on creating pollen-free flowers that are easy on people with allergies, blue roses, and other flower varieties that don't exist in nature, and even glow-in-the-dark flowers by introducing foreign DNA.

Other botanists are also genetically engineering plants that provide our food, which is much more controversial, as many are worried about the consequences of consuming genetically modified organisms (GMOs). Some think GMOs are wonderful because they can provide massive amounts of food at low costs, while others fear introducing foreign food into the biosphere will alter ecosystems.

Science

Science as Inquiry

As scientists have been able to visualize and decode DNA, they are also able to predict diseases. **Karyotypes** are pictures of individual's chromosomes, and even before birth, abnormalities such as Down syndrome (an extra chromosome 21) can be detected.

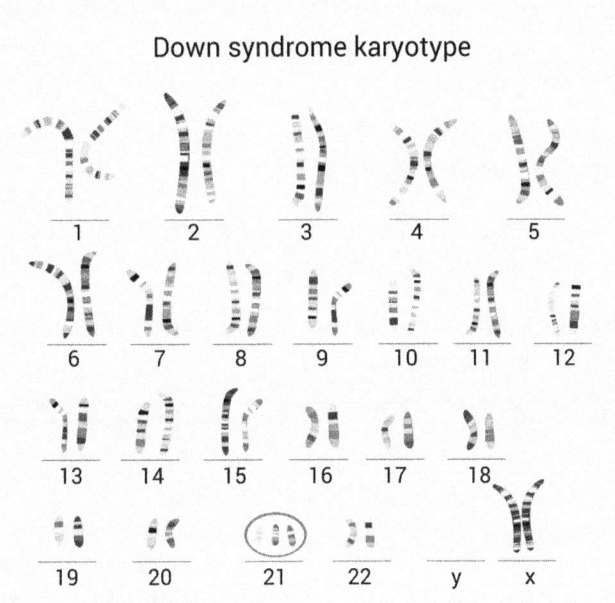

Adults can have blood tests to test their alleles and see if they have cancer-causing (or other disease-causing) genes. Being aware of possible diseases helps people to prevent and treat them.

As scientists ask more questions about disease detection, prevention, and treatment, quality of life continues to increase. For example, type 1 diabetes occurs when a person's pancreas fails to make insulin, and it is a deadly disease if left untreated. A few decades ago, scientists found a way to synthetically create insulin, and now diabetics can have long and prosperous lives.

Research

When the actor Johnny Depp flew to Australia to film a movie, he travelled with his two dogs. Australian officials immediately sanctioned him.

Australian law forbids anyone from bringing foreign species because one little change can disrupt an entire ecosystem. For example, in Hawaii, North American ducks were brought for hunting purposes, but they've endangered the native duck species. One new non-native organism can cause a natural species to become extinct.

Another danger to an ecosystem is human activity. As the human population grows and technology advances, our energy needs are polluting the atmosphere. And there are no doubts that global temperatures are climbing, which can change ecosystem dynamics. Increases in oil spills and ocean pollution is destroying aquatic ecosystems. Chopping down trees for wood as well as building parking lots and buildings is decimating terrestrial ecosystems. With these changes, biodiversity will dramatically drop. The list of endangered species continues to grow, and eventually many will become extinct. Altering populations of ecosystems can have dramatic effects.

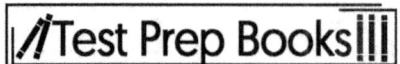

Livestock overgrazing is also detrimental to the environment. If farms don't monitor grazing animals, plants simply lose the ability to rebound, often resulting in death. The lack of producers in an ecosystem, the start of the food chain, will have disastrous consequences for the entire community.

Research is important so that society can minimize activities that interfere with ecosystems. Developing non-renewable energy (such as wind, solar, and geothermal), deliberately planning a grazing schedule to prevent overgrazing, and protecting endangered species all should be primary focuses of research.

Process of Science

Scientific research always starts as a question, followed by a hypothesis, data collection, and conclusions. Conclusions lead to further questions, repeating the process.

This was the case with the study of insect development. Long ago, scientists noticed a strange phenomenon in insects, which we now know is a process called **metamorphosis.**

There are two types of metamorphosis in insects: incomplete metamorphosis, which has three stages, and complete metamorphosis, which has four stages.

Incomplete Metamorphosis: Grasshoppers	Complete Metamorphosis: Butterflies and Beetles
<ul><li>Egg</li><li>Nymph: a mini-adult with no wings</li><li>Adult: how the organism will look for the rest of its life</li></ul>	<ul><li>Egg</li><li>Larva: a wormy, six legged, massive eater</li><li>Pupa: a larva encased in a hard shell that dramatically develops and changes in appearance</li><li>Adult: how the organism will look for the rest of its life</li></ul>

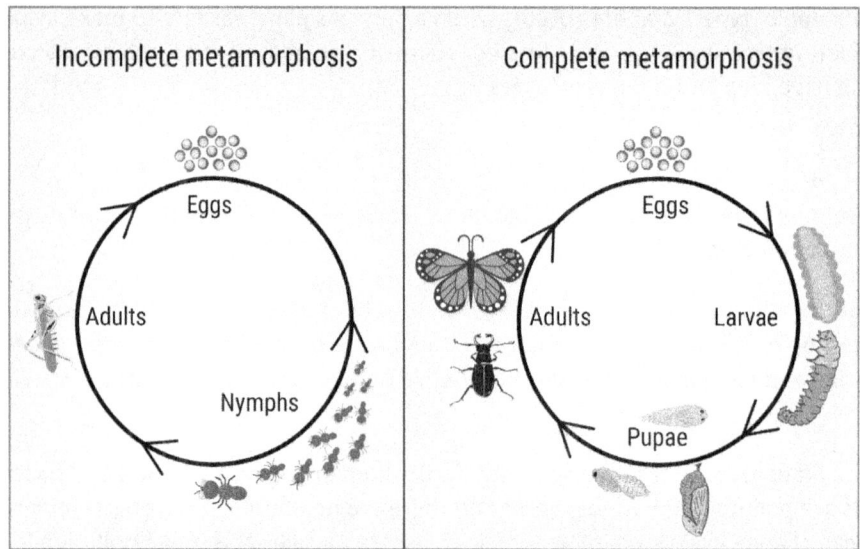

Insight into metamorphosis developed over centuries of research and goes through the scientific process, as shown below.

Problem/Question: What's happening to these insects that makes them look completely different from their younger selves?

Hypothesis: The prevailing hypotheses that were researched over the years were:

- These different creatures are from two different organisms.
- The worm-like creature is a younger version of the adult creature.

Data collection: A biologist named **Swammerdam** in the 1600s rejected the popular belief that the caterpillar and the butterfly were different organisms. Using observations from microscopic data, he confirmed that an insect (but not all insects) could go through an intermediate larval stage. Fossil evidence also confirmed the development of some insects through a larval stage. Scientists have even found genetic and protein differences from organisms that go through incomplete metamorphosis and complete metamorphosis. The insects with larval stage have a specific gene required for the process as well as differences in hormone production.

Conclusion: There is a complete metamorphosis cycle for many insects with larval and pupa stages between the egg and adult.

New problem: Why do insects go through complete metamorphosis?

New hypothesis: Complete metamorphosis is an adaptation. The intermediate "pupa egg" state between the larva and the adult stage arose so the juvenile and adult population don't compete for food, ensuring greater overall survival.

Physical Science

Physical and Chemical Properties

In the physical sciences, it is important to break things down to their simplest components in order to truly understand why they act and react the way they do. It may seem burdensome to separate out each part of an object or to diagram each movement made by an object, but these methods provide a solid basis for understanding how to accurately depict the motion of objects and then correctly predict their future movements.

Everything around us is composed of different materials. To properly understand and sort objects, we must classify what types of materials they comprise. This includes identifying the foundational properties of each object such as its reaction to chemicals, heat, water, or other materials. Some objects might not react at all and this is an important property to note. Other properties include the physical appearance of the object or whether it has any magnetic properties. The importance of being able to sort and classify objects is the first step to understanding them.

- **Matter**: anything that has mass and takes up space

- **Substance**: a type of matter that cannot be separated out into new material through a physical reaction

- **Elements**: substances that cannot be broken down by either physical or chemical reactions. Elements are in the most basic form and are grouped by identified properties using the Periodic Table. The periodic table groups elements based on similar properties. Metallic elements, inert elements, and transition elements are a few categories used to organize elements on the periodic table. New elements are added as they are discovered or created, and these newer elements tend to be heavier, fall into the metal section of the periodic table, and are often unstable. Examples of elements include carbon, gold, and helium.

- **Atoms**: the building blocks of all elements. Atoms are the smallest particles of matter that retain their identities during chemical reactions. Atoms have a central nucleus that includes positively charged protons, and neutrons, which carry no charge. Atoms are also surrounded by electrons that carry a negative charge. The amount of each component determines what type of atom is formed when the components come together. For example, two hydrogen atoms and one oxygen atom can bond together to form water, but the hydrogen and oxygen atoms still remain true to their original identities.

- **Mass**: the measure of how much of a substance exists in an object. The measure of mass is not the same as weight, area, or volume.

Physical Properties vs. Chemical Properties

Both physical and chemical properties are used to sort and classify objects:

- **Physical properties**: refers to the appearance, mass, temperature, state, size, or color of an object or fluid; a physical change indicates a change in the appearance, mass, temperature, state, size or color of an object or fluid.

- **Chemical properties**: refers to the chemical makeup of an object or fluid; a chemical change refers to an alteration in the makeup of an object or fluid and forms a new solution or compound.

Reversible Change vs. Non-Reversible Change

Reversible change (physical change) is the changing of the size or shape of an object without altering its chemical makeup. Examples include the heating or cooling of water, change of state (solid, liquid, gas), the freezing of water into ice, or cutting a piece of wood in half.

When two or more materials are combined, it is called a **mixture**. Generally, a mixture can be separated out into the original components. When one type of matter is dissolved into another type of matter (a solid into a liquid or a liquid into another liquid), and cannot easily be separated back into its original components, it is called a **solution**.

States of matter refers to the form substances take such as solid, liquid, gas, or plasma. **Solid** refers to a rigid form of matter with a flexed shape and a fixed volume. **Liquid** refers to the fluid form of matter with no fixed shape and a fixed volume. **Gas** refers to an easily compressible fluid form of matter with no fixed shape that expands to fill any space available. Finally, **plasma** refers to an ionized gas where electrons flow freely from atom to atom.

> Examples: A rock is a solid because it has a fixed shape and volume. Water is considered to be a liquid because it has a set volume, but not a set shape; therefore, you could pour it into different containers of different shapes, as long as they were large enough to contain the existing volume of the water. Oxygen is considered to be a gas. Oxygen does not have a set volume or a set shape; therefore, it could expand or contract to fill a container or even a room. Gases in fluorescent lamps become plasma when electric current is applied to them.

Matter can change from one state to another in many ways, including through heating, cooling, or a change in pressure.

Science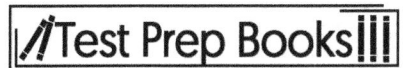

Changes of state are identified as:

- **Melting**: solid to liquid
- **Sublimation**: solid to gas
- **Evaporation**: liquid to gas
- **Freezing**: liquid to solid
- **Condensation**: gas to liquid
- **Non-reversible change** (chemical change): When one or more types of matter change and it results in the production of new materials. Examples include burning, rusting, and combining solutions. If a piece of paper is burned it cannot be turned back into its original state. It has forever been altered by a chemical change.

Forces and Motion

People have been studying the movement of objects since ancient times, sometimes prompted by curiosity, and sometimes by necessity. On earth, items move according to specific guidelines and have motion that is fairly predictable. In order to understand why an object moves along its path, it is important to understand what role forces have on influencing an object's movements. The term **force** describes an outside influence on an object. Force does not have to refer to something imparted by another object. Forces can act upon objects by touching them with a push or a pull, by friction, or without touch like a magnetic force or even gravity. Forces can affect the motion of an object.

In order to study an object's motion, the object must be locatable and describable. When locating an object's position, it can help to locate it relative to another known object, or put it into a frame of reference. This phrase means that if the placement of one object is known, it is easier to locate another object with respect to the position of the original object.

The measurement of an object's movement or change in position (x), over a change in time (t) is an object's speed. The measurement of speed with direction is **velocity**. A "change in position" refers to the difference in location of an object's starting point and an object's ending point. In science, the Greek letter **Delta, Δ,** represents a change.

Equation: $$\boldsymbol{velocity}\ (v) = \frac{\Delta x}{\Delta t}$$

Position is measured in meters, and time is measured in seconds. The standard measurement for velocity is meters/second (m/s).

$$\frac{\text{meters}}{\text{second}} = \frac{m}{s}$$

The measurement of an object's change in velocity over time is an object's **acceleration**. **Gravity** is considered to be a form of acceleration.

Equation: $$\boldsymbol{acceleration}\ (a) = \frac{\Delta v}{\Delta t}$$

Velocity is measured in meters/second and time is measured in seconds. The standard measurement for acceleration is meters/second² (m/s²).

$$\frac{\frac{\text{meters}}{\text{second}}}{\text{second}} = \frac{\text{meters}}{\text{second}^2} = \frac{m}{s^2}$$

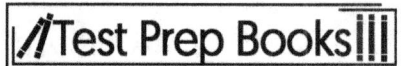

For example, consider a car traveling down the road. The speed can be measured by calculating how far the car is traveling over a certain period of time. However, since the car is traveling in a direction (north, east, south, west), the distance over time is actually the car's velocity. It can be confusing, as many people will often interchange the words speed and velocity. But if something is traveling a certain distance, during a certain time period, in a direction, this is the object's velocity. Velocity is speed with direction.

The change in an object's velocity over a certain amount of time is the object's acceleration. If the driver of that car keeps pressing on the gas pedal and increasing the velocity, the car would have a change in velocity over the change in time and would be accelerating. The reverse could be said if the driver were depressing the brake and the car was slowing down; it would have a negative acceleration, or be decelerating. Since acceleration also has a direction component, it is possible for a car to accelerate without changing speed. If an object changes direction, it is accelerating.

Motion creates something called **momentum**. This is a calculation of an object's mass multiplied by its velocity. Momentum can be described as the amount an object wants to continue moving along its current course. Momentum in a straight line is called **linear momentum**. Just as energy can be transferred and conserved, so can momentum.

For example, a car and a truck moving at the same velocity down a highway will not have the same momentum, because they do not have the same mass. The mass of the truck is greater than that of the car, therefore the truck will have more momentum. In a head-on collision, the vehicles would be expected to slide in the same direction of the truck's original motion because the truck has a greater momentum.

The amount of force during a length of time creates an **impulse**. This means that if a force acts on an object during a given amount of time, it will have a determined impulse. However, if the length of time can be extended, the force will be less, due to the conservation of momentum.

Consider another example: when catching a fast baseball, it helps soften the blow of the ball to follow through, or cradle the catch. This technique is simply extending the time of the application of the force of the ball, so the impact of the ball does not hurt the hand. As a final example, if a martial arts expert wants to break a board by executing a chop from their hand, they need to exert a force on a small point on the boards, extremely quickly. If they slow down the time of the impact from the force of their hand, they will probably injure their hand and not break the board.

Newton's Three Laws of Motion

Sir Isaac Newton spent a great deal of time studying objects, forces, and how an object's motion responds to forces. Newton made great advancements by using mathematics to describe the motion of objects and to predict future motions of objects by applying his mathematical models to situations. Through his extensive research, Newton is credited for summarizing the basic laws of motion for objects here on Earth. These laws are as follows:

First Law
The first law is the **law of inertia**. An object in motion remains in motion, unless acted upon by an outside force. An object at rest remains at rest, unless acted upon by an outside force. Simply put, inertia is the natural tendency of an object to continue along with what it is already doing; an outside force would have to act upon the object to make it change its course. This includes an object that is sitting still. The inertia of an object is relative to its momentum.

> Example: If a car is driving at a constant speed in a constant direction (also called a constant velocity), it would take a force in a different direction to change the path of the car. Conversely, if the car is sitting

still, it would take a force greater than that of friction from any direction to make that stationary car move.

Second Law

The force (F) on an object is equal to the mass (m) multiplied by the acceleration (a) on that object. **Mass** (m) refers to the amount of a substance and **acceleration** (a) refers to a rate of velocity over time. In the case of an object falling on Earth, the value of gravity will be placed in for acceleration (a). In the case of an object at rest on Earth, gravity is placed in for acceleration (a), and the force calculated by $F = ma$ is called **Weight** (W). It is important to discern that an object's mass (measured in kilograms, kg) is not the same as an object's weight (measured in Newtons, N). Weight is the mass times the gravity.

> Example: The gravity on the earth's moon is considerably less than the gravity on earth. Therefore, the weight of an object on the earth's moon would be considerably less than the weight of the object on earth. In each case, a different value for acceleration/gravity would be used in the equation $F = ma$. Mass is used to calculate weight, and they are not the same.

> Example: If a raisin is dropped into a bowl of pudding, it would make a small indentation and stick in the pudding a bit, but if a grapefruit is dropped into the same bowl of pudding, it would splatter the pudding out of the bowl and most likely hit the bottom of the bowl. Even though both items are accelerating at the same rate (gravity), the mass of the grapefruit is larger than that of the raisin; therefore, the force with which the grapefruit hits the bowl of pudding is considerably larger than the force from the raisin hitting the bowl of pudding.

Third Law

The third law of motion states that for every action there is an equal and opposite reaction. If someone pounds a fist on a table, the reactionary force from the table causes the person to feel a sharp force on the fist. The magnitude of the force felt on the fist increases the harder that they pound on the table. It should be noted that action/reaction pairs occur simultaneously. As the fist applies a force on the table, the table instantaneously applies an equal and opposite force on the fist.

> Example: Imagine a person is wearing ice skates on ice and attempts to push on a heavy sled sitting in front of them. They will be pushed in the direction opposite of their push on the sled; the push the skater is experiencing is equal and opposite to the force they are exerting on the sled. This is a good example of how the icy surface helps to lessen the effects of friction and allows the reactionary force to be more easily observed.

Forces are anything acting upon an object either in motion or at rest; this includes friction and gravity. These forces are often depicted by using a force diagram or free body diagram. A **force diagram** shows an object as the focal point, with arrows denoting all the forces acting upon the object. The direction of the head of the arrow indicates the direction of the force. The object at the center can also be exerting forces on things in its surroundings.

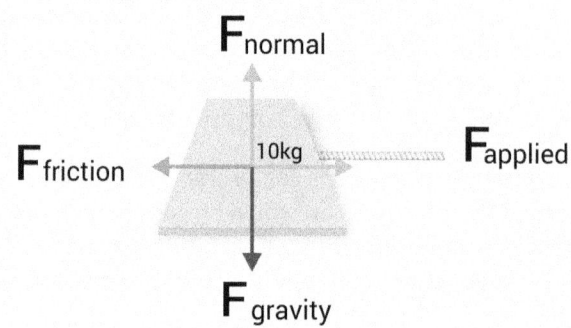

Equilibrium

If an object is in constant motion or at rest (its acceleration equals zero), the object is said to be in **equilibrium**. It does not imply that there are no forces acting upon the object, but that all of the forces are balanced in order for the situation to continue in its current state. This can be thought of as a "balanced'" situation.

Note that if an object is resting on top of a mountain peak or traveling at a constant velocity down the side of that mountain, both situations describe a state of equilibrium.

Falling Objects

Objects falling within the earth's atmosphere are all affected by gravity. Their rate of acceleration will be that of gravity. If two objects were dropped from a great height at the exact same time, regardless of mass, theoretically, they should hit the ground at the same time. This is due to gravity acting upon them at the same rate. In actuality, if this were attempted, the shape of the objects and external factors such as air resistance would affect their rates of fall and cause a discrepancy in when each lands.

Consider the traditional illustration of this principle: a feather and a rock are released at the same time in regular air versus being released at the same time in a vacuum. In the open atmosphere, the feather would slowly loft down to the ground, due to the effects of air resistance, while the rock would quickly drop to the ground. If the feather and the rock were both released at the same time in a vacuum, they would both hit the bottom at the same time. The rate of fall is not dependent upon the mass of the item or any external factors in a vacuum (there is no air resistance in a vacuum); therefore, all that would be affecting the rate of fall would be gravity. Gravity affects every object on the earth with the same rate of acceleration.

Circular Motion

An **axis** is an invisible line on which an object can rotate. This is most easily observed with a toy top. There is actually a point (or rod) through the center of the top on which the top can be observed to be spinning. This is called the axis.

When objects move in a circle by spinning on their own axis, or because they are tethered around a central point (also an axis), they exhibit circular motion. Circular motion is similar in many ways to linear (straight line) motion; however, there are a few additional points to note. A spinning object is always accelerating because it is always changing direction. The force causing this constant acceleration on or around an axis is called **centripetal force** and is often associated with centripetal acceleration. Centripetal force always pulls toward the axis of rotation. An imaginary reactionary force, called **centrifugal force**, is the outward force felt when an object is undergoing circular motion. This reactionary force is not the real force; it just feels like it is there. This has also been referred to as a "**fictional force**." The true force is the one pulling inward, or the centripetal force.

The terms centripetal and centrifugal are often mistakenly interchanged. If the centripetal force acting on an object moving with circular motion is removed, the object will continue moving in a straight line tangent to the point on the circle where the object last experienced the centripetal force. For example, when a traditional style washing machine spins a load of clothes in order to expunge the water from the load, it spins the machine barrel in a circle at a high rate of speed. A force is pulling in toward the center of the circle (centripetal force). At the same time, the wet clothes, which are attempting to move in a straight line, are colliding with the outer wall of the barrel that is moving in a circle. The interaction between the wet clothes and barrel wall causes a reactionary force to the centripetal force and expel the water out of the small holes that line the outer wall of the barrel.

Conservation of Angular Momentum

An object moving in a circular motion also has momentum; for circular motion it is called **angular momentum**. This is determined by rotational inertia and rotational velocity and the distance of the mass from the axis of rotation or center of rotation. When objects are exhibiting circular motion, they also demonstrate the conservation of **angular momentum**, meaning that the angular momentum of a system is always constant, regardless of the placement of the mass. Rotational inertia can be affected by how far the mass of the object is placed with respect to the center of rotation (axis of rotation). The larger the distance between the mass and the center of rotation, the slower the rotational velocity. Conversely, if the mass is closer to the center of rotation, the rotational velocity increases. A change in one affects the other, thus conserving the angular momentum. This holds true as long as no external forces act upon the system.

For example, an ice skater spinning on one ice skate extends their arms out for a slower rotational velocity. When the skater brings their arms in close to their body (or lessens the distance between the mass and the center of rotation), their rotational velocity increases and they spin much faster. Some skaters extend their arms straight up above their head, which causes an extension of the axis of rotation, thus removing any distance between the mass and the center of rotation and maximizing their rotational velocity.

Another example is when a person selects a horse on a merry-go-round: the placement of their horse can affect their ride experience. All of the horses are traveling with the same rotational speed, but in order to travel along the same plane as the merry-go-round turns, a horse on the outside will have a greater linear speed, due to it being farther away from the axis of rotation. Another way to think of it is that an outside horse has to cover a lot more ground than a horse on the inside, in order to keep up with the rotational speed of the merry-go-round platform. Thrill seekers should always select an outer horse.

Energy

The term **energy** typically refers to an object's ability to perform work. This can include a transfer of heat from one object to another, or from an object to its surroundings. Energy is usually measured in Joules. There are two main categories of energy: renewable and non-renewable.

- **Renewable**: energy produced from the exhaustion of a resource that can be replenished. Burning wood to produce heat, then replanting trees to replenish the resource is an instance of using renewable energy.

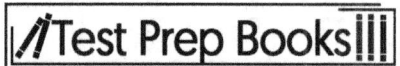

- **Non-renewable**: energy produced from the exhaustion of a resource that cannot be replenished. Burning coal to produce heat would be an example of a non-renewable energy. Although coal is a natural resource that is mined or harvested from the earth, it cannot be regrown or replenished. Other examples include oil and natural gas (fossil fuels).

Temperature is measured in degrees Celsius (°C) or Kelvin (°K). Temperature should not be confused with heat. **Heat** is a form of energy: a change in temperature or a transfer of heat can also be a measure of energy. The amount of energy measured by the change in temperature (or a transfer) is the measure of heat.

Heat energy (thermal energy) can be transferred through the following ways:

Conduction
Conduction is the heating of one object by another through the actual touching of molecules, in order to transfer heat across the objects involved. A spiral burner on an electric stovetop heats from one molecule touching another to transfer the heat via conduction.

Convection
Heat transfer due to the movement/flow of molecules from areas of high concentration to ones of low concentration. Warmer molecules tend to rise, while colder molecules tend to sink. The heat in a house will rise from the vents in the floor to the upper levels of the structure and circulate in that manner, rising and falling with the movement of the molecules. This molecular movement helps to heat or cool a house and is often called **convection current**.

Radiation
The sun warms the earth through **radiation** or radiant energy. Radiation does not need any medium for the heat to travel; therefore, the heat from the sun can radiate to the earth across space.

Greenhouse Effect
The sun transfers heat into the earth's atmosphere through radiation traveling in waves. The atmosphere helps protect the earth from extreme exposure to the sun, while reflecting some of the waves continuously within the atmosphere, creating habitable temperatures. The rest of the waves are meant to dissipate out through the atmosphere and back into space. However, humans have created pollutants and released an overabundance of certain gasses into the earth's atmosphere, causing a layer of blockage. So, the waves that should be leaving the atmosphere continue to bounce back upon the earth repeatedly, thus contributing to global warming. This is a negative effect from the extra re-radiation of the sun's energy and causes planetary overheating.

This additional warming is not something easily or quickly reversed. Because the rate of reflection within the atmosphere only multiplies the more a light wave is bounced around, it will take a concerted effort to undue past reflectance and stop future reflectance of the light waves in the earth's atmosphere. Once the re-reflectance occurs, it duplicates exponentially, along with the additional compounding of more waves. Each degree the atmospheric temperature increases has a profound effect on the delicate balance of our planet, including the melting of polar ice caps, the rise of tidal currents—which cause strong weather systems—and the depletion of specific ecosystems necessary to sustain certain species of animals or insects, to name a few.

Energy can be harnessed to operate objects, and this energy is obtained from various sources such as electricity, food, gasoline, batteries, wind, and sun. For example, wind turbines out in a field are turned by the natural power of the wind. The turbines then store that energy internally in power cells; that stored energy can be used to power the lights on a farm or run machinery.

Potential Energy vs. Kinetic Energy

Potential energy (gravitational potential energy, or PE) is stored energy, or energy due to an object's height above the ground. **Kinetic energy** (KE) is the energy of motion. If an object is moving, it has some amount of kinetic energy.

Consider a rollercoaster car sitting still on the tracks at the top of a hill. The rollercoaster has all potential energy and no kinetic energy. As it travels down the hill, the energy transfers from potential energy into kinetic energy. At the bottom of the hill, where the car is going the fastest, it has all kinetic energy, but no potential energy. If energy losses to the environment (friction, heat, sound) are ignored, the amount of potential energy at the top of the hill equals the amount of kinetic energy at the bottom of the hill.

Mechanical Energy

Mechanical energy is the sum of the potential energy plus the kinetic energy in a system, minus energy lost to non-conservative forces. Often, the effects of non-conservative forces are small enough that they can be ignored. The total mechanical energy of a system is conserved or always the same. The amount of potential energy and the amount of kinetic energy can vary to add up to this total, but the total mechanical energy in the situation remains the same.

$$ME = PE + KE$$

$$Mechanical\ Energy = Potential\ Energy + Kinetic\ Energy$$

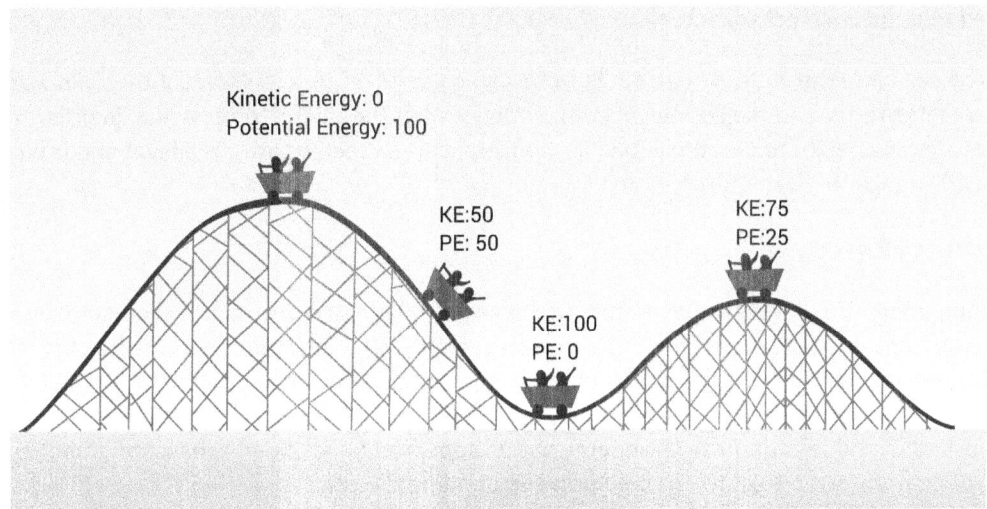

An illustration of a rollercoaster going down a hill demonstrates this point. At the top of the hill a label of $ME = PE$ describes the rollercoaster, halfway down the hill the label $ME = \frac{1}{2}PE + \frac{1}{2}KE$ describes the rollercoaster, and at the bottom of the hill, $ME = KE$ describes the rollercoaster.

Remember, energy can transfer or change forms, but it cannot be created or destroyed. This transfer can take place through waves (including light waves and sound waves), heat, impact, etc.

Simple Machines

The use of simple machines can help by requiring less force to perform a task with the same result. This is also referred to as **mechanical advantage**.

Trying to lift a child into the air to pick an apple from a tree would require less force if the child was placed on the end of a teeter-totter and the adult pushed the other end of the teeter-totter down, in order to elevate the child to the same height to pick the apple. In this instance, the teeter-totter is a lever and provides a mechanical advantage to make the job easier.

Interactions of Energy

There is a fundamental law of **thermodynamics** (the study of heat and movement) called **Conservation of Energy**. This law states that energy cannot be created or destroyed, but rather energy is transferred to different forms involved in a process. For instance, a car pushed beginning at one end of a street will not continue down that street forever; it will gradually come to a stop some distance away from where it was originally pushed. This does not mean the energy has disappeared or has been exhausted; it means the energy has been transferred to different mediums surrounding the car.

The frictional force from the road on the tires dissipates some of the energy, the air resistance from the movement of the car dissipates some of the energy, the sound from the tires on the road dissipates some of the energy, and the force of gravity pulling on the car dissipates some of the energy. Each value can be calculated in a number of ways including measuring the sound waves from the tires, measuring the temperature change in the tires, measuring the distance moved by the car from start to finish, etc. It is important to understand that many processes factor into such a small situation, but all situations follow the conservation of energy.

As in the earlier example, the rollercoaster at the top of a hill has a measurable amount of potential energy, and when it rolls down the hill, it converts most of that energy into kinetic energy. There are still additional factors like friction and air resistance working on the rollercoaster and dissipating some of the energy, but energy transfers in every situation.

Electrostatics

Electrostatics is the study of electric charges at rest. A charge comes from an atom having more or fewer electrons than protons. If an atom has more electrons than protons, it has a negative charge. If an atom has fewer electrons than protons, it has a positive charge. It is important to remember that opposite charges attract each other, while like charges repel each other. So, a negative attracts a positive, a negative repels a negative, and similarly, a positive repels a positive. Just as energy cannot be created or destroyed, neither can charge; charge is transferred. This transfer can be done through touch.

If a person wears socks and scuffs their feet across carpeting, they are transferring electrons to the carpeting through friction. If that person then goes to touch a light switch, they will receive a small shock, which is the electrons transferring from the switch to their hand. The person lost electrons to the carpet, which left them with a positive charge; therefore, the electrons from the switch attract to the person for the transfer. The shock is the electrons jumping from the switch to the person's finger.

Another method of charging an object is through induction. **Induction** is when a charged object is brought near, but not touched to, a neutral conducting object. The charged object will cause the electrons within the conductor to move. If the charged object is negative, the electrons will be induced away from the charged object and vice versa.

Yet another way to charge an object is through polarization. **Polarization** can be achieved by simply reconfiguring the electrons on an object. If a person were to rub a balloon on their hair, the balloon would then stick to a wall. This is because rubbing the balloon causes it to become negatively charged and when the balloon is held against a neutral wall, the negatively charged balloon repels all of the wall's electrons, causing a positively charged surface on the wall. This type of charge would be temporary, due to the massive size of the wall, and the charges would quickly redistribute.

Electric Current

Electrical current is the process by which electrons carry charge. In order to make the electrons move so that they can carry a charge, a change in voltage must be present. On a small scale, this is demonstrated through the electrons travelling from the light switch to a person's finger in the example where the person scuffed their socks on a carpet. The difference between the switch and the finger caused the electrons to move. On a larger and more sustained scale, this movement would need to be more controlled. This can be achieved through batteries/cells and generators. Batteries or cells have a chemical reaction that takes place inside, causing energy to be released and a charge to be able to move freely. Generators convert mechanical energy into electric energy.

If a wire is run from touching the end of a battery to the end of a light bulb, and then another is run from touching the base of the light bulb to the opposite end of the original battery, the light bulb will light up. This is due to a complete circuit being formed with the battery and the electrons being carried across the voltage drop (the two ends of the battery). The appearance of the light from the bulb is the visible heat caused by the friction of the electrons moving through the filament.

Electric Energy

Electric energy can be derived from a number of sources including coal, wind, sun, and nuclear reactions. Electricity has numerous applications, including being able to transfer into light, sound, heat, or magnetic forces.

Magnetic Forces

Magnetic forces can occur naturally in certain types of materials. If two straight rods are made from iron, they will naturally have a negative end (pole) and a positive end (pole). These charged poles react just like any charged item: opposite charges attract and like charges repel. They will attract each other when set up positive to negative, but if one rod is turned around, the two rods will repel each other due to the alignment of negative to negative and positive to positive.

These types of forces can also be created and amplified by using an electric current.

The relationship between magnetic forces and electrical forces can be explored by sending an electric current through a stretch of wire, which creates an electromagnetic force around the wire from the charge of the current, as long as the flow of electricity is sustained. This magnetic force can also attract and repel other items with magnetic properties. Depending upon the strength of the current in the wire, a smaller or larger magnetic force can be generated around this wire. As soon as the current is cut off, the magnetic force also stops.

Magnetic Energy

Magnetic energy can be harnessed, or controlled, from natural sources or from a generated source (a wire carrying electric current). Magnetic forces are used in many modern applications, including the creation of super-speed transportation. Super-magnets are used in rail systems and supply a cleaner form of energy than coal or gasoline.

Sound/Acoustic Energy

Just like light, sound travels in waves and both are forms of energy. The transmittance of a sound wave produced when plucking a guitar string sends vibrations at a specific frequency through the air, resulting in one's ear hearing a specific note or sets of notes that form a chord. If the same guitar is plugged into an electric amplifier, the strength of the wave is increased, producing what is perceived as a "louder" note. If a glass of water is set on the amplifier, the production of the sound wave can also be visually observed in the vibrations in the water. If the guitar were being plucked loudly enough and in great succession, the force created by the vibrations of the sound waves could even knock the glass off of the amplifier.

Waves can travel through different mediums. When they reach a different material (i.e., light traveling from air to water), they can bend around and through the new material. This is called **refraction**.

If one observes a straw in half a glass of water from above, the straw appears to be bent at the height of the water. The straw is still straight, but the observation of light passing from air to water (different materials) makes the straw seem as though it bends at the water line. This illusion occurs because the human eye can perceive the light travels differently through the two materials. The light might slow down in one material, or refract or reflect off of the material, causing differences in an object's appearance.

In another example, imagine a car driving straight along a paved road. If one or two of the tires hit the gravel along the side of the road, the entire car will pull in that direction, due to the tires in the gravel now traveling slower than the tires on the paved road. This is what happens when light travels from one medium to another: its path becomes warped, like the path of the car, rather than traveling in a straight line. This is why a straw appears to be bent when the light travels from water to air; the path is warped.

When waves encounter a barrier, like a closed door, parts of the wave may travel through tiny openings. Once a wave has moved through a narrow opening, the wave begins to spread out and may cause interference. This process is called **diffraction**.

Science as an Endeavor, Process, and Career

People of all cultures around the world utilize science in order to explore questions and find solutions to problems. The systematic process of designing, conducting, and analyzing experiments is universally known

Science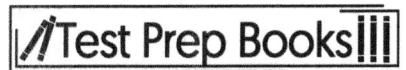

and respected. These processes are time-consuming and require specific knowledge and skills. Therefore, the pursuit of science is its own career path, with many smaller paths for each respective area of study (i.e., life sciences, chemical sciences, physical sciences). Of course, each of those paths splits into even more refined areas and requires much study and dedication. Men and women alike pursue scientific questions; some are driven by pure curiosity and others are compelled by finding a faster, or even a more economical way, of performing a task or producing an object.

Not all ideas, methods, or results are popular or accepted by society. Thus, the pursuit of science is often riddled with controversy. This has been an underlying theme since the early days of astronomical discovery. Copernicus was excommunicated from his religious establishment when he announced the belief that the sun, not the Earth, was the controlling body of the heavens known to humans at the time. Despite his having documented observations and calculations, those opposed to his theory could not be convinced. Copernicus experienced great ridicule and suffering due to his scientific research and assertions. In addition, other scientists have faced adverse scrutiny for their assertions including Galileo, Albert Einstein, and Stephen Hawking. In each case, logical thought, observations, and calculations have been used to demonstrate their ideas, yet opposition to their scientific beliefs still exists.

The possibilities for careers involving science range from conducting research, to the application of science and research (engineering), to academia (teaching). All of these avenues require intensive study and a thorough understanding of the respective branch of science and its components. An important factor of studying and applying science is being able to concisely and accurately communicate knowledge to other people. Many times this is done utilizing mathematics or even through demonstration. The necessity of communicating ideas, research, and results brings people from all nationalities together. This often lends to different cultures finding common ground for research and investigation, and opens lines of communication and cooperation.

Science as Inquiry

Scientific questions can be derived from a multitude of sources including observation, experience, or even just wondering how something is made or works. In order to answer these questions, experiments should be designed and conducted to try to achieve a solution. At the end of an experiment, there often is no clear solution and a new experiment must be designed to test the same question. If a sound, logical solution is reached through experimentation, then it must be repeatable, by the experimenter and any other person wishing to test this solution. This entire process is commonly referred to as the **scientific method**.

A question or situation exists, a **hypothesis** (or a well-educated guess) is formulated, an **experiment** is designed to test this guess, a prediction is made as to what the outcome might be based upon research, and a conclusion is formed (either the guess was correct or not). This simple method is repeated over and over, as much as necessary for each question, idea, or proposed investigation.

An experiment must be carefully designed to include concerns for safety, use of proper instrumentation for measurement, systematic methods of documentation or data collection, appropriate mathematics for analysis of data and for the interpretation to draw valid conclusions. These conclusions must be explainable and verifiable by an outside source.

The importance of having an independent party test a solution is one of the critical parts of scientific inquiry. This ensures an experiment is free from bias, truly repeatable, and documentable to multiple sources. Without this confirmation, people could make erroneous claims and cause disastrous results. There would be no order to the inquiry of science.

In scientific experimentation, safety, respect for living things, and the effect on an environment must be acknowledged and protected, as necessary. There exist universal rules for research in order to preserve these underlying tenets. Most researchers or facilities that demonstrate an adherence to these rules garner the most support from others in the scientific community when accepting ideas.

Research

Part of the process of scientific inquiry is researching a problem or question. Before an experiment can be designed, proper research should be conducted into the question. The initial question needs to be well formed and based in logical reasoning. A literature review should be conducted on existing material pertaining to the subject in question, and confirmation of any experimentation on the question that has been conducted prior should be made. If prior experimentation exists, what were the results obtained and were any conclusions drawn from those results? In addition, research should be done on all possible information regarding the initial question, the experiment, how to investigate the question, and what tools will be necessary to draw conclusions and explain any findings. Just as an experiment must be unbiased, so should any research regarding the experiment. All sources of information need to be proven reliable and accredited. For instance, a person's account of their opinion on a situation does not constitute as a valid source for research. Sources should be free of opinion or speculation.

During experimentation, research should be conducted with appropriate mechanisms for observation and measurement. Knowing the proper tools and units for accurately measuring a volume or a mass is a fundamental skill of research. Researchers also need to be held to standards of ethics and honesty. The independent repetition of an experiment helps to ensure this level of accountability. Often, the most reliable resources are those of accredited experimenters, universities, and other research laboratories. In order for such sources to publish information, they should demonstrate strict adherence to scientific methods, precise measurements for observations, and specific mathematical reporting.

It is often common for different scientists in the same place, or even separate countries, to be conducting experiments to test the same hypothesis. This does not always lead to a race to see who finishes first, but it can lead to cooperative research and shared accolades if the results prove successful. Awards for research, discoveries, and scientific application are often used by the scientific community to show appreciation for advancements in science.

Unifying Process of Science

Following the scientific method, and keeping to the standards of proper research and reporting, lends to easier communication of data and results. When information can be conveyed to multiple audiences in a manner of common understanding (i.e., mathematics), it increases the possibilities for the use of such information. Having other scientists understand an idea can also lead to further experimentation and discovery in that area. This leads to the further organization of information and a deeper understanding of our universe.

It is more systematic to group, sort, and organize information for commonalities in order to increase understanding. The organization of groups can also serve as a reference point when attempting to identify other members of that group. For instance, a newly discovered type of rock can be compared to known rocks and then better categorized as to its uses or properties, based upon how it appears and responds in experiments, when measured against known rocks. This occurs regularly when varying crystal rock structures are developed for use in super-cooled or super-conductive experiments because certain properties are more useful with regard to conduction and strength. In order to have knowledge and access to this type of variation of information, societies are formed and people from all over the world find ways to communicate and share in the scientific endeavor.

The communication of research can further questions and explorations across the world. This common goal of reaching new discoveries or uses for the application of science can bring people together. Oftentimes, the quest for scientific discovery is spawned by competition or the race to create something before another society or country. Examples of this include the race to explore space, the race for nuclear armaments, and the race to create and cure strains of deadly bacteria. In these situations, the urge to push scientific discovery ahead may not be for the most humanitarian motives; however, oftentimes these research prompts result in accidental discoveries that can solve other problems. The discoveries of vaccinations, stronger materials such as plastics, and cleaner forms of energy through superconducting crystals have all been accidental discoveries along the way of competitive scientific research. Whatever the motive for scientific discovery, it can be seen as a common thread across many nations with a potential to create unity through its demand for structure and organization.

Practice Quiz

1. How many daughter cells are formed from one parent cell during meiosis?
    a. One
    b. Two
    c. Three
    d. Four

2. What is the total mechanical energy of a system?
    a. The total potential energy
    b. The total kinetic energy
    c. Kinetic energy plus potential energy
    d. Kinetic energy minus potential energy

3. What does the Lewis dot structure of an element represent?
    a. The outer electron valence shell population
    b. The inner electron valence shell population
    c. The positioning of the element's protons
    d. The positioning of the element's neutrons

4. Which rock is formed from cooling magma underneath the Earth's surface?
    a. Extrusive sedimentary rocks
    b. Sedimentary rocks
    c. Igneous rocks
    d. Metamorphic rocks

5. Which of the following is most abundant in the Earth's atmosphere?
    a. Carbon dioxide
    b. Oxygen
    c. Nitrogen
    d. Water

See answers on next page.

Answer Explanations

1. D: Meiosis has the same phases as mitosis, except that they occur twice—once in meiosis I and once in meiosis II. During meiosis I, the cell splits into two. Each cell contains two sets of chromosomes. Next, during meiosis II, the two intermediate daughter cells divide again, producing four total haploid cells that each contain one set of chromosomes.

2. C: In any system, the total mechanical energy is the sum of the potential energy and the kinetic energy. Either value could be zero, but it still must be included in the total. Choices A and B only give the total potential or kinetic energy, respectively. Choice D gives the difference between the kinetic and potential energy.

3. A: A Lewis Dot structure shows the alignment of the valence (outer) shell electrons and how readily they can pair or bond with the valence shell electrons of other atoms to form a compound. Choice B is incorrect because the inner shell does not help us understand how likely an atom is to bond with another atom. The positioning of protons and neutrons concerns the nucleus of the atom, which again would not relate to the likelihood of bonding.

4. C: Igneous rocks are formed from the cooling of magma, both on and below the Earth's surface, which are classified as extrusive and intrusive, respectively. Sedimentary rocks are formed from deposition and cementation on the surface, and metamorphic rocks are formed from the transformation of sedimentary or igneous rocks through heat and pressure.

5. C: Nitrogen is the most abundant element in the atmosphere at 78%. Carbon dioxide and water don't make up a large percentage. Oxygen makes up only 21% of the atmosphere.

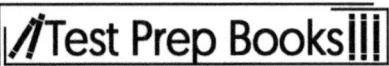

Practice Test #1

Practice Test #1

Mathematics

1. Which of the following numbers has the greatest value?
    a. 1.43785
    b. 1.07548
    c. 1.43592
    d. 0.89409

2. The value of 6×12 is the same as:
    a. $2 \times 4 \times 4 \times 2$
    b. $7 \times 4 \times 3$
    c. $6 \times 6 \times 3$
    d. $3 \times 3 \times 4 \times 2$

3. Which of the following values is the largest?
    a. 0.45
    b. 0.096
    c. 0.3
    d. 0.313

4. What is the value of b in this equation?

$$5b - 4 = 2b + 17$$

   a. 13
   b. 24
   c. 7
   d. 21

5. In 2015, it was estimated that there were 7,350,000,000 people living on Earth. Express this value in scientific notation.
    a. 7.35×10^7
    b. 7.35×10^9
    c. 73.5×10^8
    d. 73.5×10^9

6. Express the following in decimal form:

$$\frac{3}{5} \times \frac{7}{10} \div \frac{1}{2}$$

   a. 0.042
   b. 84%
   c. 0.84
   d. 0.42

Practice Test #1

7. What is the product of two irrational numbers?
    a. Irrational
    b. Rational
    c. Irrational or rational
    d. Complex and imaginary

8. The number –4 can be classified as which of the following?
    a. Real, rational, integer, whole, natural
    b. Real, rational, integer, natural
    c. Real, rational, integer
    d. Real, irrational

9. 20 is 40% of what number?
    a. 50
    b. 8
    c. 200
    d. 5,000

10. What is the product of the following expressions?

$$(4x - 8)(5x^2 + x + 6)$$

    a. $20x^3 - 36x^2 + 16x - 48$
    b. $6x^3 - 41x^2 + 12x + 15$
    c. $20x^3 + 11x^2 - 37x - 12$
    d. $2x^3 - 11x^2 - 32x + 20$

11. What is the solution for the following equation?

$$\frac{x^2 + x - 30}{x - 5} = 11$$

    a. $x = -6$
    b. There is no solution.
    c. $x = 16$
    d. $x = 5$

12. Simplify $(1.2 \times 10^{12}) \div (3.0 \times 10^8)$ and write the result in scientific notation.
    a. 0.4×10^4
    b. 4.0×10^4
    c. 4.0×10^3
    d. 3.6×10^{20}

13. Give a numerical expression for the following: "Six less than three times the sum of twice a number and one."
    a. $2x + 1 - 6$
    b. $3x + 1 - 6$
    c. $3(x + 1) - 6$
    d. $3(2x + 1) - 6$

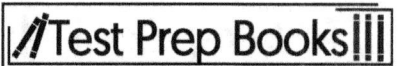

Practice Test #1

14. What is $4 \times 7 + (25 - 21)^2 \div 2$?
    a. 512
    b. 36
    c. 60.5
    d. 22

15. What value of x would solve the following equation?

$$9x + x - 7 = 16 + 2x$$

    a. $x = -4$
    b. $x = 3$
    c. $x = \frac{9}{8}$
    d. $x = \frac{23}{8}$

16. Arrange the following numbers from least to greatest value:

$$0.85, \frac{4}{5}, \frac{2}{3}, \frac{91}{100}$$

    a. $0.85, \frac{4}{5}, \frac{2}{3}, \frac{91}{100}$
    b. $\frac{4}{5}, 0.85, \frac{91}{100}, \frac{2}{3}$
    c. $\frac{2}{3}, \frac{4}{5}, 0.85, \frac{91}{100}$
    d. $0.85, \frac{91}{100}, \frac{4}{5}, \frac{2}{3}$

17. Keith's bakery had 252 customers go through its doors last week. This week, that number increased to 378. Express this increase as a percentage.
    a. 26%
    b. 50%
    c. 35%
    d. 12%

18. Simplify the following fraction:

$$\frac{\left(\frac{5}{7}\right)}{\left(\frac{9}{11}\right)}$$

    a. $\frac{55}{63}$
    b. $\frac{7}{1,000}$
    c. $\frac{13}{15}$
    d. $\frac{5}{11}$

168

Practice Test #1

19. If $\frac{5}{2} \div \frac{1}{3} = n$, then n is between:
   a. 5 and 7
   b. 7 and 9
   c. 9 and 11
   d. 3 and 5

20. This chart indicates how many sales of CDs, vinyl records, and MP3 downloads occurred over the last year. Approximately what percentage of the total sales was from CDs?

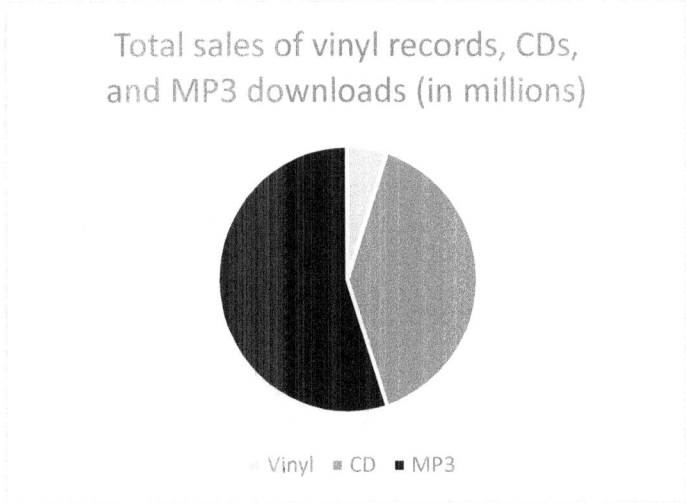

   a. 55%
   b. 25%
   c. 40%
   d. 5%

21. Express $\frac{54}{15}$ as a mixed number, reduced to lowest terms.
   a. $3\frac{3}{5}$
   b. $3\frac{1}{15}$
   c. $3\frac{3}{54}$
   d. $3\frac{1}{54}$

22. Express as an improper fraction: $8\frac{3}{7}$
   a. $\frac{11}{7}$
   b. $\frac{21}{8}$
   c. $\frac{5}{3}$
   d. $\frac{59}{7}$

23. $52.3 \times 10^{-3} =$
   a. 0.00523
   b. 0.0523
   c. 0.523
   d. 523

24. Mom's car drove 72 miles in 90 minutes. How fast did she drive in feet per second?
   a. 0.8 feet per second
   b. 48.9 feet per second
   c. 0.009 feet per second
   d. 70.4 feet per second

25. For the following similar triangles, what are the values of x and y (rounded to the nearest tenth)?

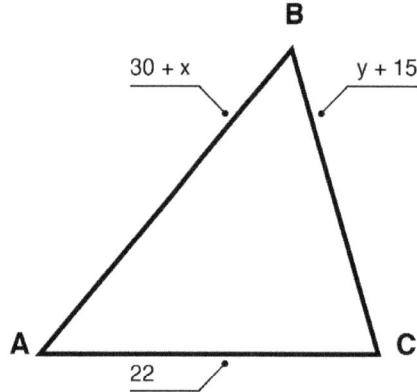
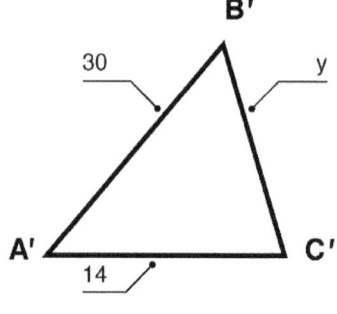

   a. $x = 16.5, y = 25.1$
   b. $x = 19.5, y = 24.1$
   c. $x = 17.1, y = 26.3$
   d. $x = 26.3, y = 17.1$

26. The triangle shown below is a right triangle. What's the value of x?

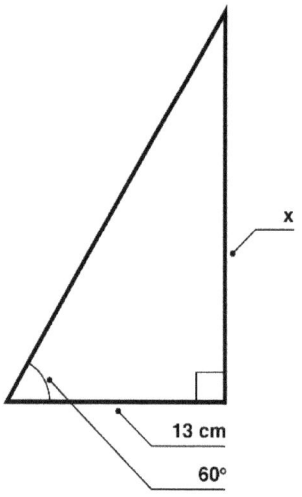

   a. $x = 1.73$ cm
   b. $x = 0.57$ cm
   c. $x = 13$ cm
   d. $x = 22.52$ cm

Practice Test #1

27. What is the solution to $9 \times 9 \div 9 + 9 - 9 \div 9$?
    a. 0
    b. 17
    c. 81
    d. 9

28. The total perimeter of a rectangle is 36 cm. If the length is 12 cm, what is the width?
    a. 3 cm
    b. 12 cm
    c. 6 cm
    d. 8 cm

29. A hospital has a bed-to-room ratio of 2 : 1. If there are 145 rooms, how many beds are there?
    a. 145 beds
    b. 2 beds
    c. 90 beds
    d. 290 beds

30. A shuffled deck of 52 cards contains 4 kings. One card is drawn and is not put back in the deck. Then, a second card is drawn. What's the probability that both cards are kings?
    a. $\frac{1}{169}$
    b. $\frac{1}{221}$
    c. $\frac{1}{13}$
    d. $\frac{4}{13}$

31. For a group of 20 men, the median weight is 180 pounds, and the range is 30 pounds. If each man gains 10 pounds, which of the following would be true?
    a. The median weight will increase, and the range will remain the same.
    b. The median weight and range will both remain the same.
    c. The median weight will stay the same, and the range will increase.
    d. The median weight and range will both increase.

32. What operation are students taught to repeat to evaluate an expression involving an exponent?
    a. Addition
    b. Multiplication
    c. Division
    d. Subtraction

33. If the point $(-3, -4)$ is reflected over the x-axis, what new point does it make?
    a. $(-3, -4)$
    b. $(3, -4)$
    c. $(3, 4)$
    d. $(-3, 4)$

34. The graph shows the position of a car over a 10-second time interval. Which of the following is the correct interpretation of the graph for the interval 1 to 3 seconds?

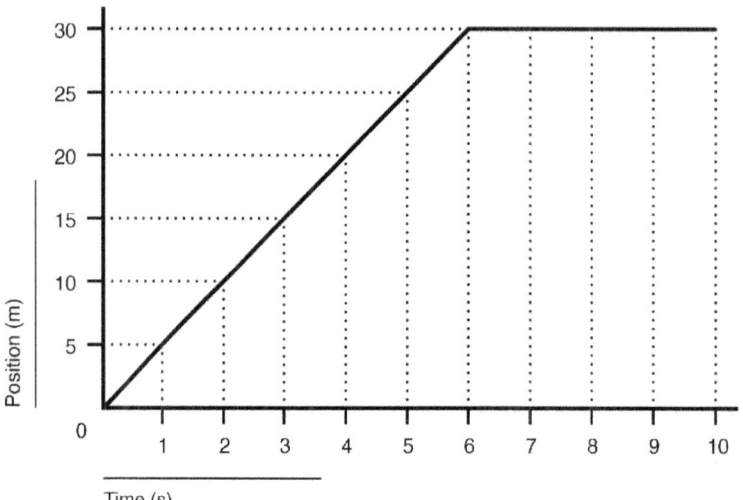

a. The car remains in the same position.
b. The car is traveling at a speed of 5 m/s.
c. The car is traveling up a hill.
d. The car is traveling at 5 mph.

35. Give a numerical expression for the following: "Six less than three times the sum of twice a number and one."
a. $2x + 1 - 6$
b. $3x + 1 - 6$
c. $3(x + 1) - 6$
d. $3(2x + 1) - 6$

36. A cube has sides that are 7 inches long. What is the cube's volume?
a. 49 in^3
b. 343 in^3
c. 294 in^3
d. 28 in^3

37. Approximately how many kilometers is 4,382 feet? There are 0.3048 meters in 1 foot.
a. 1.336 kilometers
b. 14,376 kilometers
c. 1.437 kilometers
d. 13,336 kilometers

38. What is the y-intercept for $y = x^2 + 3x - 4$?
a. $y = -3$
b. $y = -4$
c. $y = 3$
d. $y = 4$

Practice Test #1

39. Five students take a test. The scores of the first four students are 80, 85, 75, and 60. If the median score is 80, which of the following could NOT be the score of the fifth student?
   a. 60
   b. 80
   c. 85
   d. 100

40. Karen gets paid a weekly salary and a commission for every sale that she makes. The table below shows the number of sales and her pay for different weeks. The amount she makes can be represented by a linear equation. The table below shows the number of sales and her pay for different weeks.

Sales	2	7	4	8
Pay	$380	$580	$460	$620

Which of the following equations represents Karen's weekly pay?
   a. $y = 90x + 200$
   b. $y = 90x - 200$
   c. $y = 40x + 300$
   d. $y = 40x - 300$

41. Alan currently weighs 200 pounds, but he wants to lose weight to get down to 175 pounds. What is this difference in kilograms? (1 pound is approximately equal to 0.45 kilograms.)
   a. 9 kg
   b. 11.25 kg
   c. 78.75 kg
   d. 90 kg

42. Johnny earns $2,334.50 from his job each month. He pays $1,437 for monthly expenses and saves the rest. Johnny is planning a vacation in 3 months that he estimates will cost $1,750 total. How much will Johnny have left over from 3 months of saving once he pays for his vacation?
   a. $948.50
   b. $584.50
   c. $852.50
   d. $942.50

43. A line passes through the point $(1, 2)$ and crosses the y-axis at $y = 1$. Which of the following is an equation for this line?
   a. $y = 2x$
   b. $y = x + 1$
   c. $x + y = 1$
   d. $y = \frac{x}{2} - 2$

44. A line that travels from the lower left of a graph to the upper right of the graph indicates what kind of relationship between an independent and a dependent variable?
   a. Positive
   b. Negative
   c. Exponential
   d. Logarithmic

45. Which of the following is the best description of the relationship between x and y?

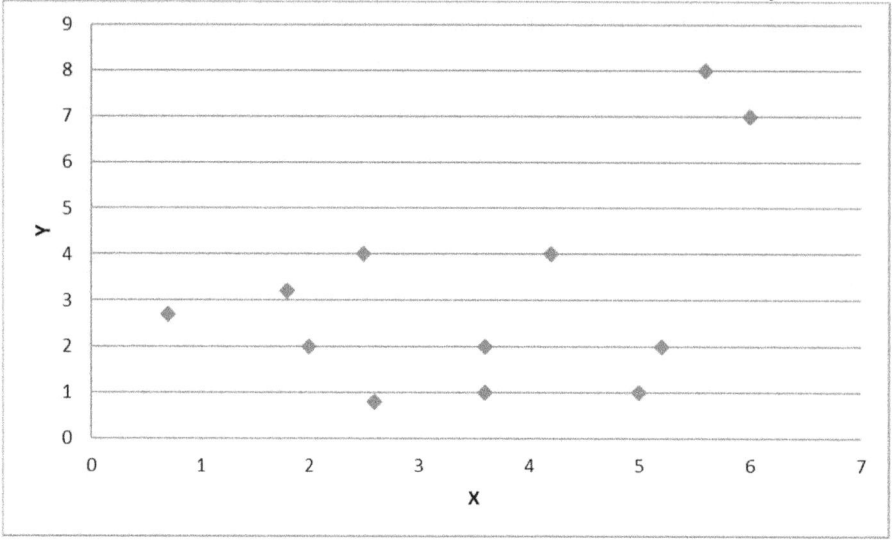

   a. The data has normal distribution.
   b. x and y have a negative relationship.
   c. x and y have no apparent relationship.
   d. x and y have a positive relationship.

46. How do you solve $V = lwh$ for h?
   a. $lwV = h$
   b. $h = \frac{V}{lw}$
   c. $h = \frac{Vl}{w}$
   d. $h = \frac{Vw}{l}$

47. What type of function is modeled by the values in the following table?

x	$f(x)$
1	2
2	4
3	8
4	16
5	32

   a. Linear
   b. Exponential
   c. Quadratic
   d. Cubic

48. Which of the following is a factor of both $x^2 + 4x + 4$ and $x^2 - x - 6$?
   a. $x - 3$
   b. $x + 2$
   c. $x - 2$
   d. $x + 3$

Practice Test #1

49. If $4x - 3 = 5$, what is the value of x?
    a. 1
    b. 2
    c. 3
    d. 4

50. A ball is drawn at random from a ball pit containing 8 red balls, 7 yellow balls, 6 green balls, and 5 purple balls. What's the probability that the ball drawn is yellow?
    a. $\frac{1}{26}$
    b. $\frac{19}{26}$
    c. $\frac{7}{26}$
    d. 1

Social Studies

1. An elementary teacher is planning a social studies lesson on individuals who have had an important historical influence to the state of Georgia. All EXCEPT which of the following individuals should be discussed in this lesson?
    a. Andrew Jackson
    b. John White
    c. William T. Sherman
    d. Booker T. Washington

2. What is NOT a responsibility for citizens of democracy?
    a. To stay aware of current issues and history
    b. To avoid political action
    c. To actively vote in elections
    d. To understand and obey laws

Question 3 is based on the following passage:

> We hold these truths to be self-evident, that all men are created equal, that they are endowed by their Creator with certain unalienable Rights, that among these are Life, Liberty and the pursuit of Happiness.—That to secure these rights, Governments are instituted among Men, deriving their just powers from the consent of the governed,—That whenever any Form of Government becomes destructive of these ends, it is the Right of the People to alter or to abolish it, and to institute new Government, laying its foundation on such principles and organizing its powers in such form, as to them shall seem most likely to effect their Safety and Happiness.
>
> Prudence, indeed, will dictate that Governments long established should not be changed for light and transient causes; and accordingly all experience hath shown that mankind are more disposed to suffer, while evils are sufferable, than to right themselves by abolishing the forms to which they are accustomed. But when a long train of abuses and usurpations, pursuing invariably the same Object evinces a design to reduce them under absolute Despotism, it is their right, it is their duty, to throw off such Government and to provide new Guards for their future security.

Excerpt from the United States Excerpt from the United States Declaration of Independence, adopted July 4, 1776

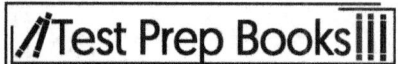

3. What is the main purpose of the excerpt?
   a. Provide a justification for revolution when the government infringes on "certain inalienable rights"
   b. Provide specific evidence of the "train of abuses"
   c. Provide an argument why "all Men are created equal"
   d. Provide an analysis of the importance of "life, liberty, and the pursuit of happiness"

4. Which member of British parliament convinced King George II in 1732 to colonize the area that is now Georgia with individuals from Britain's overflowing debtor prisons?
   a. James Oglethorpe
   b. Button Gwinnett
   c. George Walton
   d. Lyman Hall

5. A fourth-grade teacher is having students work in small groups to research and present about historical figures instrumental in leading the charge for discussion at the Constitutional Convention held in Philadelphia in 1787. Which of the following gentlemen would NOT be assigned to a group for this project?
   a. George Washington
   b. Alexander Hamilton
   c. Thomas Jefferson
   d. James Madison

6. A text read in a third-grade classroom is introducing readers to an American Indian tribe that led a nomadic lifestyle and lived in teepees that were easily moved from place to place. In which region did this tribe likely live?
   a. Plains
   b. Southwest
   c. Eastern
   d. Northwest

7. What was Britain's first permanent settlement in North America?
   a. Plymouth, Massachusetts
   b. Roanoke, Virginia
   c. Jamestown, Virginia
   d. L'Anse Meadows, Newfoundland

8. Fourth-grade students are creating timelines with landmark events of the American Revolution. Under which of the following events should they notate as where the first shot took place?
   a. At the Boston Massacre
   b. During the Boston Tea Party
   c. On Lexington Green
   d. At the Battle of Trenton

9. How many times has the US Constitution been amended in order to accommodate changes and updates?
   a. 14
   b. 18
   c. 21
   d. 27

Practice Test #1

10. Which type of map illustrates the world's climatological regions?
    a. Topographic map
    b. Conformal projection
    c. Isoline map
    d. Thematic map

11. In which manner is absolute location expressed?
    a. The cardinal directions (north, south, east, and west)
    b. Through latitudinal and longitudinal coordinates
    c. Location nearest to a more well-known location
    d. Hemispherical position on the globe

12. Which of these is NOT a true statement about culture?
    a. Culture derives from the beliefs, values, and behaviors of people in a community.
    b. All people are born into a certain culture.
    c. Cultures are stagnant and cannot be changed.
    d. Culture can be embedded within families, schools, businesses, social classes, and religions.

13. Latitudinal lines are used to measure distance in which direction?
    a. East to west
    b. North to south
    c. Between two sets of coordinates
    d. In an inexact manner

14. Which of the following statements most accurately describes the Achaemenid Empire in Persia until the fourth century BC?
    a. Islam was the official religion.
    b. Achaemenid emperors constructed the entire Silk Road network.
    c. The Achaemenid Empire successfully conquered Greece.
    d. None of the above

15. The Silk Roads caused which of the following?
    a. Spread of Buddhism from India to China
    b. The devastation of European economies
    c. Introduction of the Bubonic Plague to the New World
    d. The Great War

16. What caused the end of the Western Roman Empire in 476 AD?
    a. Invasions by Germanic tribes
    b. The Mongol invasion
    c. The assassination of Julius Caesar
    d. Introduction of Taoism in Rome

17. Which of the following statements most accurately describes the Mongol Empire?
    a. The Mongol army was largely a cavalry force.
    b. Mongol rulers did not tolerate other religions.
    c. Mongol rulers neglected foreign trade.
    d. The Mongol Empire is known for its discouragement of literacy and the arts.

18. Renaissance scholars and artists were inspired by which classical civilization?
    a. Ancient Greece
    b. Ancient Egypt
    c. The Zhou Dynasty
    c. The Ottoman Empire

19. Which of the following was a consequence of increasing nationalism in Europe in the 1800s?
    a. The unification of Spain
    b. The unification of France
    c. Increasing competition and tension between European powers
    d. More efficient trade between nations

20. Which of the following pieces of information can most likely be derived from a map indicating the addresses of persons infected with a disease?
    a. The disease's morbidity rate
    b. The disease's mortality rate
    c. Trends in victim's social status
    d. Proximity to a source of infection

21. Which political concept describes a ruling body's ability to influence the actions, behaviors, or attitudes of a person or community?
    a. Authority
    b. Sovereignty
    c. Power
    d. Legitimacy

22. Which feature differentiates a state from a nation?
    a. Shared history
    b. Common language
    c. Population
    d. Sovereignty

23. Which of the following was a consequence of World War II?
    a. The collapse of British and French empires in Asia and Africa
    b. A communist revolution in Russia
    c. The end of the Cold War
    d. The death of Franz Ferdinand, the Archduke of Austria

24. Which best describes ethnic groups?
    a. Subgroups within a population who share a common history, language, or religion
    b. Divisive groups within a nation's boundaries seeking independence
    c. People who choose to leave a location
    d. Any minority group within a nation's boundaries

25. In recent years, agricultural production has been affected by which of the following?
    a. The prevalence of biotechnology and GMOs
    b. Weaker crop yields due to poor soil
    c. Plagues of pests, which have limited food production
    d. Revolutions in irrigation, which utilize salinated water

26. Which of the following is NOT part of the Ring of Fire?
    a. Hawaii
    b. Taiwan
    c. Okinawa
    d. Easter Island

27. Which of the following is the subgroup of economics that studies large-scale economic issues such as unemployment, interest rates, price levels, and national income?
    a. Microeconomics
    b. Macroeconomics
    c. Scarcity
    d. Supply and demand

28. Which kind of market does NOT involve government interventions or monopolies while trades are made between suppliers and buyers?
    a. Free
    b. Command
    c. Gross
    d. Exchange

29. Which is NOT an indicator of economic growth?
    a. GDP (Gross Domestic Product)
    b. Unemployment
    c. Inflation
    d. Theory of the Firm

30. Which of the following consequences did NOT result from the discovery of the New World in 1492 AD?
    a. Proof that the world was round instead of flat
    b. The deaths of millions of Native Americans
    c. Biological exchange between Europe and the New World
    d. The creation of new syncretic religions

31. Which of the following was NOT a consequence of industrialization in Europe during the 1800s?
    a. The birth of the working class
    b. The expansion of European empires in Africa and Asia
    c. Improved transportation and economic efficiency
    d. The reduction of child labor

32. Which check does the legislative branch possess over the judicial branch?
    a. Appoint judges.
    b. Call special sessions of Congress.
    c. Rule legislation unconstitutional.
    d. Determine the number of Supreme Court judges.

33. Which of the following is NOT included in the Bill of Rights?
    a. Freedom to assemble
    b. Freedom against unlawful search
    c. Freedom to vote
    d. Reservation of non-enumerated powers to the states or the people

34. The United States elects the president by which of the following ways?
   a. Popular majority vote
   b. Plurality vote
   c. Electoral College
   d. Party list system

Question 35 is based on the following passage:

> Hand in hand with this we must frankly recognize the overbalance of population in our industrial centers and, by engaging on a national scale in a redistribution, endeavor to provide a better use of the land for those best fitted for the land. The task can be helped by definite efforts to raise the values of agricultural products and with this the power to purchase the output of our cities. It can be helped by preventing realistically the tragedy of the growing loss through foreclosure of our small homes and our farms. It can be helped by insistence that the Federal, State, and local governments act forthwith on the demand that their cost be drastically reduced. It can be helped by the unifying of relief activities which today are often scattered, uneconomical, and unequal. It can be helped by national planning for and supervision of all forms of transportation and of communications and other utilities which have a definitely public character. There are many ways in which it can be helped, but it can never be helped merely by talking about it. We must act and act quickly.
>
> Finally, in our progress toward a resumption of work we require two safeguards against a return of the evils of the old order; there must be a strict supervision of all banking and credits and investments; there must be an end to speculation with other people's money, and there must be provision for an adequate but sound currency.
>
> Excerpt from President Franklin D. Roosevelt's Inaugural Address, March 4, 1933

35. Which of the following best describes President Roosevelt's underlying approach to government?
   a. Government must be focused on redistribution of land.
   b. Government must "act and act quickly" to intervene and regulate the economy.
   c. Government must exercise "strict supervision of all banking."
   d. Government must prevent the "growing loss through foreclosure."

36. In the American election system, where do the candidates ultimately receive the nomination from their party?
   a. At the primary
   b. At the caucus
   c. At the debates
   d. At the party convention

37. Which part of the legislative process differs in the House and the Senate?
   a. Who may introduce the bill
   b. How debates about a bill are conducted
   c. Who may veto the bill
   d. What wording the bill contains

38. Which of the following is the primary problem with map projections?
    a. They are not detailed.
    b. They do not include physical features.
    c. They distort areas near the poles.
    d. They only focus on the Northern Hemisphere.

39. Literacy rates are more likely to be higher in which area?
    a. Developing nations
    b. Northern Hemispherical Nations
    c. Developed Nations
    d. Near centers of trade

40. All of the following are negative demographic indicators EXCEPT which of the following?
    a. High infant mortality rates
    b. Low literacy rates
    c. High population density
    d. Low life expectancy

41. Which of the following is NOT a factor in a location's climate?
    a. Latitudinal position
    b. Elevation
    c. Longitudinal position
    d. Proximity to mountains

42. All but which of the following are true of the Tropics?
    a. They are consistently hit with direct rays of the sun.
    b. They fall between the Tropics of Cancer and Capricorn.
    c. They are nearer the Equator than the Middle Latitudes.
    d. They are always warmer than other parts of the Globe.

43. The "tragedy of the commons" is best described by which of the following statements?
    a. Resources held in common are liable to be depleted beyond recovery by individuals.
    b. Societies rarely value resources that are commonly found in their environment.
    c. It is not possible to maintain resources in common and also industrialize the economy.
    d. Individuals tend to migrate toward communities that hold the greatest quantity of resources in common.

44. Which of the following is a function of a nation after it has been formed rather than a shared characteristic that would be helpful in the formation of a nation?
    a. Culture and traditions
    b. History
    c. Sovereignty
    d. Beliefs and religion

45. Of the following ideologies, which one advocates for the most radical government intervention to achieve social and economic equality?
    a. Socialism
    b. Liberalism
    c. Libertarianism
    d. Fascism

46. Of the following ideologies, which one prioritizes stability and traditional institutions within a culture?
    a. Socialism
    b. Liberalism
    c. Conservatism
    d. Libertarianism

47. The central government established under the Articles of Confederation held which of the following powers?
    a. The power to impose taxes
    b. The power to declare war
    c. The power to regulate trade
    d. The power to enforce laws enacted by Congress

48. What was a consequence of the industrialization that followed the Civil War?
    a. Decreased immigration
    b. Increased urbanization
    c. Decreased socioeconomic inequality
    d. Increased rights for workers

49. Which of the following best describes how the Treaty of Versailles contributed to the outbreak of World War II?
    a. It forced Germany to assume responsibility for all damage incurred during the war and pay billions of dollars in reparations.
    b. It failed to adequately end the violence of World War I.
    c. It left large tracts of territory unclaimed by any nation-state.
    d. It created the League of Nations.

Question 50 is based on the following passage:

> Now, therefore I, Abraham Lincoln, President of the United States, by virtue of the power in me vested as Commander-in-Chief, of the Army and Navy of the United States in time of actual armed rebellion against the authority and government of the United States, and as a fit and necessary war measure for suppressing said rebellion...
>
> And by virtue of the power, and for the purpose aforesaid, I do order and declare that all persons held as slaves within said designated States, and parts of States, are, and henceforward shall be free; and that the Executive government of the United States, including the military and naval authorities thereof, will recognize and maintain the freedom of said persons.

Excerpt from President Abraham Lincoln's Emancipation Proclamation, January 1, 1863

50. How does President Lincoln justify freeing the slaves in designated areas of the South?
    a. Emancipation is necessary since slavery is evil.
    b. Emancipation is necessary to boost the morale of the North.
    c. Emancipation is necessary to punish for the South seceding from the Union.
    d. Emancipation is necessary to strengthen the war effort of the North.

51. Federalism is described as the relationship between the federal government and which of the following?
    a. The people
    b. State governments
    c. The branches of government
    d. The Constitution

52. The case of *Brown v. Board of Education* reversed what landmark Supreme Court doctrine?
    a. Judicial review doctrine
    b. Public safety exception
    c. Due process doctrine
    d. Separate but equal doctrine

53. All EXCEPT which of the following are true of an area with an extremely high population density?
    a. Competition for resources is intense.
    b. Greater strain on public services exists.
    c. More people live in rural areas.
    d. More people live in urban areas.

54. Which of the following characteristics best defines a formal region?
    a. Homogeneity
    b. Diversity
    c. Multilingualism
    d. Social mobility

55. The process of globalization can best be described as what?
    a. The integration of the world's economic systems into a singular entity
    b. The emergence of powerful nations seeking world dominance
    c. The absence of nation-states who seek to control certain areas
    d. Efforts to establish a singular world government for the world's citizens

56. What is the name of the central bank that controls the value of money in the United States?
    a. Commodity Reserve
    b. Central Reserve
    c. Federal Reserve
    d. Bank Reserve

57. How is economic growth measured?
    a. By the rise in the inflation of a country
    b. By the amount of reserves that a country holds
    c. By the amount of exports that a country has
    d. By the GDP of a country

58. Which of the following is a region that can be identified using physical geography?
    a. New York state
    b. New York City
    c. Brooklyn
    d. Long Island

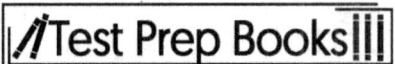

59. Which constitutional amendment gave women the right to vote in the United States?
    a. 15th
    b. 18th
    c. 19th
    d. 21st

60. What consequences did the Great Migration have?
    a. It led to conflict with Native Americans in the West in the 1800s.
    b. It led to increased racial tension in the North in the early 1900s.
    c. It led to increased conflict with Mexican immigrants in the 1900s.
    d. It led to increased conflict with Irish and German immigrants in the 1800s.

Science

1. An ecosystem that normally has moderate summers with high rainfall is experiencing a heat wave and a drought. How does this affect the rate of photosynthesis of the producers in this ecosystem?
    a. The decrease in transpiration from the high heat and the drop in rainfall decreases the number of chloroplasts, so photosynthesis rates decrease.
    b. The increase in transpiration from the high heat and the drop in rainfall results in less water. Since photosynthesis creates water, the rate increases to meet increased water demands.
    c. Increased temperature increases the number of mitochondria, so photosynthesis rates increase.
    d. The increase in transpiration from the high heat and the drop in rainfall results in less water available for photosynthesis. The rate decreases.

2. A farmer grows all of his tomato plants by vegetative propagation. He finds that one clone produces tomatoes that sell much better than any other clone. He then uses this clone to plant his entire field. Two years later a fungus wipes out his entire crop. What could the farmer have done to prevent this?

    I. Plant tomatoes that sell poorly. They are more resistant to fungus.
    II. Plant a variety of tomatoes. Genetic variation would have left some of the crop less susceptible to the fungus.
    III. Plant a variety of crops. Plants other than tomatoes might not be affected by the fungus.

    a. Choice I only
    b. Choice II only
    c. Choice I or III
    d. Choice II or III

3. What object in the solar system becomes dim during a lunar eclipse?
    a. Sun
    b. Earth
    c. Moon
    d. Earth and Moon

4. Which statement about white blood cells is true?
    a. B cells are responsible for antibody production.
    b. White blood cells are made in the white/yellow cartilage before they enter the bloodstream.
    c. Platelets, a special class of white blood cell, function to clot blood and stop bleeding.
    d. The majority of white blood cells only activate during the age of puberty, which explains why children and the elderly are particularly susceptible to disease.

Practice Test #1

5. Which locations in the digestive system are sites of chemical digestion?

   I. Mouth
   II. Stomach
   III. Small Intestine

   a. II only
   b. III only
   c. II and III only
   d. I, II, and III

6. What is the theory that certain physical and behavioral survival traits give a species an evolutionary advantage?
   a. Gradualism
   b. Evolutionary advantage
   c. Punctuated equilibrium
   d. Natural selection

7. Which of the following structures is unique to eukaryotic cells?
   a. Cell walls
   b. Nuclei
   c. Cell membranes
   d. Organelles

8. Which cellular organelle is used for digestion to recycle materials?
   a. The Golgi apparatus
   b. The lysosome
   c. The centrioles
   d. The mitochondria

9. Which of the following leads to diversity in meiotic division but not mitotic division?
   a. Tetrad formation
   b. Disassembly of the mitotic spindle
   c. Extra/fewer chromosomes due to nondisjunction
   d. Fertilization by multiple sperm

10. The sun is a major external source of energy. Which of the following is the best demonstration of this?
    a. Flowers tend to bloom in the morning, after dawn.
    b. Large animals like bears do not need to eat food when hibernating.
    c. Deserts can reach scorching temperatures in daylight but subzero temperatures at night.
    d. The tides of the ocean are highly dependent on the movement of the Moon, the celestial body that is highly reflective to sunlight.

11. Which of the following describes a typical gas?
    a. Indefinite shape and indefinite volume
    b. Indefinite shape and definite volume
    c. Definite shape and definite volume
    d. Definite shape and indefinite volume

12. What information does a genotype give that a phenotype does not?
    a. The genotype necessarily includes the proteins coded for by its alleles.
    b. The genotype will always show an organism's recessive alleles.
    c. The genotype must include the organism's physical characteristics.
    d. The genotype shows what an organism's parents looked like.

13. Which statement is supported by the Punnett square below, if "*T*" = tall and "*t*" = short?

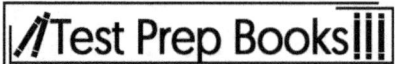

    a. Both parents are homozygous tall.
    b. 100% of the offspring will be tall because both parents are tall.
    c. There is a 25% chance that an offspring will be short.
    d. The short allele will soon die out.

14. Which of the following is a chief difference between evaporation and boiling?
    a. Liquids boil only at the surface, while they evaporate equally throughout the liquid.
    b. Evaporating substances change from gas to liquid, while boiling substances change from liquid to gas.
    c. Evaporation happens in nature, while boiling is a man-made phenomenon.
    d. Evaporation can happen below a liquid's boiling point.

15. Which of the following is a special property of water?
    a. Water easily flows through phospholipid bilayers.
    b. A water molecule's oxygen atom allows fish to breathe.
    c. Water is highly cohesive which explains its high boiling point.
    d. Water can self-hydrolyze and decompose into hydrogen and oxygen.

16. A student believes that there is an inverse relationship between sugar consumption and test scores. To test this hypothesis, he recruits several people to eat sugar, wait one hour, and take a short aptitude test afterwards. The student will compile the participants' sugar intake levels and test scores. How should the student conduct the experiment?
    a. One round of testing, where each participant consumes a different level of sugar.
    b. Two rounds of testing: The first, where each participant consumes a different level of sugar, and the second, where each participant consumes the same level as they did in round 1.
    c. Two rounds of testing: The first, where each participant consumes the same level of sugar as each other, and the second, where each participant consumes the same level of sugar as each other but at higher levels than in round 1.
    d. One round of testing, where each participant consumes the same level of sugar.

Practice Test #1

17. Which of the following is a standard or series of standards to which the results from an experiment are compared?
    a. A control
    b. A variable
    c. A constant
    d. Collected data

18. What is the last phase of mitosis?
    a. Prophase
    b. Telophase
    c. Anaphase
    d. Metaphase

19. Velocity is a measure of which of the following?
    a. Speed with direction
    b. The change in distance over the change in time
    c. Meters covered over seconds elapsed
    d. All of the above

20. Which of the following sources of energy are non-renewable?
    a. Wind energy
    b. Solar energy
    c. Fossil fuel energy
    d. Geothermal energy

21. Where is most of the Earth's weather generated?
    a. The troposphere
    b. The ionosphere
    c. The thermosphere
    d. The stratosphere

22. What type of cloud is seen when looking at the sky during a heavy rainstorm?
    a. High-clouds
    b. Altocumulus
    c. Stratus
    d. Nimbostratus

23. What is the largest planet in our solar system and what is it mostly made of?
    a. Saturn, rocks
    b. Jupiter, ammonia
    c. Jupiter, hydrogen
    d. Saturn, helium

24. Viruses belong to which of the following classifications?
    a. Domain Archaea
    b. Kingdom Monera
    c. Kingdom Protista
    d. None of the above

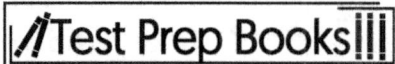

25. Consider a gas in a closed system that is kept at a constant volume. What will happen to the temperature if the pressure is increased?
    a. The temperature will stay the same.
    b. The temperature will decrease.
    c. The temperature will increase.
    d. The result cannot be determined with the information given.

26. According to Newton's three laws of motion, which of the following is true?
    a. Two objects cannot exert force on each other without touching.
    b. An object at rest has no inertia.
    c. The weight of an object is the same as the mass of the object.
    d. The weight of an object is equal to the mass of an object multiplied by the acceleration of gravity.

27. The Sun transferring heat to the Earth through space is an example of which of the following?
    a. Convection
    b. Conduction
    c. Induction
    d. Radiation

28. Which of the Earth's layers is thickest?
    a. The crust
    b. The shell
    c. The mantle
    d. The inner core

29. What is the process called in which one tectonic plate moves over another plate?
    a. Fault
    b. Diversion
    c. Subduction
    d. Drift

30. What is transpiration?
    a. Evaporation from moving water
    b. Evaporation from plant life
    c. Movement of water through the ground
    d. Precipitation that falls on trees

31. Which of the following will freeze last?
    a. Fresh water from a pond
    b. Pure water
    c. Seawater from the Pacific Ocean
    d. Seawater from the Dead Sea

32. Which of the following is true of glaciers?
    a. They form in water.
    b. They float.
    c. They form on land.
    d. They are formed from icebergs.

33. What is the broadest, or least specialized, classification of the Linnaean taxonomic system?
    a. Species
    b. Family
    c. Domain
    d. Phylum

34. Which statement is true about the pH of a solution?
    a. A solution cannot have a pH less than 1.
    b. The more hydroxide ions in the solution, the higher the pH.
    c. If an acid has a pH greater than 2, it is considered a weak base.
    d. A solution with a pH of 2 has ten times more hydrogen ions than a solution with a pH of 1.

35. Salts like sodium iodide (NaI) and potassium chloride (KCl) use what type of bond?
    a. Ionic bonds
    b. Disulfide bridges
    c. Covalent bonds
    d. London dispersion forces

36. Which of the following is unique to covalent bonds?
    a. Most covalent bonds are formed between the elements H, F, N, and O.
    b. Covalent bonds are dependent on forming dipoles.
    c. Bonding electrons are shared between two or more atoms.
    d. Molecules with covalent bonds tend to have a crystalline solid structure.

37. For any given element, an isotope is an atom with which of the following?
    a. A different atomic number
    b. A different number of protons
    c. A different number of electrons
    d. A different mass number

38. What is the electrical charge of the nucleus?
    a. A nucleus always has a positive charge.
    b. A stable nucleus has a positive charge, but a radioactive nucleus may be neutral with no charge.
    c. A nucleus is always neutral with no charge.
    d. A stable nucleus is neutral with no charge, but a radioactive nucleus may have a charge.

39. Which of the following is a representation of a natural pattern or occurrence that's difficult or impossible to experience directly?
    a. A theory
    b. A model
    c. A law
    d. An observation

40. "This flower is dead; someone must have forgotten to water it." This statement is an example of which of the following?
    a. A classification
    b. An observation
    c. An inference
    d. A collection

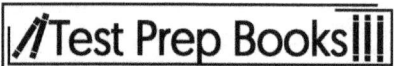

41. Which statement is true regarding atomic structure?
    a. Protons orbit around a nucleus.
    b. Neutrons have a positive charge.
    c. Electrons are in the nucleus.
    d. Protons have a positive charge.

42. What is ionization energy?
    a. One-half the distance between the nuclei of atoms of the same element
    b. A measurement of the tendency of an atom to form a chemical bond
    c. The amount of energy needed to remove a valence electron from a gas or ion
    d. The ability or tendency of an atom to accept an electron into its valence shell

43. The process of breaking down large molecules into smaller molecules to provide energy is known as which of the following?
    a. Metabolism
    b. Bioenergetics
    c. Anabolism
    d. Catabolism

44. The Human Genome Project is a worldwide research project launched in 1990 to map the entire human genome. Although the Project was faced with the monumental challenge of analyzing tons and tons of data, its objective was completed in 2003 and ahead of its deadline by two years. Which of the following inventions likely had the greatest impact on this project?
    a. The sonogram
    b. X-ray diffraction
    c. The microprocessor
    d. Magnetic Resonance Imaging (MRI)

45. Which of the following inventions likely had the greatest improvement on the ability to combat nutrition deficiencies in developing countries?
    a. Food products fortified with dietary vitamins and minerals
    b. Integrated statistical models of fish populations
    c. Advances so that microscopes can use thicker tissue samples
    d. Refrigerated train cars for transportation of food

46. Which element's atoms have the greatest number of electrons?
    a. Hydrogen
    b. Iron
    c. Copper
    d. Iodine

47. A teacher presents a science lesson to her class of second graders about physical and chemical properties. After the lesson, students create posters that highlight examples of each. Which of the following would be included on the list of examples of chemical properties?
    a. Color
    b. Malleability
    c. Reactivity
    d. Luster

48. Which of the following happens first in the scientific method?
    a. Procedure
    b. Hypothesis
    c. Observation
    d. Data collection

49. Students in a fourth-grade class are brainstorming testable hypotheses. Which of the following suggestions offered by a student is a valid hypothesis?
    a. If a cat is happy, then it purrs.
    b. If pants are softer, then they feel more comfortable.
    c. If light exposure increases, then plant height will increase.
    d. If calories are added to a dog's diet, then it will grow.

50. An elementary teacher is about to begin a new science unit of seasons and weather as part of various activities to gauge students' background knowledge. He asks each student to share what they believe to be the difference between seasons and weather. The responses of four students are presented below. Which of these students is most accurate?
    a. Carter: Seasons depend on wind and heat patterns.
    b. Darrel: Weather depends on proximity to the sun.
    c. Gloria: Seasons are day-to-day weather.
    d. Dimitri: Weather involves the water cycle.

51. Which is the best way to teach the concept of day and night to early childhood students?
    a. Showing an animated PowerPoint
    b. Going outside and talking about the Sun's location
    c. Modeling with flashlights and tennis balls
    d. Reading a book where the Sun and moon are friends

52. Why is Florida hotter than Alaska?
    a. Florida is next to the ocean.
    b. Florida is a peninsula.
    c. Alaska is farther from the equator.
    d. Alaska is larger than Florida.

53. Which of the following weather phenomena does NOT directly involve the water cycle?
    a. Hurricanes
    b. Tornadoes
    c. Snow
    d. Rain

54. Plate tectonic movement contributes to the Earth's topography by doing which of the following?
    a. Causing volcanoes
    b. Stimulating evaporation
    c. Forming deltas
    d. Stopping tornadoes

55. Which type of fossil is considered a "trace fossil"?
    a. Bone
    b. Footprint
    c. Shell
    d. Tooth

Answer Explanations #1

Mathematics

1. A: Compare each number after the decimal point to figure out which overall number is greatest. In Choices A (1.43785) and C (1.43592), both have the same tenths place (4) and hundredths place (3). However, the thousandths place is greater in Choice A (7), so it has the greatest value overall.

2. D: By rearranging and grouping the factors in Choice D, we can notice that $3 \times 3 \times 4 \times 2 = (3 \times 2) \times (4 \times 3) = 6 \times 12$, which is what we were looking for.

3. A: To figure out which value is the largest, look at the first nonzero digits. Choice B's first nonzero digit is in the hundredths place. The other three all have nonzero digits in the tenths place, so it must be Choice A, C, or D. Of these, Choice A's first nonzero digit is the largest.

4. C: To solve for the value of b, isolate the variable b on one side of the equation.

Start by moving the lower value of -4 to the other side by adding 4 to both sides:

$$5b - 4 = 2b + 17$$

$$5b - 4 + 4 = 2b + 17 + 4$$

$$5b = 2b + 21$$

Then, subtract $2b$ from both sides:

$$5b - 2b = 2b + 21 - 2b$$

$$3b = 21$$

Then, divide both sides by 3 to get the value of b:

$$\frac{3b}{3} = \frac{21}{3}$$

$$b = 7$$

5. D: The total faculty is:

$$15 + 20 = 35$$

So, the ratio is 35 : 200. Then, divide both of these numbers by 5, since 5 is a common factor to both, with a result of 7 : 40.

6. C: The first step in solving this problem is expressing the result in fraction form. Multiplication and division are typically performed in order from left to right, but they can be performed in any order. For this problem, start with the division operation between the last two fractions. When dividing one fraction by another, invert—or flip—the second fraction and then multiply the numerators and denominators.

$$\frac{7}{10} \times \frac{2}{1} = \frac{14}{10}$$

Answer Explanations #1

Next, multiply the first fraction by this value:

$$\frac{3}{5} \times \frac{14}{10} = \frac{42}{50}$$

In this instance, to find the decimal form, multiply the numerator and denominator by 2 to get 100 in the denominator. In decimal form, this would be expressed as 0.84.

7. C: The product of two irrational numbers can be rational or irrational. Sometimes the irrational parts of the two numbers cancel each other out, leaving a rational number. For example, $\sqrt{2} \times \sqrt{2} = 2$ because the roots cancel each other out. Technically, the product of two irrational numbers is a complex number, because real numbers are a type of complex number. However, Choice *D* is incorrect because the product of two irrational numbers is not an imaginary number.

8. C: The terms "whole numbers" and "natural numbers" include all the ordinary counting numbers (1, 2, 3, 4, 5, ...), and sometimes zero depending on the definition used, but no negative numbers. The term "integers" includes all those numbers, their negatives, and zero. So -4 is not a whole number or a natural number, but it is an integer. It is also rational because it can be written as a ratio of two integers ($-\frac{4}{1}$); all integers are rational. It is a real number because it does not have an imaginary component (symbolized by the letter i); all integers are real numbers.

9. A: Setting up a proportion is the easiest way to represent this situation. The proportion is $\frac{20}{x} = \frac{40}{100}$, and cross-multiplication can be used to solve for x. Here, $40x = 2,000$, so $x = 50$.

10. A: Finding the product means distributing one polynomial to the other so that each term in the first is multiplied by each term in the second. Then, like terms can be collected. Multiplying the factors yields the expression:

$$20x^3 + 4x^2 + 24x - 40x^2 - 8x - 48$$

Collecting like terms means adding the x^2 terms and adding the x terms. The final answer after simplifying the expression is:

$$20x^3 - 36x^2 + 16x - 48$$

11. B: We can try to solve the equation by factoring the numerator into $(x + 6)(x - 5)$. Since $(x - 5)$ is on the top and bottom, that factor cancels out. This leaves the equation $x + 6 = 11$. Solving the equation gives the answer $x = 5$. But when this value is substituted back into the equation, it yields a zero in the denominator of the fraction. Since this is undefined, there is no solution.

12. C: It may help to look at this problem as a fraction: $\frac{1.2 \times 10^{12}}{3.0 \times 10^8}$. We can calculate $\frac{1.2}{3} = 0.4$, and using the rules of exponents, we can see that:

$$\frac{10^{12}}{10^8} = 10^8 = 10^{(12-8)} = 10^4$$

This gives us an answer of 0.4×10^4, which is Choice *A*, but our answer is not yet in scientific notation because the first term, 0.4, is not between 1 and 10. We can rewrite 0.4×10^4, multiplying the first term by 10 and subtracting 1 from the exponent, which gives 4.0×10^3, Choice *C*.

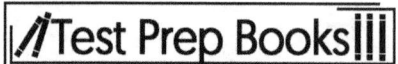

Answer Explanations #1

13. D: We can work backwards to figure this out one step at a time. "Sum" means the result of addition, so "the sum of twice a number and one" can be written as $2x + 1$. Next, "three times the sum of twice a number and one" would be $3(2x + 1)$. Finally, "three times the sum of twice a number and one, minus 6" would be $3(2x + 1) - 6$.

14. B: To solve this correctly, keep in mind the order of operations with the mnemonic PEMDAS (Please Excuse My Dear Aunt Sally). This stands for Parentheses, Exponents, Multiplication & Division, Addition & Subtraction. Taking it step by step, start with the parentheses:

$$4 \times 7 + (4)^2 \div 2$$

Then, apply the exponent:

$$4 \times 7 + 16 \div 2$$

Multiplication and division are both performed next:

$$28 + 8$$

Then finally, addition:

$$28 + 8 = 36$$

15. D:

$9x + x - 7 = 16 + 2x$	Combine $9x$ and x
$10x - 7 = 16 + 2x$	
$10x - 7 + 7 = 16 + 2x + 7$	Add 7 to both sides to remove the −7.
$10x = 23 + 2x$	
$10x - 2x = 23 + 2x - 2x$	Subtract $2x$ from both sides to move it to the other side of the equation.
$8x = 23$	
$\dfrac{8x}{8} = \dfrac{23}{8}$	Divide by 8 to get x by itself.
$x = \dfrac{23}{8}$	

16. C: The first step is to depict each number using decimals:

$$\frac{91}{100} = 0.91$$

Dividing the numerator by the denominator of $\frac{4}{5}$ to convert it to a decimal yields 0.80, while $\frac{2}{3}$ becomes 0.66 recurring. Rearrange each expression in ascending order, as found in Choice C.

17. B: First, calculate the difference between the larger value and the smaller value:

$$378 - 252 = 126$$

Answer Explanations #1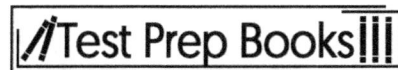

To calculate this difference as a percentage of the original value, which is the percentage *increase*, divide 126 by 252 to get 0.5, then multiply by 100 to reach the percentage 50%, Choice *B*.

18. A: First, simplify the larger fraction by separating it into two. When dividing one fraction by another, remember to invert the second fraction and multiply, like so:

$$\frac{5}{7} \times \frac{11}{9}$$

The resulting fraction $\frac{55}{63}$ cannot be simplified further, so this is the answer to the problem.

19. B: $\frac{5}{2} \div \frac{1}{3} = \frac{5}{2} \times \frac{3}{1} = \frac{15}{2} = 7.5$.

20. C: The total percentage of a pie chart equals 100%. CD sales make up less than half of the chart (50%) but more than a quarter (25%), and the only answer choice that meets these criteria is Choice *C*, 40%.

21. A: Divide 54 by 15:

$$\begin{array}{r} 3 \\ 15\overline{)54} \\ -45 \\ \hline 9 \end{array}$$

The result is 3 with a remainder of 9, which is equivalent to $3\frac{9}{15}$. Reduce the fraction $\frac{9}{15}$ for the final answer, $3\frac{3}{5}$.

22. D: $\frac{59}{7}$

The original number was $8\frac{3}{7}$. Multiply the denominator by the whole number portion. Add the numerator, and put the total over the original denominator.

$$\frac{(8 \times 7) + 3}{7} = \frac{59}{7}$$

23. B: Multiplying by 10^{-3} means moving the decimal point three places to the left, putting in zeros as necessary.

24. D: This problem can be solved by using unit conversions. The initial units are miles per minute. The final units need to be feet per second. Converting miles to feet uses the equivalence statement 1 mile = 5,280 feet. Converting minutes to seconds uses the equivalence statement 1 minute = 60 seconds. Setting up the ratios to convert the units is shown in the following equation:

$$\frac{72 \text{ miles}}{90 \text{ minutes}} \times \frac{1 \text{ minute}}{60 \text{ seconds}} \times \frac{5,280 \text{ feet}}{1 \text{ mile}} = 70.4 \text{ feet per second}$$

The initial units cancel out, and the new, desired units are left.

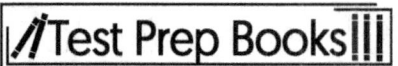

25. C: Because the triangles are similar, the lengths of the corresponding sides are proportional. Therefore, these two relationships exist:

$$\frac{30+x}{30} = \frac{22}{14}$$

$$\frac{y+15}{y} = \frac{22}{14}$$

Using cross multiplication on the first proportion results in the equation:

$$14(30+x) = 22 \times 30$$

When solved, this gives:

$$x \approx 17.1$$

Using cross multiplication on the second proportion results in the equation:

$$14(y+15) = 22y$$

When solved, this gives:

$$y \approx 26.3$$

26. D: We are given an angle (60°), the length of the opposite side (x), and the length of the adjacent side (13 cm). We can use the mnemonic "SOHCAHTOA," where the "TOA" reminds us that tangent equals the opposite side over the adjacent side. In other words, $\tan 60 = \frac{x}{13}$. Since $tan\ 60° = \sqrt{3}$, we can calculate:

$$x = 13 \tan 60 = 13 \times \sqrt{3} \approx 22.52$$

27. B: According to the order of operations, multiplication and division must be completed first from left to right. Then, addition and subtraction are completed from left to right. Therefore:

$$9 \times 9 \div 9 + 9 - 9 \div 9$$

$$81 \div 9 + 9 - 9 \div 9$$

$$9 + 9 - 9 \div 9$$

$$9 + 9 - 1$$

$$18 - 1$$

$$17$$

28. C: The formula for the perimeter of a rectangle is $P = 2L + 2W$, where P is the perimeter, L is the length, and W is the width. The first step is to substitute all of the data into the formula:

$$36 = 2(12) + 2W$$

Simplify by multiplying 2×12:

$$36 = 24 + 2W$$

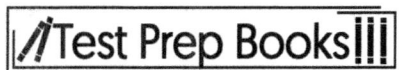

Simplifying this further by subtracting 24 on each side gives:

$$36 - 24 = 24 - 24 + 2W$$

$$12 = 2W$$

Divide by 2:

$$6 = W$$

The width is 6 cm. Remember to test this answer by substituting this value into the original formula:

$$36 = 2(12) + 2(6)$$

29. D: Using the given information of 2 beds to 1 room and 145 rooms, set up an equation to solve for the number of beds (B):

$$\frac{B}{145} = \frac{2}{1}$$

Multiply both sides by 145 to get B by itself on one side.

$$\frac{B}{1} = \frac{290}{1} = 290 \text{ beds}$$

30. B: For the first card drawn, the probability of a king being pulled is $\frac{4}{52}$. Since this card isn't replaced, if a king is drawn first, the probability of a king being drawn second is $\frac{3}{51}$. The probability of a king being drawn in both the first and second draw is the product of the two probabilities:

$$\frac{4}{52} \times \frac{3}{51} = \frac{12}{2,652}$$

To reduce this fraction, divide the top and bottom by 12 to get $\frac{1}{221}$.

31. A: If each man gains 10 pounds, every original data point will increase by 10 pounds. Therefore, the man with the original median will still have the median value, but that value will increase by 10. The smallest value and largest value will also increase by 10, so the difference between the two (the range) will remain the same.

32. B: A number raised to an exponent is a compressed form of multiplication. For example,

$$10^3 = 10 \times 10 \times 10$$

33. D: When a point is reflected over an axis, the sign of at least one of the coordinates must change. When it's reflected over the x-axis, the sign of the y coordinate must change. The x-value remains the same. Therefore, the new point is $(-3, 4)$.

34. B: The car is traveling at a speed of 5 meters per second. On the interval from 1 to 3 seconds, the position changes by 10 meters. This is 10 meters in 2 seconds, or 5 meters in each second.

35. D: "Sum" means the result of addition, so "the sum of twice a number and one" can be written as $2x + 1$. Next, "three times the sum of twice a number and one" would be $3(2x + 1)$. Finally, "six less than three times the sum of twice a number and one" would be $3(2x + 1) - 6$.

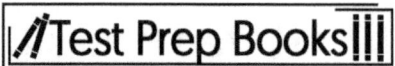

Answer Explanations #1

36. B: The formula for the volume of a cube is $V = s^3$. Substitute the side length of 7 in to get:

$$V = 7^3 = 343 \text{ in}^3$$

37. A: The conversion can be obtained by setting up and evaluating the following expression:

$$4{,}382 \text{ ft} \times \frac{0.3048 \text{ m}}{1 \text{ ft}} \times \frac{1 \text{ km}}{1{,}000 \text{ m}} = 1.336 \text{ km}$$

38. B: The y-intercept of an equation is found where the x-value is zero. Plugging zero into the equation for x allows the first two terms to cancel out, leaving -4.

39. A: Putting the scores in order from least to greatest, we have 60, 75, 80, and 85, as well as one unknown. The median is 80, so 80 must be the middle data point out of these five. Therefore, the unknown data point must be the fourth or fifth data point, meaning it must be greater than or equal to 80. The only answer that fails to meet this condition is 60.

40. C: In this scenario, the variables are the number of sales and Karen's weekly pay. The weekly pay depends on the number of sales. Therefore, weekly pay is the dependent variable (y), and the number of sales is the independent variable (x). All four answer choices are in slope-intercept form, $y = mx + b$, so we just need to find m (the slope) and b (the y-intercept). We can calculate both by picking any two points, for example, (2, 380) and (4, 460).

The slope is given by $m = \frac{(y_2 - y_1)}{(x\_2 - x\_1)}$, so $m = \frac{460 - 380}{4 - 2} = 40$.

This gives us the equation $y = 40x + b$. Now we can plug in the x and y values from our first point to find b.

Since $380 = 40(2) + b$, we find $b = 300$. This means the equation is $y = 40x + 300$.

41. B: Using the conversion rate, multiply the projected weight loss of 25 lb by $0.45 \frac{\text{kg}}{\text{lb}}$ to get the amount in kilograms (11.25 kg).

42. D: First, subtract $1,437 from $2,334.50 to find Johnny's monthly savings; this equals $897.50. Then, multiply this amount by 3 to find out how much he will have (in 3 months) before he pays for his vacation; this equals $2,692.50. Finally, subtract the cost of the vacation ($1,750) from this amount to find how much Johnny will have left: $942.50.

43. B: Since we are given the y-intercept (where the graph crosses the y-axis) as $y = 1$, we can substitute this value in for b in the slope-intercept form equation $y = mx + b$.

$$y = mx + 1$$

From here, the slope needs to be found. Given the two points (1,2) and (0,1) (from the y-intercept), use the slope formula.

$$m = \frac{y_2 - y_1}{x_2 - x_1} = \frac{2 - 1}{1 - 0} = \frac{1}{1} = 1$$

Therefore, the equation for the line is $y = 1x + 1$, or $y = x + 1$.

Answer Explanations #1

44. A: This kind of line indicates a positive relationship. A negative relationship would match a line traveling from the upper left of the graph to the lower right. Exponential and logarithmic functions aren't linear—their graphs do not make a straight line.

45. C: The data points do not appear to form any sort of line, even approximately, as we would expect for a positive or negative relationship. They also do not form the characteristic bell-shaped curve of a normal distribution. No relationship is apparent.

46. B: The formula can be manipulated by dividing both sides by the length, l, and the width, w. The length and width will cancel on the right, leaving height by itself.

47. B: The table shows values that are increasing exponentially. The differences between the inputs are the same, while the differences in the outputs are changing by a factor of 2. The values in the table can be modeled by the equation $f(x) = 2^x$.

48. B: To factor $x^2 + 4x + 4$, the numbers needed are those that add to 4 and multiply to 4. Therefore, both numbers must be 2, and the expression factors to:

$$x^2 + 4x + 4 = (x + 2)^2$$

Similarly, the second expression factors to:

$$x^2 - x - 6 = (x - 3)(x + 2)$$

Therefore, they have $x + 2$ in common.

49. B: When solving for x, add 3 to both sides to get $4x = 8$. Then, divide both sides by 4 to get $x = 2$.

50. C: The sample space is made up of:

$$8 + 7 + 6 + 5 = 26 \text{ balls}$$

The probability of pulling each individual ball is $\frac{1}{26}$. Since there are 7 yellow balls, the probability of pulling a yellow ball is $\frac{7}{26}$.

Social Studies

1. B: John White does not have an important historical influence to the state of Georgia. White was the leader of the Roanoke colony founded under the authority of Sir Walter Raleigh in what was then called Virginia and later became North Carolina. White went back to England for supplies in 1587, and when he returned, all of the colonists had mysteriously disappeared.

2. B: To avoid involvement in political processes such as voting is antithetical to the principles of a democracy. Therefore, the principal responsibility of citizens is the opposite, and they should be steadily engaged in the political processes that determine the course of government.

3. A: Heavily influenced by the Enlightenment, the Declaration of Independence repudiated the colonies' allegiance to Great Britain. The main purpose of the excerpt is to justify the colonists' revolutionary stance due to Great Britain's tyranny and the role of consent in government to protect the natural rights of citizens. Choice B is incorrect because, although the excerpt alludes to abuses, the purpose isn't to list specific evidence. This occurs later in the Declaration of Independence. Choices C and D are supporting evidence for the main purpose.

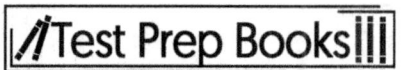

Answer Explanations #1

4. A: James Oglethorpe convinced King George II to colonize the area that is now Georgia with individuals from Britain's overflowing debtor's prisons. Button Gwinnett, George Walton, and Lyman Hall were the three Georgians who signed the Declaration of Independence in 1776. Thus, Choices *B*, *C*, and *D* are incorrect.

5. C: At the time of the Constitutional Convention, Thomas Jefferson was in Paris serving as America's foreign minister to France. Therefore, he is not a good fit for this project. George Washington led the meeting, and Alexander Hamilton and James Madison set the tone for debate, rendering *A*, *B*, and *D* incorrect.

6. A: Plains Indians followed the buffalo across the prairies, living in tent-like teepees that were easily moved from place to place. Choice *B* is incorrect because Native Americans in the Southwest relied on farming for much of their food and built adobes, which are houses made out of dried clay or earth. Native Americans in the Eastern and Northwest sections of North America survived by hunting, gathering, farming, and fishing, and lived in wooden longhouses, plank houses, or wigwams. Thus, Choices *C* and *D* are incorrect.

7. C: Established in 1607, Jamestown, Virginia was the first permanent British settlement in the New World. Plymouth was founded a bit later in 1620 when a group of Pilgrims founded the first permanent European settlement in New England, making Choice *A* incorrect. Choice *B* is incorrect because although the Roanoke Colony was founded in 1585, it isn't considered permanent – the colony's leader, John White, went back to England for supplies two years later, and he returned to find that all of the colonists had mysteriously disappeared. Choice *D* is incorrect because L'Anse Meadows was an area in Newfoundland that was briefly settled by Scandinavian Vikings around 1000 AD.

8. C: The first shot took place on Lexington Green. When the British heard that colonists were stockpiling weapons, they sent troops to Concord to seize them. However, a group of approximately seventy Minutemen confronted the British soldiers on Lexington Green. British troops killed five protesting colonists during the Boston Massacre in 1770, but this is not considered the first shot of the Revolution. Thus, Choice *A* is incorrect. Choice *B* is incorrect because the Boston Tea Party was when colonists dumped 342 chests of expensive tea into the Boston Harbor in defiance of the tea tax. The Revolution had already started when the Battle of Trenton took place on December 25, 1776, making Choice *D* incorrect.. British troops killed five protesting colonists during the Boston Massacre in 1770, but this is not considered the first shot of the Revolution. Thus, Choice *A* is incorrect. Choice *B* is incorrect because the Boston Tea Party was when colonists dumped 342 chests of expensive tea into the Boston Harbor in defiance of the tea tax. The Revolution had already started when the Battle of Trenton took place on December 25, 1776, making Choice *D* incorrect.

9. D: There are 27 amendments to the US Constitution. The 14th Amendment was adopted in 1868 to abolish slavery. The 18th Amendment was passed in 1919 and prohibited the production and sale of alcoholic beverages, but the 21st Amendment repealed it in 1933.

10. D: Thematic maps create certain themes in which they attempt to illustrate a certain phenomenon or pattern. The obvious theme of a climate map is the climates in the represented areas. Thematic maps are very extensive and can include thousands of different themes, which makes them quite useful for students of geography. Topographic maps, Choice *A*, are utilized to show physical features; conformal projections, Choice *B*, attempt to illustrate the globe in an undistorted fashion; and isoline maps, Choice *C*, illustrate differences in variables between two points on a map.

11. B: Latitudinal and longitudinal coordinates delineate absolute location. In contrast to relative location (Choice *C*), which describes a location as compared to another, better-known place, absolute location provides an exact place on the globe through the latitude and longitude system. Cardinal directions (north, south, east, west), Choice *A*, are used in absolute location, but coordinates must be added in order to have an

200

absolute location. Absolute location is far more precise than simply finding the hemispherical position on the globe (Choice *D*).

12. C: Each statement about culture is correct except for Choice *C*. Cultures often will adapt to the settings in which they are found. Improvements in technology, changes in social values, and interactions with other cultures all contribute to cultural change.

13. B: Lines of latitude measure distance north and south. The equator is zero degrees, and the Tropic of Cancer is 23.5 degrees north of the equator. The distance between those two lines measures degrees north to south, as with any other two lines of latitude. Longitudinal lines, or meridians, measure distance east and west, even though they run north and south down the globe. Latitude is not inexact, in that there are set distances between the lines. Furthermore, coordinates can only exist with the use of longitude and latitude.

14. D: During the Achaemenid Empire, Persians practiced the Zoroastrian faith and worshipped two gods. Islam only came about one thousand years later. The Achaemenids built a Royal Road that stretched across their empire, but the Silk Roads expanded throughout Asia. The Achaemenids twice tried to conquer Greece but failed both times.

15. A: The Silk Roads were a network of trade routes between Asia and the Mediterranean. Merchants and Pilgrims traveled along the Silk Roads and brought new ideas and technologies, as well as trade goods. For example, Buddhism spread from India to China. Chinese technologies also spread westward, including gunpowder and the printing press. The Silk Roads also spread the Bubonic Plague to Europe, but it did not arrive in the New World until Columbus landed there in 1492.

16. A: Large numbers of Franks, Goths, Vandals, and other Germanic peoples began moving south in the 5th century AD. They conquered Rome twice, and the Western Roman Empire finally disintegrated. The Mongol invasion, Choice *B*, pushed westward in the 13th century, long after the western Roman Empire was gone. The assassination of Julius Caesar, Choice *C*, led to the end of the Roman Republic and the birth of the Roman Empire. Taoism never spread to Rome, making Choice *D* incorrect.

17. A: The Mongols were a nomadic people who trained as horsemen from a young age. They used their highly mobile army to build a huge empire in Asia, the Middle East, and Eastern Europe. Mongol rulers were relatively tolerant of other religions because they wanted to reduce conflict within their empire, making Choice *B* incorrect. They also encouraged trade because they produced few of their own goods, making Choice *C* incorrect. The Mongol rulers also encouraged literacy and appreciated visual art, making Choice *D* incorrect.

18. A: Renaissance scholars and artists sought to emulate classical Greek and Roman culture. They translated Greek and Roman political philosophers and literature. They also copied classical architecture. Europeans had little direct contact with China until the 13th century, which was long after the Zhou Dynasty collapsed, making Choice *C* incorrect. The Renaissance Era occurred within the continent of Europe and drew from other European styles, so nations of northern Africa and the Middle East, such as ancient Egypt and the Ottoman Empire, had little to no inspiration on Renaissance scholars and artists at that time. Therefore, Choices *B* and *D* are incorrect.

19. C: In the 1800s, nationalists in different parts of Europe encouraged their countrymen to take pride in their shared backgrounds. This led to tension between different nations, as each sought to increase its status and prestige. The French and British nearly came to blows in Africa, and nationalism ultimately led to World War I in 1914. France and Spain were unified several centuries before the 1800s.

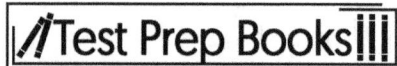

Answer Explanations #1

20. D: Mapping out the addresses of each infected person can help identify sources of disease based on how the locations are clustered. Areas with a high number of victims indicate proximity to the source of the illness. Therefore, Choice *D* is correct. Choices *A* and *B* are incorrect because the map does not provide health information about the disease's morbidity or mortality rates. Choice *C* is incorrect because without further information about the map, we cannot conclude that the geography indicates economic information.

21. C: Power is the ability of a ruling body or political entity to influence the actions, behavior, and attitude of a person or group of people. Authority, Choice *A*, is the right and justification of the government to exercise power as recognized by the citizens or influential elites. Similarly, legitimacy, Choice *D*, is another way of expressing the concept of authority. Sovereignty, Choice *B*, refers to the ability of a state to determine and control their territory without foreign interference.

22. D: Sovereignty is the feature that differentiates a state from a nation. Nations have no sovereignty, as they are unable to enact and enforce laws independently of their state. A state must possess sovereignty over the population of a territory in order to be legitimized as a state. Both a nation and a state must have a population, Choice *C*. Although sometimes present, a shared history and common language are not requirements for a state, making Choices *A* and *B* incorrect.

23. A: Devastated by World War II, Britain and France were unable to maintain their empires. Japan and Germany were also weak, which left only the United States and USSR as superpowers. The Russian Revolution had occurred during World War I, in 1917, making Choice *B* incorrect. Ideological and economic conflict between the US and the USSR led to the start of the Cold War shortly after World War II ended, making Choice *C* incorrect. Choice *D* is also incorrect; the death of Franz Ferdinand marked the beginning of World War I.

24. A: Although some ethnic groups throughout the world do engage in armed conflicts, the vast majority do not. Most ethnic groups tend to live in relative harmony with others with whom they share differences. Ethnic groups are simply a group of people with a religious, cultural, economic, or linguistic commonality. Additionally, ethnic groups don't always choose to leave places. Many have called certain locations home for centuries. Also, some ethnic groups actually make up the majority in some countries and are not always minority groups.

25. A: The use of biotechnology and GMOs has increased the total amount of food on Earth. Additionally, it has helped to sustain the Earth's growing population; however, many activists assert that scientists are creating crops that, in the long run, will be destructive to human health, even though not enough evidence exists to prove such an allegation. Agricultural production has not been affected by poorer soil, plagues of pests, or the use of saline for irrigation purposes.

26. A: The Ring of Fire is the line of frequent tectonic and volcanic activity that takes place on the edges of the Pacific Ocean's tectonic plate. Since Hawaii is in the center of the Pacific Ocean—not on the edge—it is not part of the Ring of Fire. Choice *A* is correct. Choices *B*, *C*, and *D* are incorrect because the listed places are included in the Ring of Fire.

27. B: Macroeconomics studies the economy on a large scale and focuses on issues such as unemployment, interest rates, price levels, and national income. Microeconomics studies more individual or small group behaviors such as scarcity or supply and demand. Scarcity is incorrect because it refers to the availability of goods and services. Supply and demand is also incorrect because it refers to the quantity of goods and services that is produced and/or needed.

28. A: A free market does not involve government interventions or monopolies while trading between buyers and suppliers. However, in a command market, the government determines the price of goods and services.

Answer Explanations #1

Gross and exchange markets refer to situations where brokers and traders make exchanges in the financial realm.

29. D: Behaviors of firms is not an indicator of economic growth because it refers to the behavior that firms follow to reach their desired outcome. GDP, unemployment, and inflation are all indicators that help determine economic growth.

30. A: Most scholars already knew the world was round by 1492. On the other hand, the arrival of Europeans in North and South America introduced deadly diseases that killed millions of native peoples. Europeans had developed immunity to diseases such as smallpox, while Native Americans had not. In addition, Europeans introduced a number of new plants and animals to the New World, but they also adopted many new foods as well, including potatoes, tomatoes, chocolate, and tobacco. Finally, Europeans tried to convert Native Americans to Christianity, but Native Americans did not completely give up their traditional beliefs. Instead, they blended Christianity with indigenous and African beliefs to create new syncretic religions.

31. D: The Industrial Revolution is probably one of the most important turning points in world history. The United States and Western Europe, especially Britain, were the first areas to industrialize. Steam engines were used to improve economic and transportation efficiency. They also gave western empires a military advantage over less developed countries in Asia and Africa. Finally, industrialization required large amounts of unskilled labor, which created the working class.

32. D: The Constitution granted Congress the power to decide how many justices should be on the court, and Congress first decided on six judges in the Judiciary Act of 1789. The Constitution granted the power to appoint judges and to call special sessions of Congress to the president. Only the Supreme Court may interpret the laws enacted by Congress and rule a law unconstitutional and subsequently overturn the law.

33. C: The first ten amendments to the Constitution are collectively referred to as the Bill of Rights. The Founding Fathers did not support universal suffrage, and as such, the Bill of Rights did not encompass the freedom to vote. The Fifteenth Amendment provided that the right to vote shall not be denied on the basis of race, color, or previous condition of servitude, and women did not receive the right to vote until passage of the Nineteenth Amendment. The other three answer choices are included in the Bill of Rights: the freedom to assembly is established in the First Amendment, the freedom against unlawful search is established in the Fourth Amendment, and the reservation of non-enumerated powers to the states or the people is established in the Tenth Amendment.

34. C: The president of the United States is elected by the Electoral College. The number of electors for each state depends on the state's total number of senators and representatives. The president must receive a majority (270) of the electoral votes (538), and if this doesn't occur, the Twelfth Amendment empowers the House of Representatives to elect the president. Choices *A*, *B*, and *C* are different methods for electing candidates.

35. B: President Franklin D. Roosevelt introduced the New Deal, a series of executive orders and laws passed by Congress in response to the Great Depression. The excerpt describes how President Roosevelt intended to fight poverty by using the government's power to intervene and regulate the economy. Although Choices *A*, *C*, and *D* correctly identify specific activities referenced in the excerpt, they are specific examples of the underlying philosophy in action. The underlying philosophy is an active role for government in the nation's economic affairs.

36. D: The two major political parties hold conventions to nominate their presidential candidate. The delegates are awarded based on candidates' performance in the primary elections or caucuses vote at the party convention to select the nominee. Primaries and caucuses are the democratic contests held by each

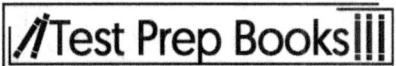

Answer Explanations #1

state to award their delegates. The candidates participate in debates on the campaign issues, but they do not receive the nomination at debates.

37. B: The process by which the House and Senate may debate a bill differs. In the House, how long a speaker may debate a bill is limited, while in the Senate, speakers may debate the bill indefinitely and delay voting on the bill by filibuster—a practice in which a speaker refuses to stop speaking until a majority vote stops the filibuster or the time for the vote passes. In both the House and the Senate, anyone may introduce a bill. Only the president of the United States may veto the bill, so neither the House nor Senate holds that power. Before the bill may be presented to the president to be signed, the wording of the bill must be identical in both houses. Another procedural difference is that the number of amendments is limited in the House but not the Senate; however, this does not appear as an answer choice.

38. C: Map projections, such as the Mercator Projection, are useful for finding positions on the globe, but they attempt to represent a spherical object on a flat surface. As a result, they distort areas nearest the poles, which misrepresent the size of Antarctica, Greenland, and other high latitudinal locations. Map projects can include great detail; some illustrate the physical features in an area, and most include both the northern and southern hemispheres.

39. C: Developed Nations have better infrastructural systems, which can include government, transportation, financial, and educational institutions. Consequently, its citizens tend to have higher rates of literacy, due to the sheer availability of educational resources and government sanctioned educational systems. In contrast, developing nations struggle to provide educational resources to their citizens. Nations in the Northern Hemisphere have no greater availability to educational resources than those in the Southern Hemisphere, and centers of trade don't necessarily equate to higher levels of education as many may exist in poorer nations with fewer resources.

40. C: Although it can place a strain on some resources, population density is not a negative demographic indicator. For example, New York City, one of the most densely populated places on Earth, enjoys one of the highest standards of living in the world. Other world cities such as Tokyo, Los Angeles, and Sydney also have tremendously high population densities and high standards of living. High infant mortality rates, low literacy rates, and low life expectancies are all poor demographic indicators that suggest a low quality of life for the citizens living in those areas.

41. C: Longitudinal position, or a place's location either east or west, has no bearing on the place's climate. In contrast, a place's latitudinal position, or its distance away from the direct rays of the sun in the Tropics, greatly affects its climate. Additionally, proximity to mountains, which can block wind patterns, and elevation, which generally lowers temperature by three degrees for every one thousand feet gained, also impact climate.

42. D: Although nearest the direct rays of the sun, the Tropics are not always warm. In fact, the nations of Ecuador and Peru, which are entirely within the Tropics, are home to the Andes Mountains, which remain snowcapped the entire year. This climatological anomaly is also due to cooler ocean currents and the orographic effect. Choices *A*, *B*, and *C* are all true of the tropics.

43. A: The "tragedy of the commons" describes a pattern in human behavior that individuals will use up resources that are held "in common" and available to all community members, unless an external restraint is in place protecting the resource from overuse. Thus, Choice *A* is correct. Choices *B*, *C*, and *D* are incorrect because these statements do not describe the depletion of communally held resources.

44. C: Sovereignty is a characteristic of a nation that is self-governing, which can only happen after the nation has been formed. Choices *A*, *B*, and *D* are incorrect because, while there are no definitive requirements to form a nation, they typically begin with a group of people bound by some shared characteristic. Examples include language, culture and traditions, history, beliefs and religion, homeland or geography, and ethnicity.

45. A: On the political spectrum, ideologies on the left side of the axis emphasize socioeconomic equality and advocate for government intervention, while ideologies on the right axis seek to preserve society's existing institutions or structures. Therefore, the correct answer will be the farthest left on the axis, making Choice *A* correct. Choice *B* is incorrect because Liberalism supports less government intervention than Socialism. Choice *C* is incorrect because Libertarianism strongly opposes government intervention. Choice *D* is incorrect because, while Fascism advocates for strong government intervention, it supports a hierarchical structure and opposes equality.

46. C: Choice *C* is correct, as it most closely corresponds to the provided definition. Conservatism prioritizes traditional institutions. In general, conservatives oppose modern developments and value stability. Choices *A* and *B* are incorrect because socialism and liberalism both feature the desire to change the government to increase equality. Choice *D* is incorrect because libertarianism is more concerned with establishing a limited government to maximize personal autonomy rather than prioritizing stability and traditional institutions.

47. B: The Articles of Confederation were the first form of government adopted in the American colonies. Under the Articles of Confederation, the central government (the Continental Congress) was granted very limited powers, rendering it largely ineffective. Although the choices describe what would appear to be basic functions of government, the central government could only declare war.

48. B: Industrialization directly caused an increase in urbanization. Factories were located near cities to draw upon a large pool of potential employees. Between 1860 and 1890, the urbanization rate increased from about 20 percent to 35 percent. The other three choices are factually incorrect. Immigration increased during industrialization, as immigrants flooded into America to search for work. Socioeconomic problems plagued the period due to the unequal distribution of wealth and the social ills caused by rapid urbanization. Labor unrest was common as unions advocated for workers' rights and organized national strikes.

49. A: The Treaty of Versailles contained a clause that required Germany to assume responsibility for damages incurred during the conflict. Thus, the Treaty ordered Germany to pay $31.4 billion, the equivalent of $442 billion in 2017. World War I ravaged the German economy, and the country couldn't afford the war debt. The resulting poverty contributed to the rise of the Nazi Party, leading to World War II.

50. D: President Lincoln issued the Emancipation Proclamation to free the slaves in the Confederacy, allowing the institution to continue in states and territories that didn't secede. The excerpt justifies the decision as a "fit and necessary war measure for suppressing said rebellion." Therefore, per the excerpt, emancipation was necessary to strengthen the war effort for the North. Choice *C* is the second-best answer, but the excerpt supports the contention that emancipation was part of an active war effort, rather than merely a punishment. Choices *A* and *B* are incorrect because nothing in the excerpt describes the evil of slavery or the effect of emancipation on morale in the North.

51. B: Federalism, at least as it was put forth by the Founders, describes the relationship between the federal and state governments wherein the powers of government are divided between the two. Choice *A* is incorrect because federalism does not refer to a relationship between the federal government and the people. Instead, the federal government interacts with the people through their state governments. Choice *C* is incorrect because the relationship between the branches of the federal government is defined by a system of checks and balances, not federalism. Choice *D* is incorrect because the Constitution lays out the system of federalism, but federalism does not describe the relationship between the federal government and the Constitution.

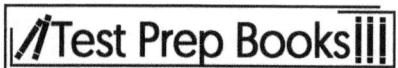

Answer Explanations #1

52. D: *Brown v. Board of Education* set the stage for the fight for civil rights throughout the United States and was the first true rebuff to segregation. It overturned the separate but equal doctrine laid out in the Plessy v. Ferguson Supreme Court case. on Supreme Court case. Choice A is incorrect because the doctrine of judicial review was established one hundred years earlier and has never been overturned. Choice B is incorrect because the public safety exception has to do with Miranda Rights. Choice C is incorrect because the due process doctrine doesn't apply here.

53. C: Population density, which is the total number of people divided by the total land area, generally tends to be much higher in urban areas than rural ones. This is true due to high-rise apartment complexes, sewage and freshwater infrastructure, and complex transportation systems, allowing for easy movement of food from nearby farms. Consequently, competition among citizens for resources is certainly higher in high-density areas, as are greater strains on infrastructure within urban centers.

54. A: Homogeneity, or the condition of similarity, is the unifying factor in most formal regions. Regions have one or more unifying characteristics, such as language, religion, history, or economic similarities, which make the area a cohesive formal region. A good example is the Southern United States. In contrast, diversity and multilingualism, Choices *B* and *C*, are factors that may cause a region to lose homogeneity and be more difficult to classify as a region. Also, social mobility, Choice *D*, is a distractor that refers to one's ability to improve their economic standing in society and is not related to formal regions.

55. A: Globalization has put students and workers in direct conflict with one another despite their relative level of physical separation. For example, students who excel in mathematics and engineering may be recruited by multinational firms who want the best talent for their business despite where they are educated. Furthermore, products produced in other nations are also in competition with global manufacturers to ensure quality craftsmanship at an affordable price. Globalization does not refer to world domination, an absence of nation-states, or a singular world government.

56. C: Federal Reserve. The Federal Reserve is the bank of banks. It is the central bank of the United States and controls the value of money. A commodity is the value of goods such as precious metals. While the Central Reserve and Bank Reserve may sound like good options, the term "bank reserve" refers to the amount of money a bank deposits into a central bank, and the Central Reserve is simply a fictitious name.

57. D: The GDP is used to measure an economy's growth. The inflation of a country doesn't tell us anything about their growth. A country may hold a lot of money in reserves but this does not tell us if they are growing or not. The same can be said for having a lot of exports. It doesn't indicate that an economy is necessarily growing.

58. D: Choice *D* is correct because *Long Island* is a physical geographical feature, rather than a region indicated by a human population. Choices *A*, *B*, and *C* are incorrect because a borough, city, or state is a geographical feature determined by society, not by landscape features.

59. C: The 19th Amendment gave women the right to vote. The 15th Amendment, Choice *A*, gave all U.S. citizens, regardless of race or color, the right to vote. The 18th Amendment, Choice *B*, introduced alcohol prohibition. The 21st Amendment, Choice *D*, repealed prohibition.

60. B: More than one million African Americans in the South went north in search of jobs during and after World War I. The Great Migration led to increased racial tension as black and white Americans competed for housing and jobs in northern cities. The Great Migration also led to the Harlem Renaissance.

Answer Explanations #1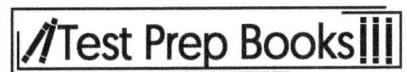

Science

1. D: Water is essential for photosynthesis. Increasing temperatures increase transpiration and drought conditions result in less water available for photosynthesis. The rate of photosynthesis will decrease.

2. D: Genetic variety in a species allows them to be more resistant to stresses. Having genetic diversity increases resilience. Growing multiple strains of tomatoes or multiple types of crops could protect the farm.

3. C: During a lunar eclipse, the Sun and Moon are on opposite sides of the Earth. They line up so that the Sun's light that normally illuminates the Moon is blocked by the Earth. This causes the Moon to become dim. Sunlight can still be seen, Choice *A*, and the Earth does not become dark, Choices *B* and *D*.

4. A: When activated, B cells create antibodies against specific antigens. White blood cells are generated in red and yellow bone marrow, not cartilage. Platelets are not a type of white blood cell and are typically cell fragments produced by megakaryocytes. White blood cells are active throughout nearly all of one's life and have not been shown to specially activate or deactivate because of life events like puberty or menopause.

5. D: Mechanical digestion is physical digestion of food by tearing it into smaller pieces using force. This occurs in the stomach and mouth. Chemical digestion involves chemically changing the food and breaking it down into small organic compounds that can be utilized by the cell to build molecules. The salivary glands in the mouth secrete amylase that breaks down starch, which begins chemical digestion. The stomach contains enzymes such as pepsinogen/pepsin and gastric lipase which chemically digest protein and fats, respectively. The small intestine continues to digest protein using the enzymes trypsin and chymotrypsin. It also digests fats with the help of bile from the liver and lipase from the pancreas. These organs act as exocrine glands because they secrete substances through a duct. Carbohydrates are digested in the small intestine with the help of pancreatic amylase, gut bacterial flora and fauna, and brush border enzymes like lactose. Brush border enzymes are contained in the towel-like microvilli in the small intestine that soak up nutrients.

6. D: Charles Darwin developed the theory of natural selection, which explains the evolutionary process. He postulated that heritable genetic differences could aid an organism's chance of survival in its environment. The organisms with favorable traits pass genes to their offspring, and because they have more reproductive success than those that do not contain the adaptation, the favorable gene spreads throughout the population. Those that do not contain the adaptation often extinguish, so their genes are not passed on. In this way, nature "selects" for the organisms that have more fitness in their environment. Birds with bright-colored feathers and cacti with spines are examples of "fit" organisms.

7. B: The structure exclusively found in eukaryotic cells is the nucleus. Animal, plant, fungi, and protist cells are all eukaryotic. DNA is contained within the nucleus of eukaryotic cells, and they also have membrane-bound organelles that perform complex intracellular metabolic activities. Prokaryotic cells (archaea and bacteria) do not have a nucleus or other membrane-bound organelles and are less complex than eukaryotic cells.

8. B: The cell structure responsible for cellular storage, digestion, and waste removal is the lysosome. Lysosomes are like recycle bins. They are filled with digestive enzymes that facilitate catabolic reactions to regenerate monomers. The Golgi apparatus is designed to tag, package, and ship out proteins destined for other cells or locations. The centrioles typically play a large role only in cell division when they ratchet the chromosomes from the mitotic plate to the poles of the cell. The mitochondria are involved in energy production and are the powerhouses of the cell.

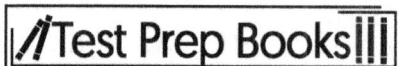

Answer Explanations #1

9. A: Crossing over, or genetic recombination, is the rearrangement of chromosomal sections in tetrads during meiosis, and it results in each gamete having a different combination of alleles than other gametes. The disassembly of the mitotic spindle happens only after telophase and is not related to diversity. While nondisjunction does cause diversity in division and is highly noticeable in gametes formed through meiosis, it can also happen through mitotic division in somatic cells. Although an egg being fertilized by multiple sperm would lead to interesting diversity in the offspring (and possibly fraternal twins), this is not strictly a byproduct of meiotic division.

10. C: Deserts' temperatures are extremely hot in the day and cold at night because of the warming effects of the sun's solar rays, so this is the best example of the sun's energy. Although some flowers do tend to bloom after dawn, this is probably due to day/night cycles regulated by the presence of light rather than intense amounts of energy. Hibernating animals tend to use large repositories of stored nutrients as energy sources rather than relying on the sun's energy, and they may in fact be in caves or hidden underground to shelter them from the sun or weather. The tides are more dependent on the moon due to its gravity rather than any effects its albedo moonlight may have.

11. A: Gases like air will move and expand to fill their container, so they are considered to have an indefinite shape and indefinite volume. Liquids like water will move and flow freely, so their shapes change constantly, but they do not change volume or density on their own. Solids change neither shape nor volume without external forces acting on them, so they have definite shapes and volumes.

12. B: Since the genotype is a depiction of the specific alleles that an organism's genes code for, it includes recessive genes that may or may not be otherwise expressed. The genotype does not have to name the proteins that its alleles code for; indeed, some of them may be unknown. The phenotype is the physical, visual manifestations of a gene, not the genotype. The genotype does not necessarily include any information about the organism's physical characteristics. Although some information about an organism's parents can be obtained from its genotype, its genotype does not actually show the parents' phenotypes.

13. C: One in four offspring (or 25%) will be short, so all four offspring cannot be tall. Although both of the parents are tall, they are hybrid or heterozygous tall, not homozygous. Although it may seem intuitive that the short allele will be expressed by lower numbers of the population than the tall allele, it still appears in 75% of the offspring (although its effects are masked in 2/3 of those). Besides, conditions could favor the recessive allele and kill off the tall offspring.

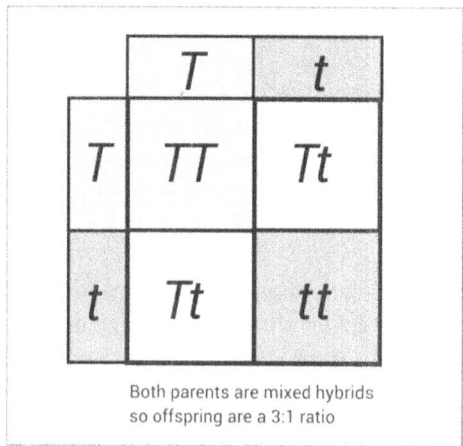

Both parents are mixed hybrids so offspring are a 3:1 ratio

14. D: Evaporation takes place at the surface of a fluid while, boiling takes place throughout the fluid. The liquid will boil when it reaches its boiling or vaporization temperature, but evaporation can happen due to a liquid's volatility. Volatile substances often coexist as a liquid and as a gas, depending on the pressure forced

Answer Explanations #1

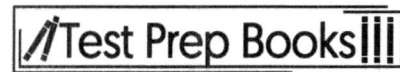

on them. The phase change from gas to liquid is condensation, and both evaporation and boiling take place in nature.

15. C: Water's polarity lends it to be extremely cohesive and adhesive; this cohesion keeps its atoms very close together. Because of this, it takes a large amount of energy to boil its liquid form. Phospholipid bilayers are made of nonpolar lipids; water, a polar liquid, cannot easily flow through it. Cell membranes use proteins called aquaporins to solve this issue and let water flow in and out. Fish breathe by capturing dissolved oxygen through their gills. Water can self-ionize, wherein it decomposes into a hydrogen ion (H+) and a hydroxide ion (OH-), but it cannot self-hydrolyze.

16. C: To gather accurate data, the student must be able compare a participant's test score from round 1 with their test score from round 2. The differing levels of intellect among the participants means that comparing participants' test scores to those of other participants would be inaccurate. This requirement excludes Choices A and D, which involve only one round of testing. The experiment must also involve different levels of sugar consumption from round 1 to round 2. In this way, the effects of different levels of sugar consumption can be seen on the same subjects. Thus, Choice B is incorrect because the experiment provides for no variation of sugar consumption. Choice C is the correct answer because it allows the student to compare each participant's test score from round 1 with their test score from round 2 after different levels of sugar consumption.

17. A: A control is the component or group in an experimental design that isn't manipulated—it's the standard against which the resultant findings are compared, so Choice A is correct. A variable is an element of the experiment that is able to be manipulated, making Choice B false. A constant is a condition of the experiment outside of the hypothesis that remains unchanged in order to isolate the changes in the variables; therefore, Choice C is incorrect. Choice D is false because collected data are simply recordings of the observed phenomena that result from the experiment.

18. B: During telophase, two nuclei form at each end of the cell and nuclear envelopes begin to form around each nucleus. The nucleoli reappear, and the chromosomes become less compact. The microtubules are broken down by the cell, and mitosis is complete. The process begins with prophase as the mitotic spindles begin to form from centrosomes. Prometaphase follows, with the breakdown of the nuclear envelope and the further condensing of the chromosomes. Next, metaphase occurs when the microtubules are stretched across the cell and the chromosomes align at the metaphase plate. Finally, in the last step before telophase, anaphase occurs as the sister chromatids break apart and form chromosomes.

19. A: Velocity is a measure of speed with direction. To calculate velocity, find the change in position over the change in time. Choices B and C are incorrect because they are both equations for speed, and do not imply a direction. A standard measurement for velocity is in meters per second (m/s).

20. C: Wind energy from turbines, solar energy from sun panels, and geothermal energy are all considered renewable and preferable alternatives to fossil fuel, of which there is a limited supply.

21. A: The troposphere is the layer of the atmosphere where the majority of the activity that creates weather conditions experienced on Earth occurs. The ozone layer is in the stratosphere; this is also where airplanes fly.

22. D: Stratus clouds are also grey, but nimbostratus clouds are the low clouds that appear during stormy weather. The other choices are usually seen on fair-weather days.

23. C: Jupiter is the largest planet in the solar system, and it is primarily composed of hydrogen and helium. Ammonia is in much lower quantity and usually found as a cloud within Jupiter's atmosphere.

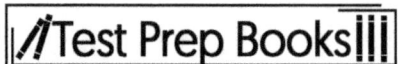

Answer Explanations #1

24. D: Viruses are not classified as living organisms. They are neither prokaryotic or eukaryotic; therefore, they don't belong to any of the answer choices.

25. C: According to the ideal gas law ($PV = nRT$), if volume is constant, the temperature is directly related to the pressure in a system. Therefore, if the pressure increases, the temperature will increase in direct proportion. Choice A would not be possible, since the system is closed and a change is occurring, so the temperature will change. Choice B incorrectly exhibits an inverse relationship between pressure and temperature, or $P = 1/T$. Choice D is incorrect because even without actual values for the variables, the relationship and proportions can be determined.

26. D: According to Newton's second law of motion, $F = m \times a$. Weight is the force resulting from a given situation, so the mass of the object needs to be multiplied by the acceleration of gravity on Earth: $W = m \times g$.

Choice A is incorrect because, according to Newton's law of universal gravitation, all objects exert some force on each other, which is based on their distance from each other and their masses. This is seen in planets, which affect each other's paths and those of their moons. Choice B is incorrect because an object in motion or at rest can have inertia; inertia is the resistance of a physical object to changing its state of motion. Choice C is incorrect because the mass of an object is a measurement of how much substance there is to the object, while the weight is gravity's effect on the mass.

27. D: Radiation can be transmitted through electromagnetic waves and needs no medium to travel; it can travel in a vacuum. This is how the Sun warms the Earth, and it typically applies to large objects with great amounts of heat or objects that have a large difference in their heat measurements. Choice A, convection, involves atoms or molecules traveling from areas of high concentration to those of low concentration and transferring energy or heat with them. Choice B, conduction, involves the touching or bumping of atoms or molecules to transfer energy or heat. Choice C, induction, deals with charges and does not apply to the transfer of energy or heat. Choices A, B, and C need a medium in which to travel, while radiation requires no medium.

28. C: The mantle is the Earth's thickest layer; it holds most of the Earth's material. The crust is thin, and the inner core is also small compared to the mantle. There is no such thing as Earth's shell.

29. C: Subduction occurs when one plate is pushed down by another. A fault is where two plates meet. Diversion occurs when two plates move apart. *Drift* isn't a term used with tectonic plates.

30. B: Transpiration is water that evaporates from pores in plants called stomata. Evaporation of moving water is still called evaporation. Infiltration is the process of water moving into the ground, and precipitation that falls on trees is called canopy interception.

31. D: Water with a higher salinity has more dissolved salt and a lower freezing point. Water from the Dead Sea has the highest salinity of the answer choices.

32. C: Glaciers are formed only on land and constantly move because of their own weight. Icebergs are formed from glaciers, and they float.

33. C: In the Linnaean system, organisms are classified as follows, moving from few and general similarities to comprehensive and specific similarities: domain, kingdom, phylum, class, order, family, genus, and species. A popular mnemonic device to remember the Linnaean system is "Dear King Philip Came Over For Good Soup."

34. B: Substances with higher amounts of hydrogen ions will have lower pHs, while substances with higher amounts of hydroxide ions will have higher pHs. Choice A is incorrect because it is possible to have an

210

Answer Explanations #1

extremely strong acid with a pH less than 1, as long as its molarity of hydrogen ions is greater than 1. Choice C is false because a weak base is determined by having a pH lower than some value, not higher. Substances with pHs greater than 2 include anything from neutral water to extremely caustic lye. Choice D is false because a solution with a pH of 2 has ten times fewer hydrogen ions than a solution of pH 1.

35. A: Salts are formed from compounds that use ionic bonds. Disulfide bridges are special bonds in protein synthesis which hold the protein in their secondary and tertiary structures. Covalent bonds are strong bonds formed through the sharing of electrons between atoms and are typically found in organic molecules like carbohydrates and lipids. London dispersion forces are fleeting, momentary bonds which occur between atoms that have instantaneous dipoles but quickly disintegrate.

36. C: Covalent bonds are special because they share electrons between multiple atoms. Most covalent bonds are formed between the elements H, F, N, O, S, and C, while hydrogen bonds are formed nearly exclusively between H and either O, N, or F of other molecules. Covalent bonds may inadvertently form dipoles, but this does not necessarily happen. For instance, dipoles do not form with similarly electronegative atoms, like carbon and hydrogen. Crystal solids are typically formed by substances with ionic bonds like the salts sodium iodide and potassium chloride.

37. D: An isotope of an element has an atomic number equal to its number of protons, but a different mass number because of the additional neutrons. Even though there are differences in the nucleus, the behavior and properties of isotopes of a given element are identical. Atoms with different atomic numbers also have different numbers of protons and are different elements, so they cannot be isotopes.

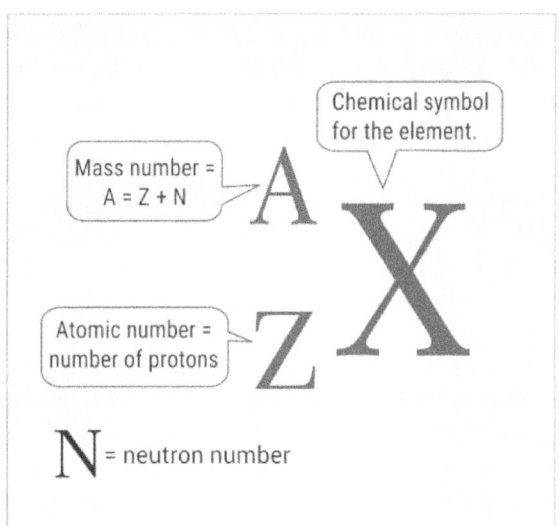

38. A: The neutrons and protons make up the nucleus of the atom. The nucleus is positively charged due to the presence of the protons. The negatively charged electrons are attracted to the positively charged nucleus by the electrostatic or Coulomb force; however, the electrons are not contained in the nucleus. The positively charged protons create the positive charge in the nucleus, and the neutrons are electrically neutral, so they have no effect. Radioactivity does not directly have a bearing on the charge of the nucleus.

39. B: Models are representations of concepts that are impossible to experience directly, such as the 3D representation of DNA, so Choice B is correct. Choice A is incorrect because theories simply explain why things happen. Choice C is incorrect because laws describe how things happen. Choice D is false because an observation analyzes situations using human senses.

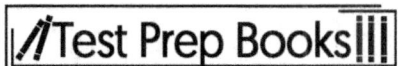

Answer Explanations #1

40. C: An inference is a logical prediction of a why an event occurred based on previous experiences or education. The person in this example knows that plants need water to survive; therefore, the prediction that someone forgot to water the plant is a reasonable inference, hence Choice *C* is correct. A classification is the grouping of events or objects into categories, so Choice *A* is incorrect. An observation analyzes situations using human senses, so Choice *B* is incorrect. Choice *D* is incorrect because collecting is the act of gathering data for analysis.

41. D: An atom is structured with a nucleus in the center that contains neutral neutrons and positive protons. Surrounding the nucleus are orbiting electrons that are negatively charged. Choice *D* is the only correct answer.

42. C: The qualitative definition of ionization energy is the amount of energy needed to remove the most loosely bound valence electron from a gaseous atom or molecule to form a cation. Choice *A* refers to atomic radius, Choice *B* refers to electronegativity, and Choice *D* refers to electron affinity. All four of these properties follow trends on the periodic table.

43. D: Catabolism is the process of breaking down large molecules into smaller molecules to release energy for work. Carbohydrates and fats are catabolized to provide energy for exercise and daily activities. Anabolism synthesizes larger molecules from smaller constituent building blocks. Bioenergetics and metabolism are more general terms involving overall energy production and usage.

44. C: Because of the vast amounts of data that needed to be processed and analyzed, technological breakthroughs like innovations to the microprocessor were directly responsible for the ease of computing handled by the Human Genome Project. Although the sonogram and MRI technology are helpful to the healthcare industry in general, they would not have provided a great deal of help for sequencing and comprehending DNA data, in general. X-ray diffraction is a technique that helps visualize the structures of crystallized proteins, but it cannot determine DNA bases with enough precision to help sequence DNA.

45. A: Many foods from developed countries are grown from plants which have been processed or bioengineered to include increased amounts of nutrients like vitamins and minerals that otherwise would be lost during manufacturing or are uncommon to the human diet. White rice, for example, is typically enriched with niacin, iron, and folic acid, while salt has been fortified with iodine for nearly a century. These help to prevent nutrition deficiencies. While it can be useful for fisheries to maintain models of fish populations so that they don't overfish their stock, this is not as immediately important to nutrition as are fortified and enriched foods. Although innovations to microscopes could lead to improved healthcare, this also has no direct effect on nutrition deficiency. Refrigerated train carts were historically a crucial invention around Civil War times and were used to transport meat and dairy products long distances without spoiling, but dietary deficiencies could be more easily remedied by supplying people with fortified foods containing those nutrients rather than spoilable meats.

46. D: Iodine has the greatest number of electrons at 53 electrons. The number of electrons increases in elements going from left to right across the periodic table. Hydrogen, Choice *A*, is at the top left corner of the periodic table, so it has the fewest electrons (one electron). Iron has 26 electrons, copper has 29 electrons, Choices *B* and *C*, respectively.

47. C: Chemical properties describe the behavior of substances, while physical properties describe their appearance. Reactivity is a behavior, and therefore it's the correct answer.

48. C: An observation typically kicks off the scientific method. The first step is to identify a problem based on an observation—the who, what, when, where, why, and how. An observation is the analysis of information using basic human senses: sight, sound, touch, taste, and smell. In this step of the scientific method, the problem is identified. Recall that designing a science investigation is based on the scientific method, which consists of the following steps: making an observation, forming a question, conducting an experiment, collecting and analyzing data, and forming a conclusion.

49. C: Choices *A* and *B* are not good choices because it's impossible to measure a cat's happiness, and there's a subjective factor involved in determining the softness of pants. Feeling more comfortable isn't objective enough. Measuring purring would also be difficult to do quantitatively; cats either do purr or don't purr. Volume could be measured with a scientific device, but that would have to be specified. Measuring the growth of a dog, Choice *D*, should be clarified—will height or mass be measured? Choice *C* has a valid independent and dependent variable, both which can be measured, so it's the correct choice.

50. D: Dimitri is correct because weather involves the water cycle. The other suggestions (and thus, answer choices) reflect misunderstandings. Weather itself changes day-to-day, and it depends on wind and heat patterns, while seasons depend on proximity to the Sun. Weather patterns such as rain and snow definitely involve the water cycle, so Choice *D* is the correct answer.

51. C: Early childhood educators should know that PowerPoint isn't an effective teaching method, and while going outside is fun, without modeling, the activity will be meaningless. The book idea would not be an effective teaching tool in this case because it's unable to model nearness, closeness, and general location. Modeling is the best option.

52. C: Climate has nothing to do with the size or shape of a state; it relates to exposure to the Sun. Places closer to the equator are hotter, so the answer is Choice *C*.

53. B: Hurricanes and rain are liquid precipitation, and snow is solid precipitation. Tornadoes only involve wind, so Choice *B* is the correct answer.

54. A: Plate tectonics involve movement in the Earth's crust that exposes areas for volcanic activities. Plates have nothing to do with evaporation or delta formation; both of those processes involve the water cycle. Plate movement also has nothing to do with tornados and wind movement.

55. B: Trace fossils are evidence of an organism as opposed to the remains of an organism. Bones, shells, and teeth were all once part of an organism and are true fossils.

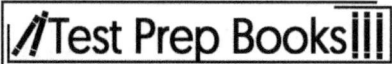

Practice Test #2

Mathematics

1. Convert $\frac{5}{8}$ to a decimal.
   a. 0.62
   b. 1.05
   c. 0.63
   d. 1.60

2. Subtract and express in reduced form: $\frac{23}{24} - \frac{1}{6}$.
   a. $\frac{22}{18}$
   b. $\frac{11}{9}$
   c. $\frac{19}{24}$
   d. $\frac{4}{5}$

3. Subtract and express in reduced form $\frac{43}{45} - \frac{11}{15}$.
   a. $\frac{10}{45}$
   b. $\frac{16}{15}$
   c. $\frac{32}{30}$
   d. $\frac{2}{9}$

4. Change 0.56 to a fraction.
   a. $\frac{5.6}{100}$
   b. $\frac{14}{25}$
   c. $\frac{56}{1,000}$
   d. $\frac{56}{10}$

5. Multiply 13,114 × 191.
   a. 2,504,774
   b. 250,477
   c. 150,474
   d. 2,514,774

6. Marty wishes to save $150 over a 4-day period. How much must Marty save each day on average?
   a. $37.50
   b. $35.00
   c. $45.50
   d. $41.00

Practice Test #2

7. Multiply and reduce $\frac{15}{23} \times \frac{54}{127}$.
   a. $\frac{810}{2,921}$
   b. $\frac{81}{292}$
   c. $\frac{69}{150}$
   d. $\frac{810}{2929}$

8. Bernard can make $80 per day. If he needs to make $300 and only works full days, how many days will this take?
   a. 6 days
   b. 3 days
   c. 5 days
   d. 4 days

9. A couple buys a house for $150,000. They sell it for $165,000. By what percentage did the house's value increase?
   a. 18%
   b. 13%
   c. 15%
   d. 10%

10. Which is closest to 17.8×9.9?
    a. 140
    b. 180
    c. 200
    d. 350

11. Taylor works two jobs. The first pays $20,000 per year. The second pays $10,000 per year. She donates 15% of her income to charity. How much does she donate each year?
    a. $4,500
    b. $5,000
    c. $5,500
    d. $6,000

12. A box with rectangular sides is 24 inches wide, 18 inches deep, and 12 inches high. What is the volume of the box in cubic feet?
    a. 2 cubic feet
    b. 6 cubic feet
    c. 3 cubic feet
    d. 5 cubic feet

13. If $f(x) = (-3x) + 17$, then what is $f(x + 1)$?
    a. $-3x + 19$
    b. $-x + 15$
    c. $-2x + 18$
    d. $-3x + 14$

14. Solve for x:

$$\frac{2x}{5} - 1 = 59$$

   a. 60
   b. 145
   c. 150
   d. 115

15. A National Hockey League store in the state of Michigan advertises 50% off all items. Sales tax in Michigan is 6%. How much would a hat originally priced at $32.99 and a jersey originally priced at $64.99 cost during this sale? Round to the nearest penny.
   a. $97.98
   b. $103.86
   c. $51.93
   d. $48.99

16. Store-brand coffee beans cost $1.23 per pound. A local coffee bean roaster charges $1.98 per $1\frac{1}{2}$ pounds. How much more would 5 pounds from the local roaster cost than 5 pounds of the store-brand?
   a. $0.55
   b. $1.55
   c. $1.45
   d. $0.45

17. Paint Inc. charges $2,000 for painting the first 1,800 feet of trim on a house and an additional $1.00 per foot for each foot beyond that. How much would it cost to paint a house with 3,125 feet of trim?
   a. $3,125
   b. $2,000
   c. $5,125
   d. $3,325

18. A bucket can hold 11.4 liters of water. A kiddie pool needs 35 gallons of water to be full. How many times will the bucket need to be filled to fill the kiddie pool? (Use the conversion 1 gallon = 3.8 liters.)
1 gallon = 3.78541 liters
   a. 12
   b. 35
   c. 11
   d. 45

19. The hospital has a nurse-to-patient ratio of 1 : 25. If a maximum of 325 patients may be admitted at a time, how many nurses are there?
   a. 13 nurses
   b. 25 nurses
   c. 325 nurses
   d. 12 nurses

Practice Test #2

20. Suppose $\frac{x+2}{x} = 2$. What is x?
    a. −1
    b. 0
    c. 2
    d. 4

21. Convert 0.351 to a percentage.
    a. 3.51%
    b. 35.1%
    c. $\frac{351}{100}$
    d. 0.00351%

22. Convert $\frac{2}{9}$ to a percentage.
    a. 22.22%
    b. 4.5%
    c. 450%
    d. 0.22%

23. If $6t + 4 = 16$, what is t?
    a. 1
    b. 2
    c. 3
    d. 4

24. The variable y is directly proportional to x. If $y = 3$ when $x = 5$, then what is y when $x = 20$?
    a. 10
    b. 12
    c. 14
    d. 16

25. There are $4x + 1$ treats in each party favor bag. If a total of $60x + 15$ treats are distributed, how many bags are given out?
    a. 15
    b. 16
    c. 20
    d. 22

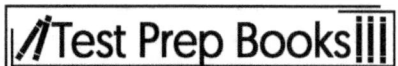

26. The following stem-and-leaf plot shows plant growth in cm for a group of tomato plants.

Stem	Leaf
2	0 2 3 6 8 8 9
3	2 6 7 7
4	7 9
5	4 6 9

What is the range of measurements for the tomato plants' growth?
   a. 29 cm
   b. 37 cm
   c. 39 cm
   d. 59 cm

27. A rectangle has a length that is 5 feet longer than 3 times its width. If the perimeter is 90 feet, what is the length in feet?
   a. 10
   b. 20
   c. 25
   d. 35

28. In an office, there are 50 workers. A total of 60% of the workers are women. 50% of the women are wearing skirts. If no men wear skirts, how many workers are wearing skirts?
   a. 12 workers
   b. 15 workers
   c. 16 workers
   d. 20 workers

29. Ten students take a test. Five students get a 50. Four students get a 70. If the average score is 55, what was the last student's score?
   a. 20
   b. 40
   c. 50
   d. 60

30. A company invests $50,000 in a building where they can produce saws. If the cost of producing one saw is $40, then which function expresses the total amount of money the company spends on producing saws? The variable y is the money paid, and x is the number of saws produced.
   a. $y = 40x + 50,000$
   b. $y + 40 = x - 50,000$
   c. $y = 40x - 50,000$
   d. $y = 50x - 400,000$

Practice Test #2

31. A six-sided die is rolled. What is the probability that the roll is 1 or 2?
    a. $\frac{1}{6}$
    b. $\frac{1}{4}$
    c. $\frac{1}{3}$
    d. $\frac{1}{2}$

32. Which of the following is NOT a way to write 40 percent of N?
    a. $(0.4)N$
    b. $\frac{2}{5}N$
    c. $40N$
    d. $\frac{4}{10}N$

33. At the store, Jan spends $90 on apples and oranges. Apples cost $1 each and oranges cost $2 each. If Jan buys the same number of apples as oranges, how many oranges did she buy?
    a. 20 oranges
    b. 25 oranges
    c. 30 oranges
    d. 35 oranges

34. A box with rectangular faces is 5 feet long, 6 feet wide, and 3 feet high. What is its volume?
    a. 60 cubic feet
    b. 75 cubic feet
    c. 90 cubic feet
    d. 14 cubic feet

35. A train traveling 50 miles per hour takes a trip lasting 3 hours. If a map has a scale of 1 inch per 10 miles, how many inches apart are the train's starting point and ending point on the map?
    a. 14 inches
    b. 12 inches
    c. 13 inches
    d. 15 inches

36. A traveler takes an hour to drive to a museum, spends three hours and 30 minutes there, and takes half an hour to drive home. What percentage of their time was spent driving?
    a. 15%
    b. 30%
    c. 40%
    d. 60%

37. A truck is carrying three cylindrical barrels. Each barrel has a diameter of 2 feet and a height of 3 feet. What is the total volume of the three barrels in cubic feet?
    a. 3π
    b. 9π
    c. 12π
    d. 15π

38. What is the value of b in this equation?

$$5b + 3 = 2b - 9$$

a. 4
b. -12
c. -4
d. 2

39. A rectangle has a length that is 5 feet longer than 3 times its width. If the perimeter is 90 feet, what is the length in feet?

a. 10
b. 20
c. 25
d. 35

40. Which of the following equations best represents the problem below?

The width of a rectangle is 2 centimeters less than the length. If the perimeter of the rectangle is 44 centimeters, then what are the dimensions of the rectangle?

a. $2l + 2(l - 2) = 44$
b. $l + 2) + (l + 2) + l = 48$
c. $l \times (l - 2) = 44$
d. $(l + 2) + (l + 2) + l = 44$

41. What is the value of x in the diagram below?

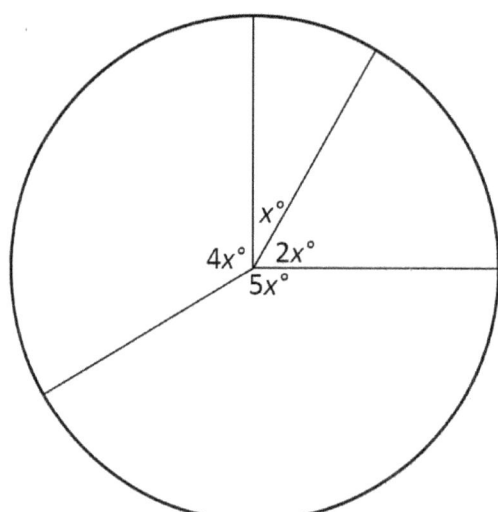

a. 60
b. 50
c. 30
d. 36

Practice Test #2

42. The width of a rectangular house is 22 feet. What is the perimeter of this house if it has the same area as a house that is 33 feet wide and 50 feet long?
    a. 184 feet
    b. 200 feet
    c. 194 feet
    d. 206 feet

43. Before a race of 4 horses, you make a random guess of which horse will get first place and which will get second place. What is the probability that both your guesses will be correct?
    a. $\frac{1}{4}$
    b. $\frac{1}{2}$
    c. $\frac{1}{16}$
    d. $\frac{1}{12}$

44. Kassidy drove for 3 hours at a speed of 60 miles per hour. Using the distance formula, $d = r \times t$ ($distance = rate \times time$), calculate how far Kassidy traveled.
    a. 20 miles
    b. 180 miles
    c. 65 miles
    d. 120 miles

45. If Amanda can eat two times as many mini cupcakes as Marty, what would the missing values be for the following input-output table?

Input (number of cupcakes eaten by Marty)	Output (number of cupcakes eaten by Amanda)
1	2
3	
5	10
7	
9	18

   a. 6, 10
   b. 3, 11
   c. 6, 14
   d. 4, 12

46. The table below shows tickets purchased during the week for entry to the local zoo. What is the mean number of adult tickets sold for the week?

Day of the Week	Age	Tickets Sold
Monday	Adult	22
Monday	Child	30
Tuesday	Adult	16
Tuesday	Child	15
Wednesday	Adult	24
Wednesday	Child	23
Thursday	Adult	19
Thursday	Child	26
Friday	Adult	29
Friday	Child	38

a. 24.2
b. 21
c. 22
d. 26.4

47. An accounting firm charted its income on the following pie graph. If the total income for the year was $500,000, how much income was received from Audit Services and Taxation Services?

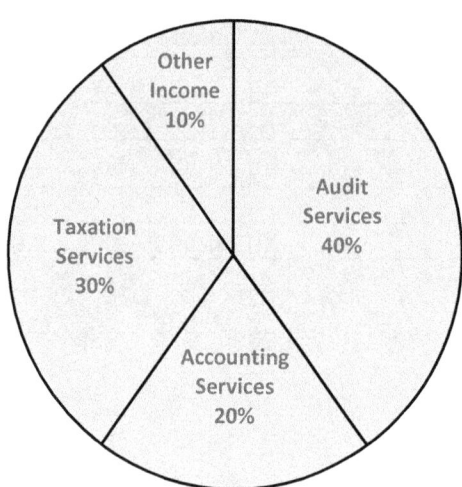

a. $200,000
b. $350,000
c. $150,000
d. $300,000

48. Which inequality represents the number line below?

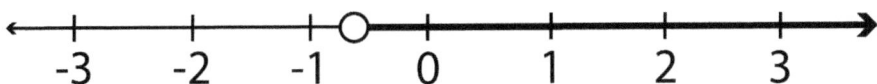

   a. $4x + 5 < 8$
   b. $-4x + 5 < 8$
   c. $-4x + 5 > 8$
   d. $4x - 5 > 8$

49. $x^4 - 16$ can be simplified to which of the following?
   a. $(x^2 - 4)(x^2 + 4)$
   b. $(x^2 + 4)(x^2 + 4)$
   c. $(x^2 - 4)(x^2 - 4)$
   d. $(x^2 - 2)(x^2 + 4)$

50. The phone bill is calculated each month using the equation $c = 50g + 75$. The cost of the phone bill per month is represented by c, and g represents the gigabytes of data used that month. Identify and interpret the slope of this equation.
   a. 75 dollars per day
   b. 75 gigabytes per day
   c. 50 dollars per day
   d. 50 dollars per gigabyte

Social Studies

1. Which of these choices BEST describes a participatory democracy?
   a. A system in which only the educated and wealthy members of society vote and decide upon the leaders of the country
   b. A system in which groups come together to advance certain select interests
   c. A system that emphasizes everyone contributing to the political system
   d. A system in which one group makes decisions for the population at large

2. Which of the following types of government intervention lowers prices, reassures the supply, and creates opportunity to compete with foreign vendors?
   a. Income redistribution
   b. Price controls
   c. Taxes
   d. Subsidies

3. What type of map would be the most useful for calculating data and differentiating between the characteristics of two places?
   a. Topographic maps
   b. Dot-density maps
   c. Isoline maps
   d. Flow-line maps

Question 4 is based on the following map:

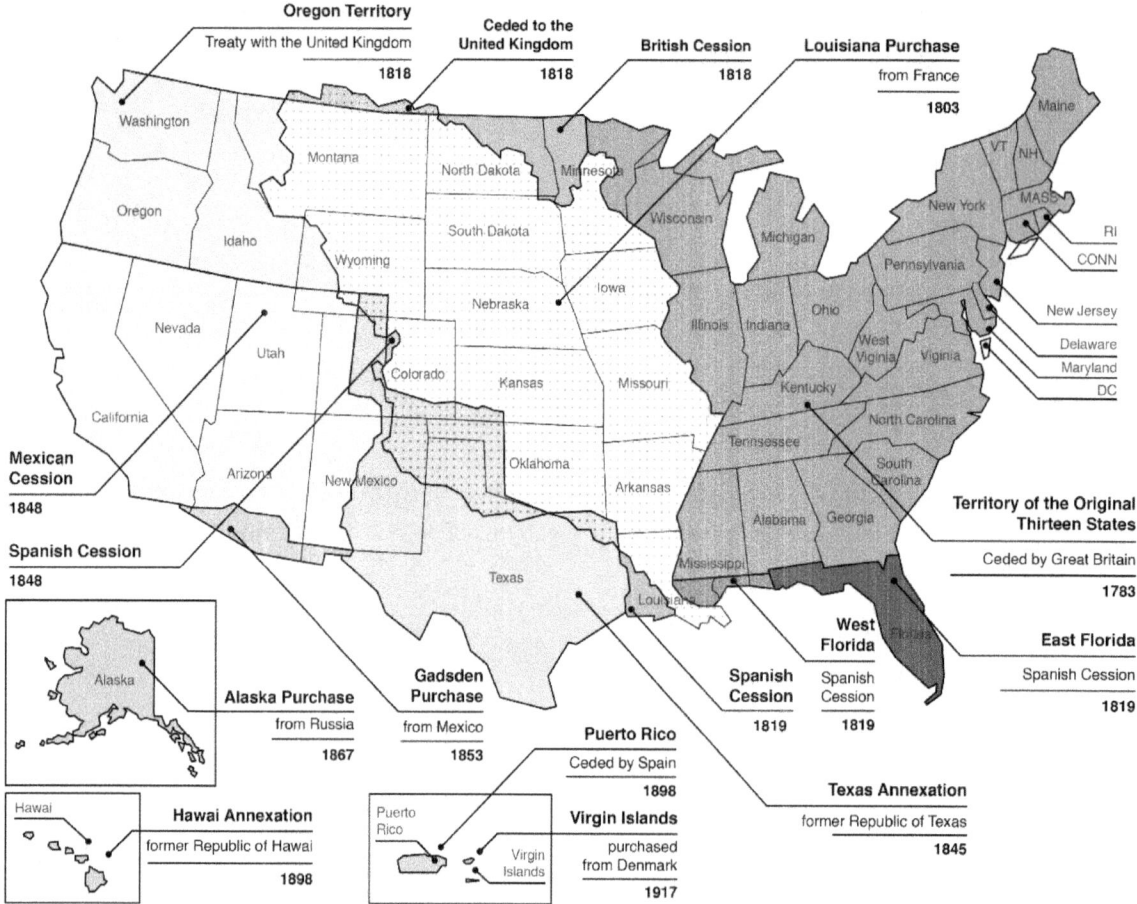

4. What current state did the United States gain through military force with a non-native nation-state?
   a. Nebraska
   b. Missouri
   c. Alaska
   d. Nevada

5. "European Union" fits best into which geographical category?
   a. Linguistic
   b. Political
   c. Ethnic
   d. Physical

6. Which of the following describes the best reason to teach students how modern unindustrialized cultures build their houses?
   a. To teach students how they could build structures without modern tools
   b. To describe how lucky students are to live in an industrialized society
   c. To understand what life was like in the distant past
   d. To emphasize how construction methods are relative to different cultures

Practice Test #2

7. Which of the following is NOT a characteristic of cultural landscapes?
   a. Ethnocentrism
   b. Industrial practices
   c. Land use patterns
   d. Physical features

8. Which of the following is an ethnic religion?
   a. Buddhism
   b. Christianity
   c. Hinduism
   d. Islam

9. Which of the following best describes the relationship between sovereignty and territoriality?
   a. Sovereignty is held by central governments, whereas subnational units of government enjoy rights to territoriality.
   b. Territoriality refers to control over territory, whereas sovereignty is related to political organization.
   c. Political entities leverage territoriality to protect their sovereignty.
   d. Territoriality is generally more valuable to political entities than sovereignty.

10. How does the division of labor in industry impact society?
    a. Specialization of laborers improves working class income.
    b. It becomes harder to globalize the economy between multiple nations.
    c. Products are produced more quickly, which makes them more readily available.
    d. The cost to produce goods increases, which results in a reduced standard of living.

11. In international relations, which of the following is NOT a basic tenet of Realism?
    a. States are the central actors.
    b. States act rationally to advance their self-interest.
    c. States should seek to form international organizations to increase global cooperation and respond to international issues.
    d. All states are interested in maintaining or expanding their power as a means of self-preservation.

12. Governments deployed large-scale propaganda for the FIRST time during which one of the following military conflicts?
    a. Russo-Turkish War
    b. First Sino-Japanese War
    c. Spanish Civil War
    d. World War I

13. Which of the following was a long-term consequence of explorers looking for a northwest passage?
    a. European powers gained a faster route to the Pacific Ocean.
    b. European powers abandoned international trade networks.
    c. European powers forged alliances with Amerindian empires.
    d. European powers colonized the Americas.

14. Which of the following was NOT a problem presented by the Articles of Confederation?
    a. Infighting between branches of government
    b. The inability to implement and collect taxes to pay off debt
    c. Slow responses from the government toward rebellions
    d. Ineffective raising of armies for wartime

Question 15 refers to the diagram below.

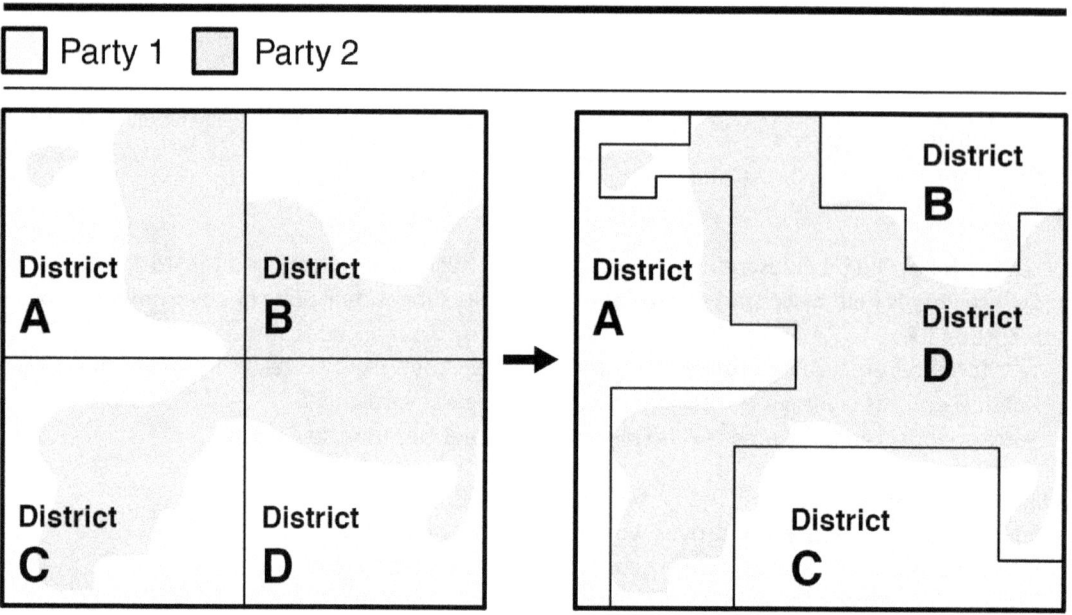

15. The diagram illustrates which of the following manipulative redistricting practices?
    a. Contiguity
    b. Gerrymandering
    c. Partisan fairness
    d. Proportional representation

16. Which of the following statements accurately describes the European Union?
    a. It was formed in 1945 after World War II.
    b. It was founded as a result of the Paris Peace Conference that ended the first World War.
    c. It aims to ensure free movement of people, goods, services, and capital within the internal market.
    d. It was founded to avoid repeating the Great War.

17. Which of the following geographical categories is a linguistic category?
    a. Greater Caucasus
    b. Anglosphere
    c. KwaZulu
    d. Arab World

18. In 1850, the ten most populous cities in the United States, in order from most populous to least, were New York, NY; Baltimore, MD; Boston, MA; Philadelphia, PA; New Orleans, LA; Cincinnati, OH; Brooklyn, NY; St. Louis, MO; Spring Garden, PA; and Albany, NY. How many of these cities are located in a state that was one of the original thirteen colonies?
    a. 6
    b. 7
    c. 8
    d. 9

19. Which term is best defined as a group of people joined by a common culture, language, heritage, history, and religion?
    a. State
    b. Nation
    c. Regime
    d. Government

20. During the 1960s–1980s, deindustrialization in cities in the Industrial North (now called the *Rust Belt*), including hubs like Buffalo, Cleveland, Chicago, and Milwaukee, would be considered an example of which of the following?
    a. Political push factor
    b. Political pull factor
    c. Economic push factor
    d. Economic pull factor

21. Which of the following best describes how culture is transmitted across society?
    a. Culture is almost always transmitted through hierarchical relationships, and it has a trickle-down effect.
    b. Culture is primarily transmitted through religion, economic activities, and government policies.
    c. Cultural exchanges on the internet have given rise to a global popular culture in recent years.
    d. Culture can be transmitted through an endless variety of activities, and the transmission can either be intentional or spontaneous.

22. Which of the following is NOT a purpose of the central bank?
    a. Manage interest rates.
    b. Set the tax rate.
    c. Backup the commercial banks.
    d. Set reserve requirements.

23. What is the name for the movement, started in the 1970s, that began the conservative pushback against the increasing role the government was taking in the economy?
    a. Fiscal policy
    b. Keynesian economics
    c. Fiscal responsibility
    d. Supply-side economics

24. Which ONE of the following best describes an economic benefit of free trade agreements?
    a. Free trade agreements increase international trade by reducing barriers to trade.
    b. Free trade agreements reduce the cost of reparations.
    c. Free trade agreements allow countries to protect domestic iron and steel production.
    d. Free trade agreements facilitate imperialism and the creation of lucrative empires.

25. What social consequences did the Black Death have in Europe?
    a. It gave birth to the concept of absolute monarchy.
    b. It ignited the Protestant Reformation.
    c. The Black Death eroded serfdom in Europe.
    d. It gave rise to child labor laws in England.

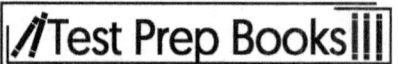

26. Nicolaus Copernicus was a key figure in which cultural phenomena?
    a. The Scientific Revolution
    b. The Age of Enlightenment
    c. The Renaissance
    d. The Protestant Reformation

27. Which of the following statements best describes King Louis XIV of France?
    a. He abdicated his throne during the French Revolution.
    b. He supported the American Revolution.
    c. He was the ultimate example of an absolute monarch.
    d. He created the concept of the Mandate of Heaven.

28. Which of the following resulted from the Age of Enlightenment?
    a. The discovery of the heliocentric theory
    b. The birth of Lutheranism
    c. The American Revolution
    d. The Renaissance

29. Which of the following statements best describes the relationship, if any, between the revolutions in America and France?
    a. The French Revolution inspired the American Revolution.
    b. The American Revolution inspired the French Revolution.
    c. They both occurred simultaneously.
    d. There was no connection between the French and American revolutions.

30. What impact, if any, did the introduction of the movable type printing press have in Europe?
    a. It increased the cost of books because the process was labor intensive.
    b. It led to an increase in literacy.
    c. The Catholic Church used it to effectively suppress the Protestant Reformation.
    d. It led to the Dark Ages.

31. Which of the following documents outlawed slavery throughout the United States?
    a. US Constitution
    b. Compromise of 1850
    c. Emancipation Proclamation
    d. 13th Amendment

32. Which event contributed to increasing sectional tension before the Civil War?
    a. Malcolm X's death
    b. The Bleeding Kansas conflict
    c. The 13th Amendment
    d. Shay's Rebellion

33. Which of the following caused America to join World War I in 1917?
    a. Germany's unrestricted submarine warfare
    b. The destruction of the USS Maine
    c. The Japanese attack on Pearl Harbor
    d. Franz Ferdinand's death in 1914

34. Which event was the last major armed conflict between US forces and Native Americans?
    a. Trail of Tears
    b. Tecumseh's War
    c. Massacre at Wounded Knee
    d. Battle of the Little Big Horn

Questions 35 and 36 are based on the following table:

Presidential Election of 1824			
Candidate	Electoral Votes	Popular Votes	State Votes in the House of Representatives
Andrew Jackson	99	153,544	7
John Quincy Adams	84	108,740	13
William H. Crawford	41	46,618	4
Henry Clay	37	47,136	0

35. Who won the presidential election of 1824?
    a. Andrew Jackson
    b. John Quincy Adams
    c. William H. Crawford
    d. Henry Clay

36. What electoral system can result in a second round of voting commonly referred to as a runoff?
    a. Majority systems
    b. Plurality systems
    c. Single transferable systems
    d. Party list systems

37. Which document established the first system of government in the United States?
    a. Declaration of Independence
    b. Constitution
    c. Articles of Confederation
    d. Bill of Rights

38. What consequences did the New Deal have?
    a. It established a number of federal agencies and programs that continue to function in the 21st century.
    b. It led to a third political party.
    c. It established a two-term limit in the White House.
    d. It led to the Great Depression.

39. What advantage did the North have over the South during the Civil War?
    a. The North was defending their homes from damage.
    b. The North had free labor at home.
    c. The North had a larger population.
    d. The North had more experienced military leaders.

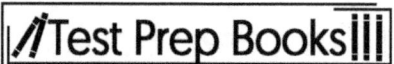

40. In which of the following areas did the United States achieve victory during the Cold War?
    a. The Korean War
    b. The Space Race
    c. The Vietnam War
    d. The Battle of Gettysburg

41. The presidential Cabinet has which of the following duties?
    a. Advise the president.
    b. Act as spokesperson for the US government administration.
    c. Solicit donations for the president's re-election campaign.
    d. Preside over the Senate.

42. Which of the following motivated Christopher Columbus to sail across the Atlantic Ocean?
    a. A desire to establish a direct trade route to Asia
    b. A desire to confirm the existence of America
    c. A desire to prove the world was round
    d. A desire to spread Judaism

43. Which of the following were characteristics of the American economy after World War II?
    a. A return to the Great Depression
    b. Increased use of computers
    c. The decline of the Sun Belt
    d. The fall of the stock market

44. Which of the following agreements allowed territories to vote on whether or not they would become free or slave states?
    a. The Connecticut Compromise
    b. The Missouri Compromise
    c. The Compromise of 1850
    d. The Three-Fifths Compromise

45. Which of the following could be considered a pull factor for a particular area?
    a. High rates of unemployment
    b. Low GDP
    c. Educational opportunity
    d. High population density

46. Differences in race, gender, sexual orientation, economic status, and language can be denoted as what?
    a. Behaviorism
    b. Peer pressure
    c. Adaptation
    d. Diversity

47. What is the difference between Mount McKinley and Mount Denali?
    a. The first uses a European name; the second uses an Indigenous name.
    b. The first is named for an American president; the second is named for a national park.
    c. The first is in the United States; the second is in Canada.
    d. The first is the original name; the second is the modern name.

48. Which of the following statements best describes how industrialization has impacted education?
    a. The increased rate of urbanization increased the quality of education through growing class sizes.
    b. An industrialized economy places greater importance on education due to the technical requirements of industrial jobs.
    c. Children can spend more time in school due to a reduced need to perform agricultural labor during the summer months.
    d. Students are less effectively socialized with their peers due to reduced social cohesion in urban environments.

49. Which political party was founded to advocate for the abolition of slavery?
    a. Constitutional Union
    b. Southern Democrat
    c. Republican
    d. Libertarian

50. The era following the Civil War is known as what?
    a. Antebellum Era
    b. Reconstruction
    c. Progressive Era
    d. Civil rights movement

51. What is the name of the policies developed by President Franklin Delano Roosevelt during the Great Depression?
    a. The Great Society
    b. The War Against Poverty
    c. Progressivism
    d. The New Deal

52. What were the consequences of the Spanish-American War?
    a. The US acquired colonies in the Caribbean and Pacific oceans.
    b. The US acquired large swaths of territory in the Southwestern United States.
    c. It led to the formation of the League of Nations.
    d. It ended the Great Depression.

53. Which Supreme Court decision struck down the separate but equal doctrine?
    a. *Roe v. Wade*
    b. *Brown v. Board of Education*
    c. *Plessy v. Ferguson*
    d. *Marbury v. Madison*

54. How does the Gulf Stream impact the climate of northwestern Europe?
    a. Increased temperature compared to latitude
    b. Increased precipitation
    c. Increased duration of the growing season
    d. Increased frequency of major storms

55. Which event helped sparked the gay and lesbian rights movement in 1969?
    a. The Stonewall Inn Riot
    b. The murder of Matthew Shepard
    c. The murder of Vincent Chin
    d. The emergence of AIDS

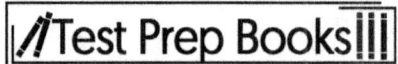

56. What became the scholarly capital of the Hellenistic world during the reign of Alexander the Great?
    a. Jerusalem
    b. Athens
    c. Alexandria
    d. Constantinople

57. Which of the following is a cultural adaptation of humans to their environment?
    a. Working together to dig a well for access to water
    b. Teaching children to drink a glass of water with each meal
    c. Irrigating fields to compensate for a lack of precipitation
    d. Sweating more heavily to cope with an arid environment

58. Which of the following fields falls under the umbrella of the social sciences?
    a. Biology
    b. English
    c. Psychology
    d. Geometry

59. Which of the following are markets that establish a few large firms as the major sellers/distributors?
    a. Free enterprise economies
    b. Pure monopolies
    c. Oligopolies
    d. Command economies

60. What is a kinship group?
    a. A pair of parents and their children
    b. A pair of grandparents, their children, and their grandchildren
    c. An extended clan of individuals related to one another
    d. A group of people with a shared historical lineage

Science

1. What is an adaptation?
    a. The original traits found in a common ancestor
    b. Changes that occur in the environment
    c. When one species begins behaving like another species
    d. An inherited characteristic that enhances survival and reproduction

2. What organelle is the site of protein synthesis?
    a. Nucleus
    b. Smooth ER
    c. Ribosome
    d. Lysosome

3. The energy from electricity results from which of the following?
    a. The atomic structure of matter
    b. The ability to do work
    c. The neutrons in an atom
    d. Conductive materials like metals

Practice Test #2

4. Which is the cellular organelle used to tag, package, and ship out proteins destined for other cells or locations?
    a. The Golgi apparatus
    b. The lysosome
    c. The centrioles
    d. The mitochondria

5. What molecule serves as the hereditary material for prokaryotic and eukaryotic cells?
    a. Proteins
    b. Carbohydrates
    c. Lipids
    d. DNA

6. Which taxonomic system is commonly used to describe the hierarchy of similar organisms today?
    a. Aristotle system
    b. Linnaean system
    c. Cesalpino system
    d. Darwin system

7. What is the Latin specific name for humans?
    a. *Homo sapiens*
    b. *Homo erectus*
    c. *Canis familiaris*
    d. *Homo habilis*

8. Which is an organelle found in a plant cell but not an animal cell?
    a. Mitochondria
    b. Chloroplast
    c. Golgi body
    d. Nucleus

9. What kind of energy do plants use in photosynthesis to create chemical energy?
    a. Light
    b. Electric
    c. Nuclear
    d. Cellular

10. What does the cell membrane do?
    a. Builds proteins
    b. Breaks down large molecules
    c. Contains the cell's DNA
    d. Controls which molecules are allowed in and out of the cell

11. What gets converted to heat inside a greenhouse?
    a. Water
    b. Sunlight
    c. Plants
    d. Oxygen

233

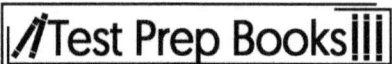

12. Circular motion occurs around what?
    a. The center of mass
    b. The center of matter
    c. An elliptical
    d. An axis

13. Which statement is true regarding electrostatic charges?
    a. Like charges attract.
    b. Like charges repel.
    c. Like charges are neutral.
    d. Like charges neither attract nor repel.

14. Which of the following list details a form of potential energy?
    a. The light given off by a lamp
    b. The gravitational pull of a black hole
    c. The heat from a microwaved burrito
    d. The motion of a pendulum

15. A car is traveling at a constant velocity of $25\ m/s$. How long does it take the car to travel 45 kilometers in a straight line?
    a. 1 hour
    b. 3,600 seconds
    c. 1,800 seconds
    d. 900 seconds

16. What is one feature that prokaryotes and eukaryotes have in common?
    a. A plasma membrane
    b. A nucleus enclosed by a membrane
    c. Organelles
    d. A nucleoid

17. With which genotype would the recessive phenotype appear, if the dominant allele is marked with A and the recessive allele is marked with a?
    a. AA
    b. aa
    c. Aa
    d. aA

18. How are fungi similar to plants?
    a. They have a cell wall.
    b. They contain chloroplasts.
    c. They perform photosynthesis.
    d. They use carbon dioxide as a source of energy.

19. What important function are the roots of plants responsible for?
    a. Absorbing water from the surrounding environment
    b. Performing photosynthesis
    c. Conducting sugars downward through the leaves
    d. Supporting the plant body

Practice Test #2

20. Which subdiscipline of biology would a botanist study?
    a. Growth of an aloe plant
    b. Evolution of monkeys
    c. Genetic changes in human brain cancer
    d. Interaction between worker bees and a queen bee

21. What shape does a water molecule form?
    a. C-shape
    b. S-shape
    c. V-shape
    d. T-shape

22. Which type of biological molecule stores information?
    a. Carbohydrates
    b. Nucleic acids
    c. Proteins
    d. Lipids

23. If a molecule was trying to enter an animal cell, which organelle would it have to pass through first?
    a. Cell wall
    b. Cell membrane
    c. Nucleus
    d. Endoplasmic reticulum

24. Which of the following is identical in both mitosis and meiosis?
    a. The number of divisions
    b. The number of daughter cells produced
    c. The synapsis of homologous chromosomes
    d. When DNA replication occurs

25. Which of following about nuclear reactions is NOT true?
    a. They involve the release of energy.
    b. The structure of the nucleus changes.
    c. They take place in the atom's nucleus.
    d. The reactants and products have equal mass.

26. The chemical reaction when a compound is broken down into its basic components is called:
    a. A synthesis reaction
    b. A decomposition reaction
    c. An organic reaction
    d. An oxidation-reduction reaction

27. What is the name of this compound: CO?
    a. Carbonite oxide
    b. Carbonic dioxide
    c. Carbonic monoxide
    d. Carbon monoxide

28. According to the periodic table, which of the following elements is the least reactive?
    a. Fluorine
    b. Silicon
    c. Neon
    d. Gallium

29. Explain the law of conservation of mass as it applies to this reaction: $2\,H_2 + O_2 \rightarrow 2\,H_2O$.
    a. Electrons are lost.
    b. The hydrogen loses mass.
    c. New oxygen atoms are formed.
    d. There is no decrease or increase of matter.

30. Dark storm clouds are usually located where?
    a. Between 5,000 and 13,000 meters above sea level
    b. Between 2,000 and 7,000 meters above sea level
    c. Less than 2,000 meters above sea level
    d. Outer space

31. Which of the following best describes this moon phase?

    a. Gibbous
    b. Waxing
    c. Waning
    d. Crescent

32. The Big Bang theory helps explain which of the following?
    a. The expanding universe
    b. Dark matter
    c. Life
    d. Gravity

Practice Test #2

33. Currently, water can be found where?
    a. On the Earth
    b. Around Saturn
    c. On Jupiter's moons
    d. All of the above

34. Which of the following correctly displays 8,600,000,000,000 in scientific notation?
    a. 8.6×10^{12}
    b. 8.6×10^{-12}
    c. 8.6×10^{11}
    d. 86×10^{11}

35. Scientist A is observing an unknown substance in the lab. Which observation describes a chemical property of the substance?
    a. She sees that it is green in color.
    b. She weighs it and measures the volume and finds the density to be 10 g/L.
    c. She applies pressure to it and finds that it breaks apart easily.
    d. She passes it through a flame and finds that it burns.

36. Which of the following processes can be solely categorized as a chemical reaction process?
    a. The condensation of water vapor around the container of an ice-cold beverage
    b. Baking brownies with chocolate chips
    c. The shattering of a glass mason jar after falling on the floor
    d. The combination of sand (SiO_2) in water

37. What is the force that opposes motion?
    a. Reactive force
    b. Responsive force
    c. Friction
    d. Momentum

38. Absolute dating involves which of the following?
    a. Measuring radioactive decay
    b. Comparing rock stratification
    c. Fossil location
    d. Fossil record

39. What is the basic unit of matter?
    a. Elementary particle
    b. Atom
    c. Molecule
    d. Photon

40. Which particle is responsible for all chemical reactions?
    a. Electrons
    b. Neutrons
    c. Protons
    d. Orbitals

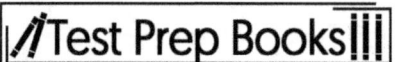

41. Which of these give atoms a negative charge?
    a. Electrons
    b. Neutrons
    c. Protons
    d. Orbital

42. In a chemical equation, the reactants are on which side of the arrow?
    a. Right
    b. Left
    c. Neither right nor left
    d. Both right and left

43. Which of these is a substance that increases the rate of a chemical reaction?
    a. Catalyst
    b. Brine
    c. Solvent
    d. Inhibitor

44. What type of eclipse occurs when the moon comes between the Earth and Sun and covers the Sun's light completely?
    a. Total solar eclipse
    b. Partial lunar eclipse
    c. Total lunar eclipse
    d. Partial solar eclipse

45. The fact that the Earth is tilted as it revolves around the Sun creates which phenomenon?
    a. Life
    b. Plate tectonics
    c. Wind
    d. Seasonality

46. Water that seeps into rock cracks and freezes will most likely result in what process?
    a. Chemical weathering
    b. Mechanical weathering
    c. Erosion
    d. Deposition

47. Which soil is the least permeable to water?
    a. Pure sand
    b. Pure silt
    c. Pure clay
    d. Loam

48. Which of the following is true regarding the Earth's southern geomagnetic pole?
    a. It's always around the same area
    b. It's near the North Pole
    c. It's near the South Pole
    d. It never moves

Practice Test #2

49. Which apparatus would be best to use to look at a solar eclipse?
    a. A telescope facing the eclipse
    b. A pinhole camera facing away from the eclipse
    c. Sunglasses facing the eclipse
    d. Binoculars facing the eclipse

50. Which type of eclipse is viewed during the daytime?
    a. Both solar and lunar
    b. Solar only
    c. Partial lunar
    d. Total lunar

51. Where do geysers get the energy to spray water?
    a. From magma
    b. From the Sun
    c. From springs
    d. From rivers

52. Which period in history dramatically increased air, water, and soil pollution?
    a. The Paleolithic Era
    b. The Big Bang Era
    c. The Industrial Revolution
    d. The Medieval Ages

53. Which greenhouse gas is a common byproduct of landfills and concentrated animal feeding operations?
    a. Carbon
    b. Corn fumes
    c. Nitrogen
    d. Methane

54. Which of the following is a drawback of geothermal power?
    a. It is less efficient than other alternative energy sources.
    b. It involves combustion, so it still contributes some amount of greenhouse gas emissions.
    c. It requires land or roof space.
    d. It requires a large amount of water.

55. Which types of geological material can serve as natural filters for water?
    a. Clay and coal particles
    b. Leaf and limb particles
    c. Granite and quartz particles
    d. Shale and calcite particles

Answer Explanations #2

Mathematics

1. C: Divide 5 by 8, which results in 0.625. This rounds up to 0.63.

2. C: To find a common denominator, look for a number that has both denominators (24 and 6) as factors. 24 works. Multiply the top and bottom of each fraction by whatever number will make the denominator 24:

$$\frac{23}{24} \times \frac{1}{1} = \frac{23}{24} \text{ and } \frac{1}{6} \times \frac{4}{4} = \frac{4}{24}$$

Now that we have a common denominator, subtract the numerators:

$$\frac{23}{24} - \frac{4}{24} = \frac{23-4}{24} = \frac{19}{24}$$

Since 19 and 24 have no common factors except 1, this fraction can't be reduced.

3. D: Set up the problem and find a common denominator for both fractions.

$$\frac{43}{45} - \frac{11}{15}$$

Multiply each fraction across by a fraction equivalent to 1 to convert to a common denominator.

$$\frac{43}{45} \times \frac{1}{1} - \frac{11}{15} \times \frac{3}{3}$$

Once over the same denominator, subtract across the top.

$$\frac{43-33}{45} = \frac{10}{45}$$

Reduce.

$$\frac{10 \div 5}{45 \div 5} = \frac{2}{9}$$

4. B: $\frac{14}{25}$

Since 0.56 goes to the hundredths place, it can be placed over 100:

$$\frac{56}{100}$$

Essentially, the way to do so is by multiplying the numerator and denominator by 100:

$$\frac{0.56}{1} \times \frac{100}{100} = \frac{56}{100}$$

Answer Explanations #2

Then, the fraction can be simplified down to $\frac{14}{25}$:

$$\frac{56}{100} \div \frac{4}{4} = \frac{14}{25}$$

5. A: 2,504,774

Line up the numbers (the number with the most digits on top) to multiply. Begin with the right column on top and the right column on bottom.

Move one column left on top, and multiply by the far-right column on the bottom. Remember to add the carry-over after you multiply. Continue that pattern for each of the numbers on the top row.

Starting on the far-right column on top, repeat this pattern for the next digit left on the bottom. Write the answers below the first line of answers; remember to begin with a zero placeholder. Continue for each number in the top row.

Starting on the far-right column on top, repeat this pattern for the next digit left on the bottom. Write the answers below the previous line of answers. Remember to begin with two zero placeholders this time.

Once this is completed, ensure the answer rows are lined up correctly, then add.

6. A: Divide the total amount by the number of days:

$$\frac{150}{4} = 37.5$$

She needs to save an average of $37.50 per day.

7. A: Multiply across the top and across the bottom.

$$\frac{15 \times 54}{23 \times 127} = \frac{810}{2,921}$$

This matches Choice A, but first look to see if the fraction can be reduced. Because the numbers are so large, it may be difficult to tell, so the easiest method may be to look at each of the other answer choices. With Choice B, the denominator, 292, is not a factor of 2,921 because $292 \times 10 = 2,920$, not 2,921. With Choice C, again, the denominator, 150, is not a factor of 2,921, because 150 is a multiple of 10 and 2,921 isn't. Finally, in Choice D, the numerator is the same as in the original fraction, but the denominator isn't, so this can't have the same value. The other choices are eliminated, so the answer must be Choice A.

8. D: The number of days can be found by taking the total amount Bernard needs to make and dividing it by the amount he earns per day:

$$\frac{300}{80} = \frac{30}{8} = \frac{15}{4} = 3.75$$

But Bernard is only working full days, so he will need to work 4 days, since 3 days is not a sufficient amount of time.

9. D: The value went up by $165,000 - $150,000 = $15,000. Out of $150,000, this is:

$$\frac{15,000}{150,000} = \frac{1}{10}$$

If we multiply the top and bottom by 10 to give us a denominator of 100, the result is $\frac{10}{100}$, or 10%.

10. B: Instead of multiplying these out, we can estimate the product by using $18 \times 10 = 180$.

11. A: Taylor's total income is $\$20,000 + \$10,000 = \$30,000$. 15% as a fraction is $\frac{15}{100} = \frac{3}{20}$. So:

$$\frac{3}{20} \times \$30,000 = \frac{\$90,000}{20} = \frac{\$9,000}{2}$$

$$\frac{\$9,000}{2} = \$4,500$$

12. C: Since the answer will be in cubic feet rather than inches, the first step is to convert from inches to feet for the dimensions of the box. There are 12 inches per foot, so the box is $\frac{24}{12} = 2$ feet wide, $\frac{18}{12} = 1.5$ feet deep, and $\frac{12}{12} = 1$ foot high. The volume is the product of these three together:

$$2 \times 1.5 \times 1 = 3 \text{ cubic feet}$$

13. D: The function presented is being evaluated for $x + 1$; therefore, $x + 1$ must be substituted into the original function as follows:

$$f(x + 1) = -3(x + 1) + 17$$

Distributing the −3 results in:

$$f(x + 1) = -3x - 3 + 17$$

Combining like terms results in:

$$-3x + 14$$

14. C: Set up the initial equation.

$$\frac{2x}{5} - 1 = 59$$

Add 1 to both sides.

$$\frac{2x}{5} - 1 + 1 = 59 + 1$$

$$\frac{2x}{5} = 60$$

Multiply both sides by $\frac{5}{2}$.

$$\frac{2x}{5} \times \frac{5}{2} = 60 \times \frac{5}{2}$$

$$x = 150$$

Answer Explanations #2

15. C: We can first find the total cost of the hat and jersey, then multiply by 0.5 to apply the 50% off:

$$(32.99 + 64.99) \times 0.5 = 48.99$$

Finally, we calculate the sales tax of 6% (that is, 0.06) and add it to the total:

$$48.99 + (48.99 \times 0.06) = 51.93$$

16. D: Five pounds of store-brand coffee would cost $\frac{\$1.23}{1\ lbs} \times 5\ lbs = \$6.15$. Five pounds of local coffee would cost $\frac{\$1.98}{1.5\ lbs} \times 5\ lbs = \$6.60$. Calculate the price difference: $\$6.60 - \$6.15 = \$0.45$.

17. D: Find how many feet are left after the first 1,800 ft:

$$3,125\ ft - 1,800\ ft = 1,325\ ft$$

At $1 per foot, this part will cost $1,325. Add this to the $2,000 for the first 1,800 ft to get the total cost:

$$\$2,000 + \$1,325 = \$3,325$$

18. A: Calculate how many gallons the bucket holds.

$$11.4\ L \times \frac{1\ gal}{3.8\ L} = 3\ gal$$

Next, calculate how many buckets are needed to fill the 35-gallon pool.

$$\frac{35}{3} = 11.67$$

Since the amount is more than 11 but less than 12, the bucket must be filled 12 times.

19. A: Using the given information of one nurse to 25 patients and 325 total patients, set up an equation to solve for the number of nurses (N):

$$\frac{N}{325} = \frac{1}{25}$$

Multiply both sides by 325 to get N by itself on one side.

$$\frac{N}{1} = \frac{325}{25} = 13\ \text{nurses}$$

20. C: Multiply both sides by x to get $x + 2 = 2x$. Then, subtract x from both sides to get $2 = x$.

21. B: 35.1%

To convert from a decimal to a percentage, move the decimal point two places to the right. In this case, that makes 0.351 become 35.1%.

22. A: Converting a fraction to a percentage takes two steps. First, divide the numerator by the denominator to turn the fraction into a decimal:

$$\frac{2}{9} = 0.2222\ ...$$

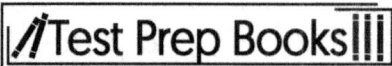

The "..." indicates a repeating decimal with an infinite number of 2's.

Now, to convert to a percentage, move the decimal point two places to the right:

$$22.22\%$$

23. B: First, subtract 4 from each side:

$$6t + 4 = 16$$

$$6t + 4 - 4 = 16 - 4$$

$$6t = 12$$

Now, divide both sides by 6:

$$\frac{6t}{6} = \frac{12}{6}$$

$$t = 2$$

24. B: The variable y is directly proportional to x, which means that whenever x is multiplied by a number, y is multiplied by that same number. When x changes from 5 to 20, it is multiplied by 4, so the original y value must also be multiplied by 4. That means $y = 3 \times 4 = 12$

25. A: The total number of treats distributed will be the number of treats per bag $(4x + 1)$ multiplied by the number of bags given out, which can be represented by the variable n. This expression is $n(4x + 1)$. Since this is the number of treats distributed, set it equal to $60x + 15$.

$$n(4x + 1) = 60x + 15.$$

In order to figure out what n is, determine what number multiplied by 4 results in 60 ($4n = 60$) and what number multiplied by 1 results in 15 ($1n = 15$). In both cases, $n = 15$. Therefore, 15 bags are given out.

26. C: The range of the entire stem-and-leaf plot is found by subtracting the lowest value from the highest value, as follows: $59 - 20 = 39$ cm. All other choices are miscalculations read from the chart.

27. D: Denote the width as w and the length as l. Then:

$$l = 3w + 5$$

The perimeter is:

$$2w + 2l = 90$$

Substituting the first expression for l into the second equation yields:

$$2(3w + 5) + 2w = 90$$

$$6w + 10 + 2w = 90$$

$$8w = 80$$

$$w = 10$$

Putting this into the first equation, it yields:

$$l = 3(10) + 5 = 35$$

28. B: If 60% of 50 workers are women, then there are 30 women working in the office. If half of them are wearing skirts, then that means 15 women wear skirts. Since nobody else wears skirts, this means there are 15 people wearing skirts.

29. A: Let the unknown score be x. The average will be:

$$\frac{5 \times 50 + 4 \times 70 + x}{10} = \frac{530 + x}{10} = 55$$

Multiply both sides by 10 to get $530 + x = 550$, or $x = 20$.

30. A: The total amount the company pays, y, equals the cost of the building ($50,000) plus the cost of the saws. Since the saws cost $40 each, the overall cost of the saws is $40 times x, where x is the number of saws. Putting all this together, we have $y = 50,000 + 40x$, which is equivalent to Choice *D*.

31. C: When a die is rolled, each outcome is equally likely. Since it has six sides, each outcome has a probability of $\frac{1}{6}$. The chance of a 1 or a 2 is therefore:

$$\frac{1}{6} + \frac{1}{6} = \frac{1}{3}$$

32. C: $40N$ would be 4,000% of N. $\frac{40}{100}$.

33. C: The best way to solve this problem is by using a system of equations. The problem states that Jan bought $90 worth of apples ($a$) and oranges ($r$) at $1 and $2, respectively. That means the first equation is:

$$1(a) + 2(r) = 90$$

It's also stated that she bought an equal number of apples and oranges, which creates the second equation: $a = r$. Then, replace a with r in the first equation to give:

$$1(r) + 2(r) = 90 \text{ or } 3(r) = 90$$

Solving for r yields:

$$r = 30$$

Thus, Jan bought 30 oranges (and 30 apples).

34. C: The formula for the volume of a box with rectangular faces is the length times the width times the height, so:

$$5 \times 6 \times 3 = 90 \text{ cubic feet}$$

35. D: First, the train's journey in the real world is:

$$3 \text{ h} \times 50 \frac{\text{mi}}{\text{h}} = 150 \text{ mi}$$

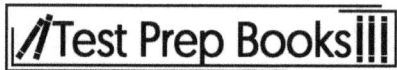

On the map, 1 inch corresponds to 10 miles, so that is equivalent to:

$$150 \text{ mi} \times \frac{1 \text{ in}}{10 \text{ mi}} = 15 \text{ in}$$

Therefore, the start and end points are 15 inches apart on the map.

36. B: The total trip time is $1 + 3.5 + 0.5 = 5$ hours. The total time driving is $1 + 0.5 = 1.5$ hours. So, the fraction of time spent driving is $\frac{1.5}{5}$ or $\frac{3}{10}$. To convert this to a percentage, multiply the top and bottom by 10 to make the denominator 100. $\frac{3}{10} \times \frac{10}{10} = \frac{30}{100}$. Since the denominator is 100, the numerator is the percentage: 30%.

37. B: The formula for the volume of a cylinder is $\pi r^2 h$, where r is the radius and h is the height. The diameter is twice the radius, so these barrels have a radius of 1 foot. That means each barrel has a volume of:

$$\pi \times (1 \text{ ft})^2 \times 3 \text{ ft} = 3\pi \text{ ft}^3$$

Since there are three of them, the total is:

$$3 \times 3\pi \text{ ft}^3 = 9\pi \text{ ft}^3$$

38. C: To solve for the value of b, isolate the variable b on one side of the equation.

Start by moving the 3 over to the other side of the equation:

$$5b + 3 = 2b - 9$$

$$5b + 3 - 3 = 2b - 3 - 9$$

$$5b = 2b - 12$$

Next, subtract $2b$ from $5b$:

$$5b - 2b = 2b - 2b - 12$$

$$3b = -12$$

Finally, divide both sides by 3 to get b on its own:

$$\frac{3b}{3} = -\frac{12}{3}$$

$$b = -4$$

39. D: Denote the width as w and the length as l. Then, $l = 3w + 5$. The perimeter is $2w + 2l = 90$. Substituting the first expression for l into the second equation yields:

$$2(3w + 5) + 2w = 90$$

$$6w + 10 + 2w = 90$$

$$8w = 80$$

$$w = 10$$

Putting this into the first equation, it yields:

$$l = 3(10) + 5 = 35$$

40. A: The perimeter of a rectangle is $P = 2l + 2w$. We are told $P = 44$, so $2l + 2w = 44$. We are also told that the width is 2 cm less than the length: $w = l - 2$. Substituting this for w in the perimeter equation, we get $2l + 2(l - 2) = 44$, which is Choice A. Although it's not necessary to answer the test question, we could solve the equation to find the length and width. The equation simplifies to $4l - 4 = 44$, or $l = 12$, and since $w = l - 2$, we find $w = 10$.

41. C: 30. A complete circle measures 360°. This circle is broken up into 4 different parts with different measures for each part. Adding these parts should give a total of 360 degrees. The equation generated from this diagram is:

$$4x + 5x + x + 2x = 360$$

Collecting like terms gives the equation $12x = 360$, which can be solved by dividing by 12 to give $x = 30$. The value of x in the diagram is 30.

42. C: First, find the area of the second house. The area is:

$$A = l \times w = 33 \times 50 = 1{,}650 \text{ square feet}$$

Then, use the area formula to determine what length gives the first house an area of 1,650 square feet. So,

$$1{,}650 = 22 \times l$$

$$l = \frac{1{,}650}{22} = 75 \text{ feet}$$

Then, use the formula for perimeter ($A = l + l + w + w$) to get:

$$75 + 75 + 22 + 22 = 194 \text{ feet}$$

43. D: The probability of picking the winner of the race is:

$$\frac{1}{4} \left(\frac{number\ of\ favorable\ outcomes}{number\ of\ total\ outcomes} \right)$$

Assuming the winner was picked on the first selection, three horses remain from which to choose the runner-up (these are dependent events). Therefore, the probability of picking the runner-up is $\frac{1}{3}$. To determine the probability that multiple events all happen, multiply the probabilities of the events:

$$\frac{1}{4} \times \frac{1}{3} = \frac{1}{12}$$

44. B: The rate, r (60 miles per hour), and time, t (3 hours), are given. To find the distance, put the values into the distance formula and evaluate:

$$d = r \times t$$

$$d = (60 \text{ mi/h}) \times (3 \text{ h}) \rightarrow d = 180 \text{ mi}$$

45. C: Since Amanda eats twice as many cupcakes as Marty, we multiply the input by 2 to get the output. Filling in for the missing numbers would result in $3 \times 2 = 6$ and $7 \times 2 = 14$.

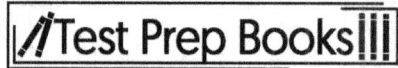

46. C: To find the mean, or average, of a set of values, add the values together and then divide by the total number of values. We will need to add up the number of adult tickets sold for the week and divide by the total number of days. The equation is as follows:

$$\frac{22 + 16 + 24 + 19 + 29}{5} = 22$$

47. B: Audit and Taxation Services total income is unknown (we can call it ATS) and its percentage of overall income is $40\% + 30\% = 70\%$. Accounting Services income is $100,000, which makes up 20% of overall income. We can use these dollar amounts and percentages to set up a proportion:

$$\frac{ATS}{\$100,000} = \frac{70}{20}$$

We can solve this equation to find Audit and Taxation Services income:

$$ATS = \left(\frac{70}{20}\right)\$100,000 = \$350,000$$

Another way of approaching the problem is to calculate the easy percentage of 10%, then multiply it by 7, because the total percentage for Audit and Taxation Services was 70%. 10% of 500,000 is 50,000. Then multiplying this number by 7 yields the same income of $350,000.

48. B: The number line shows:

$$x > -\frac{3}{4}$$

Each inequality must be solved for x to determine if it matches the number line. Choice A of $4x + 5 < 8$ results in $x < -\frac{3}{4}$, which is incorrect. Choice C of $-4x + 5 > 8$ yields $x < -\frac{3}{4}$, which is also incorrect. Choice D of $4x - 5 > 8$ results in $x > \frac{13}{4}$, which is not correct. Choice B, $-4x + 5 < 8$ is the only choice that results in the correct answer:

$$x > -\frac{3}{4}$$

49. A: This has the form $t^2 - y^2$, with $t = x^2$ and $y = 4$. It's also known that $t^2 - y^2 = (t + y)(t - y)$, and substituting the values for t and y into the right-hand side gives:

$$(x^2 - 4)(x^2 + 4)$$

50. D: The slope from this equation is 50, and it is interpreted as the cost per gigabyte used. Since the g-value represents the number of gigabytes and the equation is set equal to the cost in dollars, the slope relates these two values. For every gigabyte used on the phone, the bill goes up 50 dollars.

Social Studies

1. C: A participatory democracy in its truest form is a system in which everyone participates in the political system. Choice A describes an elite democracy, which was advocated by some of the Founders like James Madison. Choice B is a pluralist democracy—one where interest groups and advocacy for certain issues dominate the government. Choice D describes an aristocracy or an oligarchy rather than a participatory democracy.

Answer Explanations #2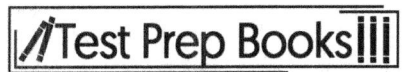

2. D: By artificially increasing supply and lowering costs of production in various sectors of the economy, subsidies can lower prices, reassure the supply, and create opportunity to compete with foreign vendors. Choice A is incorrect because income redistribution moves wealth from some people in a society to others; it does not have the effects asked for in the question. Choice B is incorrect because, while price controls can lower prices, they do have the other effects asked for in the question. Choice C is incorrect because taxes increase government revenue but do not have the effects asked for in the question.

3. C: Choice C is correct. Isoline maps are used to calculate data and differentiate between the characteristics of two places. In an isoline map, symbols represent values, and lines can be drawn between two points to determine differences. The other answer choices are maps with different purposes. Choice A is incorrect because topographic maps display contour lines, which represent the relative elevation of a particular place. Choices B and C are incorrect because dot-density maps and flow-line maps are types of thematic maps. Dot-density maps illustrate the volume and density of a characteristic of an area. Flow-line maps use lines to illustrate the movement of goods, people, or even animals between two places.

4. D: Mexico ceded Nevada as part of the peace agreement ending the Mexican-American War. Choices A, B, and C are incorrect because they are territories gained via purchase when the question asks about military force. Missouri and Nebraska became American territories through the Louisiana Purchase, and the United States purchased Alaska from Russia.

5. B: The European Union is a political entity that comprises twenty-seven independent countries in Europe. Therefore, Choice B is correct. Choices A and C are incorrect because the European Union comprises nations with diverse languages and ethnicities. Choice D is incorrect because the European Union's boundaries are defined by its member states, not land features.

6. D: Choice D is the best answer because it is important for students to internalize cultural relativism early in their education. This empowers the student to learn other social studies topics in a nonjudgmental manner. Choice D is correct. Choice A is incorrect because this construction process does not prepare students for participation in modern society. Choice B is incorrect because it values one type of society and culture over another. Choice C is incorrect because using modern preindustrial cultural practices as an example of practices of a past culture is culturally insensitive.

7. A: Ethnocentrism is a perspective on cultural differences, and it's not traditionally a characteristic of cultural landscapes. Thus, Choice A is the correct answer. Cultural landscape is an extremely broad concept to describe the relationship between physical environments and human development. Cultural landscapes include forms of economic production, including industrial practices. Therefore, Choice B is incorrect. Cultural landscapes also incorporate innumerable cultural aspects, such as land use practices. Therefore, Choice C is incorrect. Physical features of the land are a critical aspect of cultural landscapes because they shape the natural environment. Therefore, Choice D is incorrect.

8. C: Ethnic religions don't claim to hold universal truths that are applicable to all people, so they expand less aggressively than universalizing religions. As a result, ethnic religions tend to remain most popular in their hearth region of origin, and if they expand at all, it's through relocation diffusion. Hinduism is a classic ethnic religion because it has only spread from its hearth region of origin through relocation diffusion. Thus, Choice C is the correct answer. Buddhism, Choice A, Christianity, Choice B, and Islam, Choice D, are all universalizing religions. These three religions assert universal truths, and they have all spread through both relocation diffusion and expansion diffusion. Therefore, Choice A, Choice B, and Choice D are incorrect.

9. C: Sovereignty is a government's ability to project political power and authority over its territories, and territoriality refers to people's cultural, economic, and historical connections to land. Political entities have sought to increase territoriality in order to unify the state and maintain sovereign claims. Thus, Choice C is

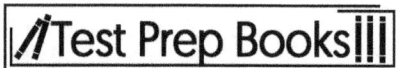

Answer Explanations #2

the correct answer. Sovereignty isn't exclusively held by central governments. In federal states, the central government shares sovereignty with subnational units of government. So, Choice A is incorrect. Sovereignty is also closely related to territorial control, and territoriality is more strongly associated with people's connections to land than political organizations. As such, Choice B is incorrect. Choice D is incorrect because all states need to exercise sovereignty in order to have a functional government.

10. C: The division of labor increases the speed with which goods can be produced. This makes luxuries more readily available at a cheaper cost. Choice C is correct. Choice A is incorrect because labor specialization often excludes those with less education from the labor pool. Choice B is incorrect because division of labor eases integrating the economies of multiple nations (which is part of the globalization process). Choice D is incorrect because the cost of production does not increase when using the division of labor.

11. C: The two major theories of international relations are Realism and Liberalism. Realism analyzes international relations through the interactions of states under the assumption that states act rationally to maintain or expand power as a means of self-preservation, which inevitably leads to conflict in an anarchical system. The question asks for the choice that doesn't adhere to Realism, and the other choices state three of the four basic tenets of Realism. In contrast, Choice C states a principle of Liberalism. Realists don't value international organizations or prioritize global cooperation.

12. D: Governments first deployed large-scale propaganda during World War I. Propaganda was a critical part of the governments' total war strategy, which called for the mobilization of every possible resource for the war effort. In order to fight this unprecedented global conflict, governments had to convince the public to sacrifice their food, goods, and lives to the war effort like never before. Thus, Choice D is the correct answer. Propaganda was used in the Russo-Turkish War (1877–1878) and First Sino-Japanese War (1894–1895), but it was not widespread and orchestrated by the government. During World War I, nearly every government created official propaganda departments for the first time in history. So, Choices A and B are incorrect. Choice C is the second best answer choice. The Spanish, German, and Soviet governments all published a significant amount of propaganda. However, World War I (1914–1918) occurred several decades before the Spanish Civil War (1936–1939). Therefore, Choice C is incorrect.

13. D: European explorers never found the Northwest Passage, but the search uncovered the Americas' economic potential. European colonization started almost immediately after Columbus reached the Caribbean, and it spread across both continents as explorers continued to search for the elusive route to Asia. Thus, Choice D is the correct answer. Although Ferdinand Magellan found a passage to Asia through the southern Atlantic, it was much slower than sailing around the Cape of Good Hope. So, Choice A is incorrect. The search for a Northwest Passage exponentially increased international trade, so Choice B is incorrect. European powers occasionally made strategic short-term alliances with individual Amerindian tribes, but alliances weren't a long-term consequence of European exploration in the Americas. As such, Choice C is incorrect.

14. A: Despite all of the issues of the Articles of Confederation, infighting among the governmental branches was not one of them. This was mainly because there weren't many branches of government, but also because the federal government didn't meet very often. Problems with debt, slow military response, and an army were all problems of the Confederation that prompted the change to a more steadfast and central solution.

15. B: Prior to redistricting, the two political parties had relatively equal support in all four voting districts. Afterward, Political Party 1 gained a decisive advantage in three political districts by packing most of Political Party 2's supporters into a single district. This manipulative redistricting practice is commonly referred to as *gerrymandering*. Thus, Choice B is the correct answer. Nearly all states require voting districts to have contiguous borders, and all of the districts depicted in the diagram are contiguous. However, contiguity isn't a manipulative practice, so Choice A is incorrect. If redistricting had occurred in accordance with the principle of partisan fairness, the voting districts wouldn't have significantly changed. In fact, Political Party 1 likely dominated the redistricting process in order to achieve such a partisan victory. Therefore, Choice C is incorrect. Choice D is incorrect because proportional representation is an electoral system, not a redistricting practice.

16. C: The European Union aims to ensure free movement of people, goods, services, and capital within the internal market. The United Nations was formed in 1945 after World War II, making Choice A incorrect. The League of Nations was founded as a result of the Paris Peace Conference that ended the first World War and was also founded to avoid repetition of the first World War, making Choices B and D incorrect.

17. B: Choice B is correct because *Anglosphere* denotes the countries in which English is the dominant language of public discourse. Thus, *Anglosphere* is a linguistic geographical category. Choice A is incorrect because the Greater Caucasus is a mountain range. Choice C is incorrect because KwaZulu is a province, a category of political geography. Choice D is incorrect because *Arab World* describes the places where people of Arab ethnicity live, so the category would be ethnic geography.

18. B: The original thirteen colonies were Virginia, New York, Massachusetts, Maryland, Rhode Island, Connecticut, New Hampshire, Delaware, North Carolina, South Carolina, New Jersey, Pennsylvania, and Georgia. Thus, all but three cities on the list (New Orleans, Cincinnati, St. Louis) are in states that were one of the original thirteen colonies, so the correct answer is Choice B, 7.

19. B: A Nation is defined as a group of people who have common traits, such as heritage, history, language, culture, and religion. It has nothing to do with borders, sovereignty, power, people in office, or the rules by which a government operates (many of which are found in the other answer terms of state, government, and regime).

20. C: Deindustrialization in cities in the Industrial North during the 1960s-1980s pushed many residents away from industrial hubs like Buffalo, Cleveland, Chicago, and Milwaukee because the number of jobs dropped significantly. Thus, people needed to move elsewhere to find employment. This is an example of an economic push factor—pushing people out of the area because of an economic downturn. Choice A is incorrect because the situation described is an economic factor, not a political factor. Choice B is incorrect because the situation described is an economic factor, not a political factor, and because economic downturn is a push factor rather than a pull factor. Choice D is incorrect because an economic downturn is a push factor rather than a pull factor.

21. D: Culture can be transmitted in nearly endless ways, ranging from governmental policies to entertainment consumption. Furthermore, culture can be transmitted intentionally or spontaneously. For example, powerful institutions can sometimes unilaterally shift the culture to achieve a goal, but other times cultural change is a natural byproduct of social interactions that spirals in an unforeseen direction. Thus, Choice D is the correct answer. Culture is not always transmitted through hierarchical relationships. For example, relocation diffusion and contagious diffusion can occur outside of hierarchical relationships, so Choice A is incorrect. Religion, economic activities, and government policies play a powerful role in cultural development, but culture can be transmitted in other important ways, such as through social interactions and digital networks. Therefore, Choice B is incorrect. Choice C is a true statement, but it does not describe how culture is transmitted across society, so it's incorrect.

22. B: The central bank is responsible for all of these except for setting the tax rate. This is done by the government.

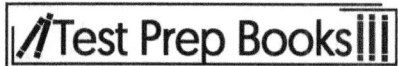

23. D: Fiscal policy is the term for what the government decides to do when it comes to its impact on the economy. Keynesian economics is the liberal economic belief that says that the government should have a role in the economy. Fiscal responsibility refers to taxation and government spending. Supply-side economics is the correct answer, as it refers to the pushback against government in the economy.

24. A: Free trade agreements seek to increase international trade by limiting or eliminating tariffs and subsidies for domestic industries. Overall, international trade increased dramatically after the signing of the General Agreement on Tariffs and Trade (1947) and formation of the World Trade Organization (1995). Thus, Choice *A* is the correct answer. Although Keynes issued proposals to reduce German reparations and establish a Free Trade Union, they are separate proposals. Reparations aren't directly related to free trade agreements. As such, Choice *B* is incorrect. Choice *C* is incorrect because free trade agreements generally prohibit countries from subsidizing or protecting domestic industries. Free trade agreements don't facilitate imperialism, so Choice *D* is incorrect.

25. C: Millions of people died during the Black Death, but those who survived found that their standard of living had improved, especially serfs. Before the Black Death, serfs had few rights and were expected to work without pay for their lord. Because labor was in such short supply after the Black Death, serfs found they were in a much better bargaining position. The Protestant Reformation was a cultural phenomenon, and the rise of absolutism was a political change. Neither had any connection to the Black Death, making Choices *A* and *B* incorrect. Choice *D* is also incorrect; although child labor laws came after the Black Death in the early 1800s, they weren't a direct result of the Black Death.

26. A: Copernicus exemplified the key techniques of the Scientific Revolution, including an emphasis on empirical data and the scientific method. He carefully observed the movement of the planets and found that his data did not match the contemporary geocentric theory, which stated that the earth was the center of the universe. He found that his data indicated that the planets revolved around the sun instead.

27. C: Louis the XIV was an absolute monarch who ruled during the seventeenth and eighteenth centuries. He concentrated power on the throne by forcing nobles to spend most of their time at the royal court. The French Revolution occurred about 75 years after he died. Absolute monarchs like Louis the XIV bolstered their prestige by claiming they were appointed by God. The Mandate of Heaven was a similar concept, but it was developed by the Zhou Dynasty in China about two thousand years before Louis XIV was born.

28. C: The Age of Enlightenment in the eighteenth century focused on political and economic philosophy as opposed to scientific discoveries. English philosopher John Locke introduced the concept of a social contract between the ruler and his subjects. His ideas helped inspire revolutions in the British colonies in North America and later France. Choice *A* is incorrect; the discovery of the heliocentric theory happened in 1543. Luther began to criticize the Catholic Church about two hundred years before the Age of Enlightenment began, making Choice *B* incorrect. Choice *D* is also incorrect, as the Renaissance happened before the Age of Enlightenment from approximately 1300-1600.

29. B: The American Revolution occurred first in 1775, and a number of European soldiers fought for the patriots. The American Revolution, in part, inspired the French Revolution. The Marquis de Lafayette came to America in 1777 and was wounded during the Battle of Brandywine. He returned to France after the American Revolution and became a leader in the French Revolution in 1789.

30. B: The printing press was much more efficient than previous methods, which required a single scribe to copy text by hand. This made books much more affordable and encouraged the growing middle class to read. No church or organization had a monopoly on the technology, so many different writers used it to spread the ideas of the Reformation, as well as the Renaissance, Scientific Revolution, and Age of Enlightenment.

Answer Explanations #2

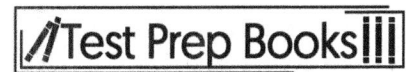

31. D: The US Constitution, Choice A, actually legalized slavery by counting slaves as three-fifths of a person. The Compromise of 1850, Choice B, banned the slave trade in Washington D.C. but also created a stronger fugitive slave law. The Emancipation Proclamation, Choice C, only banned slavery in the Confederacy. The 13th Amendment finally banned slavery throughout the country.

32. B: The Bleeding Kansas conflict contributed to sectional tension before the Civil War. The application of popular sovereignty in Kansas led to conflict as free-soil and pro-slavery forces rushed into the territory. Malcolm X's death, Choice A, was in 1965, almost 100 years after the Civil War ended. The 13th Amendment, Choice C, was ratified in 1865 and was approved at the very end of the Civil War. Shay's Rebellion, Choice D, was an uprising during 1786 and 1787 in Massachusetts.

33. A: Because the British naval blockade during World War I was so effective, Germany retaliated by using submarines to attack any ship bound for Britain or France. This led to the sinking of the RMS Lusitania in 1915, which killed more than 100 Americans. The destruction of the USS Maine, Choice B, sparked the Spanish-American War in 1898. The Japanese attack on Pearl Harbor in 1941, Choice C, brought America into World War II, not World War I. Franz Ferdinand's death in 1914, Choice D, sparked the outbreak of World War I, but America did not join the war until 1917.

34. C: The Massacre at Wounded Knee in 1890 left at least 150 Native Americans dead, including many women and children, and was the last major engagement between Native Americans and American soldiers. The Trail of Tears, Choice A, involved the forced relocation of tribes from the American Southeast in the 1830s. Although thousands of Native Americans died along the way, it was not a battle. Tecumseh launched his uprising in 1811, Choice B, and conflict between Native Americans and US soldiers would continue for decades as the country expanded further west. The Battle of Little Big Horn in 1876, Choice D, was a great Native American victory that led to the death of General Custer and more than 200 men.

35. B: The Electoral College determines the winner of presidential races, but if a candidate doesn't win a majority of electoral votes, the Twelfth Amendment requires the House of Representatives to decide the presidency, with each state delegation voting as a single bloc. The candidate with the most votes in the House wins the election. The total number of Electoral Votes in the table provided is 261; because no candidate has a majority of the votes (131), the vote went to the House of Representatives. Choice A is incorrect because the table shows that Andrew Jackson won a plurality of electoral and popular votes, but he didn't receive a majority. Choices C and D are incorrect because John Quincy Adams received the most votes in the House of Representatives, so he won the presidency.

36. A: Electoral systems dictate how the members of the ruling body are selected, how votes translate into positions, and how seats are filled in the political offices at each level of government. In a majority system, a candidate must receive a majority of the total votes in order to be awarded a seat, but if none of the candidates reach a majority, a second round of voting occurs, commonly referred to as a runoff. Choice B is incorrect because in a plurality system the candidate with the most votes, regardless of the total number, wins the election.

Choice C is incorrect because in a single transferable system the voters each only have one ballot and rank the available candidates from most to least preferred. If a candidate is eliminated, the ballots that included him/her as the voter's first choice are transferred to each voter's second choice candidate rather than being wasted or lost because the first choice candidate is no longer eligible for election. Choice D is incorrect because in a party list system a political party makes a list of candidates and divides available electoral seats between the candidates on the list based on a variety of voting systems. There would be no need for a runoff election in any of these three types of electoral system.

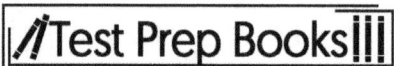

37. C: Issued in 1776, the Declaration of Independence, Choice *A*, explained why the colonists decided to break away from England but did not establish a government. That was left to the Articles of Confederation, which were adopted in 1781. The Articles of Confederation, Choice *C*, established a very weak central government that was replaced by the Constitution, Choice *B*, in 1789. It established a stronger executive branch. In 1791, the Bill of Rights, Choice *D*, amended the Constitution by guaranteeing individual rights.

38. A: The New Deal introduced a number of programs designed to increase regulation and boost the economy. Many of them remain in effect today, such as the Social Security Administration and the Securities and Exchange Commission. The New Deal also led to the Republican and Democratic parties to reverse their ideological positions on government intervention. It did not lead to a third party, Choice *B*. President Franklin D. Roosevelt was actually elected to four terms in office, and the official two-term limit was not established until the 22nd Amendment was ratified in 1951. Until then, the two-term limit had been an informal custom established by President George Washington when he left office in 1797. Thus, Choice *C* is incorrect. Choice *D* is also incorrect. The Great Depression led to the New Deal, not the other way around.

39. C: The North had a population of about 18.5 million while the South had only 5.5 million citizens and 3.5 million slaves. This meant the Union could more easily replace men while the Confederacy could not. The South was defending their homes from damage, since most of the war happened in the South, so Choice *A* is incorrect. Choice *B* is incorrect—the South had free labor at home, so they didn't have to worry about leaving their farms to go to war. Finally, Choice *D* is incorrect; the South had more experienced military leaders due to their participation in the Mexican-American War.

40. B: Although the United States initially lagged behind the Soviets, the US successfully landed the first man on the Moon in 1969. However, the Korean War resulted in a stalemate in 1953, making Choice *A* incorrect. The Vietnam War, Choice *C*, was a defeat for US forces. Despite sending more than 500,000 troops to Vietnam, the Vietnam War became increasingly unpopular and the United States eventually withdrew in 1973. The communist North Vietnamese eventually captured the southern capital of Saigon in 1975. Choice *D*, Battle of Gettysburg, is part of the Civil War.

41. A: Although the Constitution makes no provisions for a presidential Cabinet, President George Washington created one when he took office. Members of the Cabinet advise the president on a wide variety of issues including, but not limited to, defense, transportation, and education. The White House Press Secretary acts as spokesperson for the US government administration, Choice *B*. The Cabinet members are not required to raise money for the president's re-election effort, Choice *C*. The vice president, not the Cabinet, is who presides over the Senate, Choice *D*.

42. A: King Ferdinand and Queen Isabella agreed to support Columbus' mission because he promised to establish a direct trade route to Asia that would allow European merchants to bypass Middle Eastern middlemen. Columbus had no idea that America existed, Choice *B*, and he believed he had landed in India when he arrived in the Caribbean. That's why he mistakenly called the natives *Indians*. It is a common myth that Columbus sought to prove experts wrong by showing them the world was round, not flat. Most European thinkers already knew the world was round, making Choice *C* incorrect. Choice *D* is also incorrect; Christopher Columbus practiced the Christian faith, not Judaism.

43. B: World War II brought about an end to the Great Depression by switching over to wartime production. After the end of World War II, consumer demand remained high and unemployment was usually low. Computers began to become more powerful, efficient, and inexpensive in the latter part of the 20th century, and they became more common in business. The Sun Belt actually expanded after World War II as the traditional manufacturing base in the North and Midwest fell into decline. Land was cheaper in the South and West and wages were also lower too, so these regions were very attractive to businesses.

Answer Explanations #2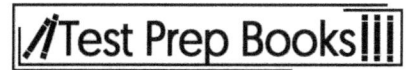

44. C: The Connecticut Compromise, Choice *A*, formed the basis for the Constitution by proposing a bicameral Congress. The Missouri Compromise, Choice *B*, banned slavery north of the 36°30' parallel in the Louisiana Territory. The Compromise of 1850, Choice *C*, essentially undid the Missouri Compromise by introducing popular sovereignty, which allowed voters in territories to decide whether or not the state constitution would ban slavery. The Three-Fifths Compromise, Choice *D*, counted slaves as three-fifths of a human being when allocating representatives.

45. C: Pull factors are reasons people immigrate to a particular area. Obviously, educational opportunities attract thousands of people on a global level and on a local level. For example, generally areas with strong schools have higher property values, due to the relative demand for housing in those districts. The same is true for nations with better educational opportunities. Unemployment, low GDP, and incredibly high population densities may serve to deter people from moving to a certain place and can be considered push factors.

46. D: Diversity refers to how everything and everyone is uniquely different. Choice *A* (behaviorism) is the study of how behavior influences the way human beings interact with their environment. Choice *B* (peer pressure) is when a group uses the majority vote to try to persuade the minority into changing their minds. Finally, Choice *C* (adaptation) is also incorrect because adaptation refers to how a human being adjusts to their surroundings to create a desired outcome. Therefore, Choice *D* (diversity) is correct.

47. A: *Mount McKinley* and *Mount Denali* both denote the same physical mountain. The first was the mountain's official name through most of the twentieth century. The second is the mountain's name as used by Indigenous people, which is now the official American name as well. Therefore, Choice *A* is correct. Choice *B* is incorrect because the national park was named for the mountain. Choice *C* is incorrect because the mountain is in Alaska, not Canada. Choice *D* is incorrect because *Mount Denali* is the indigenous name prior to European settlement.

48. B: Choice *B* is correct because industrialized societies generally need effective education for all social classes so that individuals can participate effectively in the industrial economy. For example, modern American society requires adults to have greater fluency with reading and writing than the agricultural society of the eighteenth century. Choice *A* is incorrect because increased class sizes generally correlate with *reduced* quality of education. Choice *C* is incorrect because history shows that schools continued to close during summer months, despite the reduction in agricultural work. Choice *D* is incorrect because urban environments do not necessarily indicate reduced social cohesion.

49. C: The Republican Party emerged as the abolitionist party during the Antebellum Period and succeeded in abolishing slavery after the North's victory in the Civil War. The Constitutional Union Party supported slavery but opposed Southern secession, while the Southern Democrats supported slavery and secession. The Whig Party splintered in the 1850s as a result of tension over slavery, leading to the creation of the Republican Party and Constitutional Union Party.

50. B: Reconstruction was the Postbellum Era in which the United States tried to reinstate former Confederate states into the Union and rebuild the South through occupation. The Antebellum Era, Choice *A*, was the time frame that preceded the Civil War. The Progressive Era, Choice *C*, was the era of widespread reform in the late nineteenth and early twentieth century that set the stage for Prohibition. The Civil Rights Movement, Choice *D*, is the era of US history that witnessed desegregation, reaching its culmination in the mid-1960s under the presidency of Lyndon B. Johnson.

51. D: Following his election during the Great Depression, Franklin Delano Roosevelt pledged a New Deal for the American people, inaugurating an era of social welfare and public works programs. The Great Society, Choice *A*, also set forth social welfare and public works programs, but under the presidency of Lyndon B. Johnson (LBJ). The War Against Poverty, Choice *B*, was a subcategory of LBJ's Great Society—it promised to

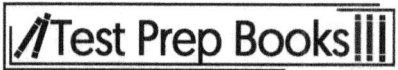

declare war on poverty like any nation would declare war on a foreign threat. Progressivism, Choice C, brought about reforms much like the New Deal, but during the early twentieth century, prior to the Great Depression and FDR's administration.

52. A: The Spanish-American War of 1898 made the US a colonial power because it acquired many former Spanish colonies. The Mexican-American War of 1846-48 led to the acquisition of California, Nevada, Utah, Arizona, and New Mexico, Choice B. World War I led to the formation of the League of Nations in 1919, Choice C. The Great Depression ended when Americans joined World War II in 1941, Choice D.

53. B: *Brown v. Board of Education* ruled that having separate schools for black and white students was inherently unequal and sparked demands for more civil rights. *Roe v. Wade* in 1973, Choice A, increased access to abortion. *Plessy v. Ferguson*, Choice C, established the "separate but equal" doctrine. *Marbury v. Madison* in 1803, Choice D, established the doctrine of judicial review.

54. A: The Gulf Stream contributes to warming the British Isles and Scandinavia, despite their northern latitudes. Therefore, Choice A is correct. Choices B and D are incorrect because the Gulf Stream does not impact weather systems. Choice C is incorrect because the Gulf Stream does not impact the duration of the region's seasons.

55. A: The Stonewall Inn Riot in 1969 helped ignite the gay and lesbian rights movement when patrons fought back against a police raid. The site became a national monument in 2016. Although he became an icon of the gay and lesbian rights movement, Matthew Shepard was murdered in 1998. Thus, Choice B is incorrect. The murder of Vincent Chin, Choice C, in 1982, became a rallying cry for Asian American activists. The gay and lesbian rights movement was well established when activists campaigned to raise awareness of AIDS during the 1980s and 1990s, making Choice D incorrect.

56. C: Alexandria became the capital. Jerusalem, Choice A, although the epicenter of Judaism and Christianity, did not host as many scholars as Alexandria during the Hellenistic period. Constantinople, Choice D, is incorrect because it was not yet created during the Hellenistic period. Athens, Choice B, the former capital of Greek scholarship, is not the answer because scholarly culture shifted from Athens to Alexandria during this period.

57. B: Choice B is correct because teaching children a life-long habit demonstrates a cultural adaptation to an arid environment. Choices A and C are incorrect because they are technological adaptations, not cultural adaptations. Choice D is incorrect because increased sweat is a biological adaptation.

58. C: Psychology is a social science that studies the ways in which the mind and cognition affect social relationships and identities. Biology, Choice A, is a hard science that studies life. English, Choice B, would be placed under the umbrella of the humanities. Geometry, Choice D, would fall under the category of mathematics.

59. C: Oligopolies are markets that establish a few large firms as the major sellers/distributors. Free market economies, Choice A, allow for more competition, while command economies, Choice D, allow for greater government control. Choice B is incorrect because pure monopolies are typically dominated by one firm rather than a few.

60. C: A kinship group designates a collection of people, loosely related to one another across multiple generations, who have certain behavioral obligations regarding one another. Thus, Choice C is correct. Choices A and B are incorrect because they designate a nuclear family and an extended family, respectively. Choice D is incorrect because the answer describes an ethnicity (such as people of Jewish descent) rather than a kinship group.

Answer Explanations #2

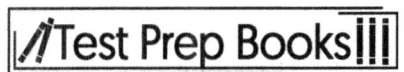

Science

1. D: Charles Darwin based the idea of adaptation around his original concept of natural selection. He believed that evolution occurred based on three observations: the unity of life, the diversity of life, and the suitability of organisms to their environments. There was unity in life based on the idea that all organisms descended from a common ancestor. Then, as the descendants of common ancestors faced changes in their environments or moved to new environments, they began adapting new features to help them. This concept explained the diversity of life and how organisms were matched to their environments. Natural selection helps to improve the fit between organisms and their environments by increasing the frequency of features that enhance survival and reproduction.

2. C: Proteins are synthesized on ribosomes. The ribosome uses messenger RNA as a template, and the transfer RNA brings amino acids to the ribosome where they are synthesized into peptide strands using the genetic code provided by the messenger RNA.

3. A: The physical structure of the atoms that compose matter lends itself to the production of electricity. The arrangement of the subatomic particles and the associated charges—mainly the negatively charged electrons in the cloud—are associated with the ability to create an electric current, which can be harnessed to do work.

4. A: The Golgi apparatus is designed to tag, package, and ship out proteins destined for other cells or locations. The centrioles typically play a large role only in cell division when they ratchet the chromosomes from the mitotic plate to the poles of the cell. The mitochondria are involved in energy production and are the powerhouses of the cell. The cell structure responsible for cellular storage, digestion, and waste removal is the lysosome. Lysosomes are like recycle bins. They are filled with digestive enzymes that facilitate catabolic reactions to regenerate monomers.

5. D: DNA serves as the hereditary material for prokaryotic and eukaryotic cells.

6. B: The Linnaean system is the most commonly used taxonomic system today. It classifies species based on their similarities and moves from comprehensive to more general similarities. The system is based on the following order: species, genus, family, order, class, phylum, and kingdom.

7. A: *Homo* is the human genus. *Sapiens* are the only remaining species in the Homo genus.

8. B: Plants use chloroplasts to turn light energy into glucose. Animal cells do not have this ability. Chloroplasts can be found in the plant cell but not the animal cell.

9. A: Photosynthesis is the process of converting light energy into chemical energy, which is then stored in sugar and other organic molecules. The photosynthetic process takes place in the thylakoids inside chloroplast in plants. Chlorophyll is a green pigment that lives in the thylakoid membranes and absorbs photons from light.

10. D: The cell membrane surrounds the cell and regulates which molecules can move in and out of the cell. Ribosomes build proteins, Choice *A*. Lysosomes break down large molecules, Choice *B*. The nucleus contains the cell's DNA, Choice *C*.

11. B: Sunlight enters the greenhouse as short-wavelength IR and gets converted to long-wavelength IR. This process also gives off heat and makes the greenhouse feel warmer than the outside climate. Water and oxygen, Choices *A* and *D*, are not involved in this reaction. The plants remain the same and do not get converted into anything else, Choice *C*.

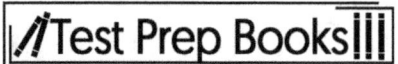

12. D: Circular motion occurs around an invisible line around which an object can rotate. This invisible line is called an axis. Choice A, center of mass, is the average location of an object's mass. Choice B, the center of matter, is not a real term. Choice C, elliptical, describes an elongated circle and is not a viable selection.

13. B: For charges, like charges repel each other and opposite charges attract each other. Negatives and positives will attract, while two positive charges or two negative charges will repel each other. Charges have an effect on each other, so Choices C and D are incorrect.

14. B: In broad terms, energy is divided into kinetic and potential energy. Kinetic energy refers to an object in motion. It is the product of mass and velocity ($KE = \frac{1}{2}mv^2$). Potential energy refers to the capacity for doing work. Its gravitational configuration is the product of mass, acceleration due to gravity, and height ($PE = mgh$). Examples of kinetic energy include heat (which is the thermal energy from atoms and molecules moving around), waves like light, and physical motion. Potential energy examples include gravitational energy and chemical energy stored in bonds.

15. C: The answer is 1,800 seconds:

$$45 \text{ km} \times \frac{1,000 \text{ m}}{1 \text{ km}} \times \frac{1 \text{ s}}{25 \text{ m}} = 1,800 \text{ seconds}$$

16. A: Both types of cells are enclosed by a cell membrane, which is selectively permeable. Selective permeability essentially means that the membrane is a gatekeeper, allowing certain molecules and ions in and out, and keeping unwanted ones at bay, at least until they are ready for use. Prokaryotes contain a nucleoid and do not have organelles; eukaryotes contain a nucleus enclosed by a membrane, as well as organelles.

17. B: Dominant alleles are considered to have stronger phenotypes and, when mixed with recessive alleles, will mask the recessive trait. The recessive trait would only appear as the phenotype when the allele combination is aa because a dominant allele is not present to mask it.

18. A: Fungal cells have a cell wall, similar to plant cells; however, they use oxygen as a source of energy and cannot perform photosynthesis. Because they do not perform photosynthesis, fungal cells do not contain chloroplasts.

19. A: Roots are responsible for absorbing water and nutrients that will get transported up through the plant. They also anchor the plant to the ground. Photosynthesis occurs in leaves, stems transport materials through the plant and support the plant body, and phloem moves sugars downward to the leaves.

20. A: Botanists study the field of botany, which is the study of plants. Neither the evolution of monkeys nor the genetic changes in human brain cancer, Choices B and C, involve studying plants. An ecologist would study how worker bees interact with a queen bee, Choice D, because that subdiscipline involves analyzing how organisms interact with each other.

21. C: Water molecules form a V-shape because of the uneven sharing of electrons between the atoms. The oxygen atom is slightly negatively charged, and the hydrogen atoms are slightly positively charged, so they pull away from each other and the molecule forms a V-shape.

22. B: Nucleic acids include DNA and RNA, which store an organism's genetic information. Carbohydrates, Choice A, are used as an energy source for an organism. Proteins, Choice C, are important for the structure and function of organisms. Lipids, Choice D, are important for energy storage and insulation.

23. B: An animal cell is surrounded by a cell membrane. The cell membrane contains proteins that regulate which molecules are allowed in and out of the cell. Only plant cells are surrounded by a cell wall, so Choice *A* is incorrect. The nucleus, Choice *C*, is located in middle of the cell and would not be the first organelle that a molecule would encounter. The endoplasmic reticulum, Choice *D*, is located within the cytoplasm, inside the cell membrane.

24. D: In both mitosis and meiosis, DNA replication occurs during interphase. Mitosis has one cell division, whereas meiosis has two cell divisions; therefore, Choice *A*, the number of divisions, is incorrect. Mitosis produces two daughter cells, whereas meiosis produces four daughter cells; therefore, Choice *B* is incorrect. Synapsis of homologous chromosomes, Choice *C*, does not occur in mitosis.

25. D: Nuclear reactions take place in the nucleus of certain unstable atoms. They involve a change in the structure of the nucleus, through some type of decomposition, and energy is released. Unlike in regular chemical reactions where mass is conserved, in nuclear reactions, there is a change in mass between the reactants and products.

26. B: A decomposition reaction breaks down a compound into its constituent elemental components. Choice *A* is incorrect because a synthesis reaction joins two or more elements into a single compound. Choice *C*, an organic reaction, is a type of reaction involving organic compounds, primarily those containing carbon and hydrogen. Choice *D*, an oxidation-reduction (redox or half) reaction, is incorrect because it involves the loss of electrons from one species (oxidation) and the gain of electrons to the other species (reduction). There is no mention of this occurring within the given reaction, so it is incorrect.

27. D: The naming of compounds focuses on the second element in a chemical compound. Elements from the nonmetal category are written with an "ide" at the end. The compound CO has one carbon and one oxygen, so it is called carbon monoxide. Choice *B* indicates that there are two oxygen atoms. Also, Choices *A*, *B*, and *C* incorrectly alter the name of the first element, which should remain "carbon."

28. C: Neon, one of the noble gases, is chemically inert or not reactive because it contains eight valence electrons in the outermost shell. The atomic number is 10, with a 2.8 electron arrangement, meaning that there are 2 electrons in the inner shell and the remaining 8 electrons in the outer shell. This is extremely stable for the atom, so it will not want to add or subtract any of its electrons and will not react under typical circumstances.

29. D: The law states that matter cannot be created or destroyed in a closed system. In this equation, there are the same number of molecules of each element on either side of the equation. Matter is not gained or lost, although a new compound is formed. As there are no ions on either side of the equation, no electrons are lost. The law prevents the hydrogen from losing mass and prevents oxygen atoms from being spontaneously spawned.

30. C: Dark storm clouds are considered nimbostratus clouds, which are located less than 2,000 meters above sea level. There are no atmospheric clouds in outer space.

31. C: When the left side of the Moon is illuminated, as it is in the given figure, it's in the waning phase. In contrast, when the right side of the Moon is illuminated, it's in its waxing phase. Gibbous describes a moon that's more than half-illuminated, and a crescent is less than half-illuminated.

32. A: The Big Bang theory explains how the universe was created from a large explosion, resulting in an expanding cloud of cosmic dust that clumped together to form stars and planets. Dark matter and life are found within the universe, and gravity is a universal law that helps explain how the Big Bang occurred.

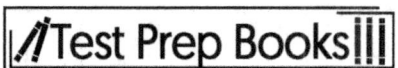

33. D: Ice (solid water) can be found in Saturn's rings. Liquid water may have recently been discovered on Jupiter's moons Europa and Callisto.

34. A: The decimal point for this value is located after the final zero. Because the decimal is moved 12 places to the left in order to get it between the *8* and the *6*, then the resulting exponent is positive, so Choice *A* is the correct answer. Choice *B* is false because the decimal has been moved in the wrong direction. Choice *C* is incorrect because the decimal has been moved an incorrect number of times. Choice *D* is false because the decimal needs to be moved to after the first non-zero number. This will always result in a significand which is less than 10.

$$8{,}600{,}000{,}000{,}000$$
$$\scriptsize 12\ 11\ 10\ 9\ \ 8\ 7\ \ 6\ \ 5\ 4\ \ 3\ \ 2\ 1$$

35. D: Chemical properties of a substance describe how they react with another substance, whereas physical properties describe the appearance of the substance by itself. Choice *D* is the correct answer because it describes how the substance reacts while burning and interacting with oxygen molecules. It is flammable because it does burn. The physical properties of color, density, and fragility are described by Choices *A*, *B*, and *C* respectively.

36. B: Recall that chemical changes involve changes to the molecular structure, whereas physical changes have to do with the appearance of the substance.

For Choice *A*, the condensation of water is represented by:

$$H_2O(g) \leftrightarrow H_2O(l)$$

This process is considered a physical change because there is no change in the identity of the substance. The process is reversible and is a common occurrence. The water vapor, or humidity, in the air tends to condense around cooler objects. If you are wearing glasses and walking from a cold building or car to the outside where it's warm, your glasses will quickly fog up due to condensation. When a glass mason jar is broken, which is the same as a glass cup, there are chemical bonds that break; however, the nature of the substance (glass, or SiO_2) is still the same. In other words, the glass is still glass. Therefore, this process is characterized as a physical change. In Choice *D*, mixing sand in water will not change the chemical structure of sand. The process is reversible if you were to evaporate out the water, leaving only sand. In Choice *B*, baking is considered a chemical process for many reasons. For example, most people have smelled the aroma that is associated with baking brownies or a cake. There is also a color change in the batter (eggs, flour, butter, chocolate chips) as it is heated. This process is not reversible, which is a key characteristic of a chemical change, because once we make the brownies, there is no way to get the eggs or butter back. New chemical bonds form as the mixture is heated (e.g., the flaky crust and slightly burnt edges around the brownie).

37. C: The force that opposes motion is called *friction*. It also provides the resistance necessary for walking, running, braking, etc. In order for something to slide down a ramp, it must be acted upon by a force stronger than that of friction. Choices *A* and *B* are not actual terms, and Choice *D* is the measure of mass multiplied by velocity $(p = mv)$.

38. A: Absolute dating involves measuring radioactive decay of elements such as carbon-14 trapped in rocks or minerals and using the known rate of decay to determine how much time has passed. Another element used is uranium-lead, which allows dating for some of the oldest rocks on the Earth.

39. B: The basic unit of matter is the atom. Each element is identified by a letter symbol for that element and an atomic number, which indicates the number of protons in that element. Atoms are the building block of each element and are comprised of a nucleus that contains protons (positive charge) and neutrons (no charge). Orbiting around the nucleus at varying distances are negatively charged electrons. An electrically neutral atom contains equal numbers of protons and electrons. Atomic mass is the combined mass of protons and neutrons in the nucleus. Electrons have such negligible mass that they are not considered in the atomic mass. Although the nucleus is compact, the electrons orbit in energy levels at great relative distances to it, making an atom mostly empty space.

40. A: Nuclear reactions involve the nucleus, and chemical reactions involve electron behavior alone. If electrons are transferred between atoms, they form ionic bonds. If they are shared between atoms, they form covalent bonds. Unequal sharing within a covalent bond results in intermolecular attractions, including hydrogen bonding. Metallic bonding involves a "sea of electrons," where they float around non-specifically, resulting in metal ductility and malleability, due to their glue-like effect of sticking neighboring atoms together. Their metallic bonding also contributes to electrical conductivity and low specific heats, due to electrons' quick response to charge and heat, given to their mobility. Their floating also results in metals' property of luster as light reflects off the mobile electrons. Electron movement in any type of bond is enhanced by photon and heat energy investments, increasing their likelihood to jump energy levels. Valence electron status is the ultimate contributor to electron behavior as it determines their likelihood to be transferred or shared.

41. A: Electrons give atoms their negative charge. Electron behavior determines their bonding, and bonding can either be covalent (electrons are shared) or ionic (electrons are transferred). The charge of an atom is determined by the electrons in its orbitals. Electrons give atoms their chemical and electromagnetic properties. Unequal numbers of protons and electrons lend either a positive or negative charge to the atom. Ions are atoms with a charge, either positive or negative.

42. B: In chemical equations, the reactants are on the left side of the arrow. The direction of the reaction is in the direction of the arrow, although sometimes reactions will be shown with arrows in both directions, meaning the reaction is reversible. The reactants are on the left, and the products of the reaction are on the right side of the arrow. Chemical equations indicate atomic and molecular bond formations, rearrangements, and dissolutions. The numbers in front of the elements are called coefficients, and they designate the number of moles of that element accounted for in the reaction. The subscript numbers tell how many atoms of that element are in the molecule, with the number "1" being understood. In H_2O, for example, there are two atoms of hydrogen bound to one atom of oxygen. The ionic charge of the element is shown in superscripts and can be either positive or negative.

43. A: A catalyst increases the rate of a chemical reaction by lowering the activation energy. Enzymes are biological protein catalysts that are utilized by organisms to facilitate anabolic and catabolic reactions. They speed up the rate of reaction by making the reaction easier (perhaps by orienting a molecule more favorably upon induced fit, for example). Catalysts are not used up by the reaction and can be used over and over again.

44. A: When the Moon comes between the Earth and Sun, a solar eclipse occurs. If the Sun is far enough away and is completely blocked by the Moon, it is a total solar eclipse. If it is only partially blocked by the Moon, it is a partial solar eclipse, Choice *D*. A lunar eclipse occurs when the Moon is on the opposite side of the Earth as the Sun, and the Sun creates a shadow of the Earth on the Moon, so that the Moon becomes completely dark, Choice *C*, or partially dark, Choice *B*.

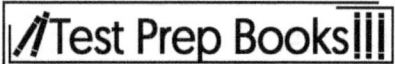

45. D: This is the only answer choice created by Earth's tilt. The Earth rotates around the Sun at an axis of 23.5 degrees, which causes different latitudes to receive varying amounts of direct sunlight throughout the year.

46. B: Freezing water expands because ice is less dense than liquid water. This expansion can break up solid rocks, which describes a form of mechanical weathering. Chemical weathering occurs when water dissolves rocks. Erosion is the movement of broken rock, and deposition is the process of laying down rocks from erosion.

47. C: Pure clay has small particles that pack together tightly and are impermeable to water. Sand is the most permeable type of soil because it has the largest grains. Loam is a combination of all three types of soil in relatively equal proportions.

48. B: Earth's southern geomagnetic pole is located near Greenland. It constantly moves around the same area, but it can intermittently flip or reverse every 100,000 years or so.

49. B: Solar eclipses should not be looked at directly. The rays of the Sun do not seem as bright as normal but can still cause damage to the eyes. A pinhole camera facing away from the eclipse allows the viewer to see a reflection of the eclipse instead of the actual eclipse. Choices *A, C,* and *D* all require looking directly at the solar eclipse.

50. B: Solar eclipses are viewed during the daytime because they involve viewing the Sun while it is out during normal daytime hours. Lunar eclipses, Choices *C* and *D*, are viewed at nighttime when the Moon is in the sky during its normal hours. The Moon is normally illuminated by the Sun that is on the other side of the Earth. When the Sun is on the other side of the Earth, it is nighttime for people looking at the Moon.

51. A: Geysers get their energy from magma within the Earth. The magma heats up water within the geyser until enough pressure builds up to create a geyser's spray.

52. C: The Industrial Revolution switched the economical focus for most of the world from agriculture to manufacturing. This period produced factories and many machines, which required the combustion of coal and other fuel sources. As a new industry, the lack of regulation did not combat the air pollution from these factories, nor were there rules on where to dump waste. While some pollution likely did occur in the other periods listed, the period of the Industrial Revolution, from approximately the mid-1760s to the early 1800s, caused a dramatic spike.

53. D: Landfills and animal waste are large contributors of methane. They do not cause significant amounts of the other greenhouse gases listed. Corn fumes are not a greenhouse gas.

54. D: Geothermal power is a renewable resource that uses the Earth's core temperature to generate energy. Unlike solar energy, which requires land or roof space for panels, geothermal energy's main drawback is that it requires a lot of water because water is injected deep underground where it is heated. As it turns to steam, it turns turbines that generate electric power. It can also cause underground and well water damage. Additionally, emergency events, such as geyser eruptions and landslides, have a high risk of being catastrophic to life. Geothermal energy does not involve combustion, so there is no greenhouse gas emission. It is also said to be three-to-five times more efficient than other alternative energy sources.

55. A: Clay and coal particles are known for their filtration properties in aquifers, as they are porous enough to let water molecules through but keep debris from passing. The other items listed typically are not porous enough for adequate filtration; rather, they just block all water.

Practice Test #3 & #4

To keep the size of this book manageable, save paper, and provide a digital test-taking experience, the 3rd and 4th practice tests can be exclusively found online. Scan the QR code or go to this link to access it:

testprepbooks.com/online387/praxis5901

The first time you access the tests, you will need to register as a "new user" and verify your email address.

If you have any issues, please email support@testprepbooks.com.

Index

1765 Quartering Act, 83
1787 Constitution of the United States, 91
Abiotic, 142
Abraham Lincoln, 85, 91, 182
Acceleration, 151, 152, 153, 154, 155, 210, 258
Acute Angle, 43
Acute Triangle, 47
Adaptive Radiation, 138
Aftershocks, 127
Alexander Fleming, 145
Alexander Hamilton, 84, 176, 200
Alexander the Great, 102, 232
Algebraic Expression, 29, 30, 31, 32, 33
Alleles, 137, 147, 186, 208, 258
Allies, 86, 103
American Revolution, 83, 84, 88, 89, 176, 228, 252
Andrew Jackson, 83, 85, 175, 229, 253
Angiosperm, 120
Angle, 41, 42, 43, 46, 47, 49, 55, 56, 111, 128
Angular Momentum, 155
Animals, 141
Anther, 146
Antibodies, 144, 145, 207
Antigen, 145
Apollo 11, 87
Apollo Missions, 87
Apothem, 56, 57
Aqueducts, 102
Arc of a Circle, 55
Archaebacteria, 141
Archduke Ferdinand of Austria, 103
Area, 22, 23, 51, 52, 53, 54, 55, 56, 57, 58, 59, 60, 61, 64, 65, 90, 93, 101, 117, 139, 144, 150, 161, 162, 176, 181, 183, 200, 204, 206, 221, 230, 238, 247, 249, 255, 262
Area Model, 22, 23
Area of a Square, 53
Area of a Trapezoid, 56
Area of a Two-Dimensional Figure, 51
Arithmetic Sequence, 38, 39
Articles of Confederation, 84, 89, 91, 93, 182, 225, 229, 250
Associative Property of Addition and Multiplication, 21
Asteroid, 123
Asthenosphere, 114, 118

Aswan Dam, 99
Atlas, 94
Atmosphere, 111, 114, 116, 117, 120, 123, 124, 125, 126, 133, 147, 154, 156, 164, 165, 209
Atomic Bomb, 87
Atoms, 150, 211, 261
ATP, 132
Autotrophs, 129, 131, 132, 141
Axon, 133
Babylon, 102
Bar Graph, 77, 78
Barter System, 105
Base, 13, 14, 25, 49, 51, 52, 53, 54, 56, 57, 59, 60, 64, 140, 159, 211, 254
Bathymetry, 95
Battle of Gettysburg, 91, 230, 254
Battle of New Orleans, 85
Big Bang Theory, 120
Bill of Rights, 84, 91, 179, 203, 229, 254
Bills, 89, 90, 132
Binary Fission, 135, 136
Binomial, 32, 140
Binomial Nomenclature, 140
Biosphere, 111, 112, 120, 142, 143, 146
Black Hole, 122, 234
Blizzards, 117
Bolshevik Revolution In 1917, 86
Book of the Dead, 102
Boston Tea Party, 83, 88, 176, 200
Box Plot, 73, 74, 75, 78
Box-and-Whisker Plot, 73
Brain, 131, 133, 140, 145, 235, 258
Brown Dwarfs, 122
Buzz Aldrin, 87
Caliphs, 101
Cambrian Explosion, 120
Canyons, 119
Capital, 105, 232, 251, 254, 256
Capsule, 131
Carbon-12, 121
Carbon-14, 121
Carolus Linnaeus, 140
Cartesian Plane, 61
Cause, 84, 88, 89, 116, 117, 119, 124, 127, 138, 144, 147, 154, 155, 156, 159, 160, 161, 206, 208, 262

Index

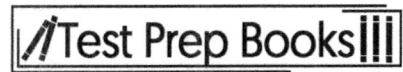

Cell Membranes, 131
Cells, 129, 130, 131, 132, 133, 135, 136, 137, 139, 141, 144, 145, 156, 159, 164, 165, 184, 185, 207, 208, 233, 235, 257, 258, 259
Cenozoic Era, 120
Center of a Data, 72
Centrifugal Force, 155
Centripetal Force, 155
Chance, 79
Charles Darwin, 137, 138, 257
Chemical Properties, 113, 150, 190
Chitin, 141
Chlorophyll, 132
Chloroplasts, 129, 131, 132, 257
Choices, 106, 110, 165, 192, 199, 200, 201, 202, 203, 204, 205, 206, 207, 209, 210, 212, 249, 250, 252, 253, 257, 258, 260, 262
Christianity, 103, 225, 249, 256
Christopher Columbus, 82, 230, 254
Chromosomes, 131, 135
Cinder Volcanoes, 118
Circumference, 54
Civil Rights Movement, 86, 87, 88, 89, 109, 110
Civil War, 85, 88, 91, 182, 212, 225, 231, 250, 253, 254, 255
Clean Water Act of 1972, 87
Climate, 93, 99, 100, 117, 143, 181, 200, 204, 257
Clouds, 115, 116, 187
Code of Hammurabi, 102
Cold War, 86, 87, 99, 103, 178, 230
Collinear, 40
Comet, 123
Command System, 107, 108
Commander-In-Chief, 89
Commensalism, 144
Common Difference, 38, 39
Common Ratio, 39
Communism, 86, 103, 108
Commutative Property of Addition, 21
Competition, 103, 128, 138, 144, 163, 178, 206, 256
Composing a Number, 13
Composing Fractions, 20
Composite Number, 27, 28
Composite Volcanoes, 118
Concave, 46
Condensation, 151
Conduction, 156, 188
Cone, 32, 49, 118

Confederate States of America, 85
Congress, 84, 89, 90, 91, 109, 110, 179, 182, 203, 205
Congruent, 48, 49, 58, 60
Conservation of Energy, 158
Constant, 31, 37, 38, 92, 120, 131, 152, 154, 155, 187, 209, 210, 234
Constitution, 84, 88, 89, 90, 91, 93, 183, 203, 228, 229, 254
Constitutional Convention In 1787, 84
Continental Army, 84
Continental Drift, 128
Continents, 82, 94, 95, 96, 101, 128, 250
Convection, 119, 124, 156, 210
Convection Current, 156
Convergent Boundary, 119
Convex, 46, 117
Coordinate Plane, 61, 62, 63, 64
Coplanar, 40
Corresponding Terms, 39
Countries, 94
Covalent Bonds, 112, 189, 211, 261
Crescent Moon, 126
Cuneiform Tablets, 101
Cylinder, 49, 50, 246
Cytokinesis, 135
Cytoplasm, 131, 132, 133, 135, 259
Cytoskeleton, 131, 133, 140
Declaration of Independence, 88, 90, 91, 200, 229, 254
Decomposing a Number, 13
Deflation, 106, 108
Degrees, 43, 55, 95, 156, 201, 247, 262
Delta, 151
Deltas, 119
Denominator, 18, 19, 20, 24, 26, 28, 193, 194, 195, 240
Dependent, 33, 75, 79, 90, 137, 154, 173, 185, 189, 208, 213, 247
Descriptive Statistics, 68
Diameter, 54
Diffraction, 160, 190
Distributive Property, 21, 30, 31
Divergent Boundary, 119
DNA, 120, 129, 130, 131, 132, 133, 135, 136, 137, 139, 140, 146, 147, 207, 211, 212, 233, 235, 257, 258, 259
DNA Replication, 135, 235, 259
Dominant Allele, 137, 234, 258

Doppler Radar, 128
Dot Plot, 77
Double Bar Graph, 77
Earth, 67, 87, 111, 112, 113, 114, 115, 116, 117, 118, 119, 120, 121, 122, 123, 124, 125, 126, 127, 143, 152, 153, 161, 164, 165, 166, 184, 187, 188, 191, 202, 204, 210, 237, 238, 260, 262
Eclipses, 126
Effects, 88, 90, 99, 100, 104, 106, 107, 145, 147, 153, 154, 157, 208, 209, 249
Elastic Rebound, 127
Electoral College System, 90
Electric Energy, 159
Electrical Current, 159
Electrostatics, 159
Elements, 149
Elliptic Orbit, 123
Emancipation Proclamation, 91, 228, 253
Empress of China, 83
Energy, 131, 132, 155, 156, 157, 158, 159, 160
Entrepreneurship, 105, 107
Equation, 27, 29, 32, 33, 34, 35, 36, 40, 54, 55, 68, 81, 132, 153, 166, 167, 168, 192, 193, 194, 195, 199, 220, 238, 242, 244, 245, 246, 247, 248, 259
Equator, 95, 117, 124, 191, 201
Equiangular Polygons, 46
Equilateral Polygons, 46
Equilateral Triangle, 47
Equilibrium, 106, 154, 185
Era of Good Feelings, 85
Erosion, 117, 118, 119, 262
Estates-General, 108
Eubacteria, 141
Eukaryotes, 129, 132, 133, 141, 258
Evaporation, 114, 186, 191, 208, 210, 213
Executive Branch, 84, 89, 92, 254
Expanded Form, 13
Experiment, 161, 162, 186, 187, 209
Faces, 48, 49, 50, 51, 52, 58, 59
Factors of a Number, 27, 28
Fall, 73, 75, 116, 117, 125, 137, 150, 154, 181, 190, 230, 256
Farewell Address, 91
Federal Aid Highway Act of 1956, 86
Federal Government, 88, 89, 90, 91, 108, 183, 250
Fertile Crescent, 101
Fictional Force, 155
Filament, 146, 159
First Trophic Level, 143

Flagellum, 131
Flowers, 146, 185
Focus, 82, 87, 88, 90, 127, 181, 262
Food Webs, 143
Force, 84, 86, 87, 88, 103, 127, 151, 152, 153, 154, 155, 158, 160, 177, 207, 210, 211, 224, 237, 249, 260
Forces, 151, 154, 159
Force Diagram, 154
Formulas, 32, 33
Fossils, 121
Fractions, 18, 19, 20, 24
Franklin D. Roosevelt, 85, 254
Freezing, 116, 151, 262
Freshwater, 112, 206
Front, 30, 31, 58, 59, 117, 153, 261
Fungi, 141
G1 Phase, 135
G2 Phase, 135
Gametes, 136, 208
Gap, 72
Gas, 150
General Circulation, 117
General Cornwallis, 84
General George Washington, 84
Genotype, 137, 186, 208, 234
Genus, 140, 257
Geology, 112
Geometric Sequence, 38, 39
George Washington, 84, 91, 176, 200, 254
Gettysburg Address, 91
Gibbous Moon, 126
Gilded Age, 85
Glucose, 131, 132, 135, 143, 257
Gravity, 151, 154, 236
Great Depression, 85, 86, 103, 229, 230, 231, 254, 256
Gregor Mendel, 137
Hail, 116
Heat, 120, 156
Henry Ford, 86
Herbert Spencer, 137
Heterotrophs, 132, 133, 141
Hieroglyphs, 102
Hippocratic Oath, 102
Histograms, 73, 78
Homo Sapiens, 140, 233
House of Representatives, 89, 203, 229, 253
Hurricanes, 117, 191

Index

Hydrosphere, 111, 112
Hypothesis, 128, 148, 149, 161, 162, 186, 191, 209
Identity Property of Addition, 21
Identity Property of Multiplication, 21
Impulse, 152
Induction, 159, 188
Industrial Revolution, 85, 107, 203, 239, 262
Industrialization, 85, 87, 98, 100, 104, 106, 179, 182, 203, 205
Inferences, 68
Inflation, 71, 106, 108, 183, 203, 206
Integer, 13, 27, 167
    Integers, 18, 24
International Date Line, 95
Inverse Operations, 15, 16, 17, 22, 34
Inverse Property of Addition, 21
Inverse Property of Multiplication, 21
Isosceles Triangle, 47
James Madison, 84, 176, 200, 248
Jim Crow, 85, 92
    Jim Crow Laws, 92
Judaism, 101, 103, 230, 254, 256
Judicial Branch, 89, 179
July 4, 1776, 90, 175
Karyotypes, 147
Kinetic Energy, 157, 164, 258
King George III, 90
King Louis XIV, 107, 108, 228
Kurtosis, 72
Kyoto Protocol, 104
Labor, 105, 179, 203, 228, 229, 252, 254
Laissez-Faire, 107
Land, 82, 83, 85, 98, 100, 105, 111, 115, 119, 120, 128, 133, 180, 188, 206, 210, 239, 249, 262
Language, 101, 104, 140, 178, 202, 205, 206, 227, 230, 251
Lava, 117, 118, 119
Law of Demand, 106
Law of Inertia, 152
Law of Supply, 106
League of Nations, 85, 92, 103, 182, 231, 256
Legislative Branch, 89, 90, 179
Like Terms, 29
Line, 22, 35, 36, 40, 41, 42, 43, 44, 54, 56, 61, 63, 75, 76, 77, 78, 86, 95, 124, 126, 135, 152, 154, 155, 160, 223, 234, 241, 249, 258
Line Graph, 76, 78
Line Plot, 77, 78
Line Segment, 42, 44

Linear Equations, 33
Linear Inequalities, 33, 34
Linear Momentum, 152
Linear Relationships, 36, 37
Linear Term, 31
Liquid, 150, 260
Lithification, 118
Lithosphere, 112, 113, 114, 118, 119
Local Governments, 90
Location, 13, 40, 61, 62, 90, 93, 98, 151, 177, 178, 181, 191, 200, 204, 213, 237, 258
Longitude, 95
Low Tide, 127
Loyalists, 84
Lunar Eclipse, 126, 184, 207, 238
Luster, 112, 261
M Phase, 135, 136
Macroeconomics, 105
Magnetic Energy, 160
Magnetic Forces, 159, 160
Malcolm X, 86, 253
Mantle, 113, 114, 117, 119, 188, 210
Market System, 107, 108
Martin Luther King Jr, 86, 88, 92, 110
Martin Luther King Jr., 86, 88, 92, 110
Mass, 65, 67, 150, 153
Matter, 149, 150, 259
Mean, 68, 69, 70, 71, 72, 97, 158, 248
Measures of Central Tendency, 69, 70
Mechanical Advantage, 158
Mechanical Energy, 157
Median, 69, 70, 71, 72, 73, 74, 171, 173, 197
Meiosis, 136, 164, 165, 208, 235, 259
Melting, 151
Mercantilism, 107, 108
Meridians, 95, 201
Mesopotamia, 101, 102
Mesosphere, 111
Mesozoic Era, 120
Metamorphosis, 139, 148, 149
Meteor, 123
Meteorite, 123
Meteoroid, 123
Meteorologists, 128
Meteorology, 128
Microeconomics, 105
Middle, 42, 69, 70, 111, 124, 135, 252, 259
Milky Way, 122
Minerals, 105, 112, 117, 121, 190, 212, 260

Mitochondria, 129, 131, 132, 233
Mixture, 150
Mode, 69, 70, 71, 72
Mode of a Data Set, 71
Momentum, 152, 155
Monera, 141, 187
Money, 65, 105
Monomial, 31
Monopolies, 106, 107, 108, 179, 232, 256
Monotheism, 103
Moons, 124, 126, 210, 237, 260
Multiples of a Given Number, 28
Mutualism, 144
Myelin, 133
Narratives, 88
National Aeronautics and Space Administration (NASA), 87
National Association for the Advancement of Colored People (NAACP), 88
Native American Tribes, 83, 88, 90, 98
Natural Phenomena, 98
Natural Resources, 98, 100, 105, 106, 138
Neil Armstrong, 87, 124
Nerve, 133, 134, 140
Net, 50, 51, 52
Neuron, 133, 134, 140
Neutron Star, 122
New Deal, 85, 89, 229, 231, 254
New Moon, 126, 127
New Spain, 82
Nile River, 99, 102
Non-Renewable, 156
Nonrenewable Resources, 105, 106
Non-Reversible Change, 151
Northwest Ordinance of 1787, 84
Nuclear Fission, 114, 119
Nuclear Fusion, 114
Nucleus, 111, 114, 129, 131, 135, 150, 189, 190, 207, 209, 211, 212, 234, 235, 257, 258, 259, 261
Nullification, 90
Number Line, 22, 24, 35, 61, 77, 80, 223, 248
Obtuse Angle, 43
Obtuse Triangle, 47
Opposites, 21
Ordered Pair, 62, 63, 75, 76
Organ Systems, 133, 135
Organic Products, 106
Organism, 121, 129, 131, 133, 134, 136, 137, 139, 140, 142, 143, 144, 147, 148, 186, 207, 208, 258

Organs, 133, 134, 135, 207
Origin, 61, 63, 249
Ottoman Empire, 82, 103, 109, 110, 178, 201
Outliers, 69, 70
Ovary, 146
Paleontology, 121
Paleozoic Era, 120
Paper Money, 106
Parallel Lines, 41
Parallelogram, 48, 56
Parallels, 95
Parasitism, 144
PEMDAS, 20, 194
Percent, 24, 25, 27, 28, 68, 71, 77, 79, 111, 112, 131, 143, 205, 219
Perimeter, 50, 52
Perimeter of a Square, 53
Phenotype, 137, 186, 208, 234, 258
Photosynthesis, 124, 132, 133, 184, 207, 233, 234, 258
Photosynthesizers, 141
Physical Properties, 150
Pi, 54
Pictograms, 101
Pie Chart, 77
Pistil, 146
Place, 13, 14, 15, 22, 24, 29, 40, 55, 70, 85, 93, 120, 127, 131, 132, 140, 157, 159, 162, 170, 176, 192, 200, 204, 208, 235, 240, 249, 255, 257, 259
Plants, 124, 131, 132, 133, 141, 143, 184, 233, 257
Plasma, 144, 150, 234
Plasma B-Cell, 144
Plot, 63, 72, 74, 77, 78, 218, 244
Point, 13, 14, 24, 35, 37, 40, 41, 42, 49, 54, 61, 62, 63, 64, 69, 70, 71, 72, 73, 76, 87, 112, 113, 116, 117, 151, 152, 154, 155, 157, 162, 186, 192, 195, 197, 210, 219, 260
Polarization, 159
Polio, 145
Polis, 102
Polygon, 44, 46, 49, 52, 56, 57, 58
Polyhedrons, 48, 49
Polymorphs, 112
Population, 68, 83, 89, 90, 94, 102, 106, 107, 108, 138, 142, 147, 149, 164, 178, 180, 183, 202, 204, 207, 208, 223, 230, 254, 255
Potential Energy, 157, 258
Potomac, 83

Index

Power of 10, 14, 15
Preamble, 90, 91
Predator-Prey Relationships, 144
President, 84, 85, 89, 90, 91, 109, 110, 180, 203, 204, 230, 254
President Eisenhower, 86
President Theodore Roosevelt, 87
President Woodrow Wilson, 85
Primary Sources, 109, 110
Prime [Greenwich] Meridian, 95
Prime Factorization, 28
Prime Number, 27, 28
Prism, 48, 49, 50, 52, 59, 60, 61
Probability, 40, 78
Prokaryotes, 129, 131, 132, 136, 141
Proportion, 25, 26, 27, 67, 68, 193, 210
Protein Enzymes, 140
Proton, 111
Pyramid, 49, 51, 105
Quadrant I, 62
Quadrant II, 62
Quadrant III, 62
Quadrant IV, 62
Quadrilaterals, 48
Radiation, 87, 114, 124, 138, 156, 210
Rain, 116, 191
Rainforest, 117
Range of a Data Set, 70
Rate, 25
Ratio, 18, 24, 25, 26, 39, 192, 216
Ratio Pieces, 25
Rational Number, 18, 21, 22, 24, 193
Ray, 41, 42
Receptor Protein, 140
Recessive Allele, 137, 186, 208, 234, 258
Reciprocal Numbers, 21
Recombination, 137, 208
Rectangle, 22, 33, 45, 48, 50, 51, 53, 58, 61, 73, 171, 196, 218, 220
Red Dwarfs, 122
Red Giant, 122
Refraction, 160
Region, 51, 82, 93, 95, 101, 103, 176, 183, 206, 249
Regular Polygon, 46, 56
Remainder, 17, 18, 23
Renewable, 155
Renewable Resources, 105, 106

Research, 114, 128, 145, 148, 152, 161, 162, 163, 176, 190
Resource, 98, 105, 106, 107, 155, 156, 250
Respiration, 132, 135
Reversible Change, 150
Revolutionary War, 84
Rhombus, 48
Ribosomes, 131, 133, 257
Richter Scale, 127
Right Angle, 41, 43, 52, 56, 59
Right Rectangular Prism, 58, 59, 60, 61
Right Triangle, 47, 57, 170
Riparian Customs, 98
RNA, 133, 140, 258
Roman Empire, 102, 103, 109, 110, 201
Rounding Numbers, 15
Royal Ice Cream Parlor, 89
S Phase, 135
Sand Dunes, 120
Scalene Triangle, 47
Scarcity, 106, 179, 202
Scatter Plot, 75, 76
Scientific Method, 161, 162, 191, 212, 252
Seawater, 112
Second Continental Congress, 90
Second Trophic Level, 143
Secondary Sources, 109
Seismic Waves, 127
Seismology, 127
Senate, 89, 180, 204, 230, 254
Sensory Neurons, 140
Sexual Reproduction, 136, 137
Shield Volcanoes, 117
Sides of the Angle, 42
Sir Isaac Newton, 152
Sleet, 116
Snow, 117, 191
Solar Eclipse, 127, 238, 239, 262
Solid, 44, 45, 48, 50, 51, 112, 113, 114, 117, 149, 150, 151, 189, 260, 262
Solution, 28, 29, 34, 35, 36, 150, 161, 167, 171, 189, 193, 211, 250
Spanish-American War In 1898, 85
Species, 97, 98, 120, 133, 137, 138, 140, 142, 144, 147, 148, 156, 185, 207, 232, 257, 259
Sphere, 49, 94
Spread of a Data Set, 72
Sputnik, 87, 128
Sputnik Satellite, 87

Square, 43, 48, 51, 52, 53, 54, 58, 61, 186, 247
Stamen, 146
Stamp Act of 1765, 83
Stars, 122
State Governments, 90, 183
States of Matter, 150
Statistics, 68
Steve Jobs, 87
Steve Wozniak, 87
Stigma, 146
Stomata, 114, 210
Straight Angle, 43
Strata, 121
Stratosphere, 111, 187, 209
Structure, 111, 129
Style, 83, 104, 146, 155
Sublimation, 151
Substance, 149
Supernovas, 122
Supply, 106, 179, 202, 227, 252
Supreme Court, 89, 93, 109, 110, 179, 183, 203, 206, 231
Surface Area, 51, 52, 59
Surface Area of a Three-Dimensional Figure, 51
Surface Area of the Prism, 52, 59
Swammerdam, 149
T-Cells, 144, 145
Tea Act, 83
Temperature, 156
Tenth Amendment, 90, 91, 203
Term, 29, 30, 31, 39, 40, 89, 101, 151, 155, 193, 206, 210, 225, 227, 229, 250, 252, 258
Tetrahedron, 49
Theory, 120, 128, 137, 138, 161, 185, 189, 228, 236, 252, 259
Theory of Adaptation, 138
Theory of Natural Selection, 137
Thermodynamics, 158
Thermosphere, 111, 187
Third Trophic Level, 143
Thomas Jefferson, 85, 176, 200
Three-Dimensional Shapes, 44, 45
Tissue, 133, 134, 190
Topography, 95, 100, 119, 191
Tories, 84

Tornadoes, 117, 191
Trait, 137, 258
Transcription, 140
Transform Boundaries, 119
Transpiration, 114, 210
Transport Protein, 140
Trapezoid, 48, 56
Treaty of Paris of 1783, 84
Treaty of Versailles, 103, 182
Triangles, 47, 53
Trinomial, 32
Triple Entente, 109, 110
Troposphere, 111, 116, 117, 187
Two-Dimensional Shapes, 44, 45
Unicellular, 133, 141
Union of Soviet Socialist Republics, 86
Unit Fraction, 20
Unit Rates, 25
United Nations, 88, 103, 104, 251
Uracil, 140
Usage, 212
Variable, 26, 27, 29, 31, 32, 33, 34, 35, 36, 40, 68, 75, 78, 90, 173, 187, 192, 209, 213, 217, 218, 246
Velocity, 151, 152, 153, 154, 155, 234, 258, 260
Vertex, 42, 43, 49, 51, 52
Vertex of the Angle, 42
Vice President, 89
Viruses, 129, 131, 187, 210
Volcanoes, 117, 118, 120, 191
Volume of a Solid, 59
Voting Rights Act of 1965, 86
Water Cycle, 114, 117, 191, 213
Weathering, 117, 118
Weight, 67, 153, 210
White Dwarf, 122
Whole Numbers, 24, 27
Woodrow Wilson's Fourteen Points, 91
Wright Brothers, 86
X-Axis, 61, 63, 75, 171
X-Ray, 190
Y-Axis, 61, 62, 63, 75, 76
Yeast, 141, 144
Zygote, 137

Dear Praxis Elementary Education Test Taker,

Thank you again for purchasing this study guide for your Praxis Elementary Education exam. We hope that we exceeded your expectations.

Our goal in creating this study guide was to cover all of the topics that you will see on the test. We also strove to make our practice questions as similar as possible to what you will encounter on test day. With that being said, if you found something that you feel was not up to your standards, please send us an email and let us know.

We would also like to let you know about other books in our catalog that may interest you.

Praxis II Social Studies

This can be found on Amazon: amazon.com/dp/1628457686

Praxis II English Language Arts

amazon.com/dp/1628458895

Praxis II General Science

amazon.com/dp/1628458550

Praxis II Mathematics

amazon.com/dp/1628458496

Praxis Core Study Guide

amazon.com/dp/1637759819

We have study guides in a wide variety of fields. If the one you are looking for isn't listed above, then try searching for it on Amazon or send us an email.

Thanks Again and Happy Testing!
Product Development Team
support@testprepbooks.com

Online Resources

Included with your purchase are multiple online resources. This includes the practice tests in an interactive format and a convenient study timer to help you manage your time.

Scan the QR code or go to this link to access this content:

testprepbooks.com/online387/praxis5901

The first time you access the page, you will need to register as a "new user" and verify your email address.

If you have any issues, please email support@testprepbooks.com.

Thank you for letting us be a part of your studying journey!

www.ingramcontent.com/pod-product-compliance
Lightning Source LLC
Chambersburg PA
CBHW060311240426
43661CB00059B/2727